D0205676

Public Relations in the Nonprofit Sector

Nonprofit organizations are managing to carry out sophisticated public relations programming that cultivates relationships with their key audiences. Their public relations challenges, however, have routinely been understudied. Budgetary and staffing restraints often limit how these organizations carry out their fundraising, public awareness and activism efforts, and client outreach. This volume explores a range of public relations theories and topics important to the management of nonprofit organizations, including crisis management, communicating to strengthen engagement online and offline, and recruiting and retaining volunteer and donor support.

Richard D. Waters is an associate professor in the University of San Francisco's School of Management. Author of more than 75 peer previewed articles and book chapters, he is the associate editor of *Case Studies in Strategic Communication* and serves on seven editorial review boards.

Routledge Research in Public Relations

Public Relations in the Nonprofit Sector

Theory and Practice

Edited by Richard D. Waters

Routledge
Taylor & Francis Group

NEW YORK AND LONDON

First published 2015
by Routledge
711 Third Avenue, New York, NY 10017

and by Routledge
2 Park Square, Milton Park, Abingdon, Oxon OX14 4RN

*Routledge is an imprint of the Taylor & Francis Group,
an informa business*

Library of Congress Cataloging-in-Publication Data
Public relations in the nonprofit sector : theory and practice / edited by
   Richard D. Waters.
      pages cm. — (Routledge research in public relations ; 6)
   Includes bibliographical references and index.
  1. Nonprofit organizations—Public relations.   2. Fund raising.
3. Nonprofit organizations—Management.   I. Waters, Richard D., 1976–
   HD62.6.P83 2015
   659.2′88—dc23
   2014045190

ISBN: 978-1-138-79508-2 (hbk)
ISBN: 978-1-315-75868-8 (ebk)

Typeset in Sabon
by Apex CoVantage, LLC

This book is dedicated to those individuals working in the nonprofit and nongovernmental sector who fight for social justice on a daily basis.

Contents

Part I
Strategic Management of Nonprofit Organizations

Part IV
New Media Challenges and Opportunities

Figures

Tables

Foreword

Richard D. Waters

Nonprofit organizations are some of the least understood segments of society, yet they are also among the most crucial. The nonprofit sector is represented by a diverse collection of private institutions that mobilize individuals to achieve common good for all. A recent study by the Center for Civil Society Studies at Johns Hopkins University estimated that the nonprofit sector employs an estimated 11 million workers, or 10.1 percent of the nation's workforce as of 2010. The nonprofit sector is the third largest of all United States industries behind retail trade and manufacturing (Salamon, Sokolowski, & Geller, 2012).

In addition to paid employees, nonprofits use a volunteer workforce equivalent to another 5.7 million full-time workers. According to the U.S. Bureau of Labor Statistics (2014), the volunteer rate for 2013 was 25.4 percent, as 62.6 million individuals volunteered for nonprofit organizations in the 2012–2013 time frame. Overall, the median number of hours volunteered at nonprofits was 50, although that number varied considerably from a high of 86 hours for those 65 years and older to a low of 36 for young adults aged 25 to 34. The Independent Sector, a nonprofit sector leadership network, reports that Americans gave 7.9 billion hours of volunteer service worth $175 billion in 2012 (Independent Sector, 2014). These volunteers help full-time and part-time employees deliver many of the programs and services provided by nonprofits to local, regional, national, and international communities.

The nonprofit sector encompasses a wide range of programs and services from multi-million dollar institutions to the far larger numbers of small entities with annual budgets of less than $25,000. Nonprofits provide communities with much of the hospital care, higher education, social services, arts and cultural entertainment, employment and training, low income housing, religious guidance, and emergency aid, just to name a few services. They also perform a crucial advocacy role by identifying unaddressed problems and bringing them to the forefront of the public attention and into the media's agenda. From the civil rights struggles of the 1960s and gay marriage battles of today, to the advancement of conservation and immigration policy, most social movements that have animated American life over the past century began with and operated in nonprofit organizations.

Despite the important contributions they make, nonprofit organizations increasingly find themselves facing challenges from multiple fronts. However, as the research compiled in this volume illustrate, public relations provides an infrastructure that can be used to overcome these obstacles. Public relations, as defined by Cutlip, Center, and Broom (2000) is "the management function that establishes and maintains mutually beneficial relationships between an organization and the publics on whom its success or failure depends" (p. 6). This hallmark definition of public relations can help the sector, individual nonprofit organizations, and nonprofit employees and volunteers respond to fiscal, effectiveness, technology, and human resource challenges.

THE FISCAL CHALLENGE

In the early 1980s, a considerable portion of America's nonprofit organizations experienced a fiscal squeeze that left a continuing fear over funding sources. Government support, which fueled much of the growth of the nonprofit sector in the 1960s and 1970s, declined sharply in the early 1980s and did not return to its 1980 level until the mid-1990s (Salamon, 2012). Although segments of the nonprofit sector saw increased levels of funding from the Clinton, Bush, and Obama presidencies, the nonprofit sector as a whole is still uncertain about the role government funding will play in its future.

The uncertainty persists in part because government support of the nonprofit sector changed during this period, as government grants and contracts that provide direct financial assistance to service providers transformed into vouchers and tax expenditures; these channel money instead to clients that shop around for nonprofit services in a competitive marketplace. By 2006, 70 percent of all federal support to nonprofit organizations took the form of these consumer-side subsidies (Salamon, 2012).

Private philanthropy, meanwhile, has continued to grow, although it has not kept pace with the growth of the overall economy or with the growth of the nonprofit sector. In 2013, the Giving USA Foundation estimated that Americans donated nearly $335 billion to the nation's charitable nonprofits (Kalugyer, 2014). Despite the near record total dollars donated to the sector, giving has steadily declined as a share of personal income since the late 1990s. As a result of the bear market from 2000 to 2002 in the American stock exchanges and the global economic crisis from 2007 to 2009, per capita giving fell significantly despite generous charitable response to the decade's disasters (September 11, 2001, terrorist attacks, the 2004 Southeastern Asian tsunami, Hurricane Katrina in 2005, and the 2010 Haitian earthquake).

Ultimately, as Natalie Tindall, Richard Waters, and Kathleen Kelly discuss in chapter 1, a fundraiser's role within a nonprofit organization impacts how he or she will approach securing support for the organization. The more enlightened managerial roles use a network of individuals to build relationships with donors. As the relationship management paradigm, as discussed by Shannon Bowen and Diana Sisson in chapter 5, illustrates that nonprofit organizations can focus on the relational outcomes of trust, satisfaction, commitment, and balanced power to bring continued interactions with a nonprofit organization by individuals. Research by public relations scholars has shown that the relationship approach can result in continued donor engagement and future donations to worthy causes (Hall, 2002; O'Neil, 2007). Likewise, in chapter 10 Giselle Auger discusses how foundations and nonprofit organizations can use online relationship-building techniques to improve harmony between the two groups. These relationship-building strategies are helpful in securing funding during times of crisis, as outlined by Emily Kinsky, Nicholas Gerlich, Kristina Drumheller, and Marc Sollosy in chapter 6.

THE EFFECTIVENESS CHALLENGE

In addition to worries concerning funding, nonprofits are also facing growing pressures to demonstrate that they are worthy of continued support. Earlier notions of the inherent trustworthiness of nonprofit organizations have faded, and nonprofits must find ways to demonstrate their fiscal and social accountability through empirical measures. Light (2002) was among the first to document the drop in public confidence of the nonprofit sector after the United Way–William Aramony scandal in the early 1990s; however, recent research shows that the public has remained skeptical of the nonprofit sector after media exposés focusing on improper use of donations, high salaries, and questionable actions by nonprofit leaders (McDougle & Lam, 2014). The public is not alone with calls for nonprofits to be more accountable in their actions. Senator Chuck Grassley (R-IA), a member of the U.S. Senate's Committee on Finance, has repeatedly called for legislation on nonprofit financial accountability. His calls have been echoed by both Democratic and Republican politicians; however, legislation has yet to come to a vote by the full Senate.

In response to these concerns, nonprofit organizations have undertaken elaborate efforts to produce and publish performance measures to demonstrate that they are worthwhile organizations. Watchdog groups, such as Charity Navigator and GuideStar, help provide overall ratings for individual organizations, but individual nonprofits can also provide their own evidence of their accountability and effectiveness. The use of public relations strategies can ensure that audiences are informed about their efforts (Starck & Kruckeberg, 2003).

Nonprofit organizations have taken actions to voluntarily adopt relevant portions of the Sarbanes–Oxley Act of 2002, which was signed into law by

George W. Bush to overhaul the financial standards for for-profit accounting firms and public corporations (Iyer & Watkins, 2008). However, nonprofit sector leaders saw that elements of the law were applicable to nonprofit organizations as well. The voluntary adoption of policies, such as having the executive director and president of the board of directors sign off on audited financials and having a formal conflict-of-interest policy, represents the proactive actions described by public relations excellence theory that help an organization remain vital in community life (Carden, 2013).

Another key characteristic of excellent public relations is being open and honest about organizational decisions and messaging. Chapter 12 on HIV/AIDS, by Erich Sommerfeldt and Sifan Xu, and chapter 13 on wind as alternative energy, by Ben Benson and Bryan Reber, highlight how two different nonprofit organizations used framing and open communication to educate others about their missions and policy goals. These modern efforts echo the campaigns for Children's Broadcasting Initiatives discussed by Rachel Kovacs in chapter 15 and the World War II gardening campaigns discussed by Cheryl Lambert in chapter 16.

Nonprofits must learn how to be more communicative about their finances and programs to meet the accountability demands of the public and demonstrate their effectiveness. In chapter 14, Liz Gardner, Trent Seltzer, Andrea Phillips, and Rachel Page reveal that message efficacy is influenced by different sources, and nonprofit communicators should consider these lessons when planning how to demonstrate their effectiveness.

THE TECHNOLOGY CHALLENGE

Rapid changes in available technology have further complicated the pressures that nonprofit organizations face. While opening new opportunities to nonprofits with their advocacy efforts and the provision of services such as education and healthcare, technology can also be a burden for nonprofits (Johnson, 1997). This is especially true for small organizations with meager budgets as it is often difficult for organizations to raise funds to pay for ever-changing technologies when donors want to see their contributions used to deliver services (Jaskyte, 2011). The cost associated with staying on top of current technologies has helped create a significant digital divide within the sector.

One of the foundation representatives interviewed by Geah Pressgrove and Brooke McKeever in chapter 20 noted that technology can be very helpful in influencing public opinion and making social change; however, nonprofit organizations must have someone who understands the technology. Nah and Saxton (2013) note that most nonprofit organizations fail to maximize their social media presence by using the platforms as broadcast channels rather than as engagement tools. Research in this volume explains how using Twitter (chapter 17 by Jeanine Guidry, Greg Saxton, and

Marcus Messner) and Facebook (chapter 18 by Moonhee Cho and Tiffany Schweickart) can be used to increase conversations about an issue and specific nonprofit organizations. These discussions also expand the discussion of social media to focus on how to transform a like on Facebook or a retweet on Twitter into meaningful off-line action. In chapter 19, Carolyn Kim and John Keeler discuss how Compassion International uses Pinterest to create significant off-line engagement with stakeholders around the globe. The lessons and insights gleaned from this research can help nonprofits advance their missions, but they must have someone capable of using it effectively.

HUMAN RESOURCE CHALLENGE

Inevitably, stresses from funding sources, increased accountability demands, and technology challenges have taken their toll on the sector's human resources. Executive directors of nonprofits not only provide the overall vision and leadership for the organization, but they must also be versed in a variety of skills that have not necessarily been written into formal job descriptions (Hoefer, 2011). For example, media relations and crisis management are two tasks that require a strong organizational representative; these typically land upon the desk of the executive director. Suzanne Horsley explains in chapter 11 that media spokespeople must be adaptive to different types of environments, especially in times of crisis. However, in chapter 2, Hilary Fussell Sisco, Randi Plake, and Erik Collins explain that many organizations have not even created a crisis management plan, much less thought about the complexities of working with the media.

Likewise, the executive director must also play an active role in fundraising for the organization either as part of an overall fundraising team or individually for specific projects (Hall, 2002). In either situation, the executive director must strive to make sure that fundraising does not intrude on other departments within the organization. Kelly (1993) first noted that the reliance of outside donations has caused fundraising to encroach upon organizations' public relations efforts, and more recent research has shown that the rate of encroachment has not changed significantly in the past 20 years (Swanger & Rodgers, 2013). In chapter 4, Christopher Wilson and Sarabdeep Kochhar explore encroachment in higher education and find that this management issue is still a concern for nonprofit leaders.

Because nonprofit employees are often required to wear multiple hats inside their organizations, the workload has become demanding, leading to considerable turnover and burnout, while employees receive relatively low wages and benefits compared to those working in the public and for-profit sectors (Kim, 2011). Public relations research highlights a variety of different ways to reduce burnout and turnover. In chapter 3, Tim Penning stresses the importance of recruiting board members who bring skill sets with them, including public relations, that complement an organization's existing talent rather than overlapping them. Jennifer Vardeman-Winter (in chapter 8) and by Brigitta Brunner and Giovanna Summerfield (in chapter 9) discuss strategies nonprofit organization employees can use to become better connected to the stakeholders they work with, thus minimizing stress and work frustrations. Denise Bortree in chapter 7 offers insights as to how nonprofit organizations can use inclusive behavioral strategies to keep male and female volunteers coming back to the organization, which helps reduce the workload of full-time and part-time employees.

Although the early foundations of public relations theory were built by studying corporate communication practices, the recent uptick in the number of scholars interested in nonprofit organizations' public relations efforts has resulted in a newfound appreciation for the unique challenges that these organizations face. As illustrated by the research in this volume, insights from public relations can assist organizational leaders with solving management dilemmas, cultivating relationships with different stakeholder groups, improving advocacy and activism efforts, and strengthening their strategic use of technology. Hopefully, this book will help nonprofit organizations address the unique challenges that they face.

The 20 chapters selected for this volume represent different aspects of public relations theory and research methods. However, together they contribute significantly to our understanding of public relations theory by filling in missing gaps in our existing public relations knowledge. Previous scholarship that has relied heavily on the study of public relations firms and corporations has built theory at the exclusion of the nonprofit sector. As pointed out by the contingency theory of accommodation (Cancel, Cameron, Sallot, & Mitrook, 1997), each organization faces different situations when it plans its public relations efforts. To truly build public relations theory, the unique position of nonprofit organizations must be examined within the public relations framework as well to develop comprehensive theoretical perspectives. Based on increasing conference presentations and publications, I am proud to say that interest in nonprofit public relations is alive and well and that this volume will serve as a guide for future nonprofit-focused studies for years to come.

REFERENCES

Bureau of Labor Statistics. (2014, February 25). Volunteering in the United States, 2013. Retrieved June 12, 2014, from http://www.bls.gov/news.release/volun.nr0.htm

Cancel, A. E., Cameron, G. T., Sallot, L. M., & Mitrook, M. A. (1997). It depends: A contingency theory of accommodation in public relations. *Journal of Public Relations Research, 9*(1), 31–63.

Carden, A. (2013). Proactivity and reactivity. In R. L. Heath (Ed.), *Encyclopedia of public relations* (pp. 686–688). Thousand Oaks, CA: Sage.

Cutlip, S. M., Center, A.H., & Broom, G.M. (2000). *Effective public relations.* Upper Saddle River, NJ: Prentice Hall.

Hall, M.R. (2002). Fundraising and public relations: A comparison of programme concepts and characteristics. *International Journal of Nonprofit and Voluntary Sector Marketing, 7*(4), 368–381.

Hoefer, R. (2011). Basic skills of nonprofit leadership. In K.A. Agard (Ed.), *Leadership in nonprofit organizations: A reference handbook* (pp. 321–328). Thousand Oaks, CA: Sage.

Independent Sector. (2014). Independent sector's value of volunteer time. Retrieved June 12, 2014, from https://www.independentsector.org/volunteer_time

Iyer, V.M., & Watkins, A.L. (2008). Adoption of Sarbanes-Oxley measures by nonprofit organizations: An empirical study. *Accounting Horizons, 22*(3), 255–277.

Jaskyte, K. (2011). Predictors of administrative and technological innovations in nonprofit organizations. *Public Administration Review, 71*(1), 77–86.

Johnson, M.A. (1997). Public relations and technology: Practitioner perspectives. *Journal of Public Relations Research, 9*, 213–236.

Kalugyer, A. D. (2014, June 17). Giving USA: Americans gave $335.17 billion to charity in 2013; total approaches pre-recession peak. Retrieved June 20, 2014, from http://www.philanthropy.iupui.edu/news/article/giving-usa-2014

Kelly, K.S. (1993). Fundraising encroachment on public relations: A clear and present danger to effective trustee leadership. *Nonprofit Management & Leadership, 4*(1), 47–68.

Kim, H. (2011). Job conditions, unmet expectations, and burnout in public child care welfare workers: How different from social workers? *Children and Youth Services Review, 33*, 358–367.

Light, P. (2002). *Trust in charitable organizations. Reform watch #6.* Washington, DC: Brookings Institution Press.

McDougle, L.M., & Lam, M. (2014). Individual- and community-level determinants of public attitudes toward nonprofit organizations. *Nonprofit & Voluntary Sector Quarterly, 43*(4), 672–692.

Nah, S., & Saxton, G.D. (2013). Modeling the adoption and use of social media by nonprofit organizations. *New Media & Society, 15*, 294–313.

O'Neil, J. (2007). The link between strong public relationships and donor support. *Public Relations Review, 33*, 99–102.

Salamon, L. M. (2012). *The state of nonprofit America.* Washington, DC: Brookings Institution Press.

Salamon, L.M., Sokolowski, S.W., & Geller, S.L. (2012). Holding the fort: Nonprofit employment during a decade of turmoil. Retrieved June 12, 2014, from http://ccss.jhu.edu/wp-content/uploads/downloads/2012/01/NED_National_2012.pdf

Starck, K., & Kruckeberg, D. (2003). Ethical obligations of public relations in an era of globalization. *Journal of Communication Management, 8*(1), 29–40.

Swang, W., & Rodgers, S. (2013). Revisiting fundraising encroachment of public relations in light of the theory of donor relations. *Public Relations Review, 39*, 566–568.

Acknowledgments

This volume would not have been possible without the contributions made by the authors of the individual chapters. I thank each and every one of them for helping advance the scholarship of nonprofit public relations.

I would like to personally thank Glenn Wickman as well as Joey, Oscar, and Brady for helping me complete this project despite some stressful and challenging times!

Part I
Strategic Management of Nonprofit Organizations

1 A Fractured Glass Ceiling in Fundraising?

Examining the Careers of Minority Healthcare Fundraisers Using Role Theory

Natalie T. J. Tindall, Richard D. Waters, and Kathleen S. Kelly

In 2013, Americans donated $335 billion to the nearly 1.6 million charitable organizations in the United States (Kalugyer, 2014). Individual fundraisers raised more than 80% of the total donations through traditional and Internet-based fundraising techniques using relationship development strategies (Waters, 2010).

In the United States, fundraising is carried out by full-time and part-time staff practitioners (Hager, Rooney, & Pollak, 2002), volunteers (Lysakowski, 2002), and outside parties, such as consultants and solicitation firms (Hooper & Stobart, 2003). In the late 1990s, Kelly (1998a) estimated that there were approximately 80,000 full-time fundraising practitioners in the United States; however, four years later, Hager and colleagues (2002) placed the number much higher, at as many as 296,000. The precise number of fundraisers is difficult to determine because practitioners hold various titles and the occupation has no set requirements for entry.

Regardless of the number of fundraisers, scholars and practitioners both agree that there is a severe shortage of minority fundraisers in the profession. Minority has been defined as "any part of the population that differs from others in some characteristics and as a result is subjected to differential treatment" (L. A. Grunig, Toth, & Hon, 2001, p. 122). In U.S. society, the designation of minority has been placed on those groups that are underrepresented or disadvantaged, not solely those who are in the statistical minority (Wu, 2002). For the purpose of this study, minority fundraisers are being defined as those practitioners with non-Caucasian backgrounds. The realities of being a minority are intertwined with the power, privilege, and control of the dominant group in a society. The dominant group oppresses and suppresses minority groups through the exclusion and denial of positions within mainstream institutions and through controlling images (Collins, 2000).

Evidence of the gap began to be published in the late 1980s as inadequate numbers of African-American/Black (Betts, 1989), Asian-American (Smith, Shue, Vest & Villarreal, 1992), Hispanic/Latino (Royce & Rodriguez, 1999), and Native American (Thorpe, 1989) fundraising practitioners. Despite awareness of a diversity problem, little was done to improve the situation throughout the 1990s. In 2005, the Association for Fundraising

Professionals (AFP) sponsored a diversity summit in conjunction with its international conference. At this meeting, global nonprofit leaders gathered to share ideas and develop a strategy for collective action to lead to greater inclusiveness in fundraising. Although many of the summit recommendations had already been brought to the sector's attention through practitioner books (e.g., Pettey, 2001), this forum allowed AFP to begin publicized talks about the issue to its membership.

Shortly after the summit, the two other major fundraising associations, the Association for Healthcare Philanthropy (AHP) and the Council for Advancement and Support of Education (CASE), began pursuing diversity recruitment initiatives. All three associations have launched public relations campaigns to highlight March as "Diversity in Fundraising" month by showcasing fundraising to minorities as a rewarding profession with opportunities for personal advancement and to help communities. AFP also regularly produces research and case studies to highlight the need for and impact of minority fundraisers, and it produces targeted publications (e.g., newsletters, listservs) to those interested in improving fundraising's diversity. In addition to organizational research, CASE also regularly highlights the need for diversification in its monthly magazine and manages a speakers' bureau to ensure the issue is discussed at chapter meetings throughout the world. AHP has demonstrated its commitment to diversity by regularly offering workshops at regional and international conferences on how to diversify the fundraising team, and also through sustained discussions in its virtual learning series.

Despite these efforts, Pettey and Wagner (2007) recently concluded that recruitment has not resulted in a greater number of minorities entering the fundraising profession. Their claim, however, is largely based on anecdotal evidence and qualitative research using small numbers of in-depth interviews. This study aims to provide a theory-based quantitative description of the careers and working environments of minority fundraisers in healthcare. With this evidence, individuals will be able to evaluate whether doors of opportunity exist in fundraising as suggested by fundraising associations.

LITERATURE REVIEW

Role Theory. Grounded in sociology and social psychology, role theory provides a suitable framework for describing an individual's daily tasks in the fundraising setting. As conceptualized by scholars, role theory focuses on "the recurring actions of an individual, appropriately interrelated with the repetitive activities of others so as to yield a predictable outcome" (Katz & Kahn, 1978, p. 189). Practitioners might perceive a set of role expectations, but modify the expected behavior based on their skills and training. Roles may also be influenced by an individual's level of autonomy, organizational expectations, or emerging standards of the profession.

Public Relations Roles. Role theory has provided significant insights for how public relations is carried out within organizations. Dozier (1992) said the study of roles has been key to the evolution of public relations as a management function. Broom (Broom & Smith, 1979) conceptualized four roles of public relations practitioners from a review of the literature: communication facilitator, expert prescriber, communication technician, and problem-solving process facilitator. To evaluate the differences between the four roles, each role has traditionally been measured through six items, resulting in a 24-item questionnaire (Broom, 1982).

Numerous studies have utilized the measurement items and have provided evidence of their high reliability (e.g., Piekos & Einsiedel, 1990; Gordon & Kelly, 1999). After 10 years of accumulated studies on the theory of public relations roles, Dozier (1992) conducted a factor analysis of the four roles and concluded that the communication facilitator, expert prescriber, and problem-solving process facilitator roles were intercorrelated. The communication technician role was not significantly related to any of the other roles. Based on the findings, Dozier (1992) argued that the public relations roles should be collapsed into two main roles, manager and technician; this was supported by other scholars (e.g., Toth & L. A. Grunig, 1993). However, it should be noted that some critical conceptual differences are lost when the three managerial roles are combined (Cutlip, Center, & Broom, 2006).

Fundraising Roles. Although fundraising has traditionally lacked a substantial body of knowledge stemming from theory and research (Kelly, 1998a), reflective practitioners have suggested that fundraisers also enact various roles. Worth and Asp (1994) identified four roles of educational fundraisers: salesperson, catalyst, manager, and leader. The salesperson role concentrates on soliciting gifts. The catalyst works behind the scenes in support of senior administrators and others involved in fundraising activities. The manager role emphasizes practitioners' skills as internal organizers. The leader role is carried out by practitioners who participate in decision making on organizational policy beyond the realm of fundraising. Worth and Asp's (1994) roles were tested by Ryan (2006). However, Ryan's survey did not measure enactment of the roles, but rather the extent to which participants believed that each role descriptor applied to "successful development officers in higher education" (p. 287). No definition of "successful" was given, mean scores on the four role indices were not reported, and reliabilities of the indices were below accepted standards. Ryan (2006) concluded that "there is no tendency for any one of the four fund-raiser roles to be given more value by the respondents" (p. 287).

Taking an organizational perspective, Fogal (1994) conceptualized three fundraising roles related to three stages of development of the fundraising function: vendor role in the formative stage, facilitator role in the normative stage, and strategist role in the integrative stage. According to Fogal (1994), in the formative stage, fundraising is "characterized by an emphasis on fundraising techniques that generate needed income, such as mass appeals through direct mail and telephone solicitation" (pp. 370–371). Organizations value practitioners who have sales skills. Fundraising is staff-centered at the normative stage, and solicitation skills are valued. At the integrative stage, fundraising is central to the nonprofit, and "donors are regarded as thoughtful participants in the organization's life and work" (Fogal, 1994, p. 371). Organizations in this stage seek fundraisers with skills in building and maintaining relationships. Importantly, Fogal argued that the three stages are not mutually exclusive, but the role assigned to fundraising "reflects the organization's style of management and institutional philosophy" (p. 371).

Derived from practitioner experience, the roles suggested by Worth and Asp (1994) and Fogal (1994) have been helpful in describing daily tasks; however, they are difficult to compare to other role theory studies because of their limitations. Kelly (1998a) combined public relations role theory with her own professional experience as a fundraiser to conceptualize four organizational roles enacted by fundraisers: liaison, expert prescriber, problem-solving process facilitator, and technician. Based on findings of a qualitative study using in-depth interviews, Kelly (1998b) explicated a new schema to measure fundraising roles. According to Kelly, the roles explain how individual fundraisers behave in carrying out their job responsibilities and predict the outcomes of the action. In describing the four roles, Kelly explained that asking fundraisers whether they solicited gifts was a weak measurement of role enactment, as that task is carried out by almost all staff fundraisers. However, routine tasks other than solicitation reveal significant insights into how fundraisers participate not only in the fundraising program but also in organizational decision making.

Kelly (1998a) hypothesized that every fundraiser plays all four roles to some extent, but enacts one predominantly. The predominant role is important as it represents the worldview held by practitioners and senior managers regarding what fundraisers do and how they contribute to organizational success. Kelly's critical analysis of the practitioner literature provided evidence that all four roles exist in fundraising practice.

Liaison is the role predominantly enacted by consultants, who do not solicit gifts but advise organizational managers and volunteers on doing so (Kelly, 1998a). The role casts practitioners as interpreters and mediators in bringing together organizational representatives with prospective donors. This is the traditional, "behind-the-scene" role of consultants. A weakness of the liaison role is its reliance on other actors, which makes fundraising vulnerable to unmet goals and inefficiency. Furthermore, practitioners enacting this role concern themselves only with fundraising; they are not involved with other aspects of the organization, such as delivering program services.

Expert prescriber is the exact opposite of liaison (Kelly, 1998a). Fundraisers in this role act and are viewed as the only ones in their organization with the skill and responsibility for raising gifts. Senior managers, trustees, and staff are content to leave fundraising in the hands of the "expert" and assume relatively passive participation. The role is attractive to managers and trustees who dislike fundraising and to fundraising practitioners who enjoy expert status. Among the role's many weaknesses, fundraising is isolated from the organization's operations, which hampers efforts to address organizational needs and establish meaningful relationships with donors.

Fundraisers usually begin their careers in the technician role, in which they primarily are concerned with producing and implementing the various tactics used in raising gifts, such as grant proposals and direct mail (Kelly, 1998a). Technicians carry out decisions made by others. They are not part of the management team and rarely participate in strategic planning, research, or budgeting decisions. Problems arise when fundraising departments consist only of technicians. In such cases, the function contributes little to advancing the organization's mission or meeting its goals.

Practitioners enacting the problem-solving process facilitator role are part of the management team. They collaborate with others in the organization, manage key actors' participation in the fundraising process, and participate in decision making on organization-wide problems. Problem-solving process facilitators rely on research and strategic planning to direct fundraising programs. Success is gauged not by the amount of money raised, but by the extent to which fundraising helped the organization achieve its goals. When fundraising departments are headed by practitioners predominantly enacting this role, the fundraising function is fully integrated in the organization's operations and aspirations.

In her exploratory study, Kelly (1998b) found qualitative evidence that the four roles accurately describe the behavior patterns of fundraisers as they go about their work for different types of charitable organizations. Wagner (2002) attested to the validity of these four roles, but called for "more research to verify and substantiate these findings" (p. 48). However, little has been done to explore the relationship between role theory and fundraising.

Tindall (2007) surveyed fundraisers at historically black colleges and universities (HBCUs) to examine which tasks they used in donor communication. She followed up that study with a more descriptive examination of the roles, using in-depth interviews (Tindall, 2009). Using Q methodology, Waters (2008) found evidence for a typology consisting of manager, technician, and researcher, fundraisers who primarily spent the day researching cultivation opportunities targeted at individuals and foundations. Waters, Kelly, and Walker (2012) explored the relationship between gender and role enactment and found that a glass ceiling exists that prevents women from taking on managerial roles. However, research has yet to explore racial diversity in relation to fundraising role theory.

Studies have shown that minority fundraisers are very successful in the field and are every bit as skilled as their Caucasian counterparts at conducing annual giving, major gift, and planned giving programs (Tindall & Waters, 2010). Regardless, little is known about the types of fundraising tasks minorities engage in on a daily basis when compared to Caucasian fundraisers. To begin to fill that void, this study poses two research questions to examine the extent to which minority fundraisers enact Kelly's (1998a) fundraising roles:

RQ1: What fundraising roles do minority fundraisers employ, and do they differ in relation to those enacted by Caucasian fundraisers?

RQ2: Do organizational characteristics limit the likelihood of individual success for minority fundraisers?

METHOD

The population selected for study was fundraisers who are members of the AHP. AHP is a professional association for fundraisers who work for charitable organizations with healthcare missions, primarily hospitals and medical centers. Founded in 1967, it currently has about 5,000 members (Association for Healthcare Philanthropy, 2014). AHP provided an appropriate population because it is one of the three major U.S. fundraising associations; healthcare organizations are one of the heaviest employers of fundraisers; and fundraisers who work for healthcare organizations are among the highest paid (Kelly, 1998a). Additionally, AHP members represent a relatively homogeneous group in that they work for one type of charitable organization and solely in fundraising, unlike members of the other two leading associations.

A random sample of 600 AHP members was selected, and questionnaires were sent to participants via the U.S. Postal Service. A follow-up mailing also requested participation in the study. The survey instrument consisted of 19 descriptive questions regarding personal demographics and organizational characteristics and the 24 role items, modified to reflect fundraising and respond to suggestions from Kelly's (1998b) earlier qualitative study. In most cases, modification required changing only one word. For example the word "fundraising" was substituted for the word "communications" in the expert prescriber indicator, "I make the fundraising policy decisions." Abbreviated versions of the statements are presented later in tables reporting results. A complete list is available from the authors.

The role statements were measured with a fractional open-end scale. Respondents were asked to indicate how well each of the 24 items described the work that they do as fundraising practitioners. They were instructed to use the scale to choose a number from zero (does not describe) to as high as they wanted to go. They were told that 100 was the score that an average practitioner would give to a typical item. Following public relations scholars who had used the same scale to measure roles (e.g., L. A. Grunig, J. E. Grunig, & Dozier, 2002), scores were transformed by computing their square roots to reduce a positive skew resulting from the open-end scale, which produced an approximately normal distribution. Mean scores were calculated, and indices were developed for each of the four roles by summing and averaging scores on the six items associated with each role.

The indices were found to be reliable, although one varied in statistical strength. The technician role (α = .86), the expert prescriber role (α = .88), and the problem-solving process facilitator role (α =.85) met the alpha standard of .80 for index reliability (Carmines & Zeller, 1979). The remaining role, liaison (α = .79), fell slightly short of the standard; however, it comfortably met the minimum alpha level of .70 that Bowers and Cartright (1984) urged communication scholars to adopt in the early phase of index development. Statistical analyses were conducted using SPSS software.

RESULTS

The research design resulted in 286 usable questionnaires being returned, a response rate of 48%. There were 101 male (35%) and 179 female (63%) participants, and six did not report gender. The average age of the fundraisers was 46; ages ranged from 23 to 80. The vast majority of the respondents (85.7%) was Caucasian; Hispanics (5.1%) were the largest minority group represented, although Asian Americans, African Americans/Blacks, and Native Americans each represented another 3% of the participants. One-fourth of the respondents earned less than $50,000 per year, whereas 56% earned between $50,000 and $100,000, and 19% earned more than $100,000. In terms of respondents' highest level of education, 5% had a doctoral degree, 33% had a master's degree, 51% had a bachelor's degree, and 10% had a high school diploma. Comparison with AHP membership statistics showed that respondents did not substantially differ from the population selected for study.

The first research question sought to determine whether minority fundraisers enacted the roles similarly to Caucasian fundraisers in AHP. To answer this question, a one-way ANOVA was conducted on the role indices. The 24 items and the indices' means are presented in Table 1–1. Minority fundraisers were more likely to enact one of the three managerial roles than the technician role (M = 7.73, SD = 3.96). Paralleling previous role theory studies in fundraising, expert prescriber (M = 11.71, SD = 3.47) was the role most often enacted by minorities, followed by problem-solving process facilitator (M = 10.73, SD = 2.98) and liaison (M = 8.93, SD = 3.19). To determine if these mean scores were significantly different for each participant, a repeated measures ANOVA was conducted. Mauchly's test of sphericity indicated that the assumption of homogeneity of variance was violated for

Table 1–1   Means and Standard Deviations for Four Fundraising Roles and Cronbach's Alpha for Role Indices.

Role Items	Caucasian Fundraisers (n = 245)	Minority Fundraisers (n = 41)
	Mean (Std Dev)	Mean (Std Dev)
Technician		
I write fundraising materials on issues and donors.	9.66 (4.26)	9.16 (3.78)
I edit fundraising materials written by others.	9.03 (4.41)	8.94 (4.28)
I produce brochures, pamphlets, etc.	9.00 (4.27)	8.19 (4.56)
I handle technical aspects of producing materials.	8.55 (4.63)	8.08 (4.67)
I coordinate photography and graphics.	7.07 (4.95)	5.48 (5.05)
I maintain media contacts and place press releases.	6.52 (4.90)	6.91 (5.51)
Index Mean (α = .86)	8.34 (3.46)	7.73 (3.96)
Liaison		
I represent the organization at events and meetings.	11.95 (3.41)	11.58 (4.42)
I inform management of donor reactions to policies.	10.32 (3.47)	10.45 (4.24)
I create opportunities for management to hear donors.	8.92 (4.28)	9.40 (3.95)
I keep the organization informed about media reports.	8.08 (4.52)	8.17 (4.72)
I report donor opinion survey results to management.	6.94 (4.74)	7.75 (4.80)
I conduct research to identify problems with donors.	5.89 (4.86)	6.47 (4.65)
Index Mean (α = .79)	8.71 (2.83)	8.93 (3.19)
Expert Prescriber		
I take responsibility for success or failure of fundraising.	12.34 (4.74)	12.47 (4.47)
Others hold me accountable for fundraising success.	11.87 (3.79)	12.16 (3.62)
Others consider me the fundraising expert.	11.31 (4.61)	11.66 (3.91)
I plan actions for pursuing fundraising opportunities.	11.18 (3.56)	11.57 (3.53)
I make the fundraising policy decisions.	10.70 (3.90)	10.54 (4.35)
I diagnose and explain fundraising opportunities.	10.48 (3.95)	11.26 (3.95)
Index Mean (α = .88)	11.29 (3.23)	11.71 (3.47)

(Continued)

Table 1–1   (Continued)

Role Items	Caucasian Fundraisers (*n* = 245)	Minority Fundraisers (*n* = 41)
Problem-Solving Process Facilitator		
I encourage mgmt. participation in fundraising decisions.	10.87 (3.32)	11.15 (3.89)
I emphasize a systematic planning process to mgmt.	10.67 (3.91)	11.74 (4.92)
I keep management involved in all phases of fundraising.	10.21 (3.43)	10.94 (3.32)
I outline alternative approaches for pursuing opportunities.	9.94 (3.79)	10.80 (3.53)
I operate as a catalyst in management's decision making.	9.31 (4.29)	10.21 (3.99)
I work with managers to increase their fundraising skills.	9.03 (4.38)	9.28 (3.83)
Index Mean (α = .85)	10.03 (2.96)	10.73 (2.98)

this data. As a result, the Huynh-Feldt test was interpreted, which indicated a significant difference between observations ($F(1.70, 62.99) = 28.87$, $p < .001$) for each individual.

Providing support for the fundraising associations' claims that minorities can advance their career and thrive in fundraising, the roles' mean scores for minorities in this study reflected those of their Caucasian counterparts. As shown in Table 1–1, Caucasians enacted the roles in the same order of the minority fundraisers, with expert prescriber ($M = 11.29$, $SD = 3.23$) being the dominant role and technician ($M = 8.34$, $SD = 3.46$) being the one least enacted. A one-way ANOVA revealed that no statistically significant differences existed for the enactment of the expert prescriber ($F(1, 284) = .54$, $p = .46$), problem-solving process facilitator ($F(1, 284) = 1.88$, $p = .17$), liaison ($F(1, 284) = .21$, $p = .65$), and technician ($F(1, 284) = .98$, $p = .32$) between minorities and Caucasian fundraisers.

The second research question sought to determine whether organizational characteristics limited the success that minority fundraisers experienced while working. On average, the respondents had 16.3 years of fundraising experience and had been with their current employer for 9.4 years. Caucasians had an average 16.8 years of fundraising experience while minorities had 13.1 years of experience in the profession. Through they had fewer years in the profession, minorities reported having longer tenure at their current organization ($M = 7.91$, $SD = 7.10$) than Caucasians ($M = 6.61$, $SD = 5.88$). When asked to estimate the amount of money raised for their organizations, Caucasians reported that they raised on average $10,379,733 ($SD = $38,274,420$) while minorities raised an average of $8,046,029 ($SD = $9,216,635$) for their organizations. This difference was not statistically significant ($F(1, 284) = .69$, $p = .41$).

One-way ANOVAs revealed that Caucasians and minorities had similar levels of organizational support in terms of the total number of people in their fundraising departments ($F(1, 284) = 2.12$, $p = .15$) and total number of fundraisers in the department ($F(1, 284) = .19$, $p = .66$). Caucasians worked in fundraising departments of 10.05 ($SD = 21.01$) people where nearly seven of those individuals worked exclusively as fundraisers ($M = 6.65$, $SD = 14.99$). The fundraising departments where minorities worked had on average 8.92 ($SD = 11.43$) people working in the office; a similar proportion ($M = 6.36$, $SD = 9.89$) of individuals worked solely as fundraisers. Because income was collected as a categorical variable, a chi-square test was conducted to determine if the participants received similar compensation for their work. Roughly 26% of Caucasian fundraisers were paid less than $50,000, compared to 30% of minority fundraisers. Nearly 56% of Caucasian fundraisers were paid between $50,000 and $99,999, compared to 45% of minority fundraisers. Thirteen percent of Caucasians were compensated between $100,000 and $149,999, compared to 15% of minority fundraisers; 5% of Caucasian and 10% of minority fundraisers received more than $150,000 in salary. Despite these differences in percentages, there is no statistical difference in the compensation received by Caucasian and minority fundraisers ($\chi^2 = 4.67$, $df = 3$, $p = .197$).

DISCUSSION

This study sought to describe the careers of minority fundraisers in the AHP using role theory and organizational characteristics and to compare those experiences to those of their Caucasian counterparts. The findings of this study echo the campaigns of AFP, AHP, and CASE, that fundraising provides rewarding opportunities for minorities. This study found no statistically significant differences between Caucasians and minorities in terms of managerial responsibilities, organizational support and compensation, and performance.

The lack of statistical significance between Caucasian and minority fundraisers is a positive finding for the fundraising profession. Contrary to previous studies—and perhaps a sign of professional growth, Caucasians were not found to be in a dominant position over minority fundraisers. Whereas previous research has shown that African-American/Black (Betts, 1989), Asian-American (Smith et al., 1992), Hispanic/Latino (Royce &

Rodriguez, 1999), and Native American (Thorpe, 1989) fundraisings were missing in managerial activities in nonprofits, the current findings actually demonstrate that minority fundraisers enacted managerial roles more often than their Caucasian counterparts. Although this difference was not statistically significant and merely a reflection of differing means, the study provides one of the first examples of a fracturing glass ceiling for minority fundraisers.

The AFP diversity summit in 2005, as well as the diversity recruitment and professional development workshops hosted by AFP, AHP, and CASE, appear to have had a positive influence on the role minority fundraisers play in their organizations. Minority participants in this study reported that they were usually placed in positions of power with fundraising endeavors. Additionally, further analysis of demographic data revealed no statistically significant differences in terms of size of the fundraisers' staff and their salaries. These results also are a positive sign for minorities in fundraising, as they provide further evidence that nonprofit management realize their value in helping achieve organizational goals. However, these findings must be interpreted cautiously.

Similar to the public relations industry, a paucity of academic research exists on fundraisers of color. Even though issues of recruitment and retention of diverse practitioners has been addressed, most of the research primarily consists of personal experiences and anecdotes (e.g., Stanfield, 2005; Stephens, 2005; Tokumura, 2005). The lack of academic research may stem from the limited visibility of practitioners of color in fundraising. Stephens (2005) proposed that the lack of certified African-American fundraising professionals was one core problem with minority recruitment. The lack of credentialed minority fundraisers may reduce the amount of professional mentorship opportunities for future fundraisers. Wagner and Ryan (2005), however, expressed greater concern for the diversification of fundraising. They acknowledged that minorities generally have lower than normal rates in terms of professional certification, but emphasized that less than 8% of the 30,000 members of the AFP (the largest fundraising association) are classified as minorities.

Discussions about diversity efforts have been started within the field's associations as a result of the 2005 diversity summit, and some efforts have been made to make fundraising an appealing field for people of color and to recruit minorities into fundraising. However, none of the organizations has an individual officer or staff member who is responsible for minority recruitment and retention strategy or activities (Wagner & Ryan, 2005).

As discussed in the introduction, the three organizations—AFP, AHP, and CASE—have all begun diversity recruitment campaigns and programs. But, they are not maximizing the impact of their programs. Despite the profession's understanding of the importance of two-way communication in the fundraising process with donors, the recruitment efforts for the diversity campaigns have largely been one-way promotional strategies. AFP's case studies and targeted publications and CASE's speakers' bureau do little to foster true discussions with potential minority fundraisers about the opportunities the profession brings. AHP has made the progression to interaction with its workshops and virtual discussion series, yet recruitment and retention specialists question the effectiveness of this strategy (McKay & Avery, 2005).

As Wagner and Ryan (2005) pointed out, the associations have not demonstrated legitimate commitment to the efforts by naming someone to oversee the programs. To be more effective, the three fundraising associations need to institutionalize diversity recruitment and retention efforts (Winston, 2001). Kreitz (2008) suggests that such a position should also work to ensure that the organizations create a culturally supportive environment and work to ensure that diversity issues are at the forefront of the organization's thinking. While both of these strategies are effective, they, too, fail to capitalize on interpersonal relationships. The most effective way to diversify the fundraising profession is through the creation of institutional alliances, which will help identify and recruit minorities interested in fundraising as they begin thinking about future career opportunities (Druker & Stanworth, 2001). None of the associations has approached leading nonprofit management training centers. Programs, such as the Center on Philanthropy at Indiana University, the Mandel Center for Nonprofit Organizations at Case Western Reserve University, or the Institute for Nonprofits at North Carolina State University, already regularly offer courses and workshops on fundraising practices. If the associations are genuinely interested in diversification, then they must approach nonprofit programs and faculty and create alliances to start their recruitment efforts with students who first express an interest in nonprofit management (Druker & Stanworth, 2001).

These strategies may result in more minorities considering fundraising as a career choice; however, scholars must continue to study the experiences of minority practitioners to determine the impact of systemic recruiting efforts (Winston, 2001). Although limited work has been done to examine the organizational roles that minorities enact, research has shown that practitioners of color are routinely satisfied and successful with their work. The current study shows that minority fundraisers have considerable authority when it comes to achieving financial well-being for their organizations. The role most often enacted was the managerial role of expert prescriber. While this role brings substantial managerial power and control over the decisions made for fundraising programs and strategic planning, this personal power and potential for success may also be inadvertently putting both the fundraisers and their organizations at risk. As Kelly (1998a) noted, fundraisers who are placed in charge of the fundraising process with little input or participation by senior managers risk organizational isolation and may devastate an organization if the fundraiser leaves the organization.

Given the parallels between public relations and fundraising role research, it is possible that Kelly's (1998a) adaptation of the four roles is not exhaustive of the career experiences of minority fundraisers. Although her examination focused on public relations practitioners, Pompper's (2004) work revealed that minorities consider themselves to be pioneers in the profession who serve as mentors and leaders for future practitioners. Other scholars have found that minority practitioners also enact a cultural interpreter role (Yamashita, 1992; Ferreria, 1993; Mallette, 1995), which primarily counsels the organization on cultural issues relevant to particular communities with which the practitioners are affiliated. These studies found that enactment of the pioneer and cultural interpreter roles also led to greater personal and professional fulfillment. Exploring these roles in relation to the fundraising profession may also provide insights that organizations can use to draw future practitioners to the profession.

One final element that associations should consider when encouraging minorities to consider careers in fundraising is compensation. Although documentation about salaries and organizational roles is scant, the findings of this study reiterate Kelly's (1998a) reported data that showed that minority practitioners received compensation that was not statistically different from their Caucasian counterparts. When considered along with the strong enactment of management responsibilities, one has to wonder just how deep the cracks are in the glass ceiling. Minority fundraisers in AHP reported having a greater proportion of the top salaries in their organizations; however, Caucasian fundraisers received salaries in the $50,000 to $99,999 range in substantially greater proportion than minority fundraisers. This discrepancy causes one to wonder whether the glass ceiling has been cracked open for minority fundraisers or merely chipped.

CONCLUSION

This study represents an important initial step in advancing theoretical knowledge on fundraising as well as providing a description of the career experiences of minority fundraisers. This research provides encouraging evidence that the nonprofit sector may be seeing results from its diversity recruitment efforts. As the diversified pool of fundraisers continues to take on leadership positions and managerial tasks, the nonprofit sector will be in an even stronger position to recruit minorities into the profession. Nonprofits will also benefit, as the organizations will be in a better strategic position to reach out to the increasingly multicultural donor database. Results of this study have important implications for recruitment strategies by professional fundraising associations to diversify the industry. But, as previously stated, this study has limitations that must be acknowledged before making sweeping generalizations about the positive career possibilities for minorities.

Limitations. This study only assessed the organizational behavior patterns of fundraising practitioners who are members of AHP. Although fundraising assumedly is conducted similarly across the nonprofit sector, the structure of hospitals and medical centers might have an impact on how fundraisers working for such organizations function. Results of this study are generalizable only to organizations represented in AHP. It may be that studies focused on respondents who are members of the other two major fundraising associations—AFP and CASE—would yield different results.

Additionally, although the research design used an appropriately conducted random sampling technique, it generated only 40 minority fundraisers. While this is reflective of AHP in terms of proportional representation, it is difficult to say that these practitioners represent the entire range of minority fundraisers. It would be helpful to examine fundraisers at a community level because practitioners who join professional associations are likely to enact managerial roles in their organizations as these roles are more closely associated with networking and are more likely to have membership dues paid for by their organization. Practitioners who predominantly enact the technician role more likely hold lower-level fundraising positions that are not associated with such benefits. An analysis of fundraisers at the community level might provide insightful data regarding the differences between role enactment by Caucasian and minority fundraisers.

REFERENCES

Association for Healthcare Philanthropy. (2014). Who we are. Retrieved February 25, 2014, from http://www.ahp.org/membership/Who/Pages/default.aspx

Betts, T. D. (1989, Autumn). Minority fund-raising in America: A historical perspective. *Journal: Contemporary Issues in Fundraising*, 6–13.

Bowers, J. W., & Courtright, J. A. (1984). *Communication research methods*. Glenview, IL: Scott, Foresman.

Broom, G. M. (1982). A comparison of sex roles in public relations. *Public Relations Review, 8*(3):17–22.

Broom, G. M., & Smith, G. D. (1979). Testing the practitioner's impact on clients. *Public Relations Review, 5*(3), 47–59.

Carmines, E. G., & Zeller, R. A. (1979). *Reliability and validity assessment*. Newbury Park, CA: SAGE University Paper.

Collins, P. H. (2000). *Black feminist thought: Knowledge, consciousness, and the politics of empowerment* (2nd ed.). New York, NY: Routledge.

Cutlip, S., Center, A., & Broom, G. (2006). *Effective Public Relations* (9th ed.). Upper Saddle River, NJ: Pearson Prentice Hall.

Dozier, D. M. (1992). The organizational roles of communications and public relations practitioners. In J. E. Grunig (Ed.), *Excellence in public relations and communication management* (pp. 327–355). Hillsdale, NJ: Lawrence Erlbaum Associates, Inc.

Druker, J., & Stanworth, C. (2001). Partnerships and the private recruitment industry. *Human Resources Management Journal, 11*(2), 73–89.

Ferreira, J. (1993). *Hispanic public relations practitioners and the glass ceiling effect*. Unpublished master's thesis, University of Maryland, College Park.

Fogal, R. E. (1994). Designing and managing the fundraising program. In R. Herman (Ed.), *The Jossey-Bass handbook of nonprofit leadership and management* (pp. 369–381). San Francisco, CA: Jossey-Bass.

Gordon, C.G., & Kelly, K.S. (1999). Public relations expertise and organizational effectiveness: A study of U.S. hospitals. *Journal of Public Relations Research, 11*(2), 143–165.

Grunig, L.A., Grunig, J.E., & Dozier, D.M. (2002). *Excellent public relations and effective organizations: A study of communication management in three countries.* Mahwah, NJ: Lawrence Erlbaum.

Grunig, L.A., Toth, E.L., & Hon, L.C. (2001). *Women in public relations: How gender influences practice.* New York, NY: Guilford Press.

Hager, M., Rooney, P., & Pollack, T. (2002). How fundraising is carried out in US nonprofit organisations. *International Journal of Nonprofit and Voluntary Sector Marketing, 7*(4), 311–324.

Hooper, P., & Stobart, S. (2003). Using third-party services to reduce the development cost and improve the effectiveness of charity websites. *International Journal of Nonprofit & Voluntary Sector Marketing, 8*(4), 328–336.

Kalugyer, A. D. (2014, June 17). Giving USA: Americans gave $335.17 billion to charity in 2013; total approaches pre-recession peak. Retrieved June 20, 2014, from http://www.philanthropy.iupui.edu/news/article/giving-usa-2014

Katz, D., & Kahn, R. (1978). *The Social Psychology of Organizations.* New York, NY: Wiley.

Kelly, K.S. (1998a). *Effective fund-raising management.* Mahwah, NJ: Lawrence Erlbaum.

Kelly, K.S. (1998b, November). *Four organizational roles of fund raisers: An exploratory study.* Paper presented to the Association for Research on Nonprofit Organizations and Voluntary Action (ARNOVA) 27th annual conference, Seattle, WA.

Kreitz, P.A. (2008). Best practices for managing organizational diversity. *Journal of Academic Leadership, 34*(2), 101–120.

Lysakowski, L. (2002). The importance of volunteers in a capital campaign. *International Journal of Nonprofit and Voluntary Sector Marketing, 7*(4), 325–333. doi: 10.1002/nvsm.189

Mallette, W.A. (1995). *African Americans in public relations: Pigeonholed practitioners or cultural interpreters?* Unpublished master's thesis, University of Maryland, College Park.

McKay, P.F., & Avery, D.R. (2005). Warning! Diversity recruitment could backfire. *Journal of Management Inquiry, 14*(4), 330–336.

Petty, J.G. (2001). *Cultivating diversity in fundraising.* San Francisco, CA: Jossey-Bass.

Petty, J.G., & Wagner, L. (2007). Introduction: Union gives us strength—diversity and fundraising. *International Journal of Educational Advancement, 7,* 171–175.

Piekos, J., & Einsiedel, E. (1990), Roles and program evaluation techniques among Canadian public relations practitioners. In J. Grunig & L. Grunig (Eds.), *Public relations research annual* (vol. 2, pp. 95–114). Hillsdale, NJ: Lawrence Erlbaum.

Pompper, D. (2004). Linking ethnic diversity & two-way symmetry: Modeling female African American practitioners' roles. *Journal of Public Relations Research, 16,* 269–299.

Royce, A.P., & Rodriguez, R. (1999). From personal charity to organized giving: Hispanic institutions and values of stewardship and philanthropy. *New Directions for Philanthropic Fundraising, 24,* 9–29.

Ryan, L.J. (2006). Behavioral characteristics of higher education fund-raisers. *International Journal of Educational Advancement, 6*(4), 282–288.

Smith, B., Shue, S., Vest, J.L., & Villarreal, J. (1992). *Asian and Hispanic philanthropy.* San Francisco, CA: University of San Francisco, Institute for Nonprofit Organization Management.

Stanfield, J. H. (2005). Race, philanthropy: Personalities, institutions, networks, and communities. *New Directions for Philanthropic Fundraising, 48*, 105–112.

Stephens, C. R. (2005). Professionalism in black philanthropy: We have a chance to get it right. *New Directions for Philanthropic Fundraising, 48*, 13–19.

Thorpe, D. (1989, Autumn). Looking at philanthropy with native eyes. *Journal: Contemporary Issues in Fundraising*, 17–20.

Tindall, N. T. J. (2007). An analysis of fund raising models at historically black colleges and universities. *Public Relations Review, 33*(2), 201–205.

Tindall, N. T. J. (2009). Working on the "short grass": Fund-raiser roles and experiences at historically black colleges and universities. *International Journal of Educational Advancement, 9*, 3–15.

Tindall, N. T. J., & Waters, R. D. (2010). The relationship between fundraising practice and job satisfaction at historically Black colleges and universities. *International Journal of Educational Advancement, 10*(3), 198–215.

Tokumura, S. S. (2005). Fundraising mores in diverse communities: The role of ethnicity and culture. *New Directions for Philanthropic Fundraising, 34*, 3–30.

Toth, E., & Grunig, L. (1993). The missing story of women in public relations. *Journal of Public Relations Research, 5*(3), 153–175.

Wagner, L. (2002). *Careers in fundraising*. San Francisco, CA: Wiley.

Wagner, L., & Ryan, J. P. (2005). Achieving diversity among fundraising professionals. *New Directions for Philanthropic Fundraising, 43*, 63–70.

Waters, R. D. (2008). The practitioner roles of fund raising: Testing the typologies using q-methodology. *Journal of Human Subjectivity, 5*(1), 45–64.

Waters, R. D. (2010). Increasing fundraising efficiency through evaluation: Applying communication theory to the nonprofit organization-donor relationship. *Nonprofit & Voluntary Sector Quarterly, 40*(3), 458–475. doi:10.1177/0899764009354322

Waters, R. D., Kelly, K. S., & Walker, M. L. (2012). Organizational roles enacted by healthcare fundraisers: A national study testing theory and assessing gender differences. *Journal of Communication Management, 16*(3), 244–263.

Winston, M. D. (2001). Recruitment theory: Identification of those who are likely to be successful as leaders. *Journal of Library Administration, 32*(3–4), 19–34.

Worth, M. J., & Asp, J. W., II. (1994). The development officer in higher education: Toward an understanding of the role. *ASHE-ERIC Higher Education Reports, 4*, 1–77.

Wu, F. (2002). *Yellow: Race in America beyond black and white*. New York, NY: Basic Books.

Yamashita, S. H. (1992). *The examination of the status and roles of Asian American public relations practitioners in the United States*. Unpublished master's thesis, University of Maryland, College Park.

2 Relying on Divine Intervention?
An Analysis of Church Crisis Management Plans

Hilary Fussell Sisco, Randi Plake, and Erik L. Collins

Virtually all organizations are susceptible to a crisis that has the ability to cause not only physical damage and financial loss, but harm to reputation as well. Because an organization's reputation is primarily based on its relations with its key publics, crisis management has become a focus of both public relations academics and professionals. Academic research has yielded a rich trove of scholarly literature regarding crisis communication management. Not surprisingly, public relations professionals in both the public and private sectors are increasingly focused on creating strategic crisis communication plans in order to prepare for and manage crisis situations.

As a whole, religious organizations appear to be an exception to this trend. Research by Kirkpatrick (2011) suggests that most individual churches have not taken the steps necessary to create coherent crisis management plans that take into account the concerns of their major stakeholders in order to enhance their relationships. For example, according to Kirkpatrick, in 2008, while 30 percent of all churches experienced a threat or emergency, 75 percent of churches reportedly had no emergency plan of any kind in place.

Although equally subject to natural disasters like hurricanes, tornados and earthquakes, houses of worship were once considered safe havens from the human strife and tumult of the everyday world (Bayer, 1998). Today, however, the news is filled with reports of robberies, assaults and even homicides occurring in places of worship (Bayer, 1998). In addition, the increased prominence in the media of church-specific crises (Tyler-Satterfield, 2009) promises even more difficulties for those charged with maintaining a positive reputation for religious organizations.

How the media report on religious organizations in times of crisis often is a product of how the organizations relate and interact with the media and on how well the organizations have communicated their positions to their other stakeholders. Although a number of scholars have investigated the kinds of crises churches have encountered (Tyler-Satterfield, 2009), there has been little published research about the current state of efforts by churches at the local level to manage the response to crises they may encounter.

The research reported in this chapter is an initial step in the investigation of this question. Employing Coombs's (2007) three-phase approach to crisis management as a guideline, the researchers conducted primary research in the form of a qualitative analysis of a sampling of church crisis management plans with a focus on their communication elements.

LITERATURE REVIEW

Crises seem to be more catastrophic and reported more frequently in the media than ever before. As Lerbinger (1997) writes, "[n]o type of organization is immune from crises" (p. 3). Furthermore, Coombs (2011) suggests, "[t]he bottom line is that all organizations should learn as much as they can about crisis management" (p. 1).

A crisis is the "perception of an unpredictable event that . . . can seriously impact an organization's performance and generate negative outcomes" (Coombs, 2007, pp. 2–3). Coombs's definition emphasizes perception of a crisis, particularly, as Crandall, Parnell, and Spillan (2010) suggest, is generally perceived to be a threat by an organization's key stakeholders.

After exploring the many definitions of a crisis, a reoccurring theme is visible: A crisis can potentially create a wide range of negative or undesirable effects. Coombs (2007) suggests that "[a] crisis can create three related threats: public safety, financial loss, and reputation loss" (p. 3). Damages from a crisis often extend beyond pecuniary loss to include injuries or death, property damage, diminution of stakeholder goodwill, and environmental harm. Because a crisis presents such potential negative outcomes for an organization and its stakeholders, managing the crisis situation in a way so as to ameliorate damage is essential.

Crises in the Church. Recognizing the many crisis vulnerabilities an organization may face is key to managing crisis situations (Coombs, 2007). Christian Security Network (CSN), a national security organization with a mission to provide churches, schools, ministries, and missionaries with training, information, and resources to become better prepared in today's world of risk, has been collecting data on church crimes since 2008, and releases an annual report every year. According to CSN, in 2010, "[a]rsonists . . . attacked an average of 100 churches, internal theft . . . cost congregations an average of more than a quarter-million dollars per incident, and almost every area of crime against Christians and their places of worship [was] rising" (Kirkpatrick, 2011, para. 1).

According to the report, robberies, violence, and bomb threats involving a church have declined since 2009. However, burglary, thefts, arson, vandalism, internal theft, and sexual offenses have increased. As Kirkpatrick (2011) writes, "[i]ncidents like internal thefts are devastating to churches in the Unites States, costing more than $15 million a year and forcing some to close their doors" (para. 6).

Tyler-Satterfield (2009) has suggested six types of church crises: moral crises, administrative crises, financial crises, legal crises, natural crises, and accidental crises. While prone to crises like other organizations, some crises that happen to a church are potentially more catastrophic. For example, Tyler-Satterfield (2009) writes, moral failures, like unethical or illegal conduct of church staff or members, "can seriously derail the overall mission and reputation of the church" (p. 3).

Although scholars have begun to explore crises in religious organizations, few have focused on the public impacts of such crises. An exception is Kauffman (2008), who examined the sex scandal crisis in the American Catholic Church. Kauffman analyzed Archbishop Cardinal Bernard Law's "Statement on the Issue of Sexual Abuse of Minors by Clergy" and image restoration activities. Kauffman's study found that the archbishop failed to restore his image despite employing many different types of crisis response strategies.

As Marra (1998, p. 461) points out, churches, just like for-profit businesses, "must be prepared to communicate during a crisis, because the ability to communicate quickly and effectively is clearly an important component of successful and effective crisis management." A communication component of a crisis management plan, therefore, is vital to a church, especially because "crises, in almost all circumstances, immediately trigger a deluge of questions from an organization's many different publics" (Marra, 1998, p. 461). The strategies and tactics within a crisis management plan help to maintain relationships with internal and external stakeholders.

Religious Organizations and the Media. A solid foundation of research has documented the ways in which religious organizations are portrayed in the media. Historically, religious organizations have been rooted in a stance of one-way communication. Recent research, however, has suggested that these organizations must adapt "from one-way preaching to symmetrical conversations between institutions and their members" (Waters & Bortree, 2012, p. 202).

Even in a technological world where interaction is easy, research (Sturgill, 2004) has found that religious organizations are not using their websites to interact with the public or its members. As Smith (2007) found, "very little dialogue is being initiated between organizations and their members, and there are few opportunities for prospective members to communicate with the organization" (p. 283).

In a case study of Greek Orthodox congregations, Patrikios (2013) found evidence that churches need to focus their messages on two audiences: the local congregation and the mass media. His research suggests that the use of similar messages for both audiences can lead to confusion and mistrust of religious organizations. Furthermore, engaging in relational dialogue with both members and the general audience has been documented to increase a religious organization's positive reputation and be seen more favorably by the public (Kosmin & Keysar, 2008; Bader-Saye, 2006).

The hesitancy to engage in dialogue with members and the media can be most damaging when religious organizations are in crisis. Courtright and Hearit (2002) noted that "the media do not cover religious news especially well" (p. 354) and that two of the most important concerns during a crisis are the increased media scrutiny and the managing of internal publics.

Stohmeier (2009) found that the type of media coverage that religious institutions face is not only determined by the content of the message. In a crisis situation, these organizations must provide context to help the media deliver information. His study posits that for the Vatican, this unwillingness to provide appropriate context has increased reputational damage to the Catholic Church.

In a study focused on a number of protestant religious organizations, Shin (2008) found that in a crisis situation, church communicators "may rely on their religious principles to resolve a crisis" (p. 405), which may not meet the expectations of the general public or the media. Therefore, it is imperative, he says, that religious organizations are able to differentiate between messages for their internal audiences and the media. These organizations must also be able to engage in dialogue with the media in order to protect its members as well as their reputations.

Crisis Management. The researchers employed Coombs's (2007) three-phase approach as a guideline for the analysis of the church crisis management plans in this study. The researchers acknowledge that Coombs's approach is not the only scholarly framework for crisis communication planning, but the three phases of crisis management were considered to be best suited for an investigation into the practice.

According to Coombs (2011), crisis management is designed to "prevent or lessen the damage a crisis can cause to an organization and its stakeholders" (p. 5). Coombs (2007) divides crisis management into three phases: (1) pre-crisis preparation, (2) crisis response, and (3) post-crisis evaluation and follow up. Coombs's (2007) approach has been used in many different organizations, including large corporations (El-Nadi, 2009), health departments (Avery et al., 2010), and higher education (Walsch, 2011).

The first phase of crisis management is the pre-crisis phase. This phase is concerned with prevention and preparation. "Preparation involves creating the crisis management plan, selecting and training the crisis management team, and conducting exercises to test the crisis management plan and crisis management team" (Coombs, 2007, p. 3). Practicing and preparing for a crisis allow faster reactions and more effective decisions. Because people want to know what has happened when a crisis occurs, Coombs recommends providing a response in the first hour after crisis so the organization can tell its side of the story (Coombs, 2007).

Crisis preparation best practices include updating the crisis management plan annually (Coombs, 2007). Research also has shown that organizations are better able to handle crises when they conduct exercises to test plans at least once a year (Barton, 2001; Coombs, 2006).

The second phase in the crisis management process is the crisis response. Coombs (2007) writes, "[t]he crisis response is what management does and says after the crisis hits" (p. 6). The crisis response "includes the first statements the spokesperson makes about the crisis" (Coombs, 2011, p. 139). The initial response must be formulated beforehand, and should be quick, accurate, and consistent. This is important because the news media are drawn to crises and an organization's response can be disseminated to reach a wide array of publics through the news media.

In the response phase, it is also important for the organization to make its initial response as quickly as feasible. According to Coombs (2011), "[s]ilence is a very passive response and reflects uncertainty and passivity" (p. 141), especially if, given the nature of the crisis, it is important for an organization to express sympathy and be ready to provide stress and trauma counseling for victims of a crisis. Having a trained spokesperson allows an organization to disseminate information in a timely manner because the news media will want an immediate response during a crisis (Coombs, 2007).

During the crisis response phase, it is imperative that an organization puts public safety first because people need to know what they must do to protect themselves. As Coombs (2007) notes, "[q]uickness and accuracy play an important role in public safety" (p. 3). However, he continues, "speed is meaningless if the information is wrong . . . inaccurate information can increase rather than decrease the threat to public safety" (p. 3).

Coombs suggests an organization should make use of all available communication channels to distribute information. These include being prepared to use a website to address crisis concerns, being prepared to use an organizational Intranet to reach employees, and being prepared to use a mass notification system for reaching employees and key stakeholders during a crisis (Coombs, 2007).

The final phase in the crisis management process is post-crisis. In this phase, an organization is attempting to return to business as usual, and the crisis is no longer the focal point. According to Coombs, follow-up communication is important after a crisis. An organization needs to "release updates on the recovery process, corrective actions, and/or investigations about the crisis" (Coombs, 2011, p. 169). Organizations must be transparent about the actions they have taken because they often have promised to provide additional information during a crisis, and may risk losing the trust of publics wanting this information if they fail to deliver (Coombs, 2007).

In the post-crisis phase, it is also critical that the crisis management plan be evaluated to see what worked, and what improvements could be made. Ultimately, says Coombs (2007), a crisis should be considered a learning experience so that an organization can apply lessons learned the next time a crisis occurs. Based on the review of literature about church-related crises and religious organizations in the media, the following research questions were developed:

RQ1: What are the major components of the church crisis management plans analyzed in this study?

RQ2: What, if any, specific threats are addressed in the church crisis management plans analyzed in this study?

Coombs's (2007) three-phase approach to crisis management has been used to study many different organizations in both the public and private sectors (El-Nadi, 2009; Avery et al., 2010; Holmes, 2011; Walsch, 2011). However, Coombs's framework has not been applied specifically to religious organizations. This led to the final research question:

RQ3: Do church crisis management plans follow Coombs's (2007) three-phase approach to crisis management?

METHOD

For this study, the researchers conducted primary research in the form of a qualitative textual analysis of church crisis management plans in order to determine their elements and structure.

Sampling Plan. To gather a sample of church crisis organizational management plans for analysis, the researchers first obtained a church directory compiled by USA Churches. Fifty churches were selected at random, representing one from each state. Church leaders in these 50 institutions were then queried about the existence of crisis management plans in their own organizations and asked for referrals to other churches that they knew had such plans. This process yielded one actual plan and one referral.

The majority of the initial respondents indicated that they neither had an organizational crisis management plan nor knew of any other churches that did. Of those few that did have such crisis management plans, most were unwilling to share them for proprietary reasons. Because of the paucity of plans obtained from the respondents, the researchers elected to employ a snowball-sampling technique, beginning with the first referral, which eventually produced a total of 14 crisis management plans for analysis. Babbie (2008) defines snowball sampling as a process in which "each person interviewed may be asked to suggest additional people for interviewing" (p. 350), and suggests that this is an appropriate technique when searching for relatively rare phenomena when traditional sampling methods would likely yield minimal results.

The organizational crisis management plans obtained came from a variety of churches. Three were Roman Catholic, two were Presbyterian, one was Anglican, one Lutheran, one Baptist, and one Unitarian; another five were classified as nondenominational Christian. A majority of respondents reported an average weekend attendance of between 301 and 2,000 people. Five churches were located in the Northeast, four in the West, three in the Midwest, and two in the Southeast.

Data Collection. The focus of this study was on church crisis management plans. Because there was little information about the contents of either actual or ideal church crisis management plans, researchers began the data collection process by selecting what appeared to be the most comprehensive plan, and then a single researcher coded all of the elements that involved the entire organization. This list was then employed as a template for reviewing each of the additional plans.

If, in this process, an item was noted not present in the initial template, it was subsequently added to compile a final inventory of elements. Notes were added for some answers that required an explanation. For example, if a plan listed the members of a crisis management team, the researcher documented the positions included.

The components of each church crisis management plan were examined to see what sections were commonly present (e.g., introduction, crisis team composition, crisis team responsibilities), and whether forms such as emergency contact lists were included. Researchers were particularly interested to note if plans contained a section for dealing with the mass media and social media. The most common threats that church crisis management plans addressed were also noted.

To determine if church crisis management plans used Coombs's (2007) approach to crisis management, the researcher analyzed the plans for sections containing information on pre-crisis, crisis response, and post-crisis evaluation. For the pre-crisis phase, the researcher noted if such elements as draft messages or exercises to test the plan were included. For the crisis response phase, the researcher looked for suggestions for initial crisis response and whether plans contained any indication of step-by-step procedures for dealing with the media. For the post-crisis evaluation phase, the researcher noted if plans included information on evaluating the success of the organization's crisis response and if they suggested releasing updates on the recovery process or any ideas for subsequent corrective actions (Coombs, 2011).

RESULTS

Research Question 1. The church crisis management plans analyzed contained many common components. For example, most of the plans had very similar formats. All of the plans included an introduction that usually included objectives and a theological perspective on disaster. As the plan of one Northeastern church noted, "[b]ecause God is our ultimate help, in the event of a crisis it is appropriate to take time to offer a prayer to God, asking for guidance and care for those affected by the crisis."

Crisis Avoidance. Although it would be uncommon for organizational crisis management plans to contain suggestions for routine stakeholder relationship nurturing, it would not be as unusual for organizations to consider the interests of stakeholders in planning specific steps to avoid or minimize the effects of a crisis. Most church crisis management plans in this study focused on what to do before and during a crisis, but did not suggest steps that could avoid the potential negative effects of a crisis on an organization's key publics. An exception was a plan by a church from the West that provided information to its stakeholders about potential risks by including forms for the safe use of parish facilities, how to obtain liability insurance, codes of conduct for chaperones, and information about how to administer medication.

Pre-crisis. The crisis management plans for most of the churches in this study were much better at preparing church personnel and other internal publics for a possible crisis. Nine of the churches had specific crisis-training information, while another two churches briefly described training plans. The majority of churches with detailed plans included information about how to form a crisis management team and how the members should be trained. For example, one Midwest church reported that it holds an annual training session that includes a review of the crisis communication management plan with crisis team members.

All but three churches included information about the composition of the crisis management team. The crisis management team often went by other names (e.g., crisis executive committee, emergency response personnel or contingency-planning group). Some crisis management team sections were more detailed than others. For example, the crisis plan in one Northeastern church noted that "[t]he Crisis Communication Team is composed of senior pastor, council chairperson, legal counsel or substitute counsel, and others as deemed appropriate." Most of the crisis management plans focused on the duties of specific people. For example, many plans had designated crisis management team members who were responsible for the safety of the church members during an emergency.

An emergency contact list was another frequently appearing component of the church crisis management plans analyzed. Only one plan, however, included a more expanded emergency contact list with telephone numbers for emergency responders (e.g., the fire department, paramedics, and police), utility emergency contacts (e.g., electricity, water, and gas providers), and telecommunication services (e.g., telephone and Internet providers).

Crisis Response. Most church crisis response plans focused on communication strategies related to external publics. For example, suggestions for a media response were included in eight of the plans. The media response sections varied in terms of complexity. For example, one Northwest church went into detail to explain that three to five talking points should be prepared and a response to the media should be made in 24 hours. The plan continued, "[t]he [crisis executive committee] CEC shall approve the talking points within 48 hours of crisis determination and all CEC members shall use these points in all communications inside and outside the church."

Seven of the church crisis management plans had specific instructions for communicating with different publics during a crisis. The most typical audience segmentations were by employees, children, handicapped guests, and ushers.

When a crisis strikes, Coombs (2007) recommends using a mass notification system so that "[c]risis managers can enter short messages into the system then tell the mass notification system who should receive which messages and which channel or channels to use for the delivery" (p. 3). None of the churches included such a mass notification system in their organizational crisis management plans, although one church in the Southeast reportedly employs a phone tree to communicate to parishioners during a crisis. Similarly, the use of social media was not addressed in any of the church organizational crisis management plans analyzed in this study.

Post-crisis. Only four of the churches included a business continuity section in their crisis management plans. One church from the West included a recovery section with information about such activities as debris removal, building repair, and inspections to help restore the parish to normal operations after an emergency. The plans of a church located in the Southeast suggested tips for ways to find alternative locations for church facilities unusable after a crisis, as well as how to continue programs in off-site locations during an emergency. This plan also suggested how to keep church websites operational in a crisis.

Coombs (2006) recommends that any actual crisis management response be carefully dissected to provide insights for dealing with a future crisis. Only a few plans contained a section on evaluation. Of those that did, a majority recommended that plans be reviewed at least every two years.

A number of additional thematic elements appeared in many of the plans. Among these were acknowledging God's protection as part of the crisis management plan, evacuation routes, safe food handling at relief functions, Christmastime loss prevention, handling of money by staff and volunteers, counseling services for victims, and designated gathering sites.

Research Question 2. Most of the church crisis management plans analyzed in this study differentiated crisis response procedures for different kinds of crises. The most typical threats addressed were potential internal crises including medical emergencies, fires, natural disasters, legal issues, financial concerns, bomb threats, chemical spills, incidents of civil unrest, and hostile intruders. None of the plans, however, contained suggestions for crisis response procedures addressed to external publics for these specific threats.

Two churches, however, did focus on outside publics, at least by implication, in discussing what Tyler-Satterfield (2009) identifies as church moral failures or heretical splits. These kinds of crises "can seriously derail the overall mission and reputation of the church" (p. 4).

Research Question 3. In general, the church crisis management plans analyzed in this study did not fit within Coombs's (2007) three-phase approach. Most of the plans focused their attention on the crisis response phase. The majority contained plans for a pre-crisis phase but differed in which elements of this phase were addressed. For example, most crisis management plans contained information on pre-crisis management team training but few had the additional information about how frequently their crisis management plans were practiced.

The majority of the church crisis plans did not have a post-crisis evaluation section. This step, according to Coombs (2007), is vital to a viable crisis management plan. In the post-crisis phase, an organization, in attempting to return to business as usual, needs to "release updates on the recovery process, corrective actions, and/or investigations on the crisis" (Coombs, 2011, p. 169). Only one church provided a section on releasing updates over time during a crisis.

According to Coombs (2007), in the final phase, the crisis management plan also must be evaluated to see what has worked and what improvements need to be made. During this phase, the organization should "seek ways to improve prevention, preparation, and/or the response" (Coombs, 2007, p. 4). Nine of the church crisis management plans did not include information on reviewing plans after a crisis strikes.

DISCUSSION

This study consisted of an analysis of 14 church crisis management plans to determine the elements contained in the plans and to ascertain if the plans follow guidelines recommended by crisis management scholars. The researchers acknowledge that this is a qualitative study, limited in the number of church crisis management plans they could locate for analysis. However, both the difficulty in finding existing crisis plans and the results of the analysis tend to support the literature that suggests churches are behind the times in terms of emergency preparedness and reputational response.

It is hard to argue with the proposition that churches should be prepared for any situations and be able to respond accordingly if they expect to be able to continue to function as normal. Previous research has shown that "a crisis management plan saves time during a crisis by pre-assigning some tasks, pre-collecting some information, and serving as a reference source" (Coombs, 2007, p. 1). Having a crisis management plan in place will help a church resolve a crisis quicker and smoother.

The results demonstrated that overall the church crisis management plans analyzed do not follow Coombs's (2007) three-phase approach to crisis management. A majority of church crisis management plans contain a minimal pre-crisis plan and mostly omit the critical post-crisis evaluation phase. Most concentrate primarily on what Coombs calls the crisis response phase.

Almost all of the communication planning in the pre-crisis phase in the crisis management plans studied was exclusively intraorganizational, focused on church internal publics rather than thinking about any external stakeholders or the media. Most of the organizations analyzed did recognize the need for establishing crisis teams and for training team members in the pre-crisis phase. They also specified who is in the team by title and name, and tended to have specific duties assigned to individuals.

In contrast, in the crisis response phase, most of the churches analyzed addressed the needs of both their internal and external publics, with particular attention to traditional mass media. Of course, this planning was geared to preparation for direct response to an incident instead of a prepared pre-crisis plan to minimize reputational damage before it occurs. Although there were elements of media planning, few crisis management plans had detailed suggestions for how to engage with the media during a crisis. None of the plans examined had a mass notification system, recommended by Coombs, which would specify what messages were appropriate and what channels should be used.

As for the post-crisis phase, most plans were silent about evaluation or any kind of post-crisis review. Similarly, there was virtually no mention of the use of nontraditional media or social media in any phase of the crisis-planning process.

Frankly, these findings did not come as a surprise to the researchers, given, as the literature suggests, that few churches appear to have crisis management plans of any kind. In fact, the researchers were encouraged to find the level of detail in the crisis response phase of the plans analyzed.

The most effective way to respond to a crisis is in a logical ordered process. Coombs (2007) writes, "[e]ffective crisis management handles the threats sequentially" (p. 1). According to Coombs, the "pre-crisis phase is . . . concerned with prevention and preparation" (p. 1), and is a critical step in reducing risks that could lead to a crisis or at least keep a crisis contained to minimize loss. Coombs adds, "planning and preparation allow crisis teams to react faster and to make more effective decisions" (p. 1). The researchers suggest that the minimal preparation evident in the pre-crisis phase in the plans analyzed should be of major concern to those tasked with devising or updating future church crisis management plans.

Of equal concern is the failure of the plans analyzed to prepare for the post-crisis phase. Coombs (2007) writes, "[t]he crisis management effort needs to be evaluated to see what is working and what needs improvement. During this phase, the organization should seek ways to improve prevention, preparation and its response" (p. 4).

Possibly the most surprising finding of this analysis is the failure to employ modern communication technology as a tool for churches in crisis. The crisis management plans analyzed did not mention social media or any kind of online communication as a way to communicate before, during, or after a crisis. The absence of social media in the plans is evidence that churches are sadly out of date when it comes to communicating directly with various publics.

This is somewhat disconcerting because both for-profit businesses and nonprofit organizations like hospitals and universities are adopting social media policies and making social media one of their primary means of communication with their stakeholders as well as the media. The researchers agree with Hoskins (2010), who suggests that not only should church crisis management plans address social media practices, but also because crises can explode via social media platforms. It would seem imperative, therefore, that churches protect themselves by creating a clear plan for employing these kinds of communication technologies (Veil, 2009).

As with almost any qualitative exploratory study, the conclusions that can be drawn are limited by the amount of data collected. To provide more generalizable results, future researchers looking at religious organizations could employ more quantitatively oriented survey methodology to gather information about crisis management plans, specifically to investigate the reasons why churches have yet to begin pre-planning for a crisis or the reasons behind their hesitation to use social media. However, future researchers should be aware of the challenges presented by religious organizations that often are reluctant to provide details of such plans because of their propriety nature.

In addition, it should be noted that the organizations analyzed in this study were churches representing various denominations. Future research could expand this analysis to include other types of organizations.

CONCLUSION

As demonstrated both by the difficulty in obtaining crisis plans of church organizations and in the analysis of the plans in this study, the religious sector, at the local level, is seemingly unprepared for a reputational crisis. If churches wish to protect their constituents and their reputations in their community, the researchers recommend that they design crisis management plans, based on suggestions by Coombs, with a full, pre-crisis preparation phase, a crisis-response phase that includes technological tools to communicate with all publics and the media, and a clear plan for evaluation and follow-up in the post-crisis phase.

REFERENCES

Avery, E., Lariscy, R., Amador, E., Ickowitz, T., Primm, C., & Taylor, A. (2010). Diffusion of social media among public relations practitioners in health departments across various community population sizes. *Journal of Public Relations Research*, 22(3), 336–358. doi:10.1080/10627261003614427

Babbie, E. R. (2008). *The basics of social research* (4th ed., pp. 349–362). Belmont, CA: Thomson Higher Education.

Bader-Saye, S. (2006). Improvising church: An introduction to the emerging church conversation. *International Journal for the Study of the Christian Church, 6*(1), 12–23.

Barton, L. (2001). *Crisis in Organization II.* Cincinnati, OH: South-Western College.

Bayer, M. (1998, May 1). Ready for a crisis. *Christianity Today, 44*(3). Retrieved April 7, 2011, from http://www.christianitytoday.com/yc/1998/mayjun/8y3070.html

Coombs, W. T. (2006). Code red in the boardroom: Crisis management as organizational DNA. Westport, CT: Praeger.

Coombs, W. T. (2007). Crisis management and communications. *Institute for Public Relations.* Retrieved May 21, 2011, from http://www.instituteforpr.org/topics/crisis-management-and-communications/

Coombs, W. T. (2011). *Ongoing crisis communication: Planning, managing, and responding* (2nd ed.). Thousand Oaks, CA: Sage.

Courtright, J. L., & Hearit, K. M. (2002). The good organization speaking well: A paradigm case for religious institutional crisis management. *Public Relations Review, 28*, 347–360.

Crandall, W., Parnell, J. A., & Spillan, J. E. (2010). *Crisis management in the new strategic landscape.* Los Angeles, CA: Sage.

El-Nadi, F.(2009, September 2). Crisis communication: A case study. Retrieved March 1, 2012, from http://fathielnadi.blogspot.com/2009/09/crisis-communication-case-study.html

Holmes, W. (2011). *Crisis communications and social media: Advantages, disadvantages and best practices.* Master's thesis, University of Tennessee, Knoxville. Retrieved June 25, 2011, from *http://trace.tennessee.edu/ccisymposium/2011/session3/2/*

Hoskins, T. (2010, April 2). 3 case studies in social media crisis management. *iMedia Connection.* Retrieved April 5, 2011, from http://www.imediaconnection.com/content/26378.asp

Kauffman, J. (2008). When sorry is not enough: Archbishop Cardinal Bernard Law's image restoration strategies in the statement on sexual abuse of minors by clergy. *Public Relations Review, 34*(1), 258–262. doi:10.1016/j.pubrev.2008.03.001

Kirkpatrick, N. (2011, January 4). Christian Security Network releases 2010 assessment. *Security Matters Magazine.* Retrieved April 5, 2011, from http://www.securitymattersmag.com/security-matters-magazine-article-detail.php?id=784

Kosmin, B. A., & Keysar, A. (2008). *American Religious Identification Survey summary report.* Hartford, CT: Trinity College. Retrieved February 10, 2014, from http://www.americanreligionsurvey-aris.org/reports/ARIS_Report_2008.pdf

Lerbinger, O. (1997). *Crisis manager* (pp. 3–6). Mahwah, NJ: Lawrence Erlbaum Associates.

Marra, F. J. (1998). Crisis communication plans: Poor predictors of excellent crisis public relations. *Public Relations Review, 24*(4), 461–474.

Patrikios, S. (2013). Comparing religious messages in the media and in the congregation: A Greek Orthodox case study. *Journal of Media and Religion, 12*(1), 25–37.

Shin, J.-H. (2008). Contingency, conflict, crisis: Strategy selection of religious public relations professionals. *Public Relations Review, 34*, 403–405.

Smith, M. (2007). Nonprofit religious organizations web sites: Underutilized avenue of communicating with group members. *Journal of Media and Religion, 6*(4), 273–290.

Stohmeier, G. (2009). The Pope in the public eye. Distortions as a result of communication deficiency. *Journal of Media Research, 4*, 37–48.

Sturgill, A. (2004). Scope and purposes of church web sites. *Journal of Media and Religion, 3*(3), 165–176.

Tyler-Satterfield, D. V. (2009, December 7). A guide for church leaders: Surviving a crisis. *Civil Agreements*. Retrieved May 28, 2011, from http://documents.jdsupra.com/e489d97b-8423-40bd-a162-395216143e8b.pdf

Veil, S. (2009, November 11). Friend vs. foe: Viewing the media as a partner in crisis response. *Institute for Public Relations*. Retrieved May 21, 2011, from http://www.instituteforpr.org/wp-content/uploads/FriendvFoe.pdf

Walsch, D.L. (2011). *A strategic communication approach to crisis situations: A case study analysis of transformative events at George Mason University and Northern Illinois University*. Doctoral dissertation, George Mason University. Retrieved June 25, 2011, from *http://hdl.handle.net/1920/6263*

Waters, R., & Bortree, D. (2012). "Can we talk about the direction of this church?": The impact of responsiveness and conflict on Millennials' relationship with religious institutions. *Journal of Media and Religion, 11*(4), 200–215.

3 PR Capacity on Nonprofit Boards

Timothy Penning

Capacity building is a common goal of nonprofit organizations. They seek to increase their capacity in various ways to further their cause or mission. Such capacity could be in the form of funding to various skills and abilities of those who work with the organization.

In this regard, boards become vital to nonprofit organizations not just for the oversight and accountability they enforce, but because each board member brings various professional capacities they can contribute to the organization. In so doing, board members become resources that contribute to a nonprofit's effectiveness and its very survival.

The literature on nonprofit organizations reveals the various methods by which board members are selected and the various roles and competencies they bring. The public relations literature, meanwhile, has addressed numerous public relations concepts using nonprofit organizations as the subject of study and to consider the practice of public relations specifically in the nonprofit sector. However, few studies have addressed whether and why nonprofit organization board members have public relations capacity or whether public relations activities are even considered a desired role for board members.

This paper attempts to fill that gap by integrating the nonprofit management and public relations literature. Research questions and hypotheses address the factors that influence the degree to which nonprofit board members are sought for public relations expertise and whether public relation is perceived as a role for boards.

LITERATURE REVIEW

The scholarship regarding the composition of organizational boards most often comes from resource dependency theory or agency theory (Hillman & Dalziel, 2003; Simmons, 2012). Agency theory presumes a conflictual relationship between the board and executives of an organization. As such, the board role is one of monitoring the behavior of executives and acting in the interest of stockholders (Brown, 2005; Simmons, 2012).

Resource dependency theory holds that the board role is less of monitoring than of providing resources from outside the organization to aid in its growth and survival (Singh, 2007). Given that perspective, board members are often selected based on the specific type of resources they can bring to an organization (Hillman & Dalziel, 2003).

It may be that resource dependency theory is more applicable to nonprofit organizations in particular since they do not have stockholders (although they do have stakeholders) and they tend to be more resource poor than corporations. Regardless, scholars have noted that the agency theory and resource dependency theory can be at work simultaneously. That is, boards may perform both a monitoring role as well as serve to provide functions and expertise. As such they are both observing organizational activity and contributing to it (Hillman & Dalziel, 2003; Simmons, 2012).

Of particular interest for this paper is the fact that among the resources board members provide organizations are those that could be considered public relations skills, perspective, and abilities. For example, a board that provides better governance and talent can enhance an organization's reputation with its stakeholders (Singh, 2007). Additionally, the range of resources nonprofits need from board members are not only material (i.e., funding and assets) but human and symbolic, which include being responsive to their environment and "legitimation and recognition of their contribution to the well being of individuals" (Schmid, 2004, p. 100).

Public relations overlaps with the theories related to nonprofit boards in stakeholder theory. Stakeholder is a term "used in public relations practice to refer to those who have an interest or stake in, and are thus likely to be affected by, the activities and plans of an organization" (Watson & Hill, 2006, p. 275). The concept of stakeholders originated in the management literature (Freeman, 1984). The term "stakeholder" has been used interchangeably with the public relations term "public" recently, although some make the distinction that publics are more active segmented subsets of stakeholder groups (deBussy & Kelly, 2010). Others have pointed out that stakeholder theory should not be limited to corporations but be extended to all forms of organization (Phillips, Freeman, & Wicks, 2003). Stakeholder theory would indicate that nonprofit organizations who are highly concerned with identifying and communicating with specified stakeholders would more likely consider public relations knowledge and experience an important capacity for board members.

Board Selection Process. Resource dependency theory would indicate that nonprofit board members are sought for the particular resources they can bring to the organization. However, the implied simple causal relationship is complicated by the variance in the board selection process, as well as what constitutes a "resource" in the minds of management, staff, other board members and various stakeholder groups.

Nonprofit organizations can fill their boards following a membership model, in which members of the organization elect a board. Another process is a board-managed model, in which a nominating committee of current board members or the executive director appoints or solicits board members based on their representation of various stakeholder groups (Rehli & Jager, 2011). Regardless of the model of board member selection, the notion of boards representing organizational stakeholders has led to the description of nonprofit boards as "boundary spanners" (Abzug & Galaskiewicz, 2001). In this context, board members, because of who they are more than what they do, provide legitimacy to organizations in the communities they serve. Abzug and Galaskiewicz (2001) found that nonprofit board members are significantly represented by those with college education and/or managerial and professional experience. However, the study did not specify which types of professional experience were seen as important.

The concept of boundary spanning has also been in the public relations literature for decades (Grunig & Hunt, 1984). It refers to the role of public relations professionals serving in a liaison capacity, representing an organization to its stakeholders or publics and the various publics to organizational management. As Grunig and Hunt (1984) put it, "they have one foot in the organization and one outside" (p. 9). In this context there is consonance between the basic roles of public relations and nonprofit boards.

Board Roles and Effectiveness. It has been noted that capabilities of individual board members contribute to the effectiveness of a board overall (Brown, 2007). As such, the specific roles and responsibilities of nonprofit boards have been studied by numerous scholars (Bradshaw, Murray, & Wolpin, 1992).

The function of nonprofit boards has been described both broadly and specifically. O'Regan and Oster (2005) described the three main functions of nonprofit boards as fundraising, monitoring management executives, and participating in the work of the organization. Their survey of more than 3,000 nonprofit board members revealed a variety of professional backgrounds, including finance, education, law, social services, and business, as well as public relations. When asked to name the top two responsibilities of boards, participants indicated strategic planning, fundraising, financial review, operational oversight, and senior management evaluation. No specification was given with regard to "operational oversight," that is, whether public relations is included.

However, further attempts to specify board responsibilities includes descriptions of what could be called public relations work. A Governance Self-Assessment Checklist (GSAC) developed for nonprofit boards includes six categories of board responsibilities: mission and planning, financial stewardship, human resources stewardship, performance monitoring and accountability, community representation and advocacy, and risk management (Gill, Flynn, & Reissing, 2005). The community representation and advocacy category is defined in a way that relates closely to public relations: "assesses communication practices, stakeholder input, and whether nomination processes generate board membership that adequately represents community diversity" (Gill et al., 2005, p. 278).

Other literature on nonprofit board composition and roles also demonstrates that public relations capacity is recommended for organizational success. In their study of nonprofit board effectiveness, Herman and Renz (2000) list public relations as well as working with volunteers and government relations as elements to be measured when assessing board effectiveness. A study of both board members and nonprofit CEOs indicated agreement that the board bears responsibility for communicating the organizational purpose, having contact with staff, encouraging community interaction, and resolution of disputes (Green & Griesinger, 1996). Cornforth (2001) identified five outputs or functions of boards, one of which is "external relations and accountability." Among the specific roles within this function are ensuring the organization meets its responsibility to stakeholders, representing the interests of stakeholders in the organization, acting as a link with important groups and organizations with which the organization interacts, and representing the organization externally. There have also been recent calls for nonprofit boards to consider oversight of the organization's sustainability practices as part of their role (Bell, 2011).

Other scholars have addressed not just the presence of certain board roles and responsibilities, but the variance with which they are enacted. For example, the life cycle of nonprofit organizations affects its board composition and activity. It is only after an entrepreneurial stage, characterized by a need for survival, and a collectivity stage, reflecting organizational growth and personalized leadership, that an organization reaches a stage of formalization and control. In that stage there is greater structural formality and complexity, which includes more specialization of board roles (Lynall, Golden, & Hillman, 2003). A survey of nonprofit executives showed that 52% feel their boards are "very active" in financial oversight and policy making, but noted low activity levels of their boards with regard to fundraising, program monitoring, community relations, and public advocacy (Hartman, 2009).

Public Relations Roles, Capacity, and Nonprofit Boards. There is virtually no research on the public relations capacity and practices of the members of nonprofit boards. The research about public relations generally in nonprofit organizations has shown that the work of public relations is often limited to fundraising. Often in nonprofits, in what is known as "encroachment" of the public relations role, fundraising manages public relations staff as opposed to public relations managing fundraising and other tasks (Kelly, 1994).

Normatively, public relations scholars advocate that public relations practitioners in nonprofit organizations take a much broader role than communication with donors. PR professionals should have primary responsibility for fundraising, but also volunteer management, event management, information campaigns, and board relations (Dyer, Buell, Harrison, & Weber, 2002). However, scholars have also noted that public relations in nonprofits should be more sophisticated than simple one-way informational messages.

The four models of public relations—press agentry, public information, two-way asymmetrical, and two-way symmetrical (Grunig & Grunig, 1992)—are not exclusive and organizations of all types may practice different models in different circumstances (Plowman, 1998). For example, a fundraising campaign may be more two-way symmetrical whereas a campaign for social change may be more asymmetrical (Kelly, 1995; Lo, 2003).

Along with variance in the models of public relations practice, scholarship in the field has focused on the paradigm of organization–public relationships (Ferguson, 1984). Multiple scales have been developed to measure the quality of relationships between organizations and their various publics (Bruning & Ledingham, 1999; Bruning & Galloway, 2003). The common scale used to measure organization–public relationships includes dimensions of trust, commitment, satisfaction, and control mutuality (Hon & Grunig, 1999).

While the specific form and practice of public relations has been advocated by scholars and practitioners, there are factors that affect presence of a PR capacity and the form it takes in any organization, including nonprofits. As mentioned above, encroachment on the public relations function by other departments within an organization can occur, such as fundraising subsuming the PR role or PR staff reporting to other functions (Fitzpatrick, 1996).

Organizational structure is another factor related to encroachment that affects the capacity and practice of public relations by nonprofit boards. If the public relations function has more authority in the organizational structure it would be more likely to have a broader role and be part of the board's capacity. The position of the public relations function or personnel in organizational structure has been viewed as its literal place on an organizational flowchart (van Ruler & de Lange, 2003), the level to which the most senior PR practitioner reports (O'Neil, 2003), who assigns whom work tasks (Heath, 1994), or the number of staff in the department (Kim & Reber, 2009).

Where public relations is placed in an organizational structure largely depends on the will of an organization's dominant coalition. This is the group of people, typically managers, who hold the most power in an organization (White & Dozier, 1992). Dominant coalitions draw power from authority as well as expertise, charisma, and other factors (Berger, 2005), and their membership can shift over time (L. Grunig, 1992).

Depending on all of the above, public relations practitioners in any organization typically enact one of two roles: technician or manager (Grunig & Grunig, 1992). While the roles may overlap, a technician primarily writes and produces communication tactics while a manager is primarily concerned with strategy, counsel, and working with management (Dozier, 1992). Also, the enacted role may not be consistent with the practitioner's perceived role (Dozier & Broom, 1995).

The way the dominant coalition views the role of public relations in an organization is called its schema or worldview, and can affect whether or not public relations staff are hired as well as how public relations is carried out by an organization (Grunig & Grunig, 1992; Dozier & Broom, 1995). These views of management, and their impact on the public relations role and its place in organizational structure, could also have a bearing on the degree to which public relations experience and knowledge is present on the organization's board.

There are several research questions and hypotheses that come from the review of literature about nonprofit boards and public relations. First, a set of research questions was created to address what skills, knowledge, or capacities nonprofit leaders desire or expect in board members; which are the most important; and which attributes of a nonprofit organization may affect whether its board has at least one member with PR knowledge or experience:

RQ1: What specific board member capacities are considered important by nonprofit leaders?

RQ2: To what extent do nonprofit leaders see communications skill and experience by board members to be important compared to other board capacities?

RQ3: Is there a difference in the size of nonprofit organizations (in number of full-time employees) or the size of its board in terms of whether or not any board member has PR expertise?

RQ4: Does the manner by which board members are selected—appointed by the president or nominated by a board committee—affect whether at least one board member has PR expertise?

The literature review, specifically the resource dependency theory, indicated a range of skills most commonly sought in board members. Few have studied the degree to which these board member capacities are valued more or less compared to each other. In addition, as the literature pointed out, smaller nonprofit organizations are prone to stress financial support primarily or exclusively. Thus it may be reasonable to expect that PR capacity is more likely to be sought or valued by organizations that are larger or have more board members, since PR skills might be sought after financial and other areas of expertise have been attained. Nevertheless, as this is a new area of research, the questions are exploratory in nature and not predictive.

In addition to these general research questions, several hypotheses were tested to determine which variables increase the likelihood that a nonprofit will have at least one board member with public relations experience or knowledge:

H1: Organizations whose leaders value communication with stakeholders as the most important board member contribution are more likely to have at least one board member with PR expertise.

H2: The more that nonprofit leaders see the role of PR as one of mutual responsiveness to stakeholders, the more likely their nonprofit organization will have at least one board member with PR expertise.

H3: The more that nonprofit leaders see the role of PR as one of mutual responsiveness to stakeholders, the more likely their nonprofit organization will have staff with full-time PR responsibilities who report to the executive director and communicate regularly with the board.

The view of public relations and its role held by presidents or the dominant coalition of any organization has been shown to have an influence on how much power and authority the public relations staff or function is given in an organization. Thus it follows that if an organization's executive director or president views public relations as a function more about relationship building than mere communication is more likely to value having a board member with such a view and expertise in the function. Similarly, organizations whose executives see public relations as something more than "getting the word out" are more likely to have a staff member dedicated to that role, at a level high enough to report directly to the president and not another function (e.g., development). Also, an organization whose nonprofit executive views the public relations role in more sophisticated management versus technician terms is more likely to encourage the public relations staff person to interact often with the board on matters of organizational strategy and governance.

METHOD

An online survey was sent to a list of nonprofit organization executive directors or presidents in a Midwestern state. There are more than 31,000 nonprofit organizations in the state, but the vast majority of them have only a director with no full-time staff and very small boards, if any. Working with a philanthropy center associated with a state university, a list of e-mail addresses for nonprofit presidents and executive directors at organizations with more than one staff member was created for the survey.

After paring down the list for bad addresses or for organizations with more than one person on the list, the final list contained 704 e-mail addresses. An e-mail invitation was sent three times, with a week between each request, to solicit respondents to click on a link and take a web-based survey. Ultimately, there were 215 responses, a rate of 30%. After data cleaning to remove some who were not the leaders of their organization or who did not complete the survey, the data included a final sample of 167 executive directors or presidents of nonprofit organizations that had a staff and board.

The questions on the survey were created for this study but derived from concepts in the literature. After a screening question to ensure that respondents were executive directors or presidents of their organizations, a series of questions about preferred board member roles and abilities were asked. For example, the GSAC mentioned by Gill and colleagues (2005) includes six categories of board roles. But others included typologies of board roles that overlapped with these six and included roles more in line with public relations (Green & Greisinger, 1996; Herman & Renz, 2000; Cornforth, 2001; Bell, 2011). Hartman (2009) determined executive directors' expectations for board activity. All of these were considered to derive seven categories of board member roles for nonprofits. Respondents could select which of seven types of role or capacity they seek in board members, checking all that apply and then selecting the one most important. Secondly, respondents were asked on each of these capacities to agree or disagree on a 5-point Likert-type scale as to whether it was important for one board member to have the listed capacity. The seven roles of board members can be seen in the tables in the results section.

Respondents were also asked their view of the function of public relations using a scale modified from Grunig & Grunig (1992) based on the four models of public relations (press agentry, publicity, two-way asymmetrical, and two-way symmetrical). Since models of public relations are not mutually exclusive and organizations practice different ones in different circumstances, a 5-point Likert-type scale (strongly agree to strongly disagree) asked executives about the purpose of public relations being to "put an organization in the best possible light," "get the word out," "ensure stakeholders respond to the organization," and "ensure that organizations are responsive to stakeholder concerns." Respondents were also asked which model best describes their organization's use of public relations overall.

A final set of questions were unique to this study and demographic in nature. They asked which capacities actually were present on their board, presence of PR staff, how the board is selected, the size of the board, the size of the organization in number of employees, and the type of nonprofit organization (social service, health, membership, trade association, etc.) based on IRS classifications.

RESULTS

A majority (88%) of the organizations represented by respondents select board members via a nomination committee of the current board. Only 12% indicated that the executive director appointed board members. The organizations were either very small or very large in terms of staff size, with few medium-sized nonprofits. Forty percent of respondents have 0–5 employees, while 24% have 25 or more employees. Of the rest, 18% have 6–10 employees, 9% have 11–15, 5% have 16–20, and 4% have 21–24. The size of their boards also varied, with number of board members as follows: 2.9% have 0–3 board members; 9.1% have 4–6; 26.8% have

Table 3–1   Capacities Sought in Nonprofit Board Members.

Board Member Capacity	%	N
Knowledge of cause	89.3%	158
Financial management	82.5%	146
Communication with stakeholders	76.3%	135
Position in community	71.2%	126
Management expertise	69.5%	123
Access to financial resources	68.4%	121
Legal counsel	58.2%	103

Note: Total N = 177. Respondents could select more than one answer.

7–9; 24% have 10–12; 15% have 13–15; and 22.2% have boards with 16 or more members.

The first research question asked which skills or abilities (i.e., capacities) nonprofit executives sought in board members. There was indication that all of the skills mentioned in the literature review were valued to a degree, but an understanding of and experience with the organization's cause or mission as well as financial management received the strongest support. Communication with the organization's various stakeholders was the third most common contribution executives said they looked for in board members. Note that the survey question asked respondents to check "all that apply" and thus the percentages do not add up to 100%. Table 3–1 summarizes the responses to this question.

The second research question sought to find more specifically how nonprofit executives valued communications skills and abilities compared to other contributions of board members. For this the respondents were presented with the same list of potential board member contributions and asked to select the one most important for their organization. In this case, communications was the fourth on the list of seven board member capacities, with only 11.5% of respondents indicating it is the most important skill. So while communications (i.e., PR) capacity seems valued by three-fourths of respondents when they could check as many as they wished, when forced to choose just one board member skill the executives responding indicated less need for PR capacity on their boards. A knowledge of the organization's mission was seen by far as the most important attribute of a nonprofit board member, with more than 40% of executives selecting this. All responses to this question are summarized in Table 3–2.

Research question three explored whether the size of a nonprofit organization in terms of the number of staff or board members mattered when it came to having at least one board member with public relations expertise.

Table 3–2   Most Important Capacities of Nonprofit Board Members.

Board Member Capacity	%	N
Knowledge of cause	40.4%	74
Access to financial resources	19.1%	35
Position in community	13.1%	24
Communication with stakeholders	11.5%	21
Management expertise	8.2%	15
Financial management	6.6%	12
Legal counsel	1.1%	2

Note: Total N = 183. Respondents could select only one answer.

To answer this question Pearson correlations were calculated between both the number of employees and the number of board members of organizations with the degree to which a respondent agreed that their board had at least one board member with PR education or expertise.

There was a weak and nonsignificant correlation between the number of employees and the presence of a board member with PR expertise ($r(163)$ = $-.148, p = .059$). The correlation is negative because the survey's Likert-type scale on the presence of a board member with PR expertise was 1 = "strongly agree." While the correlation was not significant, at $p = .059$ it is close to significance at the 95% confidence interval and thus would indicate that larger nonprofit organizations, in terms of the number of full-time staff, are more likely to have at least one board member with PR expertise.

The Pearson correlation between the number of board members and the presence of a board member with PR expertise was slightly stronger and significant ($r(162)$ = $-.283, p < .01$). This shows that organizations with more board members in total are more likely to have at least one board member with public relations education and experience.

Research question four was concerned with whether or not the method of board member selection was associated with whether or not the board had at least one member with PR expertise. Since board selection was a dichotomous variable—either the respondent said the executive appointed the board or a committee of existing board members nominated new board members—this question was investigated using independent sample t-tests. No significant difference was found ($t(131)$ = $1.047, p > .05$).

A series of simple linear regressions were calculated to test the hypotheses. Hypothesis one predicted that organizations whose leader highly values communication with stakeholders as a board member contribution would be more likely to have one board member with PR expertise. This hypothesis was not supported ($F(1,160)$ = $.885, p > .05$).

Hypothesis two, which predicted that an executive view of public relations as being mutual responsiveness to stakeholders (i.e., two-way symmetrical PR model) would lead to an organization having at least one board member with PR expertise was not supported ($F(4,157) = 1.423$, $p > .05$). All four PR model variables were included in the regression and there were no significant correlations with having PR capacity on the board. A separate regression calculated with only the two-way symmetrical PR model as independent variable was also not significant.

Finally, hypothesis three predicted that an executive's view of PR as two-way symmetrical (mutual responsiveness to stakeholders) would predict that the organization would have a staff member with full-time PR responsibilities and that the PR staff would report directly to the executive director and communicate regularly with the board. Regressions were not significant for PR staff ($F(1,162) = 2.769$, $p > .05$), PR reporting to the executive director ($F(1,162) = 2.914$, $p > .05$), or PR staff communicating regularly with the board ($F(1,162) = 2.380$, $p > .05$).

DISCUSSION

The results of this study show that executives of nonprofit organizations see public relations skills represented on their board as something that is nice to have, but not a vital requirement compared with other desired board member skills or abilities. Also, while executives speak generally to the importance of public relations ability at the board level, they tend to have only a fundamental understanding of what public relations is. Board members enacting PR roles becomes more evident when organizations and their boards are larger, showing that PR is valued only after other skills are covered and as organizations reach a later stage of maturity.

Research questions one and two show that communications (PR) is valued by nonprofit executives, but only when they could select all that apply from a list of potential board capacities derived from the literature. When forced to choose only one board contribution as important to their organization, a knowledge of the mission, access to finances, and a position in the community were the top skills of board members valued by presidents and executive directors. This is consistent with the literature that indicated specific board roles only emerge in mature organizations that are beyond the entrepreneurial and survival stage (Lynall et al., 2003), and that nonprofit boards are generally not active in public relations activities (Hartman, 2009).

Research question three revealed that nonprofit organizations with more employees and more board members are somewhat more likely to have at least one board member with PR expertise. This may reflect the fact that organizations with more staff members engage more stakeholders and stakeholder groups and therefore executives see the value in having public relations skill as a capacity present on the board. The fact that organizations with larger boards are clearly more likely to have at least one board member with PR expertise makes sense given resource dependency theory, which would indicate that a board member with public relations knowledge would be sought only once public relations is seen as a necessary resource for the organization (Hillman & Dalziel, 2003). In this study, other resources are clearly seen as primary, such as the more preferred board capacities found in research questions one and two. In other words, larger boards can satisfy the preferred capacities or resources including knowledge of mission, access to financial resources and representing key positions in the community first, and as boards grow they can include board members who contribute PR skills to existing board competencies. Another way of saying this might be that PR skills among board members are "nice to have" but not a "must have."

The result of research question four is that there is no difference in preferences for PR capacity on the board if the board members are appointed by the executive or nominated by a board committee. This may be because 88% of respondents said their board members are nominated by a board committee, so there was not enough variance in the sample for there to be a meaningful or significant difference revealed in the results. Another possibility is that neither current board members nor executives are inclined to advocate for board members with PR capacity, which echoes the findings from research questions one, two, and three. Therefore, the process of board member selection is less of an influential variable as the size of the organization or the board.

While none of the hypotheses was statistically significant, there is value in examining these results. For example, we learn that executives value communications with stakeholders but they also see PR as "get the word out" (75%) and not a more sophisticated view of the profession as relationship building (Hon & Grunig, 1999; Bruning & Galloway, 2003) or strategic planning function. Given this view of PR as a technician and not a management role, many nonprofit executives may see that such a function could be carried out by staff and therefore does not require board members to be involved in what they consider PR. This is consistent with the research on public relations role enactment (Grunig & Grunig, 1992; Dozier & Broom, 2006), particular at the organizational level where the stated understanding of public relations is not what is actually practiced. This finding also adds confirmation to the fact that the dominant coalition schema or worldview about public relations affects its practice and level of influence within organizations (L. Grunig, 1992; Grunig & Grunig, 1992; Dozier & Broom, 2006).

While only 29% of respondents said they have staff dedicated full time to PR, that could reflect the fact that PR (i.e., mere one-way communications tactics) is part of the role of another staff member, including clerical staff. Another possibility is that executives perceive that such a function does not require PR expertise but involves board members giving speeches to various stakeholder groups or leveraging their "position in the community," which at 13% was the third-highest preferred capacity of respondents. However, this study did not answer why executives value a board member's position in a community. It is implied that this will be a "resource" that will bring some value to the organization. But it would seem that many executives do not have a full grasp of "stakeholders" as persons not just to be targeted but who may be affected by an organization (Watson & Hill, 2006), and thus require a more managed and strategic communication approach.

It should be noted that the responses of nonprofit executives to some of the survey questions may not be valid because they do not have a complete or accurate understanding of "PR." For example, 75% see "get the word out" as a definition of the PR role in their organization, whereas 10.8% said present the organization in the "best possible light," and only 6.8% each defined PR as ensuring that stakeholders respond to organizational objectives (two-way asymmetrical) or that the organization is responsive to stakeholders (two-way symmetrical).

Nevertheless, regressions for predicting that an executive view of PR as two-way symmetrical would increase the likelihood of an organization having full-time PR staff, and that PR staff report to the executive director, were approaching significance, with $p = .098$ and $.090$, respectively. This may merit further study on how a nonprofit leader's view about the role of public relations may be associated with the presence and role of PR practitioners in nonprofit organizations, which could confirm the notion that membership in the dominant coalition is based on expertise as well as authority (Berger, 2005).

While the hypotheses tested in this study did not receive statistical support, that may simply be due to the fact that the sample in this study represents the reality in nonprofit organizations—that leaders have a limited or narrow view of the function of public relations and do not see it as more than "getting the word out," and therefore many nonprofits, apart from budgetary reasons, do not employ full-time public relations staff because they do not appreciate the value or resource such staff would provide. In other words, because nonprofit executives have a limited view of the function of public relations and so few have PR capacity represented on their boards, it is hard to determine the causal variables that predict those cases. The study therefore shows practitioners the need to explain to executive directors that public relations is a management function enabling organizations to build and maintain mutual relationships with multiple publics, and not a mere one-way communication "technician" role.

CONCLUSION

This study provides mixed results with regard to the presence and appreciation for public relations on nonprofit boards. Executives of nonprofit organizations express some appreciation for the role of public relations on their boards, but only after some other functions or areas of expertise are addressed. So, public relations is not seen as a primary or vital interest of boards.

Also, few nonprofit organizations have a staff person dedicated to public relations. It may be that nonprofits have freelancers or public relations firms to handle public relations functions, but even then public relations is most often limited to a technician role and not integrated into leadership, strategy, and interaction with management and board.

Finally, executives of nonprofit organizations appear to have a remedial understanding of public relations, seeing it primarily as "getting the word out" in a one-way communication task. This represents an opportunity cost, in that nonprofit executives are missing the benefits of public relations by not seeing it as a management—or even a board—function dedicated to building relationships of mutual benefit between the organization and all of its publics.

There are several limitations to this study. One is the survey method and the problem of respondents self-reporting on answers. There can be a tendency for respondents to inflate their answers or express something that is not accurate for their organization. Also, the lack of a full comprehension of public relations could limit the validity of the responses.

Future research could employ qualitative methods such as focus groups to determine the source of executive directors' understanding of what "public relations" actually is. Additional questions in such a method would allow more deeper exploration and determination of other variables that may prevent or encourage nonprofit executives from having staff and board members with more advanced public relations capacity as a management function.

Also, this study shows there is opportunity in future research to examine nonprofit executives' understanding of the term stakeholder. Stakeholder theory originated in management studies (Freeman, 1984) but others have pointed out that it should not be limited to corporations (Phillips et al., 2003). For example, research could examine if nonprofits see stakeholders as targets of one-way communication to achieve organizational goals, or if they grasp the definition of stakeholders as being people who could be affected by the organization and thus need more two-way and strategic communication (Watson & Hill, 2006). Related to this, future research could examine causes of the apparent disconnect between recommended responsibilities of nonprofit boards that include communication functions (Ingram, 1996) and the lack of those capacities represented on boards.

This study also points to the need for future research to examine whether and how nonprofit organizations segment their publics and measure the nature of their relationships with them. While 76% of the respondents in this study claimed to value communication with stakeholders as a board function, a more focused study could apply the growing literature on relationship management and measuring organization–public relationships (OPRs) (Bruning & Ledingham, 1999; Hon & Grunig, 1999; Bruning & Galloway, 2003) to the perception and actions of nonprofit executives and board members.

REFERENCES

Abzug, R., & Galaskiewicz, J. (2001). Nonprofit boards: Crucibles of expertise of symbols of local identities? *Nonprofit and Voluntary Sector Quarterly, 30*(1), 51–73.

Bell, J. (2011, April 26). Beyond financial oversight: Expanding the board's role in pursuit of sustainability. *Nonprofit Quarterly*. Retrieved May 7, 2012, from http://nonprofitquarterly.org/governancevoice/11921-beyond-financial-oversight-expanding-the-boards-role-in-pursuit-of-sustainability.html

Berger, B. (2005). Power over, power with, and power to relations: Critical reflections on public relations, the dominant coalition and activism. *Journal of Public Relations Research, 17*(1), 5–28.

Bradshaw, P., Murray, V., & Wolpin, J. (1992). Do nonprofit boards make a difference? An exploration of the relationship among board structure, process, and effectiveness. *Nonprofit and Voluntary Sector Quarterly, 21*, 227–249.

Brown, W.A. (2005). Exploring the association between board and organizational performance in nonprofit organizations. *Nonprofit Management & Leadership, 15*(3), 317–339.

Brown, W.A. (2007). Board development practices and competent board members: Implications for performance. *Nonprofit Management & Leadership, 17*(3), 301–317.

Bruning, S., & Galloway, T. (2003). Expanding the organization-public relationship scale: Exploring the role that structural and personal committment play in organization-public relationships. *Public Relations Review, 29*(3), 309–319.

Bruning, S., & Ledingham, J. (1999). Relationships between organization and publics: Development of a multi-dimensional organization-public scale. *Public Relations Review, 25*(2), 157–170.

Cornforth, C. (2001). What makes boards effective? An examination of the relationship between board inputs, structures, processes, and effectiveness in nonprofit organizations. *Corporate Governance, 9*(3), 217–227.

deBussy, N.M., & Kelly, L. (2010). Stakeholders, politics, and power: Towards an understanding of stakeholder identification and salience in government. *Journal of Communication Management, 14*(4), 289–305.

Dozier, D.M. (1992). The organizational roles of communications and public relations practitioners. In J. Grunig & J. Grunig (Eds.), *Excellence in public relations and communication management* (pp. 327–355). Hillsdale, NJ: Lawrence Erlbaum Associates.

Dozier, D., & Broom, G. (1995). Evolution of the manager role in public relations practice. *Journal of Public Relations Research, 7*(1), 3–26.

Dozier, D., & Broom, G. (2006). The centrality of practitioner roles to public relations theory. In C. Botan & V. Hazleton (Eds.), *Public relations theory II* (pp. 137–170). Mahwah, NJ: Lawrence Erlbaum.

Dyer, S., Buell, T., Harrison, M., & Weber, S. (2002, Winter). Managing public relations in nonprofit organizations. *Public Relations Quarterly*, 13–17.

Ferguson, M. (1984). *Building theory in public relations: Interorganizational relationships*. Paper presented at the Public Relations Division, Association for Education in Journalism and Mass Communications, Gainesville, FL.

Fitzpatrick, K. (1996). Public relations and the law: A survey of practitioners. *Public Relations Review, 22*(1), 1–8.

Freeman, R. (1984). *Strategic management: A stakeholder approach.* Boston, MA: Pitman.

Gill, M., Flynn, R.J., & Reissing, E. (2005). The governance self-assessment check-lists: An instrument for assessing board effectiveness. *Nonprofit Management & Leadership, 15*(3), 271–295.

Green, J.C., & Griesinger, D.W. (1996). Board performance and organizational effectiveness in nonprofit social service organizations. *Nonprofit Management & Leadership, 6*(4), 381–402.

Grunig, J., & Grunig, L. (1992). Models of public relations in communication. In J. Grunig (Ed.), *Excellence in public relations and communication management* (pp. 285–325). Hillsdale, NJ: Lawrence Erlbaum Associates.

Grunig, J.E., & Hunt, T. (1984). *Managing public relations.* New York: Holt, Rinehart & Winston.

Grunig, L. (1992). Power in the public relations department. In J. Grunig & J. Grunig (Eds.), *Excellence in public relations and communiction management* (pp. 483–501). Hillsdale, NJ: Lawrence Erlbaum Associates.

Hartman, R.D. (2009, May/June). Are public service nonprofit boards meeting their responsibilities? *Public Administration Review*, 387–390.

Heath, R. (1994). *Management of corporate communication: From interpersonal contacts to external affairs.* Hillsdale, NJ: Lawrence Erlbaum Associates.

Herman, R.D., & Renz, D.O. (2000). Board practices of especially effective and less effective local nonprofit organizations. *American Review of Public Administration, 30*, 146–160.

Hillman, A.J., & Dalziel, T. (2003). Boards of directors and firm performance: Integrating agency and resource dependency theories. *Academy of Management Review, 28*(3), 383–396.

Hon, L., & Grunig, J. (1999). *Guidelines for measuring relationships in public relations.* Gainesville, FL: Institute for Public Relations.

Ingram, R. (1996). *Ten basic responsibilities of nonprofit boards.* Washington, DC: National Center for Nonprofit Boards.

Kelly, K.S. (1994). Fund-raising encroachment and the potential of public relations departments in the nonprofit sector. *Journal of Public Relations Research, 6*(1), 1–22.

Kelly, K.S. (1995). Utilizing public relations theory to conceptualize and test models of fundraising. *Journalism & Mass Communication Quarterly, 72*, 106–127.

Kim, S.Y., & Reber, B. (2009). How public relations professionalism influences corporate social responsibility: A survey of practitioners. *Journalism & Mass Communication Quarterly, 86*(1), 157–174.

Lo, Y. (2003). *A public relations guide to nonprofits.* Exeter, NH: PR Publishing.

Lynall, M.D., Golden, B.R., & Hillman, A.J. (2003). Board composition from adolescence to maturity: A multitheoretic view. *Academy of Management Review, 28*(3), 416–431.

O'Neil, J. (2003). An investigation into the sources of influence of corporate public relations practitioners. *Public Relations Review, 29*, 159–169.

O'Regan, K., & Oster, S.M. (2005). Does the structure and composition of the board matter? The case of nonprofit organizations. *Journal of Law, Economics, and Organization, 21*(1), 205–227.

Phillips, R., Freeman, R., & Wicks, A. (2003). What stakeholder theory is not. *Business Ethics Quarterly, 13*(4), 479–502.

Plowman, K. (1998). Power in conflict for public relations. *Journal of Public Relations Research, 10*(4), 237–261.

Rehli, F., & Jager, U.P. (2011). The governance of international nongovernmental organizations: How funding and volunteer involvement affect board nomination modes and stakeholder representation in international nongovernmental organizations. *Voluntas, 22,* 587–612.

Schmid, H. (2004). Organization-environment relationships: Theory for management practice in human service organizations. *Administration in Social Work, 28*(1), 97–113.

Simmons, C. (2012). Will you be on our board of directors? We need help: Media corporations, environmental change, and resource dependency theory. *Journalism & Mass Communication Quarterly, 89*(1), 55–72.

Singh, V. (2007). Ethnic diversity on top corporate boards: A resource dependency perspective. *International Journal of Human Resource Management, 18,* 2128–2146.

van Ruler, B., & de Lange, R. (2003). Barriers to communication management in the executive suite. *Public Relations Review, 29*(1), 145–158.

Watson, J., & Hill, A. (2006). *Dictionary of media and communication studies* (vol. 7). London: Hodder Arnold.

White, J., & Dozier, D. (1992). Public relations and management decision making. In J. Grunig (Ed.), *Excellence in public relations and commmunication management* (pp. 91–108). Hillsdale, NJ: Lawrence Erlbaum Associates.

4 The Billion-Dollar Question
Examining the Extent of Fundraising Encroachment on Public Relations in Higher Education

Christopher Wilson and Sarabdeep K. Kochhar

U.S. colleges and universities have engaged in systematic public relations and fundraising activities since the early 1900s (Cutlip, 1994; Kelly, 1998). However, as both of these functions have been integrated into the complex organizational structure of today's institutions of higher learning, the activities of public relations and fundraising departments have become more sophisticated and effective in achieving organizational goals. Now, public relations departments at modern universities have the same capacity for excellent public relations as similar departments in for-profit businesses (L.A. Grunig, J.E. Grunig, & Dozier, 2002) and often provide strategic counsel to governing board members and executive officers about the consequences of policy decisions on external publics (Lum, 2013).

Likewise, fundraising departments in colleges and universities employ principles of excellent public relations to cultivate relationships with donors and solicit gifts (Hall, 2002; Waters, 2008). In fact, fundraising efforts have become so effective that Stanford University reported raising $1 billion in 2012, becoming the first university to raise that amount of money in a single year (Gonzales, 2013). In addition, statistics compiled by Giving USA show that colleges and universities received 13% of all giving in 2011 (Hall, 2012). In 2012, the top fundraising colleges and universities raised $18.6 billion from private sources, more money than any other nonprofit category (Philanthropy 400, 2012), and charitable giving to all U.S. colleges and universities exceeded $31 billion (Council for Aid to Education, 2013).

While public relations and fundraising have been defined as conceptually distinct organizational functions (Kelly, 1991), the similarities between the two functions (Hall, 2002) have resulted in confusion and disagreement about how the two departments should be structured in a university setting (Satchwell, 2010). This is in spite of the fact that the Council for Advancement and Support of Education (CASE) has long supported a combined "advancement" department of public relations, fundraising, and alumni relations. However, evidence suggests that colleges and universities have not uniformly adopted the integrated advancement model (DiConsiglio, 2011). Furthermore, these disagreements are often exacerbated by fundraising's ability to demonstrate its monetary contribution to the organization

(Mesh & Rooney, 2008) and public relations' struggles to demonstrate its value to management (L. A. Grunig et al., 2002). As a result, strong fundraising departments often encroach on weaker public relations departments. Encroachment disrupts the direct reporting relationship of public relations to the CEO and can produce negative consequences for the public relations function and the entire organization (Kelly, 1994).

The purpose of this exploratory study is to test and advance theory about fundraising encroachment on public relations in higher education. Specifically, it aims to examine the extent of structural fundraising encroachment on public relations in colleges and universities that raise the most money. This research addresses this issue through a content analysis of the organizational charts and websites of 80 colleges and universities on the 2012 Philanthropy 400 list. These institutions were selected for study because the large gifts secured by their fundraising departments make them especially likely to show signs of encroachment. In addition, colleges and universities have historically employed the greatest proportion of fundraisers, a factor that can also contribute to encroachment (Kelly, 1998).

LITERATURE REVIEW

Encroachment on Public Relations. Public relations has been defined consistently by scholars (e.g., Grunig & Hunt, 1984) and practitioners (e.g., Arthur W. Page Society, 2012) as a management function that "establishes and maintains mutually beneficial relationships between an organization and the publics on whom its success or failure depends" (Broom, 2009, p. 7). While a great deal of public relations research explores the conditions that empower public relations as a management function (e.g., L. A. Grunig et al., 2002), scholars also have studied the condition of weak public relations management known as encroachment (e.g., Lauzen, 1991). Dozier (1988) defined encroachment as "the practice of assigning the top management role in the public relations department to someone from outside public relations" (p. 9). Encroachment is a concern to public relations scholars and practitioners because it diminishes the ability of the public relations function to manage an organization's interdependencies with strategic publics by distancing it from organizational decision making. When public relations is not included in organizational decision making, it becomes a low-level support function (Broom & Dozier, 1986). As a result, public relations managers are not able to bring important information about an organization's publics to the management table.

Lauzen (1992a) explained the reason for encroachment on public relations by situating public relations roles theory within strategic contingencies theory (Hickson, Hinings, Lee, Schneck, & Pennings, 1971). Strategic contingencies theory proposes that an organizational subunit has more power in an organization when it is central (i.e., critical for the success and survival of the organization), is not substitutable (i.e., its activities cannot be accomplished by another unit), and helps the organization cope with uncertainty (Hickson et al., 1971). Therefore, according to the strategic contingencies approach, the public relations manager role has more power, and is subsequently more resistant to encroachment, than the technician role because it has high centrality, low substitutability, and the necessary skills to reduce organizational uncertainty. Encroachment on public relations primarily has been studied in for-profit organizations (Lauzen, 1991; 1992a; 1992b). Findings indicated that marketing imperialism (Lauzen, 1991) and gender (i.e., when the top public relations practitioner is female rather than a male; Lauzen 1992b) were positively related to public relations encroachment. Additionally, recent research by van Ruler and de Lange (2003) found evidence of encroachment among for-profit, nonprofit, and semi-government organizations in the Netherlands.

Fundraising Encroachment on Public Relations. In the nonprofit sector, the public relations department frequently operates in the shadow of the fundraising department. Lee (2011) examined the history of nonprofit public relations and concluded that it had only achieved second-tier status in the nonprofit sector because public relations has "largely been practiced and researched as an extension of fundraising, thus ghettoizing it from broader sectorial applications and benefits" (p. 329). Moreover, fundraising is a powerful organizational function. MacKeith's (1994) study of interdepartmental relationships revealed that fundraising department priorities often dominate over the priorities of service-providing departments. Additionally, research has demonstrated that public relations practices are similar to fundraising activities (Kelly, 1991). As Hall (2002) suggests, the similarity in approaches can facilitate cooperation and collaboration between the two departments; however, these similarities also could facilitate encroachment of public relations by powerful fundraising departments that seek to monopolize the communication expertise of the public relations department.

Few scholars have addressed the issue of fundraising encroachment on public relations in the nonprofit sector. A review of the major public relations and nonprofit journals produced only four studies: three by Kelly (1993a; 1993b; 1994), one by Hall and Baker (2003), and one by Swanger and Rodgers (2013). These studies are based on Kelly's (1991) contention that fundraising is a specialization of public relations focused on managing relationships with one particular public: donors. Kelly (1998) explained that the public relations function in nonprofit organizations should be concerned about organizational relationships with all of the organization's publics. From this perspective, fundraising encroachment occurs when the public relations function is subordinate to fundraising (Kelly, 1993a). Additionally, fundraising encroachment on public relations has the potential to generate negative consequences for nonprofit organizations, such as loss of support and possible aggressive action from neglected publics (Kelly, 1994).

Kelly (1993b) explained that "fundraising encroachment forces public relations practitioners to concentrate on the concerns and demands of only one public, effectively placing 'environmental blinders' on the function and the organizations they strive to serve" (p. 354).

Exploratory qualitative research on the structural relationship between public relations and fundraising led Kelly (1993b) to conclude that fundraising had encroached on public relations in "an alarming proportion" of charitable nonprofit organizations (p. 49). Subsequent qualitative research identified three different types of structural relationships between public relations and fundraising. The most prevalent relationship (63%) was that public relations and fundraising were in separate departments. The second most prevalent relationship (37%) involved fundraising encroachment, where public relations was subordinate to fundraising. There were no observed cases of the third relationship structure (0%), where public relations is dominant over fundraising. In related quantitative studies, Kelly (1993a; 1994) again found that the most prevalent structural relationship (43%) was separate public relations and fundraising departments where the senior managers of both departments reported to the CEO. In terms of encroachment, she reported that there was structural fundraising encroachment in 23% of the charitable nonprofits studied. However, she also found that public relations reported to a manager who was not a fundraiser or a public relations practitioner in 13% of the organizations. When these percentages are added together, encroachment on public relations occurred in 36% of the organizations. Unlike the previous qualitative study (Kelly, 1993b), these quantitative studies found that public relations managed the fundraising function in 13% of the organizations (Kelly, 1993a; 1994).

Of particular relevance to the present study, Kelly (1993a; 1994) found that education had the highest and lowest proportions of encroachment. Private universities and colleges had the highest proportion of fundraising encroachment (50%), while public comprehensive and doctorate-granting universities had the lowest proportion (8%). Kelly (1994) explained that this finding reflects the traditional funding patterns for different types of educational institutions. Educational institutions that are perceived to depend more on fundraising have high levels of encroachment, while institutions that depend more on public funding have low levels of encroachment. According to Kelly, private educational institutions typically raise more money from private donations than public institutions. Likewise, public research universities typically raise more money than public comprehensive and doctorate-granting universities. Public comprehensive and doctorate-granting universities typically raise more money than two- and four-year colleges.

Kelly (1993a) also compared the titles of senior public relations and fundraising managers as an indicator of organizational power. She found that 52% of senior fundraising managers were vice presidents or executive directors, while only 26% of senior public relations managers had similar titles. Kelly explained that when senior fundraisers possess executive-level titles and senior public relations managers do not, "fundraisers' voices are more likely to be heard by trustees, as well as senior managers, than are the voices of lower-titled PR practitioners" (p. 61).

Hall and Baker (2003) studied encroachment in the context of public relations management in higher education. They conducted a survey of chief public relations officers at the 63 member universities of the Association of American Universities (AAU) to determine how organizational structure affected perceptions of the value of excellent public relations. They reported that 24% of the universities had a single vice president who was responsible for both public relations and fundraising. The other 74% had separate public relations and fundraising functions. In addition, they found that 35% of the chief public relations officers had the title of "vice president" or "vice chancellor," while 24% were associate or assistant vice presidents. Moreover, 20% had director-level titles. They also found that chief public relations officers in the combined department had lower perceptions of the importance of excellence public relations practices than the chief public relations officers in separate departments. This led the researchers to conclude that their data provided empirical support for Kelly's contention that fundraising encroachment causes the public relations function to be perceived as "less important than when it stands independent of fund raising" (p. 142).

Swanger and Rodgers (2013) used in-depth interviews of public relations and fundraising practitioners to investigate fundraising encroachment in a large nonprofit social service network. They reported levels of encroachment similar to those of Kelly (1993b). Swanger and Rodgers (2013) found that fundraising encroachment was present in 31% of the organizations in their study. They also reported strong support from both public relations practitioners (62%) and fundraising practitioners (75%) that the two departments should be separate but equal in organizational influence. In addition, they discovered that only one of eight fundraising practitioners interviewed thought that public relations should report to fundraising. Similarly, only one of the eight public relations practitioners interviewed thought fundraising should report to public relations.

Research Question and Hypotheses. The following research question was proposed to investigate the state of fundraising encroachment on public relations in the educational nonprofit subsector:

> RQ1: What is the rate of occurrence of structural fundraising encroachment on the public relations function in the top U.S. colleges and universities that raise the most gift dollars?

The following hypotheses were proposed based on Kelly's (1993a; 1994) observations that encroachment rates differed among private and public colleges and universities, as well as among research, comprehensive and doctorate-granting universities and two- and four-year colleges:

H1: Structural fundraising encroachment on public relations will be more prevalent in private colleges and universities than in public colleges and universities.

H2: Structural fundraising encroachment on public relations will be more prevalent in research universities than in universities and colleges with other missions.

METHOD

Quantitative content analysis was employed to answer the research question and test the hypotheses. This method was selected because the information needed to accomplish the study's purpose was available on college and university websites and relevant public databases. The unit of analysis for this study was the individual college or university. The primary units of observation were executive-level organizational charts and the educational institutions' websites.

Organizational charts provide a visual representation of various organizational functions, their interrelationships, and their positions within the whole organization (Daft, 2010). These charts can be important for public relations practitioners and scholars because they provide approximations of how the public relations department fits into the chain of command (Broom, 2009). Of particular relevance to this study, executive-level organizational charts were used to explain which functions report directly to the CEO and form part of the official decision-making body of the organization (Broom, 2009).

Population. The population of interest was nonprofit colleges and universities in the United States that fundraise. For the purposes of this research, the population defined for actual study was the 106 nonprofit colleges and universities on the 2012 Philanthropy 400 list (Philanthropy 400, 2012). The Philanthropy 400 is an annual ranking compiled by *The Chronicle of Philanthropy* of the charities that have raised the most money from private sources (López-Rivera, 2012). This population was deemed appropriate for study because of its reliance on fundraising, and its influence on peer institutions and on the charitable nonprofit sector as a whole. Previous research on charitable nonprofits has used the Philanthropy 400 for sampling purposes (e.g., Waters & Lemanski, 2011).

Because executive-level organizational charts were required to study fundraising encroachment in this study, the authors searched the websites of all the colleges and universities on the 2012 Philanthropy 400 list for current executive-level organizational charts. Results of this preliminary analysis found that 23 (21%) of the colleges and universities on the list did not have current executive-level organizational charts on their websites. These organizations were removed from the population list. In addition, three university systems were included on the 2012 Philanthropy 400 list. These also were removed because of the difficulty inherent in comparing a multi-university system with a single university. These deletions resulted in a total sample of 80 colleges and universities.

Coder Training. The authors of the study served as coders. Both participated in three hours of coder training and independent practice coding. During the independent practice phase, the authors coded for the measures presented in the next section using three randomly selected colleges and universities on the 2012 Philanthropy 400 list. After the coder training, intercoder reliability was assessed between the two coders. The authors coded ten (13%) colleges and universities selected randomly from the 2012 Philanthropy 400 list. Because this study contains nominal and ratio level data, the authors used Krippendorff's alpha to calculate intercoder reliability (Hayes & Krippendorff, 2007). Its value is reported for each variable in the following section.

Measures. Structural encroachment was defined as the subordination of the public relations function to some other function (Kelly, 1993a). This construct was measured by observing the positions of the public relations and fundraising departments on the executive-level organizational chart, their relationship with each other, and the nature of their reporting relationship to the CEO. Definitions of fundraising and public relations were adopted from CASE ("About CASE," n.d.). To interpret the information on the organizational charts, the authors adopted the organizational chart conventions described by Kelly (1998) and Liebler and McConnell (2012).

Observations of structural encroachment were captured using four indicators. The first indicator included four categories of structural relationships based on Kelly's (1994) classification scheme. The first category was a combined public relations and fundraising department. In this configuration, only one senior manager represents both functions in reporting directly to the organization's chief executive officer. This consolidated structure represents the "advancement" model of university relations (see Kelly, 1998). The second category was separate public relations and fundraising departments where the senior manager of each reports directly to the CEO. The third category was a peripheral relationship to the organization. In this relationship, one of the functions has a peripheral or affiliated relationship to the institution's executive line functions. This structure was created to accommodate the different ways that universities incorporate affiliated foundations into their governance structures (see Kelly, 1998). The fourth category consisted of any other structural relationship. Intercoder reliability for structural relationship was acceptable ($\alpha = 1$).

The second indicator of structural fundraising encroachment was the direction of structural encroachment (i.e., whether public relations reports to fundraising or fundraising reports to public relations). When public relations and fundraising were both in the same department, coders used organizational websites to determine the education and professional background of the senior manager of the combined department. When the individual's educational history and professional experiences clearly were related to public relations, coders indicated that fundraising answered to public relations. When the individual's educational history and professional experiences clearly were related to fundraising, coders indicated that public relations answered to fundraising. If the education and background reflected a discipline other than fundraising or public relations, coders selected an "other" option. If there was not enough information to determine the manager's background, coders selected a "cannot tell" option. Intercoder reliability for direction of structural encroachment was satisfactory ($\alpha = 1$).

The third indicator was the titles of the senior public relations and fundraising officers. Titles were gathered from organizational charts and websites. First, coders determined whether the titles of the senior public relations officer and the senior fundraising officer were equivalent. Next, coders recorded the level of the titles of these officers as (a) president/CEO, (b) vice president, (c) chief, (d) director, (e) manager, and (f) other. Finally coders indicated any title modifiers using seven categories: (a) senior, (b) executive, (c) associate, (d) assistant, (e) managing, (f) none, and (g) other. Intercoder reliabilities for title equivalence ($\alpha = 1$), public relations titles ($\alpha = 1$), and modifiers ($\alpha = 1$), as well as fundraising titles ($\alpha = 1$) and modifiers ($\alpha = 1$), were satisfactory.

The fourth indicator was the number of staff members in the public relations and fundraising departments. This information was also obtained from organizational websites. Coders first searched each department website for a listing of staff members. If there was not a complete listing, coders searched the university website for directory information. If the number of staff members was obviously incomplete or not available, coders indicated that the number was not available (n/a). If the number was available, coders marked that the information was available and counted the number of staff members in each department. Intercoder reliabilities for presence of public staff members ($\alpha = 1$), number of public relations staff members ($\alpha = .99$); and presence of fundraising staff members ($\alpha = 1$), number of fundraising staff members ($\alpha = .99$) were satisfactory.

RESULTS

The purposive sample used in this study included a mix of public (66.3%, $n = 53$), and private (33.8%, $n = 27$), colleges and universities. All of the colleges and universities in the sample (100%, or $n = 80$) were four-year universities; however, 91.3% ($n = 73$) of them were research universities, 5.0% ($n = 4$) were four-year colleges that also offered two-year programs, 1.3% ($n = 1$) was a comprehensive or doctoral-granting university, and 2.5% ($n = 2$) were other.

Research Question 1. The first research question investigated the rate of structural encroachment on public relations among the 80 colleges and universities in the sample. To determine this rate, the universities were grouped into the four structural categories explained in the method section. Results reveal that 21% ($n = 17$) have a reporting structure where public relations and fundraising are in the same organizational department, 64% ($n = 51$) have separate public relations and fundraising departments that report to the CEO, 11% ($n = 9$) have a structure where public relations or fundraising is included in the organizational hierarchy but the other is not, and 4% ($n = 3$) have some other type of structural organization of the two functions.

To further explore the direction of structural encroachment, the educational and professional backgrounds of the senior managers in the 17 combined departments were analyzed. Results show that in 15 of the combined departments, public relations reports to a senior manager with a fundraising background. In the other two departments, the senior manager of the combined department had a background other than public relations: the background of the senior manager of the combined department at the University of Notre Dame was religion, whereas for the senior manager at the University of Alabama it was marketing. There were no cases where fundraising reported to a manager with a public relations background. Based on these results, there is a 19% rate of fundraising encroachment on public relations among the top fundraising colleges and universities. Additionally, adding in the other two cases where public relations answers to a manager from a different discipline, encroachment on the public relations function climbs to 21%.

Further evidence of encroachment in these 15 colleges and universities can be seen in the titles of the senior fundraiser and the senior public relations officer. A chi-square test found that title equivalence between senior fundraisers and senior public relations officers was significantly different between organizations that had structural fundraising encroachment and those that did not, $\chi^2 = 9.94$, $df = 1$, $p = .002$. In every case (100%, or $n = 15$) where a college or university had structural fundraising encroachment, the titles of the senior fundraiser and the senior public relations officer were not equivalent. There were no cases (0%, or $n = 0$) where senior fundraisers and senior public relations officers had equivalent titles under conditions of encroachment. In addition, in colleges and universities where fundraising did not structurally encroach on public relations, 43% ($n = 28$) of these senior leaders had equivalent titles while 57% ($n = 37$) did not.

Further analysis of the titles in the 15 institutions with fundraising encroachment revealed that senior fundraisers represented the highest levels of university governance, including vice chancellor (27%, or $n = 4$), senior vice president (40%, or $n = 6$), and vice president (33%, or $n = 5$). Meanwhile, the titles of the senior public relations officers had more variation and were clearly subordinate to the titles of the senior fundraisers. These titles included associate vice chancellor (27%, or $n = 4$), vice president (13%, or $n = 2$), associate vice president (20%, or $n = 3$), assistant vice president (13%, or

$n = 2$), chief communications officer (7%, or $n = 1$), executive director (7%, or $n = 1$), and director (13%, or $n = 2$). Additionally, an analysis of the number of public relations and fundraising staff members highlights the extent of structural encroachment of fundraising on public relations. As shown in Table 4–1, 13 out of the 15 universities had a greater number of fundraising staff members than public relations staff members. However, there were two organizations (North Carolina State and University of California at Berkeley) that did not have a listing of public relations staff members available on their organizational websites. Three out of the 17 organizations (Case Western Reserve University, Dartmouth College, and University of California at Berkeley) did not make available the number of fundraisings staff members on their organizational websites. An important trend to note is that in all the cases with available data, the number of fundraising staff members was more than double that of public relations staff members, except in the case of the University of California at Los Angeles, which had slightly more public relations staff members than fundraising staff members. Furthermore, a paired-samples t-test found there was a significant difference between the number of public relations ($M = 32.73$, $SD = 13.2$) and fundraising staff members ($M = 111.8$, $SD = 51.3$), $t(10) = -4.9$, $p < .001$.

Hypothesis 1. A chi-square test was conducted to determine the extent to which the frequency of structural fundraising encroachment differed between public and private colleges and universities (i.e., institutional governance). Prior to performing this analysis, the structural relationship variable was combined with the direction of encroachment variable to produce a dichotomous dummy variable that indicated the presence or absence of fundraising encroachment. Structural fundraising encroachment was present in the 15 cases where public relations and fundraising were in the same organizational department and the head of the department was from a fundraising background. As shown in Table 4–2, the chi-square test revealed that the frequency of structural fundraising encroachment was not significantly different in public and private colleges and universities, $\chi^2 = .32$, $df = 1$, $p = .570$. Therefore, hypothesis 1 was not supported.

Hypothesis 2. A Fisher's exact test was performed to investigate the extent to which the frequency of structural fundraising encroachment differed according to college and university mission (i.e., two- or four-year college, comprehensive and doctoral universities, and research universities). Because of the small number of comprehensive and doctoral universities in the sample ($n = 1$), this category was combined with the two- or four-year college category prior to performing the analysis. The structural fundraising encroachment dummy variable explained in the previous section was used in this analysis as well. Fisher's exact test was used instead of a chi-square test because the expected count for one of the cells was less than five. As reported in Table 4–2, the test found that there was not a significant difference, $p = 1.0$, in structural

Table 4–1 Comparison of the 17 Universities Where Public Relations and Fundraising Were in the Same Department.

University	Direction of Structural Encroachment	Senior Public Relations Officer's Title	Senior Fundraising Officer's Title	Public Relations Staff (*n*)	Fundraising Staff (*n*)
Case Western Reserve University	Fundraising	Vice President	Senior Vice President	16	n/a
Dartmouth College	Fundraising	Assistant Vice President	Senior Vice President	36	n/a
North Carolina State University	Fundraising	Director	Senior Vice President	n/a	276
Southern Methodist University	Fundraising	Associate Vice President	Vice Chancellor	40	120
University of Alabama	Other	Associate Vice President	Vice President	37	115
University of California at Berkeley	Fundraising	Associate Vice Chancellor	Vice President	n/a	n/a
University of California at Los Angeles	Fundraising	Associate Vice Chancellor	Vice Chancellor	66	58
University of California Irvine	Fundraising	Director	Vice Chancellor	39	120
University of Houston	Fundraising	Associate Vice Chancellor	Senior Vice President	32	63
University of Louisville	Fundraising	Associate Vice President	Vice Chancellor	22	70
University of Maryland at College Park	Fundraising	Assistant Vice President	Vice President	32	192
University of Miami	Fundraising	Vice President	Vice President	26	143
University of North Carolina at Chapel Hill	Fundraising	Associate Vice Chancellor	Senior Vice President	28	113
University of Notre Dame	Other	Associate Vice President	Vice Chancellor	37	106
University of Virginia	Fundraising	Chief Communication Officer	Vice President	35	195
Wake Forest University	Fundraising	Associate Vice President	Senior Vice President	24	114
Washington and Lee University	Fundraising	Executive Director	Vice President	16	42

Table 4–2 Frequency of Structural Fundraising Encroachment by University Governance and Mission.

	Structural Fundraising Encroachment		
Governance	Present	Absent	Row total
Public	9 (17%)	44 (83%)	53 (100%)
Private	6 (22%)	21 (78%)	27 (100%)
Column total	15 (19%)	65 (81%)	80 (100%)

$\chi^2 = .32$, $df = 1$, $p = .570$, $N = 80$

	Structural Fundraising Encroachment		
Mission	Present	Absent	Row total
Research	14 (19%)	59 (81%)	73 (100%)
Other missions	1 (14%)	6 (86%)	7 (100%)
Column total	15 (19%)	65 (81%)	80 (100%)

$p = 1.0$, $N = 80$

fundraising encroachment between research universities and colleges and universities with other missions. Therefore, hypothesis 2 was not supported.

DISCUSSION

This study found that structural fundraising encroachment was present at a rate of 19% among the 80 colleges and universities sampled from the 2012 Philanthropy 400 list. When encroachment by disciplines other than fundraising are included, the percentage of structural encroachment reaches 21%. Previous research found structural encroachment rates across different types of nonprofits to be considerably higher than the rate found in this study. Kelly (1993b) found that fundraising encroachment was present in 37% of the nonprofits studied. Kelly (1993a; 1994) reported an encroachment rate of 36%. Hall and Baker (2003) observed a 24% encroachment rate among institutions of higher education. Additionally, Swanger and Rodgers (2013) found that fundraising encroachment was present in 31% of the organizations in their study.

While the encroachment rate reported in this study is lower than the rates found in previous studies, the percentage of organizations adopting separate public relations and fundraising departments is fairly consistent with previous research. This study found that 64% of the 80 colleges and universities from the 2012 Philanthropy 400 list considered in this study were organized into separate public relations and fundraising departments. Kelly (1993b) reported that the most prevalent structural relationship (63%) was separate public relations and fundraising departments. Similarly, Kelly (1993a; 1994) found that fundraising and public relations were separate departments in 43% of the organizations. Additionally, Hall and Baker (2003) reported separate departments in 74% of colleges and universities in their sample. Finally, Swanger and Rodgers (2013) found support from both public relations practitioners (62%) and fundraising practitioners (75%) that the two departments should be separate but equal in organizational influence. These findings are interesting in light of CASE's long-standing recommendation that public relations, fundraising, and alumni relations should be housed in an integrated advancement department. It appears that the preferred organizational structure among the U.S. colleges and universities that raise the most gift dollars is to have separate public relations and fundraising departments.

The lower rate of structural encroachment and the prevalence of separate public relations and fundraising departments found in this study bodes well for public relations in higher education. These findings may be an indication that public relations has made inroads in this subsector in terms of the three components of strategic contingencies theory: centrality, substitutability, and the ability to cope with uncertainty (Hickson et al., 1971). One reason for this may be increased environmental uncertainty. It is reasonable to assume that the leaders of extremely complex organizations, like the top U.S. colleges and universities, are aware that they have to pay attention to a variety of external publics, not just donors. As colleges and universities become larger and require more private support for their operations, the decisions of these influential organizations affect a wider array of stakeholder groups. At the same time, the environment in which these organizations operate is becoming more complex and unpredictable. It is likely that under these conditions public relations acquires more centrality (i.e., its contributions are critical for the success and survival of the organization) and becomes less substitutable (i.e., public relations activities cannot be handled by fundraising).

However, the fact that there were no cases of fundraising reporting to public relations demonstrates the strength of the fundraising function among these top gift-raising colleges and universities. While public relations appears to have gained some ground, fundraising certainly does not appear to have lost any. Another reason public relations departments in these institutions may be in a stronger position is that independent public relations departments place a higher value on excellent public relations practices than does a combined advancement department (Hall & Baker, 2003). As the public relations department's potential to provide excellent communication increases, the department is likely to gain more organizational power, which is needed to counter the often dominating priorities of the fundraising department (MacKeith, 1994).

These findings also demonstrate that the patterns of encroachment among colleges and universities reported in previous studies do not hold true for today's top fundraising schools. Over two studies, Kelly (1993a; 1994) found that educational institutions that depend more on fundraising, such as private colleges and universities, had higher levels of encroachment than public institutions that depend more on public funding. The results of statistical tests conducted for this study found no differences in the frequency of structural fundraising encroachment due to institutional governance or mission. These results may be due to the fact that there was not much variation in the level of dependence on fundraising dollars among the colleges and universities that raise the most money. Once a college or university reaches the highest levels of fundraising, differences due to institutional characteristics, such as governance and mission, probably do not make a difference.

This similarity between public and private institutions may be due to public institutions becoming increasingly reliant on fundraising during the last 30 years. State or public support has greatly diminished since the early 1980s. Now, what are formally referred to as state institutions receive only a small portion of their operating budgets from state revenue. For example, Seigel (2012) reported that 30 years ago states provided enough funding to cover nearly three-quarters of universities' budgets. However, in 2012, the percentage of their budgets covered by state funds was down to only a quarter. Similarly, Kelderman (2012) reported that state support for public colleges fell 7.6% in 2012 alone. Therefore, because public colleges and universities have had to rely increasingly on private dollars to fund their operations, there was little difference in encroachment between public and private institutions of higher learning.

CONCLUSION

The top fundraising colleges and universities in 2012 experienced less fundraising encroachment on public relations than has been reported for colleges and universities in previous studies. However, existing theory could not explain why some of these institutions chose an encroachment model while others did not. Other factors should be considered to understand encroachment when organizations face not only complex and uncertain environments but also increasing dependence on private donations. In addition, a limitation of this research is that it only looked at colleges and universities that were included on the Philanthropy 400. It did not take into account large universities that did not raise enough money to be considered on the list or smaller institutions of higher education that may not have the resources to staff distinct fundraising and public relations offices. It may be found that Kelly's (1994) explanation of differences in encroachment may hold true among these organizations.

REFERENCES

About CASE. (n.d.). Council for Advancement and Support of Education. Retrieved March 26, 2013, from http://www.case.org/About_CASE.html

Arthur W. Page Society. (2012). Building belief: A new model for activating corporate character and authentic advocacy. Retrieved January 30, 2014, from http://www.awpagesociety.com/insights/building-belief/

Broom, G.M. (2009). *Cutlip & Center's effective public relations* (10th ed.). Upper Saddle River, NJ: Prentice Hall.

Broom, G.M., & Dozier, D.M. (1986). Advancement for public relations role models. *Public Relations Review, 12*(1), 37–56.

Council for Aid to Education. (2013, February 20). Colleges and universities raise $31 billion in 2012 [News release]. Retrieved March 28, 2013, from http://www.cae.org/content/pdf/VSE_2012_Press_Release.pdf

Cutlip, S.M. (1994). *The unseen power: PR. A history.* Hillsdale, NJ: Lawrence Erlbaum.

Daft, R.L. (2010). *Organization theory and design.* Mason, OH: Cengage Learning.

DiConsiglio, J. (2011, November/December). United by goals: There is no integrated advancement without communications and marketing. *CASE Currents, 37*(9), 30–36.

Dozier, D.M. (1988). Breaking public relations' glass ceiling. *Public Relations Review, 14*(3), 6–14.

Gonzales, R. (2013, February 20). Stanford tops college fundraising list. Retrieved March 27, 2013, from http://www.npr.org/2013/02/20/172519482/stanford-tops-college-fundraising-list

Grunig, J.E., & Hunt, T. (1984). *Managing public relations.* Fort Worth, TX: Holt, Rinehart and Winston.

Grunig, L.A., Grunig, J.E., & Dozier, D.M. (2002). *Excellent public relations and effective organizations.* Mahwah, NJ: Lawrence Erlbaum Associates.

Hall, H. (2012, June 19). Charitable donations barely grew last year, "Giving USA" finds. *Chronicle of Higher Education.* Retrieved March 27, 2013, from http://chronicle.com/article/Charitable-Donations-Barely/132375/

Hall, M.R. (2002). Fundraising and public relations: A comparison of programme concepts and characteristics. *International Journal of Nonprofit and Voluntary Sector Marketing, 7*(4), 368–381.

Hall, M.R., & Baker, G.F. (2003). Public relations from the ivory tower: Comparing research universities with corporate/business models. *International Journal of Educational Advancement, 4*(2), 127–154.

Hayes, A.F., & Krippendorff, K. (2007). Answering the call for a standard reliability measure for coding data. *Communication Methods and Measures, 1*(1), 77–89.

Hickson, D.J., Hinings, C.R., Lee, C.A., Schneck, R.E., & Pennings, J.M. (1971). A strategic contingencies' theory of intraorganizational power. *Administrative Science Quarterly, 16*(2), 216–229.

Kelderman, E. (2012, January 23). State support for colleges falls 7.6% in 2012 fiscal year. *Chronicle of Higher Education.* Retrieved October 28, 2013, from http://chronicle.com/article/State-Support-for-Higher/130414/

Kelly, K.S. (1991). *Fundraising and public relations: A critical analysis.* Hillsdale, NJ: Lawrence Erlbaum Associates.

Kelly, K.S. (1993a). Fundraising encroachment on public relations: A clear and present danger to effective trustee leadership. *Nonprofit Management and Leadership, 4*(1), 47–68.

Kelly, K.S. (1993b). Public relations and fundraising encroachment: Losing control in the non-profit sector. *Public Relations Review, 19*(4), 349–365.

Kelly, K. S. (1994). Fundraising encroachment and the potential of public relations departments in the nonprofit sector. *Journal of Public Relations Research,* 6(1), 1–22.

Kelly, K. S. (1998). *Effective fundraising management.* Mahwah, NJ: Lawrence Erlbaum Associates.

Lauzen, M. M. (1991). Imperialism and encroachment in public relations. *Public Relations Review,* 17(3), 245–255.

Lauzen, M. M. (1992a). Public relations roles, intraorganizational power, and encroachment. *Journal of Public Relations Research,* 4(2), 61–80.

Lauzen, M. (1992b). Effects of gender on professional encroachment in public relations. *Journalism & Mass Communication Quarterly,* 69(1), 173–180.

Lee, M. (2011). Historical milestones in the emergence of nonprofit public relations in the United States, 1900–1956. *Nonprofit and Voluntary Sector Quarterly,* 40(2), 318–335.

Liebler, J. G. & McConnell, C. R. (2012). *Management principles for health professionals* (6th ed.). Sudbury, MA: Jones & Bartlett Learning.

López-Rivera, M. (2012, October, 14). How the *Chronicle* compiled its Philanthropy 400 rankings. *Chronicle of Philanthropy.* Retrieved February 7, 2013, from http://philanthropy.com/article/How-The-Chronicle-s/134990/

Lum, L. (2013, February). Communicating up. *CASE Currents,* 39(2), 28–33.

MacKeith, J. (1994). Interdepartmental relations and voluntary organizations: An exploration of tensions and why they arise. *Nonprofit Management and Leadership,* 4(4), 431–446.

Philanthropy 400. (2012). *The Chronicle of Philanthropy.* Retrieved March 26, 2013, from http://philanthropy.com/section/Philanthropy-400/237/

Satchwell, C. M. (2010). At the fundraising core: Strategic public relations in fundraising practice [White paper]. Retrieved March 26, 2013, from http://www.case.org/Documents/protected/whitepapers/Satchwell_StrategicPR.pdf

Seigel, R. (2012, June 21). Are public universities still public? [Interview]. Retrieved October 28, 2013, from http://www.npr.org/2012/06/21/155524647/are-public-universities-still-public

Swanger, W., & Rodgers, S. (2013). Revisiting fundraising encroachment of public relations in light of the theory of donor relations. *Public Relations Review,* 39(5), 566–568.

Van Ruler, B., & De Lange, R. (2003). Barriers to communication management in the executive suite. *Public Relations Review,* 29(2), 145–158.

Waters, R. D. (2008). Applying relationship management theory to the fundraising process for individual donors. *Journal of Communication Management,* 12(1), 73–87.

Waters, R. D., & Lemanski, J. L. (2011). Revisiting strategic communication's past to understand the present: Examining the direction and nature of communication on Fortune 500 and Philanthropy 400 web sites. *Corporate Communications: An International Journal,* 16(2), 150–169.

5 Alumni Commitment, Organization–Public Relationships, and Ethics

Shannon A. Bowen and Diana C. Sisson

In the ever-changing media landscape, organization–public relationships (OPRs) are amplified, particularly in social media where organizations can receive immediate feedback from their respective publics. Further, relationships must be maintained in an ethical manner to build the trust and credibility that allows long-term relationships to flourish. In this chapter, we review the literature on organization–public relationships and combine it with the perspectives of utilitarianism and deontology from moral philosophy. We are unaware of any other studies that have filled the gap in the literature combining OPR variables and ethics in the nonprofit world of relationship building.

Evaluating OPR theory in our case study, the University of South Carolina's *No Limits* campaign, provides an in-depth look at OPRs in social media for an academic organization, particularly in the commitment dimension. The *No Limits* campaign is an initiative by the University of South Carolina that "honors the individuals who work, study, teach and graduate" by communicating "our values, our aspirations and our personality" (University of South Carolina, n.d.).

Although the nonprofit or for-profit status of a university may vary, based on public or private funding, the vast majority of university alumni associations are founded as nonprofit organizations. Nationally, the number of higher education nonprofit organizations has increased from 1.58 million in 2011, which is "an increase of 21.5 percent since 2001" (Pettijohn, 2013). Their nonprofit 501(c)(3) status allows them special tax privileges, including making alumni donations tax deductible. The University of South Carolina's My Carolina Alumni Association, a 501(c)(3) charitable organization founded in 1846, is under the governance of the Office of University Foundations. In 2012, the University of South Carolina had $1,887,817,316 of total assets (University of South Carolina, 2012). As an entity that collects membership dues and is a 501(c)(3) charitable organization, the University of South Carolina's My Carolina Alumni Association provided an opportunity for the study of relationships between a nonprofit organization and an alumni public. This research did not explore why the University preferred to use the term "charitable organization" rather than "nonprofit organization," but assumes it places an emphasis on the tax-deductible nature of donations.

The purpose of comparing the alumni survey (*n* = 103) and social media comments was to explore what variables were connected to the commitment felt by alumni to the University. An ethical analysis of the campaign allowed us to make both positive observations and normative recommendations for social media use.

LITERATURE REVIEW

Reputations and Organization–Public Relationships. OPRs are thought of as processes of forming and maintaining relationships between an organization and its publics (Yang & Grunig, 2005). Commitment is the dimension of OPRs explored in this chapter. Commitment is defined as the "extent to which each party believes and feels that the relationship is worth spending energy to maintain and promote" (Hon & Grunig, 1999, p. 3). Scholars examined OPRs in an academic setting in terms of measurement validation (Jo, Hon, & Brunner, 2004) and relational quality (Yang, Alessandri, & Kinsey, 2008).

Reputations play an important role in OPRs. Reputations are "perceptual representations of a company's past actions and future prospects," particularly in terms of how attractive a company or organization is to consumers within an industry (Fombrun, 1996, p. 72). Reputations provide advantages within an industry, which is the basis of a competitive advantage. Websites (Bowen, 2010a) and social media (Wright & Hinson, 2011) have been found to emphasize the existent reputation of an organization rather than being a tool to create or change a reputation. Social media and social networking sites (SNS) are online tools that help foster active relationships between an organization and its target publics through reciprocal communication (Bowen, 2013).

Reputations result from competition; thus, reputations provided a competitive advantage grounded in trust and respect. Typically, reputations are centered on a unique product or service an organization provides. Moreover, Fombrun (1996) argued that reputations inform consumers and publics about an organization's products and services, what its values are, and whether it is financially stable for investments by stakeholders.

Given that reputations have financial implications, Fombrun (1996) asserted that an organization's reputation is linked to an organization's identity, which Dukerich and Carter (2000) argued consists of external perceptions of an organization's actions. Perceptions regarding an organization's actions contribute to how it approaches building and maintaining relationships with its publics.

Lee and Park (2013) explicated OPRs through an examination of message interactivity and its effects on organizational reputation. Lee and Park (2013) argued that organizations were evaluated in a positive manner when they responded. More so, comments elicited perceptions of higher trustworthiness, as well as perceptions of "having better control of mutuality and communal relationships, and higher satisfaction, compared to organizations that did not respond back" (p. 188). They asserted that "actively responding to the public's comments posted on organizational Web sites and blog sites positively influence both perceptions of relationship management and corporate reputation" (p. 201).

Both reputations and identity can be important in the nonprofit sector, as demands for accountability are heightened in donorship-based organizations (Doh, 2006). In member organizations, demands for ethical rectitude are high due to the idea of advocacy on behalf of a shared belief or cause, requiring an equally high level of trust to be built (Jiang & Bowen, 2011). Furthermore, Sargeant and Lee (2004) argued that "higher degrees of trust in a voluntary organization may be associated with a greater willingness to (a) become a donor and (b) give greater sums" (p. 616). Trust is viewed as a foundational element of relationship building. Some scholars argued that social media are comprised of relationship networks that facilitate trust building (Smitko, 2012).

Satisfaction and Commitment. Perceived satisfaction seemed to positively impact OPRs and attitudes towards brands, particularly when pertaining to purchasing products. Kim and Chan-Olmsted (2005) explored how different aspects of OPRs affect brand attitudes. They found that perceptions of relationships with an organization affect customers' brand attitudes of the organization and perception of satisfaction seemed to have a significant impact on customers' attitudes toward a brand (Kim & Chan-Olmsted, 2005). Furthermore, Sha and Dozier (2014) argued "identification with the academic unit, past unit engagement . . . identification with alumni's major (e.g., public relations), and number of campus organizational membership while a student" were significant in predicting whether an individual would maintain a financial commitment with a university (p. 1).

Because perceived satisfaction played an integral role in determining the quality of OPRs, perceived satisfaction also contributed to the willingness to maintain relationships. Surveying college students, Johnson and Acquavella (2012) extended OPRs through an examination of customer satisfaction and willingness to maintain relationships with cell phone service providers. They found that there was an association between personal commitment, anthropomorphism, perceived satisfaction, and willingness to maintain relationships with an organization. Citing Brunig and Galloway (2003), Johnson and Acquavella (2012) defined anthropomorphism as when an organization "embodies human characteristics," which included trustworthiness, meeting expectations of its respective publics, and community involvement (p. 164).

Stakeholders' subjective views may also contribute to perceptions of relational quality in OPRs. Yang and colleagues (2008) explicated OPRs between students and universities through an evaluation of relational quality and subjective stakeholder views. By evaluating reputational quality, Yang and colleagues (2008) asserted that relational quality and reputation are rooted in subjective views of "their experience, interactions, and information" (p. 162). It stands to reason that those stakeholder views can be enhanced by credibility and attention to ethics.

Ethics, Trust, and Relationships. Using ethical behavior to enhance relationships between organizations and publics is not a concept that is unique to the nonprofit world, as ethics was emphasized in public relations theory (Vercic, Grunig, & Grunig, 1996) and as a principle of public relations excellence (Bowen, 2004). Although ethics is considered a primary factor in the success of public relations efforts, the connection between ethics and trust among publics has yet to be fully explored. Bowen and Hung-Baesecke (2013) conducted research that found ethics was a precursor to authentically good relationships between organizations and publics. Ethical behavior as a foundational basis of organizational decision making appeared to enhance all types of relationships between an organization and its publics (Bowen & Hung-Baesecke, 2013).

Ethics enhances all forms of trust in relationships; however, the importance of trust in those relationships may be emphasized in nonprofits. Donor and member publics engage in a high degree of scrutiny of organizational actions, expenditures, policies, and lobbying activities (Bowen, 2011). Jiang and Bowen (2011) found that the activist groups tend to hold to a deontological belief system, emphasizing autonomy, equality, duty, and good will or good intentions. They also found that the activist groups' member publics expected a high degree of transparency and respect.

The publics of nonprofits expect them to engage in dialogue surrounding matters of ethics or policy. Pearson (1989), basing his ethics on the sociological theory of Habermas, explained that public relations has an obligation of dialogue that it must meet to ethically engage with its publics. Although dialogue is an ethical requirement, we need further means of analysis and parameters for decision making that go beyond dialogue. In ethical terms, how does an organization define what it values and what it wants to foster in relationships with its publics?

Bowen (2010b) argued that trust is built on consistency, ethics, and organizations meeting the expectations of publics over time. In creating these relationship qualities, there are two primary approaches to normative ethics that an organization could take: utilitarianism or deontology. These two perspectives go far beyond the obligation of dialogue to provide a decision-making framework of what should be considered to be ethical.

Utilitarianism. Utilitarian ethics originated with Jeremy Bentham and were refined by John Stuart Mill (DeGeorge, 2010). Utilitarianism is a consequentialist form of ethics: The ethics of the decision are determined by the predicted outcomes or consequences of different options. Predicting how those options can potentially affect publics allows an ethical analysis based on the consequences of different decision options, weighing the good and bad outcomes of each.

Although there are various forms of utilitarian ethics, the type that is used most often defines the good in terms of public interest or creating happiness for the greatest number of people, as opposed to creating harm. Mill's utilitarian theory argues that the ethical alternative creates the greatest good for the greatest number of people, while minimizing harms (Elliot, 2007). It is important that all affected publics be considered and all potential outcomes be weighed before one can truly determine what creates the greatest good for the greatest number of people.

The utilitarian approach to ethics has the strength of aligning well with the strategic constituencies approach to public relations; that is, both perspectives view consequences on publics as integral to ethical decision making. Utilitarianism has the weaknesses of always maintaining majority rule, which can reinforce the status quo at the expense of a minority, and asking the decision maker to accurately predict future outcomes, a difficult task. Still, a utilitarian approach to ethics allows a thorough consideration of the organizations consequences on publics.

Deontology. Deontological ethics is a non-consequentialist form of ethical decision making: decisions are based on duty to uphold moral principle rather than potential outcomes. Immanuel Kant (1783/1964) pioneered deontology as a way to make the virtue ethics of ancient Greece more definitive, testable, and applicable to currently ongoing moral dilemmas. In deontology, the moral autonomy or maximal objectivity of the decision maker is crucial to rule out bias in the decision. Decisions are made using reason alone, examining moral principle from every possible vantage point, including that of various publics. Moral principles that are thought to be universal are those which should be acted upon.

Universal moral principles are those which appeal to the obligation of the decision maker regardless of culture, circumstance, or outcome. Decisions should be reversible, that is, still ethical if the decision maker should be on the receiving end of the decision. Finally, decision should also be made using good intention or good moral will to drive the decision, as opposed to self-interest, greed, or other factors that may bias the decision. Deontology encourages decisions to be made by reason alone, examining the underlying principle that upholds moral duty. Those principles are normally broad considerations of moral duty, such as honesty, fairness, respect, or equity.

A deontological approach to public relations ethics in the nonprofit world requires research to assess the decision from many varied perspectives. Public relations managers must understand the needs and values of internal and management publics and the values of key public around the organization. Conducting such a rigorous ethical analysis has the weakness of requiring time and a research budget to understand the values of publics, but also has the strength of resulting in an extremely thorough ethical analysis that may save the organization from further problems.

Who Uses These Approaches? Wright (1985) found that entry- and mid-level public relations practitioners tended to use a utilitarian form of analysis, based on the potential consequences of their decisions. He found that more executive management public relations professionals preferred a deontological approach to ethical decision making over a utilitarian analysis. Age, moral development, career experience, and the sophistication of ethical analysis ability were explored in Wright's (1985) study to explain the growing preference for deontology.

Other studies have also found a preference for deontology among managerial public relations professionals (Bowen et al., 2006). Deontology seems to lend itself naturally to the policy type of decisions that must be made in executive positions. Those who preferred deontology were found to have more years of experience in public relations and a high rate of reporting directly to their organization's CEO (Bowen, 2008). Although both of the approaches to ethical decision making are used in various levels of public relations, combining them for a multisided analysis is also possible, as explained in Bowen and Gallicano (2013).

Combining reputation management, OPR variables, and ethics is a new area of study. To understand how these variables operate within the context of a nonprofit environment, the authors designed a case study to explore these questions. In the following case study, we look at a branding campaign in an effort to understand the linkages between these variables, as well as to make strategic normative recommendations for future use in nonprofit public relations.

METHOD

Evaluating OPRs in University of South Carolina's *No Limits* campaign through an adaptation of Hon and Grunig's (1999) *PR Relationship Measurement Scale* provided an exploratory, in-depth look at OPRs in social media for an educational institution, particularly with regard to the commitment dimension of OPR theory. Thus, relationships can be enhanced through tailored campaigns with social media components.

A post-hoc ethical analysis of the case allowed us to assess the ethics of the communication in the campaign. We analyzed the case using utilitarian and deontological theory to make normative recommendations for nonprofit public relations. This case study examined university–alumni relationships, but it also stands to reason that ethical management of a nonprofit campaign can further the relationships of any nonprofit organization with any type of public.

In this mixed-method study (Tashakkori & Teddlie, 1998), we used an online survey and a qualitative analysis to explore alumni commitment in OPRs within the University of South Carolina's *No Limits* campaign. We explore whether the relationship variable "commitment" could help tailor academic campaigns' social media components. Online survey method was employed in the examination of the OPR found amid the University of South Carolina's *No Limits* campaign, specifically pertaining to the commitment dimension of OPRs. Informal thematic analysis of Facebook user comments on University of South Carolina's *No Limits* Facebook posts was also employed to enhance understanding of the social media component.

Survey Data Collection. We used a cross-sectional design (Shoemaker & McCombs, 2003) based on an alumni population. Using a sampling frame of 7,000 e-mail addresses supplied by the alumni relations office, we collected 238 responses. Two screening questions brought the final sample size to 103 usable responses from alumni who are familiar with the *No Limits* campaign. Questions focused on the commitment dimension of OPRs and were constructed using 7-point Likert scales, with 1 = strongly agree and 7 = strongly disagree, which were modeled after the Hon and Grunig (1999) scale. All statistical tests, including one-way ANOVAs and chi-square tests, used $p < 0.05$ to determine significance. Institutional review board approval was obtained prior to the distribution of the online survey.

The qualitative component of this study examined Facebook posts ($n = 11$) containing *No Limits* campaign verbiage and any comments ($n = 77$) on those posts. Facebook posts and comments informed the extent to which an OPR existed in the social media component of the campaign. Data collected from the University of South Carolina's Facebook page was dated from the beginning of the *No Limits* campaign's soft launch in September 2012 through July 19, 2013.

Facebook posts pertaining to the organization's *No Limits* campaign messaging were grouped by common themes found in reputation management strategies as they were the antecedents found in the maintenance of OPRs (Hon & Grunig, 1999). Using pattern matching, Facebook user responses to the organization's *No Limits* campaign were grouped together by themes found in the outcomes of OPRs (Hon & Grunig, 1999).

FINDINGS

Given the small sample size, this study is considered to be exploratory and can shed light into the complex relationships between a university's nonprofit arm and its alumni. Because we used mixed methods, we believe that our findings captured several dimensions of the case under study. Findings revealed that alumni who were connected to the University's Facebook page desired to maintain a relationship or affiliation, as well as interact with the University. More so, alumni who desired to maintain a relationship or association with the University realized that the University wanted to maintain a long-term commitment, as well as a relationship with alumni through the *No Limits* campaign. Relationship management strategies used by the University in the social media component of its *No Limits* campaign focused on strategies of positivity and relationship nurturing—elements of stewardship.

Alumni Commitment to the University of South Carolina. When asked if there was a long-lasting bond between the University of South Carolina and its alumni, survey respondents tended to agree (38.8%) or strongly agree (24.3%). Responses about the prominence of the value of an alumnus's relationship with the University above other institutions were mixed. When asked whether their relationship with the University of South Carolina had greater prominence than a relationship with any other institution, responses showed varying levels of agreement (59.2%) and varying levels of disagreement (27.2%). Responses about whether an alumnus's relationship with the University was "very important" indicated overall agreement. Respondents strongly agreed (32%) or agreed (40.8%).

As illustrated in Table 5–1, survey respondents overwhelmingly indicated that they wanted to maintain a relationship or affiliation with the University.

Table 5–1 Alumni Commitment to the University of South Carolina.

	N	Min	Max	Mean	SD
The University of South Carolina is trying to maintain a long-term commitment to alumni through the *No Limits campaign.*	103	1	7	3.10	1.35
The University of South Carolina wants to maintain a relationship with alumni through its *No Limits campaign.*	103	1	7	3.00	1.35
There is a long-lasting bond between the University of South Carolina and alumni.	103	1	6	2.53	1.26
I value my relationship with the University of South Carolina more than with any other institution or organization.	103	1	7	3.19	1.82
My relationship with the University of South Carolina is very important to me.	103	1	7	2.53	1.33
I want to maintain a relationship or affiliation with the University of South Carolina.	103	1	5	2.35	1.06
I am very loyal to the University of South Carolina.	103	1	7	2.30	1.31
I do not care to interact with the University of South Carolina.[a]	103	2	7	5.86	1.18

[a]Reverse Coded.

Responses showed that respondents agreed (50.5%) or strongly agreed (33%) that they wanted to maintain a relationship with the University.

Responses surrounding whether the University's *No Limits* campaign was an attempt to maintain a long-term commitment with alumni or to maintain a relationship with alumni were mixed. When asked whether the University of South Carolina was trying to maintain a long-term commitment to alumni through the *No Limits* campaign, respondents indicated that they were unsure or neutral (40.8%) or agreed (20.4%). Survey respondents also indicated that they were unsure or neutral (35.9%) or agreed (26.2%) that the University of South Carolina wanted to maintain a relationship with alumni through its *No Limits* campaign.

Respondents indicated that they are very loyal to the University of South Carolina. Responses showed that respondents strongly agreed (40.8%) or agreed (32%). When asked if they did not want to interact with the University, respondents indicated that they did want to interact with the University by strongly disagreeing (44.7%) or disagreeing (35%) with this reversed item.

Alumni Commitment and Interaction with the *No Limits* Campaign on Social Media. Findings from this online survey revealed that when asked whether they were connected to the University on its various social media platforms, there was an almost even split among respondents who indicated they were connected (46.6%) and those who were not (47.6%).

Being connected to the University of South Carolina on its various social media accounts seemed to indicate that alumni wanted to interact with the University, χ^2 (10, $N = 103$) = 18.78, $p < 0.05$. An alumnus who desired to maintain a relationship or affiliation with the University of South Carolina also seemed to value his or her relationship with it more than any other institution, χ^2 (24, $N = 103$) = 127.51, $p < 0.05$, which was statistically significant.

The desire to maintain an association or relationship with the University seemed to indicate that the individual's relationship with the University of South Carolina was very important to them, χ^2 (24, $N = 103$) = 159.29, $p < 0.05$. The desire to maintain an association or relationship with the University seemed to indicate that the individual was very loyal to the University of South Carolina, χ^2 (20, $N = 103$) = 140.24, $p < 0.05$. Additionally, the state in which the individual resided, χ^2 (65, $N = 103$) = 89.80, $p < 0.05$, as well as whether the individual was a member of the My Carolina Alumni Association, χ^2 (5, $N = 103$) = 16.56, $p < 0.05$, were statistically significant when examining whether an alumnus felt loyal to the University of South Carolina. Membership in the My Carolina Alumni Association also was associated with an individual's desire to maintain a relationship or affiliation with the University of South Carolina, χ^2 (4, $N = 103$) = 18.43, $p < 0.05$.

Alumni who desired to maintain a relationship or an affiliation with the University of South Carolina seemed to realize that the University wanted to maintain a long-term commitment, χ^2 (24, $N = 103$) = 46.83, $p < 0.05$, as well as a relationship with alumni through its *No Limits* campaign, χ^2 (24, N = 103) = 43.89, $p < 0.05$.

A one-way ANOVA was used to determine if different levels of employment affected whether or not alumni wanted to interact with the University of South Carolina. Respondents tended to have full-time employment (67%), while some respondents indicated that they were unemployed (13.6%). This analysis revealed that the effects of different levels of employment on interaction with the University were significant, $F(3, 88) = 4.60$, $p < 0.05$. Post-hoc analysis using a Tukey HSD showed that the mean for full-time employment ($M = 6.04$, $SD = 1.12$) was significantly different than unemployment ($M = 4.86$, $SD = 0.95$) and graduate student ($M = 5.00$, $SD = 2.83$). Contrarily, the mean for full-time employment differed little from part-time employment ($M = 5.86$, $SD = 1.22$). Based on this important finding, it appeared that alumni who were employed full-time or part-time wanted to interact with the University of South Carolina.

Organization–Public Relationship Presence in *No Limits* Campaign Social Media. Guided by Hon and Grunig (1999), dominant relationship management themes found through an informal qualitative analysis of *No Limits* campaign messages posted by the University of South Carolina on its Facebook page showed an emphasis on positivity and relationship nurturing, an element of stewardship. Stewardship, a relationship management strategy, was defined as "recogniz[ing] the strategic value of previously established relationships" (Hon & Grunig, 1999, p. 17).

Positivity, defined as actions an "organization or public does to enhance the enjoyment in a relationship" (Hon & Grunig, 1999, p. 14), presented itself in at least six of the 10 University of South Carolina's *No Limits* Facebook posts. Using verbiage from the campaign, Facebook posts focused on the positive aspects of the University, particularly topics like beautiful weather, pride, humor, heart, spirit, potential, and love that would elicit a positive emotional response from a member of any of its target publics.

Relationship nurturing, one of the four elements of stewardship, is when an "organization accepts the importance of supportive publics and keeps them central to the organization's consciousness" (Hon & Grunig, 1999, p. 17). Facebook posts pertaining to the *No Limits* campaign messaging placed prominence primarily on students and their achievements in their respective areas of study, as well as in their extracurricular activities like volunteerism. For example, one Facebook post portrayed a doctoral student in biological anthropology who examines skeletal remains to discover different ways of diagnosing breast cancer. Other Facebook posts centered on a student giving an inspirational speech during Black History Month, another focused on a student's service and volunteerism, and so on.

Relationship Outcomes. Dominant OPR outcomes found through an informal qualitative analysis of Facebook user comments about *No Limits* campaign messages posted by the University of South Carolina on its Facebook page include control mutuality, trust, satisfaction, commitment, and exchange relationships. Interestingly, communal relationship was not a significant theme in the informal qualitative analysis of Facebook comments regarding the University's *No Limits* campaign.

Control mutuality and exchange relationship themes emerged in comments on the University of South Carolina's Facebook posts regarding its *No Limits* campaign in the form of critique of the University's first *No Limits* television advertisement. Some Facebook commenters indicated that the television advertisement was "uninspiring" and was "made for a much older audience." Examples of trust include one commenter wishing she could be at the University because it was one of her top schools she hoped to attend, which speaks to the integrity of the University's admissions process. Satisfaction was expressed in comments on the University's Facebook page about the campaign's slogan, student feature stories, the first *No Limits* television advertisement, and winning a football game.

Commitment themes emerged in comments on the University of South Carolina's Facebook posts regarding its *No Limits* campaign when it was related to sharing April Fool's jokes and sports, particularly football. The affective dimension of commitment centered on emotions, whereas the continuance dimension centered on action (Hon & Grunig, 1999). Two Facebook user comments showed crossover between the affective and continuance dimensions of commitment.

Ethical Analyses. Conducting a campaign with ethical rectitude is important in the overall success of any organization, but perhaps more so in nonprofits and other organizations because publics may expect higher levels of transparency, accountability, and work in the public interest. The obligation of dialogue means that both organizations and publics should engage in conversation with one another. Likewise, power differentials may disrupt the equilibrium of that relationship, meaning that it may be in danger unless ethics is prominent in decision making.

In addition to the moral obligation of dialogue, engaging in ethical decision making in campaigns between organization and publics makes good practical sense. Trust, as a precursor of good OPRs, means that ethical decision making or attention to ethics is necessary to build trust. More structured forms of ethical analyses, utilitarianism and deontology, allow us to shed additional light on this case.

Utilitarianism. As described above, a utilitarian moral analysis seeks to provide the greatest good for the greatest number of people, while creating the least amount of negative outcomes. Using that perspective, it appears in the data presented above that the *No Limits* campaign has achieved its goal of the greater number of alumni that have been disaffected or negatively impacted by it. In a utilitarian analysis, public interest in creating a relationship with the University, and furthering the variables of loyalty and commitment, were outcomes of the *No Limits* campaign.

A utilitarian analysis of the campaign also revealed that the stewardship and positivity strategies used by the University benefited the majority of alumni, and did not bring harm to the minority. Therefore, the University's strategy meets the utilitarian test of benefiting the greater good of the greater number of people and is ethical.

Negative consequences of the campaign were that those respondents who were currently unemployed or seeking higher levels of employment did not feel committed to maintaining a relationship with the University. Although that outcome is negative, it does not meet the standard to be avoided of causing harm as an outcome in utilitarian ethics. Therefore, we can conclude that the *No Limits* campaign is ethical when examined through utilitarianism, because it promotes the greater good for the greater number of publics (alumni) in maintaining a relationship with the University.

Deontology. When using a deontological analysis, the *No Limits* campaign becomes more problematic. The *No Limits* campaign is more of a one-sided dissemination of information than is ideal. A more symmetrical or dialogical approach to the campaign would likely engender greater commitment from alumni publics. Although the *No Limits* campaign upholds its moral duty to provide accurate information, it does not appear to respect the dignity of publics by engaging them in dialogue, seeking to completely understand the perspectives of various kinds of alumni, including employed and unemployed.

The perspective of alumni should be sought and included by the University because those publics are worthy of respect in and of themselves, and by virtue of their rationality obligate the University to engage in dialogue with them. Failing the obligation of dialogue and the deontological obligation for treating publics as equals, worthy of dignity and respect in and of themselves, means of the campaign should be reenvisioned to become more dialogical to be considered truly ethical. Instead of providing persuasive messages based on what the University would like publics to do, the University should also ask alumni publics what they want from it as an institution. Making the relationship more reciprocal and allowing alumni publics to experience more control mutuality would, in theory, strengthen the relationship between the alumni and the University. Engaging in dialogue with alumni publics and conducting more in-depth research on their viewpoints would allow the University the insight it needs to incorporate some of its ideas and perspectives into the campaign. If the University took that extra step to make the campaign more dialogical, respecting diverse viewpoints, it would meet the second ethical test of the deontological moral theory.

To meet the deontological standard of communicating with good intention, the campaign should be tailored by the University. Research asking alumni publics what information they need or want from the University could allow the campaign to be designed with good intention, not only filling the information needs of alumni publics, but also creating support and commitment for the University among alumni. The University should avoid communicating with alumni only as a means to only achieving its own goals, but should consider the alumni valuable community members in and of themselves. Then the University would truly be communicating with good intention, without bias or exploitation, and based upon the rational and autonomous perspectives of multiple publics. Trust among all publics would be enhanced, and if the above theory holds true, commitment to an ongoing relationship would also be fostered. In this manner, the *No Limits* campaign would meet all of the rigorous tests of deontological ethics.

Although the *No Limits* campaign is already successful, we believe that even great campaigns can be improved in terms of their responsiveness and ethical rectitude. Other nonprofit organizations can learn from this already successful campaign by improving upon responsiveness, dialogical communication, respect and dignity of alumni publics, and good intention. Admittedly, these ethical guidelines are normative in nature; theory in this chapter provides a sound basis for the enhancement of trust and relationship commitment.

DISCUSSION

In a dynamic social media environment, OPRs become more challenging (Yang & Grunig, 2005). In a social media environment, organizations can receive immediate feedback from their publics (Bowen, 2013). Feedback from these relationships, as well as an understanding of why publics participate in OPRs, can help organizations tailor their communication campaigns. The University of South Carolina appeared to understand the different facets of OPRs, which reflected in the social media component of the *No Limits* campaign, and used it to tailor its reputation management strategies to resonate with alumni.

Positivity and relationship nurturing were key reputation management strategies that the University of South Carolina used in the social media component of its *No Limits* campaign. As a result, the outcomes indicated that there was an effective organization–public relationship within the social component of the campaign. Facebook user comments centered on trust, satisfaction, control mutuality, commitment, and exchange relationships. However, a focus on alumni in Facebook posts with *No Limits* campaign messaging could enhance the University of South Carolina's relationship-nurturing strategies and increase interaction with alumni on Facebook. *No Limits* campaign messaging in the University's Facebook posts reflect the achievements of current students. A possible strategy may be to focus on alumni experiences at the University of South Carolina that prepared them for achievements made post-graduation. Incorporating the perspectives of alumni publics, and genuinely looking for their insights to add to the campaign, would strengthen the ethical nature of the communication and help it to pass the stringent tests of deontology.

Based on the informal qualitative analysis in this study, communal relationships were not as significant as other organization–public relationship outcomes. While some members of the University of South Carolina's Facebook community did provide support around the critique of the first *No Limits* television advertisement, this support was not as frequent as those who critiqued the advertisement. Perhaps strengthening these communal relationships might foster greater online community advocates for the University on social media.

Quantitative data collected through an online survey examined the commitment dimension of the organization–public relationship found in the social media component of the *No Limits* campaign. Commitment is defined as the "extent to which each party believes and feels that the relationship is worth spending energy to maintain and promote" (Hon & Grunig, 1999, p. 3). Examining the extent to which alumni felt committed to the University of South Carolina provided insights about the extent that commitment caused alumni to interact with the campaign messaging on the University's Facebook page. Although being connected to the University on its various social media accounts seemed to indicate that alumni wanted to interact with it, the degree of commitment seemed to be affected most by the desire to maintain an association or relationship with the University of South Carolina.

Value and importance of the relationship with the University and loyalty to it seemed to also be significant. Interestingly, My Carolina Alumni Association membership, geographic location, and employment also seemed to have significant associations with alumni desire to interact with the social media component of the University of South Carolina's *No Limits* campaign, as well as their desire to maintain an association or relationship with the University. Finally, our analysis indicated that the intention of the University must be to maintain positive relationships with alumni regardless of their ability to contribute financially. By emphasizing stewardship and positivity in its relationships, and incorporating good intention in relating with all alumni publics, this campaign can meet the most stringent test of ethics and deontological moral theory.

Implications: Keys for Ethical Nonprofit OPRs. As this chapter reaches its conclusion, we make normative recommendations for managing public relations campaigns in the nonprofit arena. Although our case study was not generalizable, the theory and practice presented in this chapter offers some key takeaways that can assist in the ethical management of nonprofit public relations.

Positivity and relationship-nurturing strategies, one of the four elements of stewardship, are effective approaches to fostering alumni commitment in social media components of a communication campaign. As social media efforts become more prominent in nonprofit campaigns, it is critical to understand the role that stewardship can play in furthering relationships. Furthermore, alumnus commitment was affected most by the alumnus's desire to maintain an association or relationship with the University of South Carolina, allowing us to understand the desire to stay connected.

Commitment may not be the most important variable in the building of successful relationships between nonprofits and their publics. Our qualitative findings indicate that both symmetrical dialogue and trust may foster more effective and beneficial relationships with members of the University's online alumni public. Again, social media can play a vital role in allowing and supporting asymmetrical dialogue between an organization and its publics, fostering mutual understanding.

Dialogue is not only an ethical obligation between organizations and publics; it also helps to build and engender trust. As Bowen and Hung-Baesecke (2013) argued, trust can be seen as a precursor to building authentic relationships. Trust can be viewed as a precondition for positive relationships between an organization and its publics that allows dialogue to create mutual understanding.

Ethics should be a key component of OPRs. Because nonprofits have to be trustworthy to be successful, ethics must be a high priority for the organization. Although commitment was not a linchpin variable in this case, commitment was heightened when publics wanted to maintain an association with the organization.

Public relations practitioners must be empowered to make ethical decisions, and they must have some knowledge of ethical decision making to engage in routine and autonomous moral analyses. They should be involved in the strategic management of the nonprofit, and their ethical analyses should be invited by the dominant coalition on a routine basis. Routinely examining matters of ethics normally leads to a higher level of ethical responsibility in an organization's strategic management.

Ethical analyses require that many sides of an issue be considered before decision is reached. One-sided thinking means that an ethical decision cannot be reached. Using a rigorous framework such as utilitarianism or deontology results in more thoroughly considered and long-lasting ethical decisions. Although the case in this study was ethical when using a utilitarian framework, deontology revealed that more symmetry, inclusiveness, and a more dialogical approach were needed.

CONCLUSION

Listening is extremely important, and it is required in deontological ethics. When organizations offer the dignity and respect to publics that listening entails, relationships should improve. Conflicts can be openly discussed, priorities can be accurately ascertained, and integrated solutions can be created. Over time, trust between nonprofit organizations and publics should then be enhanced, resulting in more satisfactory, long-term relationships on each end of the equation. By engaging in trustworthy behavior carried out with good will and good intention, the ethical rectitude of nonprofits is also heightened; one could argue that increased ethical responsibility should be a higher-order goal of all who work in the nonprofit arena.

Limitations of This Study. Given that this survey has been conducted in the summer, response rates were lower than the ideal rate of 20%. Although we planned on sending a second wave of invitations to participate in our survey to alumni, we were constrained from doing so; this constraint is a significant limitation of our study. In the collection and analysis of Facebook comments, it was unclear whether individuals were either alumni or students; therefore, all comments were coded for the presence of organization–public relationship outcomes.

ACKNOWLEDGMENTS

The researchers would like to thank the University of South Carolina's Division of Communication, as well as the My Carolina Alumni Association for their help in the distribution of the online survey.

REFERENCES

Bowen, S. A. (2004). Expansion of ethics as the tenth generic principle of excellent public relations: A Kantian theory and model for managing ethical issues. *Journal of Public Relations Research, 16*(1), 65–92.

Bowen, S. A. (2008). A state of neglect: Public relations as corporate conscience or ethics counsel. *Journal of Public Relations Research, 20*(3), 271–296.

Bowen, S. A. (2010a). An examination of applied ethics and stakeholder management on top corporate websites. *Public Relations Journal, 4*(1). Retrieved December 1, 2013, from http://www.prsa.org/Intelligence/PRJournal/

Bowen, S. A. (2010b). The nature of good in public relations: What should be its normative ethic? In R. L. Heath (Ed.), *Handbook of public relations* (pp. 569–583). Thousand Oaks, CA: Sage.

Bowen, S. A. (2011). Ethics in government public relations. In K. Stewart, M. Lee, & G. Neeley (Eds.), The practice of government public relations (pp. 155–177). London: Taylor & Francis.

Bowen, S. A. (2013). Using classic social media cases to distill ethical guidelines for digital engagement. *Journal of Mass Media Ethics, 28*(2), 119–133. doi:10.1080/08900523.2013.793523

Bowen, S. A., & Gallicano, T. D. (2013). A philosophy of reflective ethical symmetry: Comprehensive historical and future moral approaches in the excellence theory. In K. Sriramesh, A. Zerfass, & J.-N. Kim (Eds.), *Public relations and communication management: current trends and emerging topics*. New York, NY: Routledge.

Bowen, S. A., Heath, R. L., Lee, J., Painter, G., Agraz, F., McKie, D., & Toledano, M. (2006). *The business of truth: A guide to ethical communication*. San Francisco, CA: International Association of Business Communicators.

Bowen, S. A. & Hung-Baesecke, C. J. (2013, May). *Is ethics a precursor to authentic organization-public relationships?* Paper presented at the 11th Annual International Conference on Communication & Mass Media (Atiner), Athens, Greece.

Bruning, S. D., & Galloway, T. (2003). Expanding the organization-public relationship scale: Exploring the role that structural and personal commitment play in organization-public relationships. *Public Relations Review, 29*, 309–319. doi:10.1016=50363–8111(03)00042–0

DeGeorge, R. T. (2010). *Business ethics* (7th ed.). Boston, MA: Prentice-Hall.

Doh, J. P. (2006). Global governance, social responsibility and corporate-NGO collaboration. In S. Vachani (Ed.), *Transformations in global governance: Implications for multinationals and other stakeholders* (pp. 209–224). Cheltenham, UK: Edward Elgar.

Dukerich, J. M., & Carter, S. M. (2000). Distorted images and reputation repair. In M. Schultz, M. J. Hatch, & M. H. Larsen (Eds.), *The expressive organization: Linking identity, reputation, and the corporate brand* (pp. 97–112). Oxford: Oxford University Press.

Elliot, D. (2007). Getting Mill right. *Journal of Mass Media Ethics, 22*(2 & 3), 100–112.

Fombrun, C. J. (1996). *Reputation: Realizing value from the corporate image*. Boston, MA: Harvard Business School Press.

Hon, L. C., & Grunig, J. E. (1999). Guidelines for measuring relationships in public relations. *Institute for Public Relations*. Retrieved December 1, 2013, from http://www.instituteforpr.org/research_single/guidelines_measuring_relationships

Jiang, H., & Bowen, S. A. (2011). Ethical decision making in issues management and activist groups. *Public Relations Journal, 5*(1), n.p.

Jo, S., Hon, L. C., & Brunner, B. R. (2004). Organisation-public relationships: Measurement validation in a university setting. *Journal of Communication Management, 9*(1), 14–27.

Johnson, D. I., & Acquavella, G. (2012). Organization-public relationship: Satisfaction and intention to retain a relationship with a cell phone service provider. *Southern Communication Journal, 77*(3), 163–179. doi:10.1080/1041794X.2011. 634478

Kant, I. (1964). *Groundwork of the metaphysic of morals* (H. J. Paton, Trans.). New York, NY: Harper & Row. (Original publication 1785.)

Kim, J., & Chan-Olmsted, S. M. (2005). Comparative effects of organization–public relationships and product-related attributes on brand attitude. *Journal of Marketing Communications, 11*(3), 145–170.

Lee, H., & Park, H. (2013). Testing the impact of message interactivity on relationship management and organizational reputation. *Journal of Public Relations Research, 25*(2), 188–206. doi:10.1080/1062726X.2013.739103

Pearson, R. (1989). Beyond ethical relativism in public relations: Coorientation, rules, and the idea of communication symmetry. In J. E. Grunig & L. A. Grunig (Eds.), *Public relations research annual* (vol. 1, pp. 67–86). Hillsdale, NJ: Lawrence Erlbaum Associates.

Pettijohn, S. L. (2013). The nonprofit sector in brief: Public charities, giving, and volunteering, 2013. Washington, DC: Urban Institute. Retrieved December 1, 2013, from http://www.urban.org/UploadedPDF/412923-The-Nonprofit-Sector-in-Brief.pdf

Sargeant, A., & Lee, S. (2004). Trust and relationship commitment in the United Kingdom voluntary sector: Determinants of donor behavior. *Psychology & Marketing, 21*(8), 613–635. doi:10.1002/mar.20021

Sha, B.-L., & Dozier, D. M. (2014, March). *The rules of engagement: How donor identification relates to donation intention.* Paper presented to the International Public Relations Research Conference, Miami, FL.

Shoemaker, P. J., & McCombs, M. E. (2003). Survey research. In G. H. Stempel, D. H. Weaver, & G. C. Wilhoit (Eds.), *Mass communication research and theory.* Boston, MA: Allyn and Bacon.

Smitko, K. (2012). Donor engagement through Twitter. *Public Relations Review, 38*(4), 633–635. doi:10.1016/j.pubrev.2012.05.012

Tashakkori, A., & Teddlie, C. (1998). *Mixed methodology: Combining qualitative and quantitative approaches* (vol. 46). Thousand Oaks, CA: SAGE.

University of South Carolina. (n.d.). No limits campaign. *University of South Carolina Marketing Toolbox.* Retrieved February 19, 2014, from http://sc.edu/toolbox/noLimits_overview.php

University of South Carolina. (2012). USC System Financial Statement and Schedules. Retrieved December 1, 2013, from http://web.admin.sc.edu/fr/files/USC-System-FinancialStatement-ElliottDavis-FY1112.pdf

Vercic, D., Grunig, L. A., & Grunig, J. E. (1996). Global and specific principles of public relations: Evidence from Slovenia. In H. Culbertson & N. Chen (Eds.), *International Public Relations: A Comparative Analysis* (pp. 31–65). Mahwah, NJ: Lawrence Erlbaum Associates.

Wright, D. K. (1985). Can age predict the moral values of public relations practitioners? *Public Relations Review, 11*(1), 51–60.

Wright, D. K., & Hinson, M. (2011). A three-year longitudinal analysis of social and emerging media use in public relations practice. *Public Relations Journal, 5*(3). Retrieved June 26, 2014, from http://www.prsa.org/intelligence/prjournal/documents/2011wrighthinson.pdf

Yang, S.-U., Alessandri, S. W., & Kinsey, D. F. (2008). An integrative analysis of reputation and relational quality: A study of university-student relationships. *Journal of Marketing for Higher Education, 18*(2), 145–170.

Yang, S.-U., & Grunig, J. E. (2005). Decomposing organisational reputation: The effects of organisation-public relationship outcomes on cognitive representations of organisations and evaluations of organisational performance. *Journal of Communication Management, 9*(4), 305–325.

6 Race for Crisis Control

Attitudes and Giving Responses after Susan G. Komen for the Cure Pulled Planned Parenthood Funding

Emily S. Kinsky, R. Nicholas Gerlich, Kristina Drumheller, and Marc Sollosy

Nonprofit organizations (NPOs) seek to help society. To do so, they must have donors who share their passions for a cause, so they are in a particularly delicate position when a crisis hits. On Jan. 31, 2012, an Associated Press story revealed that Susan G. Komen for the Cure (Komen) was pulling its grants for breast cancer screening from Planned Parenthood ("Timeline," 2012; see Appendix). A firestorm of activity ensued with pro-life groups supporting the decision, while the impassioned messages of Planned Parenthood supporters went viral via social media. When the decision was first made, the managing director for community health programs at Komen resigned in protest (Goldberg, 2012). A few days after the news went public, however, the policy was changed and a senior Komen official resigned because of the reversal. Even after the shift, critics continued their rhetoric against the organization, and supporters derided Komen's decision to reverse the policy change. The tenor of discussion on social media was heated, and donations and event participation for Komen were both negatively affected.

Using the theory of planned behavior (TPB), U.S. citizens' responses to the funding-related crisis at Komen were examined. TPB has seen a recent resurgence as researchers recognize its benefit to consumer behavior and stakeholder relations. We see potential for TPB's application in studying nonprofit organizations; and in this study, we specifically look at its application during a crisis.

LITERATURE REVIEW

Susan G. Komen for the Cure. Susan G. Komen was diagnosed with breast cancer at age 33. Throughout Susan's diagnosis and treatment, she tried to think of ways to improve the lives of others battling breast cancer. Komen's dedication became her sister Nancy's inspiration for creating Susan G. Komen for the Cure. Soon after its introduction in 1982, it became the leader in the breast cancer movement ("About Us," 2012), focusing on research, education, screening, and treatment.

The Susan G. Komen Breast Cancer Foundation, Inc. does business as Susan G. Komen for the Cure and Affiliates, dedicated to the eradication of cancer.

The organization has built relationships with medical centers across the globe. According to Komen's Consolidated Financial Statements by Ernst & Young (2012), the Race for the Cure walks/runs were held in 133 cities across the United States in 2012; the funds raised from these events each year are a primary source of revenue. Of the funds raised by its 120 affiliates, 75% of the net proceeds are used at the local level for breast cancer–related education, treatment, and screenings, while the remaining proceeds are used to fund research and grants nationally (Ernst & Young, 2012).

Komen has invested almost $2 billion into breast cancer research and community screenings; however, it has not completed this task alone. This organization thrives off of its donations from large corporate and small party sponsors and partners. In 2012, the Komen website ("Partners & Sponsors," 2012) listed three groups of sponsors: Million Dollar Council Elite (40 brands that donated at least $1 million), Race for the Cure National Sponsors (11 organizations), and Corporate Sponsors (120 organizations). These sponsors helped raise more than $47 million in the 2011 fiscal year.

Planned Parenthood. Planned Parenthood provides education, screenings, and information on reproductive health care to millions of people every year, including men, women, and young adults. This international organization has been around for nearly a century and advocates for people's rights to make their own decisions about their future family, sex, and overall health. According to Planned Parenthood (2012), it is the largest provider of reproductive services in the United States—services that include abortions and, thus, have prompted controversy.

Planned Parenthood operates in almost 800 health centers around the world providing a wide range of healthcare. The organization not only provides care, but it also advocates for women's health rights issues through Planned Parenthood Federation of America. This section of the organization focuses on educating the public and paying for legislative advocacy, education campaigns, and organizing. This organization tries to stay present throughout the world whether in courts, on campuses, in local communities, or online to advocate for the services the organization provides, including contraceptives and education (Planned Parenthood, 2012).

Komen–Planned Parenthood Grant. Komen bases decisions to fund local organizations and clinics from assessments done by associates within those areas. If these affiliates determine that there is a particular need, then they provide grants to fund education, screening, and support for local residents of that specific community. Of the 121 affiliates Komen had in 2011, 19 worked directly through Planned Parenthood to provide "breast health education and breast screenings for hundreds of thousands of low-income, uninsured or medically under-served women" ("Regarding," 2011, para. 3). During the 5 years leading up to the crisis, this grant had funded 4,866 mammograms, 139,000 breast exams, breast health education for 160,000 women, and detected 177 cases of breast cancer ("Regarding," 2011).

The Crisis. On January 31, 2012, news agencies reported that Komen would pull funding from Planned Parenthood because of Komen's new policy not to fund any organization undergoing government investigation. Planned Parenthood was under Congressional investigation beginning in the fall of 2011 related to the funding of abortions (Kliff & Sun, 2012).

Speculators stated that Komen succumbed to the pressure of pro-life activists when the organization withdrew its funding (Phillips, 2012). According to some, it was viewed as a political move, and that insertion of politics collided with stakeholders' expectations of Komen as an apolitical organization with an apolitical cause. The policy change for the Komen foundation granting criteria was made under Senior Vice President for Public Policy Karen Handel, who had been with the organization approximately one year. One of the reasons some saw this as a political move was because Handel previously advocated for cutting funding to Planned Parenthood in 2010 when running for governor of Georgia (Kliff & Sun, 2012).

Komen's decision to cut funding to Planned Parenthood resulted in increased donations to Planned Parenthood by various activists and supporters. Within 24 hours, the organization received more than $650,000; $400,000 from online donations and $250,000 from Lee Fikes and his wife to replace what Komen grants would have provided (Kliff & Sun, 2012). New York Mayor Michael Bloomberg also gave $250,000 (Phillips, 2012).

Komen's retraction of the decision to cut funding from Planned Parenthood took only three days. On February 3, 2012, a statement was released by the organization: "We will continue to fund existing grants, including those of Planned Parenthood, and preserve their eligibility to apply for future grants, while maintaining the ability of our affiliates to make funding decisions that meet the needs of their communities" (Phillips, 2012, para. 11). After the political crisis of defunding Planned Parenthood erupted, Handel resigned on February 7.

Crisis Communication. Seeger, Sellnow, and Ulmer (1998) explain that an organizational crisis is a "specific, unexpected, and nonroutine event or series of events that create high levels of uncertainty and threaten or are perceived to threaten an organization's high priority goals" (p. 233). In February 2012, Komen faced an unexpected series of events that threatened the funding of Komen. Because of its nonprofit status and dependence on donations, a crisis of this magnitude could impact its very existence.

Coombs (2012) points out that crises are unpredictable rather than unexpected; in other words, organizations know a crisis will happen, just not when. Organizational crises, unlike natural disasters, are generally a result of mistakes, oversights, and organizational deficiencies. When a crisis threatens an organization, the organization's image is often at stake (Benoit, 1995). In this case, Komen "failed to think it through" (Brinker, 2012, para. 6) and faced a barrage of complaints and boycott threats. According to Eric Brinker (2012), "Accustomed to triaging breast cancer, not PR debacles, we stumbled" (para. 6). However, like any organization, NPOs need to be savvy in crisis preparations to avoid detrimental mistakes.

When organizations face a crisis, good leadership is critical as a response is considered. According to Coombs (2012), "Crisis management seeks to prevent or lessen the negative outcomes of a crisis and thereby protect the organization, stakeholders, and industry from harm" (p. 5). As an organizational communicator, one must strategically evaluate communication options and must consider the organizational values and vision as well as environmental factors (Pauchant & Mitroff, 1992). During a crisis, organizations must keep lines of communication open. Openness "allows the organization to be proactive in presenting its view of the crisis to the media" (Seeger, 1997, p. 245). Although the preference is for open and quick responses by the organization in crisis, stress can complicate good decision making (Benoit & Brinson, 1994; Drumheller & Benoit, 2004).

With the rise of social networks like Facebook and Twitter, organizations can engage with stakeholders more openly and more quickly; however, the increased speed and intensity of stakeholder engagement via social media—with good or bad news—has stunned a growing number of organizations. Effective crisis management takes on a new dimension when boycotts can be organized with the click of a button, as Komen quickly discovered. Whereas some research has been conducted on nonprofits in crisis (e.g., Sisco, 2012), the lion's share has focused on corporations. Social media, too, has been receiving more attention on its role as a communication channel for organizations (e.g., DiStaso & Bortree, 2012), but this is an area that requires more examination. NPOs need to understand how their communication affects donors, which could potentially be explained using the theory of planned behavior.

Theory of Planned Behavior and Consumer Ethics. The theory of planned behavior (TPB) posits that a person's intentions to behave a certain way are an indicator of the likelihood of actually behaving that way in the future (Ajzen, 1985; 1991). According to Wang (2009), "The TPB is central to our understanding of the psychological processes underlying human behavior" (p. 431). The theory of planned behavior is an extension of Ajzen and Fishbein's (1980) theory of reasoned action. It adds the concept of behavioral intentions, which are a function of attitudes, subjective norms, and perceived behavioral control. According to Ajzen (1985; 1991), an increase in favorable attitudes and subjective norms and an increase in the perception of having control over one's behavior will increase the person's intention to take part in that behavior. The TPB proposes that people are more likely to perform certain behaviors when there is an increased motivation or intention to perform that behavior. Perugini and Bagozzi (2001) built on this by contending that desire to behave a certain way is the antecedent of intent to behave in that manner. They defined desire as "a state of mind whereby an agent has a personal motivation to perform an action or to achieve a goal" (Perugini & Bagozzi, 2004, p. 71). They attempted to expand and deepen TPB with their model of goal-directed behavior, which included adding the concept of anticipated emotions as "parallel predictors" of behavior (Perugini & Bagozzi, 2001, p. 83).

Shaw and Shiu (2003) expanded TPB to create a model for understanding the role of ethical concerns in consumer choices, such as purchasing goods manufactured by sweatshop labor. "Ethical concerns are often ongoing and irresolvable" (Shaw & Shiu, 2003, p. 1486), requiring more effort in decision making. Ethical considerations present a complexity not found in most models, which focus primarily on hedonic and utilitarian behaviors. The nuance of contemplating a choice that, all other matters aside, may present the logical selection is complicated when ethical concerns tug at a person. Shaw, Shiu, Hassan, Bekin, and Hogg (2007) sought to address this complexity by proposing the examination of attitude, subjective norms, and perceived behavioral control, along with social identity and ethical concerns.

The TPB is not without criticism because of its lack of focus on motivations and volition. Shaw and colleagues (2007) recognized this criticism, and view the model with plan and desire being separate from intention. In addition, the influence of opinion leaders is not to be underestimated. These important others "can serve to impact personal motivation to act in terms of desire by positively supporting personal motivation or through negatively influencing desire to avoid sweatshop apparel" (p. 2). By extension, the influence of others could potentially impact ethical decisions related to philanthropic giving. Before social media, these important others might be limited to an individual's intimate circle, but that circle has become much larger with social networking.

Social networking is a new aspect to consider with regard to TPB. Social media could affect TPB via the introduction of multiple voices that may exert pressure on user attitudes. Thus far, findings on this effect are mixed. In relation to online communities, Bagozzi, Dholakia, and Mookerjee (2006) found that group norms and social identity significantly predicted behavioral intentions. This implies that comments made online could solidify norms and identity, which could subsequently influence consumer decisions. In contrast, Bagozzi, Dholakia, and Pearo (2007) found that subjective norms failed to significantly predict intentions related to online communities, while Thorbjørnsen, Pedersen, and Nysveen (2007) found that subjective norms were not sufficient for capturing the means by which consumer self and social identity influence consumer intentions.

Whereas Shaw and colleagues (2007) studied the context of avoiding clothing made by sweatshop labor, the current study examines planned donations to a nonprofit in the aftermath of a communication crisis. The purpose of this study is to extend research related to TPB to include donations to nonprofits, specifically within the context of planned donations or avoidance of donations to Komen. Hypotheses were constructed based on previous TPB findings related to consumer attitudes, desires and intent toward purchasing sweatshop clothing (Shaw et al., 2007) and based on the negative media coverage following Komen's change in policy. Thus, we hypothesize:

H1a: Attitude will have a strong positive relationship with desire to avoid donating to Komen.

H1b: Subjective norms will have a strong positive relationship with desire to avoid donating to Komen.

H1c: Perceived behavioral control will have a strong positive relationship with desire to avoid donating to Komen.

H2a: Attitude will have a strong positive relationship with intent to avoid donating to Komen.

H2b: Subjective norms will have a strong positive relationship with intent to avoid donating to Komen.

H2c: Perceived behavioral control will have a strong positive relationship with intent to avoid donating to Komen.

The model by Shaw et al. (2007) examines desire, intent, and plans to avoid buying sweatshop clothing. They discovered "desire was found to be pertinent in fully mediating the effect of attitude and partially mediating the effect of subjective norm on intention" (p. 2). Furthermore, they found desire to be distinct from intention. Moreover, desire was found to be a requirement, because attitude by itself did not change intention. They concluded that consumers must desire the "positive attitude" connected to the avoidance of sweatshop clothing before intent would kick in. Based on these findings, we posit:

H3: The relationship between attitude, subjective norms, perceived behavioral control, and intent is mediated by desire.

H4: The relationship between attitude, subjective norms, perceived behavioral control, and plan is mediated by desire and intent.

METHOD

Procedure and Sample. A survey was created using Qualtrics Survey Software and distributed online through a Mechanical Turk panel and social media sites. This helped ensure a geographically diverse and statistically valid sample (Mason & Watts, 2009; Paolacci, Chandler, & Ipeirotis, 2010; Buhrmester, Kwang, & Gosling, 2011; Mason & Suri, 2012), and one most likely to have been exposed to the online dialogue related to the controversy. Data were collected February 3, three days after the grant criteria announcement and the day of the Komen apology, through February 8. Participants were asked basic demographic questions, philanthropic giving practices, and intention to give to Komen and Planned Parenthood.

Measures

Demographics. Information was collected regarding each participant's age, gender, ethnicity, marital status, education, political affiliation, and state of residence.

Planned Behavior. Scale items in the TPB survey were adjusted to fit the Komen situation, with the primary goal being to assess respondents' planned giving or avoidance of giving to Komen. Wording of these items remained as close as possible to the original from Shaw and colleagues (2007); instead of a focus on purchasing products manufactured by sweatshop labor, questions were adapted to reflect attitudes and intent toward donating to Komen following the organization's controversial decision to stop funding Planned Parenthood.

Scales were designed based on prior studies (e.g., Ajzen & Fishbein, 1980; Ajzen & Madden, 1986; Shaw et al., 2007). Overall attitudes toward Komen were measured through five 7-point semantic differential scales. Participants chose between the following adjectives to describe Komen: (a) foolish–wise; (b) harmful–beneficial; (c) boring–exciting; (d) enjoyable–unenjoyable (reverse coded); and, (e) good–bad (reverse coded). The attitude subscale of the TPB had a Cronbach's alpha of .96.

Subjective norms (SN) were evaluated by asking whether respondents thought those who are important to them would think they should or should not donate to Komen and whether those important others would approve of the behavior. Responses to these two items were made on a 7-point scale (should to should not). The subjective norms subscale of the TPB had a Cronbach's alpha of .63.

Perceived behavioral control (PBC) was measured using three items to assess the participants' perception of control over donating to Komen. Responses were made on a 7-point scale (strongly disagree to strongly agree). The perceived behavioral control subscale of the TPB had a Cronbach's alpha of .79.

Respondents' desire to avoid donating to Komen was assessed via two items. Participants responded based on a 7-point scale (strongly disagree to strongly agree). This desire subscale of the TPB had a Cronbach's alpha of .87.

Behavioral intentions (BI) were measured with two items asking participants their likelihood of avoiding donating to Komen and intent of avoiding donating to Komen. Participants responded using a 7-point scale (very unlikely to very likely). The subscale for behavioral intentions had a Cronbach's alpha of .94.

Next, planned behavior was evaluated through two items. Consistent with past research, the plans participants made to avoid donating to Komen were measured. Answers were made on a 7-point scale (strongly disagree to strongly agree). The desire subscale of the TPB had a Cronbach's alpha of .93.

Finally (and separate from TPB scales), respondents' planned giving to both Komen and Planned Parenthood was measured via a pair of identical questions (one per organization), in which participants were asked to indicate whether they planned to start giving to the charity, increase giving, decrease giving, quit giving, or maintain the same level (which may or may not include prior giving).

RESULTS

A total of 270 completed surveys were usable. Of the participants, 37.3% were males and 62.7% were females, with most being Caucasian (84.8%). Other ethnicities identified include Asian (5.1%), Hispanic (3.3%), Black/African American (3.3%), Native American (.7%), and Other (2.9%). Nearly 52% were single; 48% were married or living with a partner. One-third of the sample held a 4-year degree (38%), with 18% holding an advanced degree. Those who had some college or completed a 2-year degree made up 37.5% of the sample, with less than 6% having only a high school diploma. In the sample, respondents identified as Democrat (39%), Independent (33%), Republican (20%), Libertarian (5%), or Other (3%).

Forty-three states were represented, with Texas having the most respondents (n = 84). Half of the sample lived in suburban areas (49.3%), with the rest of the sample living in cities (33.7%) and rural areas (16.7%). Around 50% of the sample made less than $40,000 annually. Given the income distribution, it is not surprising that one-half of the sample said that less than 20% of their income was expendable, nor that the majority gave less than $1000 per year to charitable organizations (75%).

Confirmatory factor analysis (CFA) and structural equation modeling (SEM) analyses were performed with AMOS 4.0 software (Wothke & Arbuckle, 1996) with maximum-likelihood estimation. Structural Equation Models were computed for a Base Model (attitude, subjective norms, and perceived behavioral control effect on plan), Partially Mediated Model 1 (attitude, subjective norms, and perceived behavioral control relationship to plan as mediated by desire), Partially Mediated Model 2 (attitude, subjective norms, and perceived behavioral control relationship to plan as mediated by intent), and Fully Mediated Model (attitude, subjective norms, and perceived behavioral control relationship to plan as mediated by desire and intent). An assessment of the variations between the measured model (CFA) and the proposed models (SEM) showed reasonably good overall fits. Table 6–1 presents the goodness of fit comparisons between the models, in addition to other relevant measures. A comparison of the four proposed models and the measured model (CFA) supported the fully mediated model

Table 6–1 Model Comparison for Theory of Planned Behavior Variables.

	Base Model	Partially-Mediated Model 1	Partially-Mediated Model 2	Fully-Mediated Model	Measured Model
		SEM			CFA
χ^2	71.791	101.470	103.670	125.731	122.215
Degrees of Freedom	38	58	58	79	75
Probability	.000	.000	.000	.001	.000
GFI	.952	.941	.941	.939	.941
RMSEA	.060	.056	.056	.049	.050
CI of RMSEA	.038–.073	.036–.072	.038–.073	.032–.064	.033–.066
Normed χ^2	1.889	1.749	1.787	1.592	1.630
Incremental Fit					
NFI	.968	.964	.964	.965	.966
CFI	.985	.984	.984	.987	.986
RFI	.954	.952	.952	.954	.952
Parsimony					
AGFI	.916	.910	.910	.907	.905
PNFI	.669	.717	.717	.726	.690

as demonstrating the most acceptable path relative to the measured model. This was determined by comparing the χ^2's and the normed χ^2's of the models. The fully mediated model presented no significant change of the χ^2 nor a significant increase in the normed χ^2, with only a decrease of .038 from the measured χ^2 of 1.630 to 1.592 for the fully mediated model. The model also returned a CFI of .987 (CFI; Bentler, 1990) and a RMSEA of .049 (RMSEA; Steiger & Lind, 1980), suggesting an acceptable fit (Bentler & Bonett, 1980; Browne & Cudeck, 1992; Hu & Bentler, 1999). This result indicated that no alternative path was needed.

Table 6–2 reports the regression weights for the path model, and Figure 6–1 depicts the relationships between attitude, social norms, perceived behavioral control, desire, intent, and plan. Results show that attitude had a moderate and significant relationship to desire, while desire mediated intent. The role of subjective norms and perceived behavioral control were significant as they affected desire, and subsequently intent and plan. Attitude had a weak, yet significant, effect on intent. The effect of social norms is manifest, although weak, at both levels (desire and intent). While perceived behavioral control is still significant, it is felt primarily at the stage of desire. Based on these results, all hypotheses except H2c were supported (see Table 6–2).

Table 6–2   Fully Mediated Model of Theory of Planned Behavior Variables.

Hypothesis	Construct	Estimate	S.E.	C.R.	P	Conclusion
H1a	DES ← ATT	0.605	.066	9.205	***	Supported
H1b	DES ← SN	0.281	.125	2.259	.023	Supported
H1c	DES ← PBC	0.346	.109	3.189	.001	Supported
H2a	INTENT ← ATT	0.227	.050	4.528	***	Supported
H2b	INTENT ← SN	0.162	.077	2.099	.037	Supported
H2c	INTENT ← PBC	0.064	.078	0.939	.346	Not Supported
H3	INTENT ← DES	0.623	.056	11.075	***	Supported
H4	PLAN ← INTENT	1.050	.067	15.666	***	Supported

(***) denotes probability ≤ .001

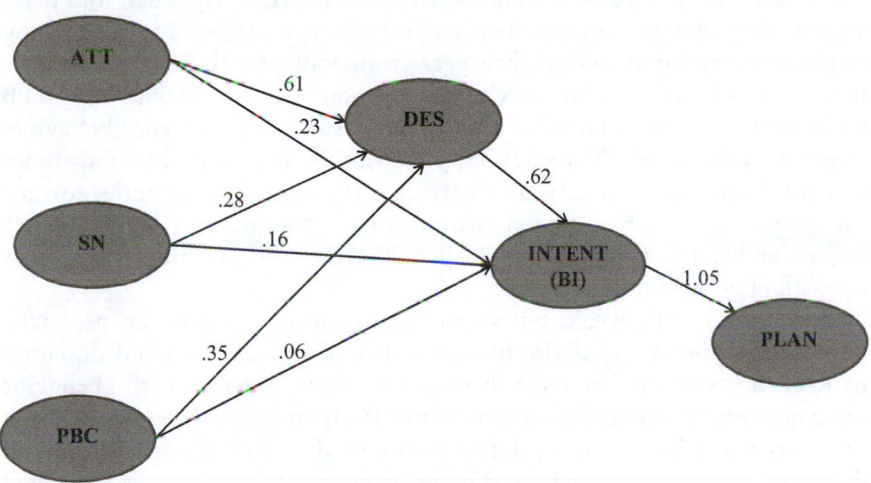

Figure 6–1   Fully Mediated Path Model for the Theory of Planned Behavior.

It should also be noted that Planned Parenthood is the unwitting beneficiary of the Komen controversy. Collectively, 41% of respondents said they would either start giving to Planned Parenthood or increase their donation levels, while only 2.5% said they would decrease or discontinue funding Planned Parenthood. In contrast, only 18.1% said they would increase support or start giving to Komen, while 17.8% said they would decrease or discontinue support. Komen may have gained some support, but also lost a nearly equal percentage of givers. Reports of giving in the wake of the controversy support these results as certain affiliates reported lower donations and race participation. For example, in the 2012 Race for the Cure in Washington, DC, 37,000 crossed the finish line, about 25,000 fewer racers than in previous years (Fessler, 2012). Concurrently, the New Jersey chapter was down at least $300,000 in donations received (Lee, 2012). According to Ernst & Young's consolidated financial statements (2012), the amount of public support and revenue at March 31, 2012 was $42,853,910 less than March 31, 2011.

DISCUSSION

The results indicate that a respondent's attitude toward giving to Komen is the strongest factor in his or her decision to avoid/not avoid donating to that nonprofit (.61). According to Miller (2005), "attitudes are defined as the sum of beliefs about a particular behavior weighted by evaluations of those beliefs" (p. 126). Perceived behavioral control followed in influence (.35), and social norms also wielded some influence (.28). Thus, the strong positive relationship between attitude and desire, and subsequently intent and plan, suggest participants are more focused on their own attitudes toward giving to the organization than how their peer group will view them or toward any perceived lack of control in the choice to donate. Consistent with early TPB findings that "attitudes toward a particular issue might influence behaviors relevant to the issue" (Miller, 2005, p. 126), this study found that attitudes toward Komen as an organization are at play as much as attitudes toward the general behavior of giving. Attitudes have traditionally had a greater impact on behavioral intentions (Miller, 2005), so the current research lines up with previous findings in other fields.

Furthermore, the weak, but significant, relationship between perceived behavioral control and desire indicates that being able to avoid donating to Komen is not the key issue. It may have been different if the behavior were not entirely voluntary, but this is not likely the case. Whereas avoiding products made by sweatshop labor (Shaw et al., 2007) reflects a nuanced decision of commonly purchased items, donating to a charity is volitional and is derived from available discretionary household funds.

The findings also allude to the potential impact social media may have on an individual's planned behavior. The forum of an organizational Facebook page, in addition to the unregulated and unfiltered Twitter feeds of the public, allows anyone with an opinion to voice it easily. These opinions shared with others may influence people's attitudes, and thus, their behavior. It is possible that the responses reported herein were affected by this phenomenon.

While much of the information disseminated about Komen's decision was delivered via traditional media, individuals and Planned Parenthood took to social media to make it viral. With three official Twitter feeds (@PPFAQ, with health information for 9,859 followers as of July 2012; @PPact, for the advocacy arm with 56,201 followers; and @HeyPP, for teens with 1,124 followers), Planned Parenthood is quite active in social media. In 2012, Komen had two official feeds: @KomenfortheCure and @Komenadvocacy, with 43,581 and 2,748 followers respectively. According to Panepento (2012), Planned Parenthood posted the news on both Twitter and Facebook on Tuesday, while Komen waited until Wednesday to post news on its Facebook page. Some suggest that the delay to speak out in social media made things worse for Komen (Panepento, 2012). This would certainly seem consistent with these results. If influential peers were not inspired by Komen to share more positive statements about the organization through social media, the only voices would be the dissenters, thus creating an exodus of Komen supporters.

Besides impacting attitudes, the effects of subjective norms might be intensified in the social media era because the perception of an individual's peer group has been redefined. People are no longer limited to face-to-face interactions, nor are they restricted by time and place. Instead, social media permit interactions between people and their acquaintances across multiple layers of life, and, in the case of company and organizational pages, with people completely unknown to the user.

This research helps public relations practitioners in the nonprofit realm by expanding the theories available for their use. Applying the theory of planned behavior, once relegated to psychology and consumer behavior (Shaw et al., 2007), adds another tool in the PR practitioner's toolbox for better understanding the organization's stakeholders. In other words, the theory of planned behavior is not only useful in understanding *buying* behavior but also *giving* behavior. In this case, we found that intent to donate was mediated by desire, and respondents' plan to donate was mediated by their intent. In addition, attitude was the best predictor of giving; what mattered more was what respondents thought of donating to the organization than what they perceived others thought—the perceived social norms—although those perceptions still held a weak influence over desire.

Although giving is a different activity from consumer shopping, the application of the theory of planned behavior to this scenario is still valid, and demonstrates the possible influences of others on the decisions individuals make. In other words, attitudes and peer pressure can affect planned giving as much as they do planned buying. In the social media era, peer influence can extend far beyond immediate family, friends, and coworkers, because the social graph connects people who may or may not even know each other. What current social media networks have also introduced is the power of archival data. Although an organization can control the information it posts on its own website (DiStaso & Bortree, 2012), stakeholders can search Twitter based on a hashtag used by dissenters, which is completely out of the control of an organization. In another example, Facebook's Timeline layout can be beneficial for an organization as it tells its story through time, but when crises hit, it can keep that stamp of a crisis on the organization forever. The organization can choose to erase information from that time period leaving an obvious hole, which Lowe's chose to do on its Facebook page after the crisis resulting from pulling advertising from *All-American Muslim* (Kinsky, Gerlich, Drumheller & Brock Baskin, 2014). This, however, is unwise and could potentially lead to further damage to an image. Organizations, including NPOs, need to use social media with extreme caution. It is important to engage with stakeholders, to listen, to be part of the conversation and to counter negative stories, but it should not be used lightly. For nonprofits that likely cannot afford professional monitoring services, this may suggest a new role for trustworthy volunteers.

CONCLUSION

Respondent attitudes were the biggest predictor of their desire to give to Komen, followed by perceived behavioral control and social norms. Thus, compared to social norms and perceived behavioral control, a person's attitude toward donating to Komen was the biggest predictor of the desire to give and of the intent to give.

The attitude toward giving to a particular entity must be impacted by the organization image and brand perception (in this case, that of Komen and the pink ribbon used by the organization). Komen's brand, and thus the attitude toward giving to it, cannot help but be impacted by the framing of the institution via traditional and social media. Through social media, many voices share their opinions, and those voices can influence readers'/viewers' attitudes. The impact in this instance trended toward a plan to avoid donating to Komen, which should be a cautionary tale for NPOs. Crisis management is an imperative function for any organization (Coombs, 2012), regardless of profit status.

Limitations. The study's limitations include its small sample of self-reported Facebook users. Despite that limitation, the sample is diverse geographically, with good representation across age groups and gender. Thus, there is little reason to suspect another sample would respond differently.

It is also limited in that the TPB was applied to only the Komen controversy, and not the ancillary subject of Planned Parenthood. While it would be interesting to apply the TPB framework to Planned Parenthood giving, it would have been a time-consuming (and likely confusing) task to have respondents complete two batteries of TPB questions. Thus, the TPB was applied to only the principal player in this controversy (Komen).

Finally, one must consider that plan is not necessarily action. Although respondents may indicate (via the model) they will avoid donating to Komen, and report their plans with regard to Komen and Planned Parenthood, only a longitudinal study would permit an examination of actual donations (or non-donations) resulting from the controversy.

Nonprofit organizations, like any organization, need to develop and practice crisis management plans inclusive of social media. Finding ways to connect to opinion leaders within social media can help an organization better manage crisis communication efforts. As such, volunteers could serve key roles as social media managers and assistants in strategic communication. Donations are the lifeblood of any NPO, deserving of the protection of effective crisis communication.

REFERENCES

About us. (2012). Susan G. Komen for the Cure. Retrieved February 5, 2012, from http://ww5.komen.org/AboutUs/AboutUs.html

Ajzen, I. (1985). From intentions to actions: A theory of planned behavior. In J. Kuhl and J. Beckman (Eds.), *Action-control: From cognition to behavior* (pp. 11–39). Heidelberg: Springer.

Ajzen, I. (1991). The theory of planned behavior. *Organizational Behavior and Human Decision Processes, 50*, 179–211.

Ajzen, I., & Fishbein, M. (1980). *Understanding attitudes and predicting social behavior*. Englewood Cliffs, NJ: Prentice-Hall.

Ajzen, I., & Madden, T. J. (1986). Prediction of goal-directed behavior: Attitudes, intentions, and perceived behavioral control. *Journal of Experimental Social Psychology, 22*(5), 453–474.

Bagozzi, R. P., Dholakia, U. M., & Mookerjee, A. (2006). Individual and group bases of social influence in online environments. *Media Psychology, 8*, 95–126.

Bagozzi, R. P., Dholakia, U. M., & Pearo, L. R. K. (2007). Antecedents and consequences of online social interactions. *Media Psychology, 9*(1), 77–114. doi:10.1080/15213260701279572

Benoit, W. L. (1995). *Accounts, excuses, and apologies: A theory of image restoration strategies*. Albany: University of New York Press.

Benoit, W. L., & Brinson, S. L. (1994). AT&T: Apologies are not enough. *Communication Quarterly, 42*, 75–88.

Bentler, P. M. (1990). Comparative fit indexes in structural models. *Psychological Bulletin, 107*(2), 238–246.

Bentler, P. M., & Bonett, D. G. (1980). Significance tests and goodness of fit in the analysis of covariance structures. *Psychological Bulletin, 88*, 588–606.

Brinker, E. (2012, May 10). Mother's Day in the mud. Retrieved July 7, 2012, from http://blog.komen.org/?p=1038

Browne, M. W., & Cudeck, R. (1992). Alternative ways of assessing model fit. *Sociological Methods Research, 21*(2), 230–258.

Buhrmester, M. D., Kwang, T., & Gosling, S. D. (2011). Amazon's Mechanical Turk: A new source of inexpensive, yet high-quality, data? *Perspectives on Psychological Science, 6*(1), 3–5.

Coombs, W. T. (2012). *Ongoing crisis communication: Planning, managing, and responding* (3rd ed.). Thousand Oaks, CA: Sage.

DiStaso, M. W., & Bortree, D. S. (2012). Multi-method analysis of transparency in social media practices: Survey, interviews and content analysis. *Public Relations Review, 38*, 511–514. doi:10.1016/j.pubrev.2012.01.003

Drumheller, K., & Benoit, W. L. (2004). USS Greeneville collides with Japan's Ehime Maru: Cultural issues in image repair discourse. *Public Relations Review, 30*, 177–185.

Ernst & Young. (2012). Consolidated financial statements and supplemental financial information. Retrieved October 26, 2013, from http://ww5.komen.org/uploadedFiles/Content/AboutUs/Financial/1207–1375237%20Financial%20Statements%20as%20of%2010.31.12_eissue.pdf

Fessler, P. (2012, June 1). Planned Parenthood issue haunts Komen's races [Transcript]. *NPR*. Retrieved August 1, 2013, from http://www.npr.org/2012/06/01/154121920/komen-donations-down-after-planned-parenthood-dispute

Goldberg, J. (2012, February 3). Ex-Komen official Mollie Williams has no plans to return to group. *Atlantic*. Retrieved July 13, 2012, from http://www.theatlantic.com/health/archive/2012/02/ex-komen-official-mollie-williams-has-no-plans-to-return-to-group/252563/

Hu, L., & Bentler, P. M. (1999). Cutoff criteria for fit indexes in covariance structure analysis: Conventional criteria versus new alternatives. *Structural Equation Modeling: A Multidisciplinary Journal, 6*(1), 1–55.

Kinsky, E. S., Gerlich, R. N., Drumheller, K., & Brock Baskin, M. (2014). Pulling ads, making apologies: Lowe's use of Facebook to communicate with stakeholders. *Public Relations Review, 40*(3), 556–558. doi:10.1016/j.pubrev.2014.03.005

Kliff, S., & Sun, L. H. (2012, February 1). Planned Parenthood says Komen decision causes donation spike. *Washington Post*: Health & Science. Retrieved July 12, 2012, from http://www.washingtonpost.com/national/health-science/planned-parenthood-says-komen-decision-causes-donation-spike/2012/02/01/gIQAGLsxiQ_story.html

Lee, E. (2012, June 21). Northern N.J. chapter of Susan G. Komen for the Cure falls $300K short of fundraising goal. *Star Ledger*. Retrieved August 1, 2013, from http://www.nj.com/news/index.ssf/2012/06/northern_nj_chapter_of_susan_g.html

Mason, W. A., & Suri, S. (2012). Conducting behavioral research on Amazon's Mechanical Turk. *Behavioral Research Methods, 44*(1), 1–23.

Mason, W. A., & Watts, D. J. (2009). Financial incentives and the "performance of crowds." *Association for Computing Machinery Explorations Newsletter, 11*(2), 100–108.

Miller, K. (2005). *Communication theories: Perspectives, processes, and contexts* (2nd ed.). Boston, MA: McGraw Hill.

Panepento, P. (2012, February 1). Social media fuel debate as a big charity cuts off Planned Parenthood aid. *Chronicle of Philanthropy*. Retrieved August 1, 2013, from http://philanthropy.com/blogs/social-philanthropy/social-media-fuel-debate-as-a-big-charity-cuts-off-planned-parenthood-aid/29976

Paolacci, G., Chandler, J., & Ipeirotis, P. (2010). Running experiments on Amazon Mechanical Turk. *Judgment and Decision Making, 5*, 411–419.

Partners & sponsors. (2012). Susan G. Komen for the Cure. Retrieved July 14, 2012, from http://ww5.komen.org/Partners/PartnersSponsors.html

Pauchant, T. C., & Mitroff, I. I. (1992). *Transforming the crisis-prone organization: Preventing individual, organizational, and environmental tragedies.* San Francisco, CA: Jossey-Bass.

Perugini, M., & Bagozzi, R. P. (2001). The role of desires and anticipated emotions in goal-directed behaviours: Broadening and deepening the theory of planned behavior. *British Journal of Social Psychology, 40*, 79–98. doi:10.1348/014466601164704

Perugini, M., & Bagozzi, R. P. (2004). The distinction between desires and intent. *European Journal of Social Psychology, 34*, 69–84. doi:10.1002/ejsp.186

Phillips, A. (2012, February 8). Susan G. Komen versus Planned Parenthood: Did anyone really win? *Washington Times*: Communities. Retrieved February 14, 2012, from http://communities.washingtontimes.com/neighborhood/60-second-attention-span/2012/feb/8/susan-g-komen-versus-planned-parenthood-did-anyone/

Planned Parenthood. (2012). Who we are. *Planned Parenthood Federation of America, Inc.* Retrieved February 14, 2012, from http://www.plannedparenthood.org/about-us/who-we-are-4648.htm

Regarding Susan G. Komen for the Cure and Planned Parenthood. (2011, June 24). Retrieved February 14, 2012, from http://www.komenie.org/assets/controversial-issues-and-komen/planned-parenthood-2011.pdf

Seeger, M. W. (1997). *Ethics and organizational communication.* Cresskill, NJ: Hampton Press.

Seeger, M. W., Sellnow, T. L., & Ulmer, R. R. (1998). Communication, organization, and crisis. *Communication Yearbook, 21*, 231–275.

Shaw, D., & Shiu, E. (2003). Ethics in consumer choice: A multivariate modelling approach. *European Journal of Marketing, 37*(10), 1485–1498. doi:10.1108/03090560310487202

Shaw, D., Shiu, E., Hassan, L., Bekin, C., & Hogg, G. (2007). *Intending to be ethical: An examination of consumer choice in sweatshop avoidance.* Advances in Consumer Research (ACR), Orlando, FL.

Sisco, H. F. (2012). Nonprofit in crisis: An examination of the applicability of situational crisis communication theory. *Journal of Public Relations Research, 24*, 1–17.

Steiger, J. H., & Lind, J. C. (1980, May). *Statistically-based tests for the number of common factors.* Paper presented at the annual Spring meeting of the Psychometric Society, Iowa City, IA.

Thorbjørnsen, H., Pedersen, P. E., & Nysveen, H. (2007). "This is who I am": Identity expressiveness and the theory of planned behavior. *Psychology & Marketing, 24*, 763–785. doi:10.1002/mar.20183

Timeline of key events in Komen controversy. (2012, February 7). *Washington Post.* Retrieved July 12, 2012, from http://www.washingtonpost.com/national/health-science/timeline-of-key-events-in-komen-controversy/2012/02/07/gIQAX4EWxQ_story.html

Wang, X. (2009). Integrating the theory of planned behavior and attitude functions: Implications for health campaign design. *Health Communication, 24*(5), 426–434. doi:10.1080/10410230903023477

Wothke, W., & Arbuckle, J. L. (1996). Full-information missing data analysis with Amos. In G. A. Marcoulides and R. E. Schumacker (Eds.), *Advanced structural equation modeling techniques: Issues and techniques.* Mahwah, NJ: Lawrence Erlbaum Associates.

Appendix: Timeline of the Komen Controversy

January 2011—Karen Handel becomes a consultant for Susan G. Komen for the Cure.

April 2011—Handel hired as senior vice president of policy for Komen.

Spring 2011—A three-member subcommittee of the Komen board examines Planned Parenthood funding.

September 29, 2011—Rep. Cliff Stearns (R-FL) notifies Planned Parenthood of Congressional investigation regarding the illegal use of federal funds to pay for abortions.

November 29, 2011—Komen board unanimously votes for policy that eliminates Planned Parenthood funding.

November 30, 2011—Mollie Williams, managing director, Community Health Programs at Susan G. Komen for the Cure, resigns in protest.

December 16, 2011—Komen president phones Planned Parenthood president to notify her of the new policy.

January 31, 2012—Story breaks about new Komen policy that stops Planned Parenthood funding.

February 3, 2012—Komen reverses decision and adds the term "criminal" to the policy; Planned Parenthood now eligible again to apply for funds.

February 7, 2012—Handel submits resignation e-mail to Brinker; Brinker publishes statement on organization website.

Part II

Stakeholder Relations

7 New Dimensions in Relationship Management
Exploring Gender and Inclusion in the Nonprofit Organization–Volunteer Relationship

Denise Sevick Bortree

Gender differences among publics are an important area of study in public relations. Although most studies have focused on differences among practitioners (Toth & Grunig, 1993; Aldoory & Toth, 2002; Choi & Hon, 2002; Aldoory & Toth, 2004, Frohlich & Peters, 2007), scholarship also should examine gender differences among publics. Studies have shown that some organizations, intentionally or not, behave differently toward employees along the lines of gender (Mor Barak & Cherin, 1998), which may impact the way individuals perceive their relationship with the organization. For nonprofit organizations, this may hold true for the volunteer public. By exploring teen volunteers' experiences, this study examines whether experiences vary along the lines of gender and whether the degree to which teen volunteers feel included by the communication and behaviors of organizations differs based on gender.

Volunteers are an important public for nonprofit organizations contributing valuable ideas and manpower that allow organizations to fulfill their missions (Brown, 1999). There are more than 1.9 million nonprofits in the United States (IRS, 2006), which receive 8.1 billion volunteer hours from more than 61 million individuals (Corporation for National and Community Service, 2007). Over 15.5 million of these individuals are under the age of 20 (Corporation for National and Community Service, 2005). However, recent numbers from the Bureau of Labor Statistics (2014) indicate that volunteering is on the decline across all demographic groups, including teens.

However, other studies show that one in three volunteers does not continue serving an organization from year to year (Corporation for National and Community Service, 2005). Cultivating strong relationships with volunteers is important for nonprofit organizations (Bortree & Waters, 2008), specifically teen volunteers, who experience long-term benefits from their community service (Bortree, 2010). Studies have shown that the motivations for volunteering differ for males and females. The purpose of this study is to explore how gender impacts the nonprofit organization–volunteer relationship particularly in terms of how the genders feel included in various aspects of the nonprofits where they volunteer. Using the relationship management and organizational inclusion frameworks, this study explores how teen volunteers experience the organization relationship differently along the lines of gender and how inclusion can predict the quality of the relationship.

LITERATURE REVIEW

Public relations plays a role in building and maintaining relationships with key publics of nonprofit organizations including volunteers (Bortree & Waters, 2008; Bortree, 2010; Bortree & Waters, 2010; Waters & Bortree, 2010). Building relationships by creating effective communication (Henley, 2001) and encouraging volunteers to voice their opinions (Garner & Garner, 2011) are two of the most effective ways to relate to and retain volunteers. These are key elements of relationship building.

Relationship Management. The relationship management paradigm provides a solid foundation for examining how nonprofit organizations manage and cultivate relationships with volunteers. It also provides suggestions for the evaluation of the relationship based on measurement of feelings of trust, commitment, satisfaction, and control mutuality (Hon & Grunig, 1999). Nonprofit literature has found that a strong feeling of *trust* predicts the donation of time to work for an organization (Passey & Tonkis, 2000); commitment of volunteers can be increased by actively seeking out and listening to suggestions (Ryan, Kaplan, & Reese, 2001). *Satisfaction* with volunteer positions increases when nonprofits match volunteers to tasks appropriate to their levels of skills and expertise (Tschirhart, Mesch, Perry, Miller & Lee, 2001), and control *mutuality* is a key predictor of the other relationship indicators (trust, commitment, and satisfaction) among teen volunteers (Bortree, 2010). Given the purpose of this study is to examine how gender impacts the nonprofit organization–volunteer relationship, the first research question was created:

> RQ1: Do male and female volunteers differ in their evaluations of the four relationship dimensions?

Previous relationship management studies have demonstrated a predictive power of the four outcomes suggested by Hon and Grunig (1999). Specifically, these studies have been able to predict future involvement with the organization (e.g., Ki, 2006; Waters, 2008). To evaluate the predictive power of the relationship dimensions in the volunteer setting, a second research question was created:

> RQ2: Can one's intent to continue volunteering be predicted by his or her evaluation of the relationship using the four dimensions?

Gender Differences and Volunteerism. Empirical research indicates that gender, defined as the socialization of males and females, makes a difference in volunteer experience in terms of frequency of volunteering (Rosenthal, Feiring, & Lewis, 1998), motives for volunteering (Maslanka, 1993), interest in volunteering (Trudeau & Devlin, 1996), leadership roles (Thompson, 1995), the nature of the institution (Schlozman, Burns, & Verba, 1994), and volunteer commitment (Lammers, 1991). Recent empirical research suggests that women appear to be more charitable than their male counterparts, especially when it involves volunteering (Belfield & Beney, 2000; Andreoni & Vesterlund, 2001). Among current volunteers, men and women donate hours to organizations in similar proportions (Hodgkinson & Weitzman, 1996). However, females are much more likely to volunteer than males across all age groups (Gaskin & Smith, 1997; Independent Sector, 2001). Research has found that women consistently outnumber male volunteers by a ratio of 3 to 1 (Lammers, 1991; Mesch, Rooney, Steinberg, & Denton, 2006).

One explanation for the higher volunteerism among females is that altruistic behavior is more highly developed in women than in men (Eisenberg, 1992). Wilson and Musick (1997) found that women score higher on standardized measures of altruism and volunteering. Others suggest that feelings of nurturance lead women to be more involved in volunteer activities involving the caring of others while men often chose more public and politically oriented volunteer activities (Cable, 1992; Thompson, 1993, Schlozman et al., 1994). Little (1997) found that men are more likely to view volunteering as being complementary to their actual work while women are more likely to view volunteering as an opportunity to care for others while strengthening existing friendships (Gallager, 1994).

Among teen volunteers ages 13–18, females are more likely to volunteer than males, with 28% of teen girls reporting volunteer activity in 2008 and 24% of teen boys volunteering (Bureau, 2009). Sundeen and Raskoff (2000) found that females were much more likely to express a desire to volunteer for community organizations than their male counterparts.

Regardless of reasons for volunteerism, it is important to understand the role that gender plays in the relationship that develops between a nonprofit organization and its volunteers. Little research has been done on the differences between male's and female's experiences in the volunteer relationships and how organizations can cultivate relationships with the genders (Little, 1997). As public relations research moves from examining stakeholders as monolithic groups to the understanding of individual differences, the question of how to cultivate relationships with volunteers along the lines of gender becomes an important one.

Organizational Inclusion. Whether working as a volunteer or a paid employee, feeling included by coworkers and management in an organization is a critical component of workplace harmony (Mor Barak & Cherin, 1998). Inclusion in various aspects of the organization leads to feelings of acceptance, which corresponds to feelings of satisfaction with the organization and commitment to continued involvement (Lawler, 1995). On the other hand, feelings of exclusion result in decreased levels of productivity and greater levels of organizational segregation. Individuals who feel excluded are likely to distrust their coworkers and the organization (Stein, 2002). They are also more likely to leave an organization because they feel powerless (Mor Barak, Levin, Nissly, & Lane, 2006).

Studies of inclusion in the workplace have found that female employees tend to feel less included than their male counterparts (Mor Barak, 2005). This aligns with the studies of gender in public relations in which females have indicated exclusion from important networks (Hon, 1995) and have less structural power than males (O'Neil, 2003).

Despite being a fundamental component of nonprofit organizations (Salamon, 2002), volunteers often find themselves in situations where they may feel excluded. Volunteers may work exclusively with paid staff or primarily with other volunteers. Depending on their assignment, volunteers may work repeatedly in the same division of an organization or on the same program, and others may work throughout the organization depending on the daily needs (Grube & Piliavin, 2000). Volunteers' assignments may influence the connections made with others and feelings of organizational inclusion.

Volunteers are often excluded from the organization's decision-making process (Markham, Johnson, & Bonjean, 1999). Teenage volunteers may be perceived as temporary help and less valuable an asset to the nonprofit. They may be perceived as not as invested in the organization, and therefore, not as important to include in organizational events. If the patterns of exclusion of female workers extend to volunteers, then female volunteers may be less likely than males to receive important information from the organization, to be invited to important meetings, and to be included in decision making. This could lead to lower levels of satisfaction with and commitment to the organization. For many teens, volunteering is an important source of learning about the workplace (Johnson et al., 1998). If female teen volunteers are included less than males, this may shape their perceptions of future work experiences.

Individuals who are asked for their advice are more likely to feel included in an organization's decision-making process (Mor Barak & Cherin, 1998). Inclusion in the informational network is enhanced when individuals are kept informed about activities and announcements. Participative inclusion results from being invited and encouraged to attend meetings and events held by individuals throughout the organization. As defined by Mor Barak (2005), these three levels—decision making, information networks and participative inclusion—represent personal inclusion.

Inclusion, however, is not solely defined in terms of one's personal inclusion in organizational actions. Feeling connected to and accepted by different social groupings in an organization is also a vital component of inclusion. Organizational inclusion can be measured at five levels (Mor Barak, 2005). Radiating outward in terms of social distance, these levels are the social group that immediately works with the volunteer, the department where the volunteer works, the volunteer coordinator in charge of hiring volunteers, the upper management and leadership of the organization, and the entire organization structure. Based on prior research showing that female employees are less included by organizations than are males, the following hypothesis is offered:

H1: Female teen volunteers experience significantly less inclusion in the nonprofit organization–volunteer relationship than do male teens.

Research has shown that the eight levels of personal and organizational inclusion impact the way individuals view their relationships with organizations that offer paid employment in Fortune 500 companies (Mor Barak & Levin, 2002) and social work organizations (Mor Barak, 2000). However, levels of inclusion have not been evaluated in the context of volunteering. To study the connection in the nonprofit sector, the study's third research question was posed:

RQ3: Do the feelings of inclusion experienced by male and female volunteers impact how they evaluate their relationship with the nonprofit organizations where they volunteer differently?

Feelings of inclusion are linked to relationships that volunteers build with other volunteers. Gender differences emerge around this issue. Research has found that teenage females are more likely to volunteer in the company of friends, to see volunteering as a social outlet, and to seek the peer approval by volunteering (Wuthnow 1995:163). Teenage males, on the other hand, are likely to volunteer individually and express more desire to work with adults rather than their own peers (Sundeen & Raskoff, 1995). The study's final research question was created to evaluate the social nature of teenagers' volunteer experiences:

RQ4: Does volunteering with one's own peer group/social circle impact inclusion differently for males and females?

METHOD

Surveys were administered to teenage volunteers at five library systems in one northeastern and two southeastern states in the United States. Libraries that participated offered teen volunteers one hour of community service credit for completing the survey. The volunteer responsibilities of the participants included activities such as working in the children's libraries, shelving books, checking out books, and planning events for peers. Participants under the age of 18 were required to secure the signature from a parent or guardian. Volunteer coordinators distributed and collected sealed packets to ensure anonymity for the survey respondents. Of the 950 teen volunteers in the library systems, 343 completed usable surveys, achieving a 36% response rate. Although they were a convenience sample that limits the generalizability of the results to the study participants, the systems were located in three different states and represented different cultural and socioeconomic communities. The library systems represent urban and suburban communities from small and medium-sized cities. Sampling from a range of communities should help ensure that a wide variety of teenage perspectives were collected.

The survey used existing scales from public relations and organizational communication. Specifically, Hon and J. Grunig's (1999) abbreviated relationship outcome scales were used to measure the organization–public relationship, and Mor Barak's (2005) 15-item questionnaire was used to measure the eight inclusion indices. These items can be grouped in two ways. First, the measures give an indication of organizational inclusion on five levels: workgroup, social group, supervisor, higher management, and organization. Each level is measured separately based on three questions. These items can then be regrouped into three additional scales (decision making, information networks, and level of participation) to measure personal inclusion.

Additionally, the survey measured the volunteers' intent to continue volunteering with the organization in the future. This question and all scale items were measured using a 9-point Likert-type scale design. Participants also anonymously provided information about their demographics, including gender and age. The gender question was used to categorize individuals as male or female. Results were calculated for these two groups of participants. Indicating a gender of male or female is a way for individuals to identify with a social group, and as such, we feel that this was a reasonable way to measure for gender.

All four relationship dimension variables were found to be reliable using Cronbach's alpha values. Trust ($\alpha = .90$), control mutuality ($\alpha = .87$), commitment ($\alpha = .85$), and satisfaction ($\alpha = .89$) all exceeded Carmines and Zellers's (1979) alpha level of .70. Seven of the eight inclusion indices also met this level. Workgroup ($\alpha = .81$), organization ($\alpha = .71$), supervisor ($\alpha = .76$), higher management ($\alpha = .77$), decision making ($\alpha = .80$), information networks ($\alpha = .75$), and participation ($\alpha = .71$) all were deemed reliable.

Although the social group inclusion index ($\alpha = .58$) was lower than the desired .70 level, it was moderately reliable. One reason this index may not have been as reliable in this study as it has in previous studies concerns the participants. The inclusion indices were designed to be used with adults. The current study focused on teenage volunteers. Even though the majority of the indices were reliable with the different age grouping, the social group index may need to be refocused in future studies examining teenagers and young adults.

RESULTS

Females represented the majority of the respondents (68%) compared to males (32%). The mean age was 16 years, ranging from a low of 13 to a high of 19. An exploration of the interaction between gender and age found the

Table 7–1 One-Way ANOVA on Relationship Evaluation between Male and Female Volunteers.

Relationship Outcome	Males ($n = 111$)	Females ($n = 232$)	MS	$F(1, 341)$	p-value
Trust	7.30 (1.15)	7.03 (1.17)	5.27	3.84*	.05
Commitment	6.85 (1.08)	7.07 (.98)	3.59	3.50	.06
Satisfaction	7.23 (1.16)	7.20 (1.02)	.07	.06	.81
Control Mutuality	6.93 (1.22)	6.14 (1.11)	46.75	35.72***	<.001

Note: ***$p < .001$; **$p < .01$; *$p < .05$.

male and female participants in this study were not significantly different in age ($F(1, 340) = .69, p = .41$).

The first research question sought to determine whether male and female teenage volunteers evaluate their relationships with the library systems differently. Table 7–1 presents the results of the one-way ANOVA that was conducted to examine the differences between male and female volunteers. Two relationship dimensions were evaluated significantly more positively by male volunteers—trust and control mutuality—meaning that males trust the organization more and felt that power was more balanced between themselves and the organization. A nearly significant difference existed for the dimension of commitment as females rated their committed to the relationship higher than males. No significant difference was detected for satisfaction.

The second research question sought to determine if the relationship dimensions could predict which volunteers were most likely to continue volunteering in the future. Volunteering intent was converted from an interval to categorical variable by dividing participants into three roughly equal groups (high, medium, and low intent), and discriminant analysis was conducted to see if the four relationship dimensions could predict membership into the high and low volunteer inclusion groupings.

As Table 7–2 shows, the most important variable that led to group prediction was trust. Its Wilks' λ value means that 55% of the variance is not explained by the group differences. When examining the interaction of the relationship dimensions, trust, commitment and control mutuality differentiated between the two groups the most. However, all were used to create the model to predict whether individuals were likely to volunteer in the future:

Discriminant Function Score = −1.35 + 1.05(trust) − .20(satisfaction) − .27(commitment) − .44(control mutuality)

The canonical correlation of the discriminant function, $R = .67$, indicating a moderate correlation between the independent variables and the

Table 7–2   Discriminant Analysis of Overall Relationship with Nonprofit Organization.

	B	B	Wilks' λ	F (1, 249)	Low Intent Group (*n* = 124)		High Intent Group (*n* = 127)	
					Mean	SD	Mean	SD
Constant	–1.35							
Trust	1.05	1.11	.68	116.78***	7.91	0.76	6.48	1.27
Satisfaction	–.20	–.22	.99	1.12	7.20	0.98	7.35	1.21
Commitment	–.27	–.28	.97	7.68**	6.89	0.92	7.24	1.11
Control Mutuality	–.44	–.52	.98	4.34*	6.32	1.17	6.63	1.21

Note: R = .67, Wilks' λ of function = .55, χ^2 = 144.31, *df* = 4, *p* < .001, centroids = (.89, –.87); ***p < .001; **p < .01; *p < .05.

discriminant function score. The Wilks' λ of the function was statistically significant (χ^2 = 144.31, *df* = 4, *p* <. 001). The group centroids for the groups of this function are .89 and –.87, respectively, indicating that the function is fairly discriminating between the groupings.

Given the statistical significance, the model was tested to see if it could predict group membership. Based on a cross tabulation, the model was very accurate in predicting group membership for individuals who had low intentions of continuing to volunteer with the organization in the future as it correctly predicted 100 of 126 cases (χ^2 = 90.87, *df* = 1, *p* <.001). The model also was able to predict most of those who intended to continue volunteering. Of the 125 cases predicted to continue volunteering, only 24 were predicted incorrectly. Overall, the success rate of this model at predicting the group membership was 80%; the hit rate was statistically significant (*t* = 10.17, *df* = 249, *p* < .001). Therefore, it is possible to predict intent to continue volunteering by measuring the relationship evaluation.

The study's hypothesis sought to test whether female teenage volunteers felt less included in the organization than did their male counterparts. Table 7–3 presents the results of the one-way ANOVA. As predicted, females scored lower in overall inclusion (*F*(1, 341) = 5.22, *p* = .02). The hypothesis was supported. Examination of the eight dimensions of inclusion revealed that females scored significantly lower in four types of inclusion: work group (*F*(1, 315) = 5.20, *p* = .02), organizational level inclusion (*F*(1, 341) = 4.59, *p* = .03), decision making (*F*(1, 341) = 4.97, *p* = .03), and information networks (*F*(1, 315) = 5.37, *p* = .02). Two additional items, supervisor (*F*(1, 341) = 5.59, *p* = .06) and participation (*F*(1, 341) = 3.19, *p* = .08), were leaning toward statistical significance with males scoring higher than

Table 7–3   One-Way ANOVA on Feelings of Inclusion between Male and Female Volunteers.

Inclusion Type	Males ($n = 111$)	Females ($n = 232$)	df	MS	F-score	p-value
Organizational						
Work Group	6.65 (1.33)	6.29 (1.11)	1, 341	9.41	6.70**	.01
Social Group	5.60 (1.22)	5.46 (.92)	1, 340	1.50	1.42	.24
Supervisor	5.53 (1.31)	5.26 (1.19)	1, 341	5.60	3.68	.06
Higher Management	3.87 (1.42)	3.73 (1.09)	1, 341	1.40	.96	.33
Organization	4.90 (1.40)	4.61 (1.09)	1, 341	6.52	4.59*	.03
Personal						
Decision Making	5.53 (1.12)	5.05 (.98)	1, 341	4.97	4.70*	.03
Information Networks	5.41 (1.11)	5.16 (.93)	1, 341	4.82	4.90*	.03
Participation	5.19 (1.24)	4.99 (.88)	1, 341	3.25	3.19	.08
Total Inclusion	5.30 (1.05)	5.07 (.82)	1, 341	4.25	5.22*	.02

Note: $***p < .001$; $**p < .01$; $*p < .05$.

females. However, these measures did not reach the standard social scientific criteria for statistical significance.

The third research question sought to determine whether the eight types of inclusion impacted the male and female volunteers' evaluation of the relationship differently. First, linear regression analysis was used to measure the relationship between overall inclusion and relationship quality. The results indicate that inclusion is a strong predictor of relationship quality ($\beta = .50$, $p < .001$, $r^2 = .25$) with inclusion explaining 25% of the variance in relationship quality.

Path analyses were conducted separately for male and female volunteers to test the linkage between each type of inclusion and the four relationship dimensions using AMOS 17.0. The model examined all possible paths between the variables. The model tested for males and females is represented in Figure 7–1. The data fit the models as all of the criteria outlined by Raykov and Marcoulides (2000) were successfully met for both the five levels of personal inclusion ($\chi^2 = 1.08$, CFI = 1.0, GFI = .99, NFI = .98, and RMSEA = .02) and the three levels of organizational inclusion ($\chi^2 = 1.31$, CFI = .99, GFI = .97, NFI = .96, and RMSEA = .03).

Table 7–4 highlights the significant paths that resulted from the statistical tests. Interestingly, a combination of positive and negative paths emerged from the analysis. Work group inclusion and information networks had the most impact on all four relationship dimensions for both genders.

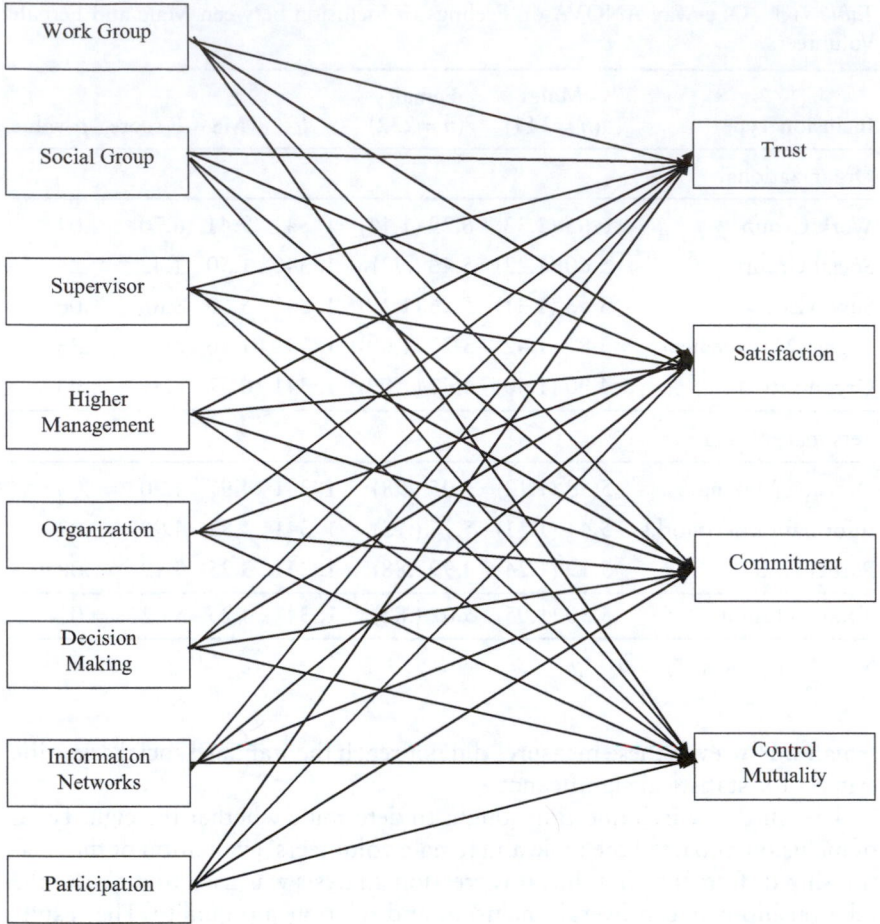

Figure 7–1 Model Tested to Determine the Impact of Inclusion on Relationship Outcomes for Volunteers.

Information networks had a strong positive impact on all four dimensions for females, and it positively impacted trust and control mutuality for males. The only type of inclusion that did not impact the relationship dimensions was feeling included in decision making. Workgroup inclusion had the strongest impact for males predicting control mutuality (β = .54, p < .001) and trust (β = .54, p < .001). For females information networks strongly predicted satisfaction (β = .53, p < .001), followed closely by work group, which greatly impacted trust (β = .51, p < .001).

The final research question tested whether the composition of teens' workgroups impacted the level of inclusion that they felt in the organization. First, a cross tabulation was conducted to determine if the genders worked

Table 7–4   Path Analysis of Levels of Inclusion on the Evaluation of the Relationship Dimensions.

Path	Standardized coefficient	Standardized Error
Male Volunteers		
Personal Inclusion		
Information Networks → Control Mutuality	.34***	.10
Information Networks → Trust	.45***	.09
Information Networks → Commitment	.32***	.09
Information Networks → Satisfaction	.49***	.13
Participation → Satisfaction	−.35**	.12
Organizational Inclusion		
Work Group → Trust	.54***	.07
Work Group → Control Mutuality	.54***	.08
Work Group → Satisfaction	.35***	.09
Work Group → Commitment	.30**	.09
Higher Level Management → Satisfaction	−.29**	.08
Organization → Commitment	.39**	.11
Social Group → Commitment	−.23*	.03
Female Volunteers		
Personal Inclusion		
Information Networks → Control Mutuality	.43***	.07
Information Networks → Trust	.41***	.08
Information Networks → Commitment	.40***	.06
Information Networks → Satisfaction	.52***	.09
Participation → Satisfaction	−2.0**	.10
Organizational Inclusion		
Work Group → Trust	.51***	.06
Work Group → Control Mutuality	.37***	.07
Work Group → Satisfaction	.27***	.06
Work Group → Commitment	.24**	.07
Social Group → Control Mutuality	.16*	.08
Supervisor → Commitment	.17***	.07
Organizational → Satisfaction	.20**	.07
Higher Management → Control Mutuality	−.13*	.06
Higher Management → Commitment	−.20**	.07

Note: ***$p < .001$; **$p < .01$; *$p < .05$.

in different proportions primarily with their own peer group, with adults, or with a combination of both age groups. Male teenage volunteers reported that they were more likely to work with adults (41%) than female volunteers did (20%). Females were most likely to work with an even number of both adults and teens (42%). Only 24% of males reported that they worked with both age groups. A higher percentage of female volunteers (38%) reported working primarily with their peers than teenage male volunteers (28%). These differences were statistically significant ($\chi^2 = 23.57$, $df = 2$, $p < .001$). To test for an interaction of gender and workgroup in the prediction of inclusion, an ANOVA was run with both gender and workgroup as independent variables and inclusion as the dependent variable. No significant interaction was detected ($F(2, 335) = .076$, $p = .91$). However, workgroup composition was a significant predictor of inclusion, with those who worked with adults ($M = 5.29$, $SD = .91$) experiencing higher inclusion than those who work primarily with their peers ($M = 4.97$, $SD = .98$). Working with about the same number of peers and adults did not produce significantly different results from the other groups ($M = 5.20$, $SD = .91$). One can conclude that males are more likely to work with adults, females are more likely to work with a balance of both peers and adults, and teen volunteers who work with adults tend to feel the most included in the organization.

DISCUSSION

This study examined the differences in the nonprofit organization–volunteer relationship as experienced by male and female teenagers. Results indicate that teens' inclusion in the relationship was low, that inclusion predicts overall quality of the relationship, and that relationship quality can predict future intentions to continue volunteering. While teens generally feel excluded in their volunteer workplace setting, an increase in inclusion may lead to a better immediate volunteering experience and to a longer period of volunteering. Female teenage volunteers experienced lower feelings of inclusion and lower relationship quality. However, their intention to continue to volunteer with the organization was not significantly different from male volunteers. This study raised an important issue of gender differences in the organization–public relationship.

Looking at teenage volunteers, workgroup and information network inclusion appear to be the most strongly linked to relationship quality. Organization-level inclusion also positively predicted relationship quality for both genders. All three of these types of inclusion were experienced by males at a significantly higher level than females, resulting in a less-fulfilling volunteer experience for females. Two of these inclusion types, workgroup and information networks, predict all three relationship quality outcomes, so it is not surprising to find that females also rated their relationship as significantly lower than did male volunteers in two of the four quality outcomes.

Workgroup level inclusion is a measure of the degree to which volunteers feels that they are given enough information about their work, that they are consulted about issues that arise in their workgroup, and that they are invited to participate in work and workgroup activities. The power of workgroup inclusion is not surprising given the importance of interpersonal relationships during adolescence. Significant personal development happens during this time occurs in the context of peer relationships (Ladd, 2004). When teens experience positive relationships with other teens and adults, it allows them to work toward positive identity development. Nonprofit organizations' encouragement of workgroup inclusion through team building activities results in higher quality relationships within the workgroup, which ultimately enhances the overall relationship with the nonprofit organization.

The findings indicate points of concern for nonprofit organizations when female teen volunteers feel less included. If volunteer coordinators are more likely to keep their male teen volunteers informed or ask for their feedback, this could create an environment of subtle discrimination against female teens. The differences detected in this study may be due to male teens being perceived as more valuable because substantially fewer male teens volunteer. In an effort to keep male teen volunteers, volunteer coordinators and workgroup leaders may provide them with more information and solicit their opinion more often.

Males are also often socialized to be more aggressive in the workplace, and this may begin with early work-related experiences, such as volunteering. Male volunteers may be socialized to ask more questions and make workgroup decisions while similar behaviors are not expected of female teens. Regardless of reason, the lack of inclusion at this early stage in teens' work life begins a dangerous pattern of gender exclusion. Over time, the decision to systematically include one gender over another culminates in larger societal problems, such as a disproportionate number of males in management and uneven power balance in male and female structural roles.

The other type of inclusion that predicted all four relationship qualities for both genders was information networks. Volunteers are included in information networks when they receive information from all levels of the organization. This includes receiving information that a volunteer needs to perform a task and receiving information from upper-level management about the future direction of the organization. This has important implications for public relations and internal communication.

Despite perceptions of having little investment in the nonprofit, teen volunteers want to receive information about the organization, their jobs, and their workgroup. They want to be "in the know" about upcoming events and organizational changes. When teens feel that they are receiving inside information, they feel better about their volunteer experience, as reflected in the assessment of relationship quality. As with workgroup inclusion, female teen volunteers indicated a lower level of information network inclusion than male volunteers. This difference could be due to a higher need for information among female teen volunteers, but it could also mean that nonprofit organizations give its male teen volunteers more information than females.

Informal networks, such as those between teenage male volunteers and adults could facilitate this exclusive information sharing. Results indicate that males are more likely to work with adults exclusively than are female volunteers. Males may receive more information than females simply because of who they work with. However, the organization is ultimately responsible for its actions toward both genders and should work to be sure they are equally included in any information networks. This means ensuring that there is no bias in the way information about their tasks and organizational matters is shared with teen volunteers regardless of their gender.

The third type of inclusion that positively impacted relationship quality for both genders was organizational-level inclusion. This is an indication of the power that volunteers have to influence the organization and the degree to which they are kept informed about the direction of the organization. For males this type of inclusion leads to increased commitment to the organization while it led to greater relationship satisfaction for females. When an organization keeps teen volunteers informed about changes and upcoming events, it demonstrates that it recognizes their value, which leads to a more positive relationship between volunteer and organization. Organizational inclusion lead to males feeling that the organization is worthy of their time and investment and to females feeling pleased with their overall experience with the nonprofit.

Unfortunately, females feel significantly less included at the organizational level than males, who feel more informed about the organization and feel they have more power to affect organizational changes. As nonprofit organizations consider their communication strategies at an organizational level, they need to be aware of the information and inclusion needs of males and females and strive to meet the needs equally for both genders. Further research about the specific needs of the genders and the values they attach to sources and types of information would aid in constructing more effective communication plans.

Social group inclusion and supervisor level inclusion had small but significant positive impact on control mutuality and commitment, respectively, for female teen volunteers. Teen girls who feel more included in their social group are more likely to feel a power balance in the organization. Likely social peer groups develop from workgroups, so inclusion in a social group would mean more power to make suggestions and changes in your workgroup. Teen girls also experience more commitment to the organization when their supervisor includes them in decision making and shares information with them. The emergence of social group inclusion as a significant predictor of relationship quality is not surprising given the literature that female teens volunteer with friends and perceive volunteering as a social activity (Wuthnow, 1995, 163). Female teens appear to couple their need for social interaction with a desire to volunteer in a way that benefits their relationship with peers and their relationship with the organization.

Inclusion involving higher-level management and participation negatively impacted relationship evaluation for both genders while social group inclusion had a similar effect for males. Conceptually, these negative relationships are difficult to explain, but likely the negative relationship between higher-level management and relationship quality is due to types of activities in which teen volunteers engage. Some are assigned to groups that have significantly more interactions with other volunteers while others work with staff. It could be that those who spend a great deal of time with other volunteers perceive themselves as having less interaction with higher-level management than do those who have limited interaction with other volunteers. More interaction with staff and management and less with other volunteers could create a negative relationship with the organization. On the other hand, the nature of the interaction between higher-level management and teen volunteers was not specified in the questionnaire. It is possible that interactions with management are negative, for example, delivering bad news. As well, if higher-level management does not value teen volunteers, then the quality of the interactions may not be high. Any one of these could have created the negative relationship between higher-level management and relationship quality.

Participative inclusion explores the degree to which volunteers feel they are invited to participate in organizational events. Perhaps, volunteers who put a high value on social aspects and organizational events are less interested in the mission of the organization; thus, they are less likely to value the relationship. Social group inclusion had a negative impact on relationship evaluation for males. Prior research has not suggested that inclusion in a social peer group is important to male teens. Instead, research has shown that male volunteers focus more on work and skill development rather than socialization.

Of the four relationship indicators, teen males reflect higher feelings of trust and control mutuality than females. Considering that they feel more included in the organization and have more power to make suggestions at the workgroup and organization levels, it is not surprising to find that they assess the balance of power between themselves and the organization more favorably than females. Males also appear to trust the organization more, which is linked to respect. Volunteers who believe strongly in an organization's mission and see the organization behaving in a manner that takes their concerns into consideration often are more trusting. If workgroup leaders and management are soliciting the feedback of teen males more than teen females, then the assessment of greater feelings of trust is expected.

Statistically speaking, female teens were close to significance in their higher expressions of organizational commitment. Past research connects inclusion to feelings of satisfaction and commitment. However, this study found stronger connections to an individual's feelings of trust and balanced power. This may be due to gender differences in perceptions of inclusion and the relationship; however, it suggests that more research is needed to explore the intricacies of inclusion and relationship indicators.

The last research question searched for a significant interaction between gender, workgroup members, and inclusion. No interaction was found, meaning that the composition of a workgroup (primarily teens, primarily adults, or an even number of each) does not impact one gender's inclusion more than the other. The analysis revealed that teen males work more with adults while females work more with a mixture of both age groups. In general, those who work with adults experience significantly more inclusion than those who work primarily with peers, but those who work with a mix of both are not significantly different from the other groups. This is noteworthy for nonprofit organizations as they make assignments for teen volunteers. Assigning teens to workgroups with some adults will result in a more inclusive experience for teen volunteers.

Implications for Nonprofit Organizations. As nonprofits consider how to improve relationships with teen volunteers, they should consider that teens reported low levels of inclusion. But results suggest that through increased inclusion, teenage volunteers may feel better about their current experiences and continue volunteering. Inclusion throughout the organization is important, but workgroup inclusion is most important for teens. Equipping workgroup leaders and volunteer coordinators with skills to effectively include teens in day-to-day decisions, such as asking for feedback, providing timely and relevant task-oriented information, and allowing teens to participate in task-related decision making, will contribute to increased feelings of inclusion. Investing time and effort in teen volunteers will result in a longer relationship. To improve the quality of the relationship with teen volunteers, nonprofits should place teens in workgroups with adults, consider inviting teens to sit in on decision-making meetings, and make sure teens are receiving adequate communication from the organization. All organizations need to be aware of the way their communications and behaviors impact gender. Volunteering frequently acts as a gateway to the workforce for teens, so their volunteering experiences educate them about the work environment and contribute to gender socialization. If teen females experience less inclusion than males, this may create negative expectations carried forward into future careers. Management and volunteer coordinators should actively solicit the opinions of female volunteers and seek ways to empower them to take active roles in organizational decision making.

Implications for Public Relations. While public relations may have limited impact at the workgroup level, it does exert control over the communication flow within the organization. Both groups indicated that receiving organizational information and being informed about important changes and events at the organizational level were important and lead to a more positive relationship. Finding ways to engage teens and ways to deliver information related to all levels of the organization is important for organizations and their teen volunteers. Considering the nature of media use by teens, public relations practitioners in nonprofit organizations should consider using multiple channels to reach out to their young volunteers. While the use of traditional newsletters, meetings, and even e-mail are appropriate, new media and social media channels may be a way for organizations to deliver information to youth and engage with them in a format that they value. Some nonprofit organizations have created blogs, web sites, and social networks for their teen clients. Doing the same for teen volunteers could reap long-term benefits. As a discipline, public relations has struggled with gender issues as female practitioners often report discrimination, exclusion, and imbalanced power between the groups. But this issue is not exclusive to practitioners in public relations. Other disciplines have experienced gender inequities, and it appears that organizational stakeholder groups may also be adversely affected. The role of public relations is to bring balance to the relationship between an organization and its publics by serving as an advocate for the needs of both. It is reasonable to think this mission could extend to bringing balance in gender treatment when differences emerge around communication and organizational behavior. As an advocate for the inclusion of women at organizational levels from unpaid volunteer to chief executive, public relations may find its voice in regard to organizational gender issues.

Inclusiveness in nonprofit organizations leads to higher quality relationships, but the types of inclusion and their degree of impact differ between males and females. Prior studies of the organization–public relationship have focused on publics as monolithic groups in which all individuals experience the relationship similarly despite Holtzhausen's (2000) urging that everyone has different perspectives and life histories that impact individual perceptions of the organization–public relationship. This study suggests that there are differences along lines of diversity, specifically in this case, gender.

CONCLUSION

This study found a significant disparity between the inclusion of female teen volunteers and their male counterparts. It also found that females rated their relationship with the nonprofit organization lower than did males. This has implications for how nonprofit organizations relate to their teen volunteers along gender lines.

There were a number of limitations in this study. This study used a convenience sample, so results cannot be generalized across the nonprofit sector despite the researchers' attempts to select diverse library systems. Additionally, this is one of the first applications of the inclusion scales to volunteers and to a teen audience. As a result, one of the dimensions of inclusion scored rather low on reliability. It is possible that some measures need future work in order to be applied accurately to a teen audience.

This study conceptualized gender as a social construction; however, the definition and conceptualization of gender varies within the public relations literature. Gender was measured with a single question that asked participants to indicate male or female. This is a limitation of the study.

REFERENCES

Aldoory, L., & Toth, E. (2002). Gender discrepancies in a gendered profession: A developing theory for public relations. *Journal of Public Relations Research, 14,* 103–126.

Aldoory, L., & Toth, E. (2004). Leadership and gender in public relations: Perceived effectiveness of transformational and transactional leadership styles. *Journal of Public Relations Research, 16,* 157–183.

Andreoni, J., & Vesterlund, L. (2001). Which is the fair sex? Gender differences in altruism. *Quarterly Journal of Economics, 116,* 293–312.

Belfield, C. R., & Beney, A. P. (2000). What determines alumni generosity? Evidence for the UK, *Educational Economics, 8,* 65–80.

Bortree, D. S. (2010). Exploring adolescent-organization relationships: A study of effective relationship strategies with adolescent volunteers. *Journal of Public Relations Research, 22,* 1–25.

Bortree, D. S., & Waters, R. D. (2008). Admiring the organization: A study of the relational quality outcomes of the nonprofit organization-volunteer relationship. *Public Relations Journal, 2*(3). Retrieved November 24, 2008, from http://www. prsa.org/prjournal/Vol2No3/BortreeWaters.pdf

Bortree, D. S. & Waters, R. (2010). The impact of involvement in the organisation-public relationship: Measuring the mediating role of involvement between organisation behavior and perceived relationship quality. *Prism, 7*(2). Retrieved from http://praxis.massey.ac.nz/prism_on-line_journ.html

Brown, E. (1999). Assessing the value of volunteer activity. *Nonprofit and Voluntary Sector Quarterly, 28,* 3–17.

Bureau of Labor Statistics. (2014). Volunteering in the United States, 2013. Retrieved from http://www.bls.gov/news.release/volun.nr0.htm

Cable, S. (1992). Women's social movement involvement: The role of structural availability in recruitment and participation processes. *Sociological Quarterly, 33,* 35–51.

Carmines, E. G., & Zeller, R. A. (1979). *Reliability and validity assessment.* Newbury Park, CA: Sage.

Choi, Y., & Hon, L. C. (2002). The influence of gender composition in powerful positions on public relations practitioners' gender-related perceptions. *Journal of Public Relations Research, 14,* 229–263.

Corporation for National and Community Service. (2005). *Youth helping America: Building active citizens: The role of social institutions in teen volunteering.* Retrieved April 18, 2008, from http://www.nationalservice.gov/pdf/05_1130_LSA_YHA_study.pdf

Corporation for National and Community Service. (2007). *Volunteering in America: 2007 state trends and rankings in civic life.* Retrieved April 18, 2008, from http://www.nationalservice.gov/pdf/VIA/VIA_fullreport.pdf

Eisenberg, N. (1992). *The caring child.* Cambridge, MA: Harvard University Press.

Frohlich, R., & Peters, S. B. (2007). PR bunnies caught in the agency ghetto? Gender stereotypes, organizational factors, and women's careers in PR agencies. *Journal of Public Relations Research, 19,* 229–254.

Gallagher, S. K. (1994). Doing their share: Comparing patterns of help given by older and younger adults. *Journal of Marriage and the Family, 56,* 567–578.

Garner, J. T., & Garner, L. T. (2011). Volunteering an opinion: Organizational voice and volunteer retention in nonprofit organizations. *Nonprofit and Voluntary Sector Quarterly, 40*(5), 813–828. doi:10.1177/0899764010366181

Gaskin, K., & Smith, J. D. (1997). *A new civil Europe? A study of the extent and role of volunteering.* London: The National Volunteering Centre.

Grube, J. A., & Piliavin, J. A. (2000). Role identity, organizational experiences, and volunteer performance. *Personality and Social Psychology Bulletin, 26,* 1108–1119.

Henley, T. K. (2001). Integrated marketing communications for local nonprofit organizations: Messages in nonprofit communications. *Journal of Nonprofit & Public Sector Marketing, 9,* 179–184.

Hodgkinson, V., & Weitzman, M. (1996). *Giving and volunteering in the United States.* Washington, DC: Independent Sector.

Holtzhausen, D. R. (2000). Postmodern values in public relations. *Journal of Public Relations Research, 12,* 93–114.

Hon, L. C. (1995). Toward a feminist theory of public relations. *Journal of Public Relations Research, 7*(1), 27–88.

Hon, L. C., & Grunig, J. (1999). *Guidelines for measuring relationships in public relations.* Gainesville, FL: Institute for Public Relations Research.

Independent Sector. (2001). *Giving and volunteering in the United States: Key findings.* Washington, DC: Author.

Internal Revenue Service (2006). Tax-exempt organization and other entities listed on the exempt organization business master file, by type of organization and internal revenue code section, fiscal years 2002–2005. In R. Schwartz (Ed.), *Internal Revenue Service Data Book 2006* (p. 55). Washington, DC: Author. Retrieved March 3, 2008, from http://www.irs.gov/pub/irs-soi/06databk.pdf

Johnson, M. K., Beebe, T., Mortimer, J. T., & Snyder, M. (1998). Volunteerism in adolescence: A process perspective. *Journal of Research on Adolescence, 8,* 309–332.

Ki, E. J. (2006). *Linkages among relationship maintenance strategies, relationship quality outcomes, attitude, and behavioral intentions.* Unpublished doctoral dissertation, University of Florida, Gainesville.

Ladd, G. W. (2004). *Children's peer relations and social competence: A century of progress.* London: Yale University Press.

Lammers, J. C. (1991). Attitudes, motives, and demographic predictors of volunteer commitment and service duration. *Journal of Social Service Research, 14,* 125–140.

Lawler, E. E. (1995). *Creating high performance organizations.* San Francisco: Jossey-Bass.

Little, J. (1997). Constructions of rural women's voluntary work. *Gender, Place, and Culture, 4,* 197–209.

Markham, W. T., Johnson, M. A., & Bonjean, C. M. (1999). Nonprofit decision making and resource allocation: The importance of membership preferences, community needs, and interorganizational ties. *Nonprofit and Voluntary Sector Quarterly, 28,* 152–184.

Maslanka, H. (1993). Women volunteers at GMHC. In C. Squire (Ed.), *Women and AIDS: Psychological perspectives: Gender & psychology series* (pp. 110–125). Newbury Park, CA: Sage.

Mesch, D. J., Rooney, P. M., Steinberg, K. S., Denton, B. (2006). The effects of race, gender and marital status on giving and volunteering in Indiana. *Nonprofit and Voluntary Sector Quarterly, 35*, 565–587.

Mor Barak, M. E. (2000). The inclusive workplace: An eco-systems approach to diversity management. *Social Work, 45*, 339–354.

Mor Barak, M. E. (2005). *Managing diversity: Toward a globally inclusive workplace*. Thousand Oaks, CA: Sage.

Mor Barak, M. E., & Cherin, D. A. (1998). A tool to expand organization understanding of workforce diversity: Exploring a measure of inclusion-exclusion. *Administration in Social Work, 22*, 47–64.

Mor Barak, M. E., & Levin, A. (2002). Outside of the corporate mainstream and excluded from the work community: A study of diversity, job satisfaction and well-being. *Community, Work & Family, 5*, 133–157.

Mor Barak, M. E., Levin, A., Nissly, J. A., & Lane, C. J. (2006). Why do they leave? Modeling child welfare workers' turnover intentions. *Children and Youth Services Review, 28*(5), 548–577.

O'Neil, J. (2003). An analysis of the relationships among structure, influence, and gender: Helping to build a feminist theory of public relations. *Journal of Public Relations Research, 15*, 151–179.

Passey, A., & Tonkis, F. (2000). Trust, voluntary association and civil society. In F. Tonkis, A. Passey, N. Fenton, & L. C. Hems (Eds.), *Trust and civil society* (pp. 52–71). New York: St. Martin's Press.

Raykov, T., & Marcoulides, G. A. (2000). *A first course in structural equation modeling* (2nd ed.). Mahwah, NJ: Lawrence Erlbaum.

Rosenthal, S., Feiring, C., & Lewis, M. (1998). Political volunteering from late adolescence to young adulthood: Patterns and predictors. *Journal of Social Issues, 54*, 471–493.

Ryan, R. L., Kaplan, R., & Grese, R. E. (2001). Predicting volunteer commitment in environmental stewardship programmes. *Journal of Environmental Planning and Management, 44*, 629–648.

Salamon, L. M. (2002). *The state of nonprofit America*. Washington, DC: Brookings Institution.

Schlozman, D., Burns, N., & Verba, S. (1994). Gender and the pathways to participation: The role of resources. *Journal of Politics, 56*, 963–990.

Stein, T. B. (2002). *Workforce transitions from the profit to the nonprofit sector*. New York: Kluwer Academic/Plenum.

Sundeen, R. A., & Raskoff, S. A. (1995). Teenage volunteers and their values. *Nonprofit and Voluntary Sector Quarterly, 24*, 383–403.

Sundeen, R. A., & Raskoff, S. A. (2000). Ports of entry and obstacles: Teenagers' access to volunteer activities. *Nonprofit Management & Leadership, 11*, 179–197.

Thompson, A. (1993). Volunteers and their communities: A comparative analysis of firefighters. *Nonprofit and Voluntary Sector Quarterly, 22*, 155–166.

Thompson, A. (1995). The sexual division of leadership in volunteer emergency medical service squads. *Nonprofit Management and Leadership, 6*, 55–66.

Toth, E. L., & Grunig, L. A. (1993). The missing story of women in public relations. *Journal of Public Relations Research, 5*, 153–175.

Trudeau, K. J., & Devlin, A. L. (1996). College students and community service: Who, with whom, and why? *Journal of Applied Social Psychology, 26*, 1867–1888.

Tschirhart, M., Mesch, D. J., Perry, J. L., Miller, T. K., & Lee, G. (2001). Stipended volunteers: Their goals, experiences, satisfaction, and likelihood of future services. *Nonprofit and Voluntary Sector Quarterly, 30*, 422–443.

Waters, R.D. (2008). Applying relationship management theory to the fundraising process for individual donors. *Journal of Communication Management, 12,* 73–87.

Waters, R. D. & Bortree, D. S. (2010). Preparing for the expanding role of cybervolunteerism in the new millennium: An application of the ROPES model of public relations. *International Journal of Volunteer Administration, 28*(1). Retrieved from http://www.ijova.org/PDF/VOL27_NO1/WatersBortree.pdf

Wilson, J., & Musick, M. (1997). Who cares? Toward an integrated theory of volunteer work. *American Sociological Review, 62,* 694–713.

Wuthnow, R. (1995). *Learning to care.* New York: Oxford University Press.

8 Navigation and Grounded Communication

Grassroots Strategies for Public Relations Practitioners Working with Underserved Communities

Jennifer Vardeman-Winter

Critical health public relations scholars suggest that culture-based approaches are the basis for employing effective, community-based initiatives (e.g., Aldoory, 2009). In public relations literature, local culture has close linkages with grassroots movements. Grassroots groups emerge from within a community, for a community, and studying their strategies is key to understanding how to achieve authentic culture-centered communication. But, an ethnographic study surveying various grassroots approaches has not yet been conducted. Thus this project explores how intersections of identity affect communication at local levels. To do this, I investigated how communicators in grassroots groups are working with women[1] from underserved communities about salient risks.

To do this, I review literature about communicating with underserved populations, critical health/risk public relations, and grassroots communication from a public relations perspective. Put together, these bodies of literature highlight the central problem of communicator–publics gaps. Next, I explain the qualitative data collection and analysis methods used. I then present the results according to emerging themes of public participation in decision making, an inside-out approach, and practices of identity reflexivity. Finally, I pose a theory of grounded communication that communicators can use in grassroots efforts.

LITERATURE REVIEW

The Context of Communicating with Underserved Populations. Underserved populations are generally regarded as those who have little or no access to health care because of cultural, linguistic, and economic reasons. Specific reasons they cannot access health care are varied and multiple, and usually include reasons of poverty, lack of insurance, and myriad barriers to obtaining care like lack of transportation, childcare, and local, qualified medical personnel. However, reasons groups are underserved also include "high-risk behaviors, vulnerable lifestyles, or social stigma . . . [and] cultural divides and disconnects between group members and healthcare professionals" (Patsdaughter, 2005, p. 124).

Thus, underserved populations are important to study from a public relations perspective because campaigns targeting them expend significant dollars and represent a sizeable portion (approximately 20%) of public relations services (Council of Public Relations Firms, n.d.). Also, previous studies suggest that because of the limited resources, these populations tend to be inactive health information seekers (Dutta & King, 2008). The confluence of social, economic, and political factors represents a significant, persistent communication context that practitioners work to resolve (Len-Ríos, 2012).

Critical Health/Risk Public Relations. The majority of cultural work in health, risk, and crisis communication focuses on how to engage communities in campaigns. One complicating factor is the extent to which communicators and policymakers share characteristics—namely, involvement with a risk—with focus communities. Thus, an emerging research agenda in critical health/risk public relations examines identity reflexivity, a line of inquiry that examines specific factors in producing culturally competent campaigns: the absence of publics in programming; the communicator–publics gaps; and the essentialization of identities and dilution of cultural characteristics.

Absence of Publics in Programming. Historically, risk communication places a physical distance between the programmers of a campaign—program managers, communicators, and policymakers—and members of the focus community during the programming steps and procedures (Lupton, 1994). Dutta (2010) critiqued this locational distance as an "assumption of criteria," citing "large-scale projects that often remove [health communicators] from the actual sites of data gathering" (p. 538), which result in inauthentic and unhelpful communication to publics.

Addressing this, Palenchar (2010) marked an evolution in risk communication, largely by the increasing scholarship and recognition in practice toward "participatory-transparent" (Lofstedt, 2004, cited by Palenchar, 2010, p. 452) programming. The inclusion of publics in programming requires digging into specific rhetorical discourses for meaning (Heath, 2009) and "foregrounding the community as an active meaning-making participant" (Dutta, 2010, p. 537). This can be accomplished by a number of methods of community engagement, from advisory boards to consensus-building workshops as well as via ethnographic research (e.g., Palenchar & Heath, 2007). Separately, some scholars have linked this absence of publics to the social distance between communicators and publics, based on their different intersecting identities (e.g., Vardeman-Winter, 2011).

Communicator–Publics Gaps. Social distance refers to the cultural, socio-economic, and psychographic differences between groups (Nedim, 2009), such as those producing campaigns and those affected by campaigns (Curtin & Gaither, 2007). Social distance creates different knowledges and perspectives because different groups may not interact often, they may not have natural empathy for one another, and/or they use their perceived differences for social cohesion (Nedim, 2009). As scholars have examined the politics of gender in the composition of the public relations workforce, some have shifted to focus on how the consequences of identities affect the quality of campaigns, as argued by Vardeman-Winter (2011): "Although campaign designers and publics may be of a similar race and gender, differences in income, educational background, and experience working in a White-collar job like public relations result in significant incongruence in meaning-making about fundamental daily decisions" (p. 426).

To address these "systematic erasure[s] of local communities as these communities have been turned into passive target audiences for interventions"[2] (Dutta, 2010, p. 537), a critical cultural health communication "privilege[s] native and indigenous ethnographies as entry points for making knowledge claims, highlighting the capacity of local participants in co-creating knowledge that is more meaningful, compared to top-down knowledge about the community produced by outside experts" (Dutta, 2010, p. 538). To reduce communicator–publics gaps, scholars have begun to advocate for the work of community-based participatory research (CBPR), which relies heavily on employing cultural "insiders" to liaise communication between scholars, researchers, and communication programmers and community members (e.g., Palenchar, 2010). However, the use of CBPR and other "bridging" communication efforts exists on a spectrum in that communicators must make negotiations between the acceptability by a public of the community liaison and the parameters of the grant/organizational mission to employ the liaison (Dutta, 2010). This fine line can result in "cultural misses" because of essentialization of identities and dilution of culture (Vardeman-Winter & Tindall, 2010).

Essentialization of Identities and Dilution of Cultural Characteristics. Cultural misses occur when meanings are misappropriated into campaign messages (Vardeman-Winter & Tindall, 2010). The research investigating women's meaning-making of health has revealed that women are often essentialized as a homogenous group in their preferences for media, brands, and representations of themselves, despite their racial, national, religious, socioeconomic, and sexual orientation differences (Aldoory, 2009). Similarly, Dutta (2010) pinpointed these "assumptions of universality" that privilege West-centric, biomedical, "scientific claims" of health and marginalize "local sciences, indigenous sciences, feminist sciences" (Dutta, 2010, p. 536). To avoid these campaign faults, communicators must seize continuous opportunities for message testing, at the very least, and systematically engage with publics during the entirety of programming and implementation to produce meaningful representations and cultural adaptations of health/risk projects. Such calls for culture-centric campaigns seem to align with grassroots movements, particularly in which communities are given full control over the entire media programming process.

Grassroots Communication and Public Relations. Coverage of grassroots communication by public relations scholars is limited, apolitical, and "has the feel of a resource manual, as opposed to scholarly inquiry" (Curnalia, Mermer, & Tyus, 2009, p. 6). Recent literature on grassroots communication focuses on the advent of social media in empowering groups to reach their intended publics (Carty, 2010). From the public relations perspective, discourse about grassroots communication focuses on media placements, interpersonal, door-to-door campaigning, and gimmicks (Curnalia et al., 2009).

Mostly, grassroots efforts rely on face-to-face communication. *Public relationships* are the basic unit of grassroots mobilization. They are forged to bolster support at the community level, are different from private or professional relationships, and are meant to develop trust and accountability over time, meanwhile being challenged by environmental constraints (Reed, 2008, cited by Christens, 2010). According to Christens (2010), the only way to accomplish these tasks is through face-to-face, interpersonal conversations called one-on-ones, which focuses on listening to another person and asking three basic questions: "First, what is the person's history? . . . Second, what is their present situation? . . . Third, what do they think about their future? What are their hopes and dreams and what are the future threats they perceive?" (p. 889)

Much of this work about critical-cultural health and risk public relations has been written theoretically and abstractly. But, the lessons are difficult to adopt from reading alone without submersion in the field. Thus, I studied the most basic, ground-level communication currently being done in health and risk to find out from communicators how they are doing the "bridging" work. The research question guiding this study was:

RQ: How do grassroots communicators overcome the challenges they face in working with publics from underserved communities?

METHOD

My assumption going into this research was that grassroots organizations do a better job of communicating with underserved communities and enacting change than large-scale, top-down, high-dollar campaigns, like those conducted by pharmaceutical companies, federal government agencies, hospitals, consumer product manufacturers, and even some large nonprofit organizations. However, communication research is scarce about contemporary, innovative grassroots strategies used. Therefore, the research question called for qualitative data collection and analysis because of its exploratory purpose (Potter, 1996).

Sampling and Participants. The original purpose of the study was to interview public relations practitioners and communicators at grassroots organizations to learn their strategies. Thus, purposive and convenience sampling strategies (Rubin & Rubin, 1995) were used to recruit people in positions at organizations that have local, city-, county-, and state-wide reach. I began recruitment by sending e-mails to communicators at several organizations I knew through my previous research, community service, and personal contacts. Snowball sampling was also used because some participants referred me to people in similar positions.

Concurrently, I began volunteering with a recently formed health care advocacy group I found through the first participant in the study. She suggested another meeting with the executive director of a new initiative to combine women's health organizations together and speak on behalf of all groups at the capitol during the state's current legislative session. The executive director invited me to attend steering committee meetings, where I met executive directors and communicators from similar local organizations focusing on women's health. I recruited from this group's membership.

Summary of Participants. All organizations had missions focused on women's and/or girls' causes like breast cancer advocacy and prevention, reproductive rights, pregnancy prevention, self-esteem development, advocacy for equal access to health care, and ovarian and cervical cancer awareness, among others. Furthermore, in my recruitment e-mail and explanation about the study to the group's membership, I explained that I could interview anyone who performs communication tasks with women at a grassroots level. Therefore, I talked with women who were not necessarily tasked with performing public relations or communication duties, per se, and who did not have those job titles. Rather, some participants represented roles of executive director, health educator, community health worker (CHW), communication manager, professor, outreach manager, and program coordinator.

I talked with a total of 10 participants (four CHWs/health educators, three executive directors, and three program/outreach managers and communicators). All participants signed a voluntary participant information sheet, and each one described herself as having performed communication with women for an average of 10.5 years. All participants were women. All participants worked in Houston, Texas. Eight were White, and two were African American. This lack of racial diversity is a major limitation to this study, particularly as no Hispanic women/Latinas or Asians were recruited.

Procedures. Once participants expressed interest in being interviewed, we decided on a mutual time and place to meet. Half of the interviews were conducted in participants' offices, and half were conducted in local cafés. When we met, I asked them to read the informed consent form, which was approved by my university's institutional review board. I answered questions they had. Finally, before proceeding through the interview guide, I gave them a $25 gift card to Target to thank them for their time.[3] After obtaining participants' permission, I audio-recorded the conversations for accuracy purposes. Interviews lasted approximately 60–75 minutes each. I transcribed all the interviews.

Interview Guide. The semi-structured interview guide consisted of 26 questions that explore basic concepts in this study: organizational mission and participant's role; public communication factors; grassroots programming and women; cultural factors in programming; dynamics of publics-incorporation in programming; and dynamics of communicator–publics differences. Sample questions were "in what ways are publics invited to participate in decision-making?" and, "would you say the identities of the people in your organization and the identities of your publics are similar or different? Why/not?"

Data Analysis. The most appropriate way to allow a theory about grassroots strategies to emerge was to use a grounded theory approach to analysis. Inductive data analysis was performed (Miles & Huberman, 1994). Analytical techniques derived from grounded theory allowed themes to emerge autonomously from the data, and the methods of constant comparison and integration were used (Glaser & Strauss, 1967). Themes were coded using a qualitative software program, HyperResearch, and axial coding was used to connect the themes to the research question (Miles & Huberman, 1994). Finally, I conducted member checks throughout the study to ensure I accurately portrayed a participant's data in the report. During the interviews, I periodically checked in with the participants to ensure I understood them correctly, and I summarized at the end of the interviews what I believe I heard from them.

RESULTS

I set out to study grassroots strategies to communicate with underserved publics about health. Without asking about the increasingly important role of patient navigation in modern health care, I quickly learned about the role of CHWs in improving health outcomes among women in underserved populations. Thus, although I began recruiting public relations practitioners doing grassroots communication with women, I broadened the participant pool to any person using grassroots communication with women about health.

The participants, then, included varying professional roles. Four were CHWs/health educators, three were executive directors, and three were program/outreach coordinators and communicators. Although these groups are disparate in some ways, they all work directly with women and advocate for the navigation-based model of communication with women.

To overcome the challenges communicators face in working with women from underserved communities—which are largely challenges of varying manifestations of cultural difference—organizations are implementing a number of grassroots-based strategies. These strategies are considered grassroots because they (a) rely heavily on one-on-one or small group interpersonal communication, (b) focus on commonalities among the group, like gender and associated social roles, and (c) work at a strictly local level (Curnalia et al., 2009; Christens, 2010). The grassroots communicators working with women from underserved communities in this study used public participation in decision making, an inside-out approach, and practices of identity reflexivity to overcome barriers largely created by communicator–publics gaps.

Public Participation in Decision Making. The participants overwhelmingly talked about the need to include publics in decision making. But, the extent to which publics were invited to participate varied, from letting publics guide the conversation during an education lesson to asking publics at the start of programming what the needs of their communities were. For example, two executive directors talked about how their feedback systems at their events guide programming for future events. For example, Tammy explained that her organization's board of directors mandates that a certain portion of future topics at meetings must be based on topics past attendees have asked for in surveys.

On another end of the spectrum of public participation, Cami said she hires facilitators from a community to ask what needs should be addressed:

> Instead of just going in [to a community] and running a program, we first try to locate some kind of successful community organization with some kind of charismatic, organized person who has already proven to get people together on some level . . . Then we go into the community and do a short presentation, and have that person lead the presentation. If needed, we will just use our efforts to train that person to teach the program instead of going there ourselves.

To effectively work with a community, all participants voiced that the methods for change must come from within the community first rather than being "imposed on a community." Becky, a CHW, said the best way to help a community is through the "inside-out" approach in which you "find out from the women, what is it you need? . . . What are the barriers for you to get healthcare?" The inside-out approach is the basis for the CHW approach that most participating organizations used.

Inside-Out Approach. The inside-out approach is the philosophical and methodological basis for the work CHWs do. Tammy and Elaine, the executive director and program coordinator, respectively, of a collaborative of organizations focusing on a common women's health risk, discussed working with CHWs, particularly when the publics are different from them.

> We do supportive navigation of community health workers. We work with [local community college], with the first accredited community health worker program. CHWs are extremely important with uninsured,

low-income women to help them navigate the system . . . by helping the CHWs being out in the community, staying in tune with what their patients need, that ensures better access for all women.

In Elaine and Tammy's case, they are both educated, White, middle- and upper-class women who are tasked with helping communities of low-income, African-American women achieve quality health care. They felt that they could not gain credibility with this community alone:

> There's definitely some challenges because we are not from those neighborhoods. So it's trying to get that buy-in, that we are trying to help, and we definitely realize that when we meet with them, we have to bring one of our own—a partner from that culture . . . Because there is definitely a lingo; there's definitely a different approach about how you are upfront; but it's harder for us.

The approach Elaine and Tammy attempted at first before bringing in a CHW to do the "cultural bridging" is called the "outside-in" approach, according to another participant. Lara is an adjunct professor at a community college training CHWs, drawing upon her 30 years of experience as an educator, nurse, communicator, and CHW. She gave examples of working with nongovernmental organizations (NGOs) and local health agencies that would enact a behavior change campaign among an underserved community, use their own facilitators and employ messaging and tactics that were organizationally generated, and then realize that their campaign failed. She explained that communicating with underserved communities can take two tracks. The first is called outside in, which is the traditional model of communication campaigns, and the second is called inside out, the grassroots-based community education:

> [Outside-in] brings [campaign materials] in, drops it, and leaves, and takes all their results with them so then they can go to another place, drop it. Inside out—when I worked a project here, there were 20 women . . . It's not what I told them what to do, it's what they themselves wanted to do on their terms, within their community . . . A real community organizer is someone who starts from the bottom up.

Employing this inside-out approach requires the help of CHWs and navigators.

Navigation and Community Health Workers. CHWs are individuals from local communities who assist in the patient navigation process. They are employed in the health care system and provide "medical and cultural translation, health education, information and referrals, intake and eligibility services, case management, and advocacy to diverse patient populations"

(Love, Gardner, & Legion, 1997, p. 511). Specifically, they provide guidance for fellow community members via " 'high-talk' interventions that take place upstream from the point of cure: systematic outreach, consistent follow-up, preventive services, the education of community members on self-care and behavior change, and the organizing of community-level and policy interventions" (Love et al., 1997, p. 520). CHWs advocate for listening, supporting, and encouraging clients to advocate for themselves (Becker, Kovach, & Gronseth, 2004).

To these points, most participants talked about the multiple barriers low-income women of color face in accessing health care. Tammy explained that CHWs—also sometimes called patient navigators and promoters—help navigate women through the health/medical system, focusing particularly on the barriers to accessing care like lack of transportation, lack of child or elder care, lack of finances/insurance, linguistic differences, low literacy, and faith restrictions:

> They are more hands-on. There are patient navigators that might stay with that patient not only through diagnosis but through treatment and survivorship afterwards. . .kind of like having a nice friend throughout . . . like saying, hey, I can't pay my rent this month, do you know if there's anything out there that can help me . . . So knowing all those systems that are out there and helping them, as a whole family, help them find services.

As "a nice friend," CHWs are "insider[s]" to a community (Love et al., 1997, p. 510), acting as "links between healthcare professionals and populations viewed as at-risk and difficult to reach" (Becker et al., 2004, p. 328).

The role of CHW is loosely defined and variably applied, thereby making the professionalization and institutionalization of CHWs difficult. Furthermore, the CHW is not a new role but is newly recognized by public health researchers, policymakers, and communicators (Lehmann & Sanders, 2007). Myriad social, economic, and cultural issues result in the increased need for CHWs. These include recent shifts in managed care structures—a paradigm shift in the health care model from treatment to preventive care, which also has meant a managed, "cost-conscious" model (Love et al., 1997, p. 511); shortages of workers trained to administer care in underserved areas; rising morbidity and mortality rates of preventable disease (Lehmann & Sanders, 2007); and increasing diversity in the U.S. population (Love et al., 1997), coupled with persistent health disparities factors like poverty, language barriers, immigration status, and racism (Landers & Stover, 2011, p. 2198). CHWs fill in gaps the public health and medical systems cannot fill through " 'task-shifting'—a review and subsequent delegation of tasks to the 'lowest' category that can perform them successfully" (Lehmann & Sanders, 2007, p. 1).

This task shifting is where most grassroots communication occurs between an organization and publics. A medical professional diagnoses and treats specific problems, but the CHW or patient navigator does the "everyday" work to bring individuals into the public health care setting, physically, linguistically, and mentally. Elaine explained the work done by CHWs, which exemplifies the type of *public relationship* essential in grassroots organizing (Christens, 2010):

> They put CHWs on the ground in the communities, and they go door-to-door to ask, does your family need any health resources? They say, yeah, OK, here's an FQHC[4] down the block. Here's somebody who will help you with your rent, and here's something that will help you with this . . . They are super grassroots.

As Becky, a CHW, put it, CHWs "remove the barriers" to getting to the site of health care, whereas doctors and nurses treat the actual medical condition. Different from other medical professionals, CHWs typically do not have a health or medical background, but rather, they know how to work through the system from the perspective of a lay patient. The grounding of the CHW within the community—and not elevated to a specialized knowledge and position within the medical field—is the reason the CHW is effective in helping a patient access care. Taylor—a CHW from a collaborative who works with Elaine and Tammy—explained the importance of a CHW being from the community:

> The CHW working in that segment should be from that community. I'm not necessarily saying from that person's zip code or community . . . but if you're dealing with the African American population, you should be African American . . . So once you get in there, they say, oh, they know about us . . . they understand we're a highly faith-based community. They understand what it means to not have transportation, they understand the choice between feeding your two little ones and getting a mammogram. They get it.

Becky illustrated what she's learned it is like for women she works with to seek care at a major hospital system located across a highway from them, which she notes is the major reason patient navigation is vital to having women's health care needs met:

> It's intimidating for most. Take [name of hospital]. Nobody knows where that breast center is. There are many buildings, so many parking garages, so many people clustered together . . . There's very little assistance or direction for any of our minorities . . . Some women are just lost to the system because it's just so overwhelming to try to navigate through the paperwork: where do I go? What do I do? . . . What doctor is going to treat me? Who's gonna take care of my children? Especially among the minority races.

Practices of Identity Reflexivity. Because of the recognition of fundamental differences between the participants—primarily based on their organizational identities and in some cases, their physical and social identities—participants had processes and philosophies they followed to ensure they did not "elevate themselves" above their publics, as one participant called it. Participants discussed how they recognized their assumptions as communicators and as people with more privileged health information than their publics, as Cami, an executive director, explained:

> The first assumption we have to work off of all the time is that not all people got the information that we got . . . I'd say we have a pretty diverse staff, but we all came from families where both parents took interest in our lives, our learning, and tried to give us the skills we needed to push ahead. But just because we had that doesn't mean that everybody we meet ever got that.

Several participants seemed to suggest that acknowledging a lack of understanding between themselves and publics was most important in doing cultural bridging. One communicator said that when "talking to a group of individuals, and you think you know about them, you are probably already wrong. You would feel like you would know people of your own ethnicity, or your own religion, or whatever, and you're wrong." Unequivocally, participants discussed the need to "not judge" community members for the decisions they make, even though it is difficult not to do this at times because of the communicator–publics gaps. For example, Becky knows the judgments that are made of her publics for not getting mammograms, but she works to understand "where [women] are coming from":

> A lot of people think, oh my gosh, she hasn't gotten a mammogram, there's healthcare all over the [city], that's dumb, why didn't she go get a mammogram? Well, insurance, or lack thereof; transportation; babysitting; some husbands want their wives to stay home during the day—they don't go out, they don't do anything outside of the home. It gives you a better understanding of where they're coming from rather than just judging.

Participants also talked about self-monitoring their behaviors to ensure they don't reveal their biases and risk losing rapport with community members. Jasmine told multiple stories about monitoring her verbal and nonverbal cues when observing risky behaviors among the population she educates:

> It can be difficult at times . . . I've had to turn away because there's things that make me cringe sometimes. I had to make sure that my facial

expressions, my tone of voice, that no judgment came through. I had to take a step back and say, you have knowledge that they don't necessarily have. If I didn't have the knowledge that I necessarily have, I might make some of the same mistakes.

Finally, participants believed they had better reactions from community members and felt their approach was well respected when they explicitly voiced the differences that exist between themselves as communicators and the publics, as one executive director explained:

Even verbally recognizing that you don't look like them, you don't come from the same neighborhood as them, and that you're just sharing information they can use . . . I usually recognize that I don't claim to be an expert on this community. I know we have different backgrounds.

Communicators also expressed to women that although they have some information, that the women know what's best for themselves because they have information that is most relevant for their community.

DISCUSSION

I conducted qualitative, in-depth interviews with 10 communicators working with women from underserved communities to find evidence for how communicators cross cultural gaps. I observed a breadth and depth of ways communicators are bringing publics into decision making and programming, approaching programming from the inside out, employing CHWs to do cultural bridging, and checking their assumptions and behaviors to maintain rapport and trust with publics. These findings extend current discussions about critical health/risk public relations and contribute to a developing theory of grounded communication.

Renaissance of Grassroots Strategies. Some evidence in this study supported findings from previous public relations studies about the use of grassroots strategies. Whereas most previous work discussed public relations' use of digital grassroots strategies (Carty, 2010), the practitioners using social media to bolster support conducted traditional public relations in the sense that they created a message themselves and disseminated it to publics via popular social networking sites. Differently, practitioners using interpersonal communication conducted unconventional messaging strategies because they allowed for public participation in decision making. According to the executive directors and program managers that oversee the work of CHWs and health educators, those interpersonal conversations that allow for public autonomy to trickle up to the organizational philosophies that engender empowerment and co-construction of meaning between organizations and publics.

Thus, the individual work of CHWs poses some provocative questions to public relations as a practice: is our field oversaturated with mass-mediated campaigns that have lost sight of publics? Despite the potential cost inefficiencies of doing CHW-type work, the practices of identity reflexivity, the inside-out approach, and public-driven programming explained by the participants demonstrate that at the very minimum, considering assumptions and biases, communicator–public gaps, and ways we contribute to cultural misses can only improve our communication in an increasingly mediated communication society.

Furthermore, all participants talked about a grounded approach to research, with the understanding of not knowing what will be the topic of discussion or the intervention behavior until they enter a community and find out what its members need. Lara, for example, explained the best process for conducting a true inside-out practice if the communicator is not from a community is starting by analyzing communities' health risks according to the zip code and data available on Census Tract and the county appraisal district. After identifying underserved areas according to factors like number of children per household, where they receive their meals, rental versus ownership percentages, school outcomes scores, number of local primary care physicians, and other related information, the communicator should then enter the field as a volunteer:

> You go down some of the streets ... look at the churches, look at the schools ... You introduce yourself as someone who would like to volunteer ... you just go and listen. If they ask who you are, you just say you are interested in who they are and that you are a teacher, and I don't really have a good grasp on what the textbooks say and what's really going on. There will be suspicion at first ... you just keep coming back and keep coming back and then one day, somebody will say to you, now what did you say you were doing? [You say] would you take me to the grocery store with you? I'm really interested in, uh, y'all talk a lot about food.

Theory of Grounded Communication. Lara and other CHWs interviewed emphasized a truly impartial, grounded form of communication in which an organization may not know what health risk it will be ultimately working to improve when communicators initiate a relationship with community members. This paradigm shift likely is extremely difficult to conceive of for organizational communicators, and executive directors and high-level communicators may encounter many barriers in gaining other publics' support of such campaigns. However, according to participants, the outcomes of such grounded approaches to communication are significant. For example, Peg, an executive director, described that since adopting the navigation model in helping lesbians and transgender men in her community access quality health care, she has seen health outcomes like increased screenings for cancers and heart disease, which she has used to gain attention from health agencies at the federal level. Thus, a theory of grounded communication suggests that as communicators employ more grassroots, inside-out missions, strategies, and messaging with publics, the quality of communication outcomes and the number of relevant partnerships increases.

Critical Health/Risk Public Relations. This study confirmed previous findings and propositions of critical health/risk communication and public relations, specifically in the area of "assumptions of criteria" (Dutta, 2010). As part of nonprofit organizations, all participants expressed a persistent tension between their organizational missions in working with women and the limitations of grants and funding sources. In one way, this problem is lessening, as evidenced by Cami's, Tammy's, and Marianne's organizations, as they have sought and received grant money from federal health agencies aimed specifically at hiring individuals from within target communities to liaise for their organizations. However, the traditional model of funding health and risk threats continues to focus on specific risks rather than ecological, infrastructural, and cultural threats.

The participants also confirmed previous assertions of "assumptions of universality" (Dutta, 2010), because all participants talked easily when asked about how communicator–publics differences were perceived and negotiated. The CHWs, in particular, emphasized that a *discourse of barriers* is a production of public health, medical, communication, and scholarly knowledge through which we frame underserved communities. Marianne, a CHW trainer, expressed strongly that "healthcare is its own culture. The bureaucracy is its own culture. So we are bridging from one culture to another." Participants in the study suggested the barrier is ours: that we cannot see past our culture of access and medical knowledge to see the lives of others without access.

Practical Implications. The importance of advanced scientific and behavioral knowledge and communication technologies is not to be underestimated: These innovations continue to save lives and improve quality of health for many. But these critiques of health and risk public relations are important to improve communication practices to reach publics that are not privileged with access to digital communication technologies and easy gateways to quality health care; revisit the quality of the basic unit of communication—the relationship—to ensure communication is undeterred and meaningful; and advance a new model of health/risk public relations, particularly as the climate for health care and communication change as policies and processes for health care administration changes.

CONCLUSION

This study provides some important ideas and theoretical developments for nonprofit communicators and scholars. First, public relations scholars have not yet bridged the concept of the cultural/community practices of public relations with the emerging role of CHWs/navigators as public relations liaisons.

These workers suggest an alternative model of public relations, particularly for nonprofit organizations that rely heavily on interpersonal communication tactics to accomplish goals. Furthermore, the study provides some of the necessary practical skills—such as employing navigators and conducting identity reflexivity—and the important philosophies—like the inside-out approach for interventions—for accomplishing relationship building in today's dynamic communication environment. Finally, scholars have previously endorsed grounded approaches to communication campaigns (e.g., Dutta, 2007; 2010), and this study provides actionable ways to accomplish this and provides some premises upon which to build testable theory about the relationships between grounded strategies and tactics and health communication outcomes.

Limitations and Future Research. As this study was an exploratory, qualitative study, the results cannot be generalizable to all nonprofit communication work. Thus, quantitative studies should chronicle and compare the outcomes of campaigns employing CHWs/navigators and those employing traditional intervention methods. Also as many of these participants worked in similarly structured organizations and programs, researchers should look for benchmark campaigns that are not limited by grant parameters but rather employ donations raised to conduct grounded communication. To this point, a study should examine grant programs that are still problem focused versus ecological focused, and compare success rates. Finally, the study was limited geographically to Houston-based participants; therefore, future research should expand the scope of CHWs in other states and working with additional populations.

NOTES

1. The original purpose of the study was to interview practitioners communicating with women because they are the primary purchases of food and healthcare. But, all participants recruited worked with women from underserved communities. For the purposes of highlighting grassroots strategies, the context of underserved publics is salient.
2. The term "intervention" is a commonly used word among public health practitioners to mean the set of practices that focus on improving the quality of life among a population. As interventions and campaigns employ identical strategies and tactics, the words are used interchangeably in this article.
3. I received an internal grant from my university to provide incentives to participants.
4. Federally qualified health center.

REFERENCES

Aldoory, L. (2009). The ecological perspective and other ways to (re)consider cultural factors in risk communication. In R.L. Heath & H.D. O'Hair (Eds.), *Handbook of risk and crisis and crisis communication* (pp. 227–246). New York, NY: Routledge.

Becker, J., Kovach, A.C., & Gronseth, D.L. (2004). Individual empowerment: How community health workers operationalize self-determination, self-sufficiency, and decision-making abilities of low-income mothers. *Journal of Community Psychology, 32*, 327–342. doi:10.1002/jcop.20000

Carty, V. (2010). New information communication technologies and grassroots mobilization. *Information, Communication, & Society, 13*(2), 155–173.

Christens, B.D. (2010). Public relationship building in grassroots community organizing: relational intervention for individual and systems change. *Journal of Community Psychology, 38*, 886–900. doi:10.1002/jcop.20403

Council of Public Relations Firms. (n.d.). *Inside PR: Healthcare*. Retrieved March 31, 2013, from http://prfirms.org/inside-pr/healthcare

Curnalia, R., Mermer, D.L., & Tyus, J. (2009, November). *A qualitative exploration of the group processes and public relations strategies in local grassroots campaigns*. Paper presented at the annual meeting of the National Communication Association, Chicago, IL.

Curtin, P. A., & Gaither, T. K. (2007). *International public relations: Negotiating culture, identity, and power*. Thousand Oaks, CA: Sage.

Dutta, M.J. (2007). Communicating about culture and health: Theorizing culture-centered and cultural sensitivity approaches. *Communication Theory, 17*, 304–328.

Dutta, M.J. (2010). The critical cultural turn in health communication: Reflexivity, solidarity, and praxis. *Health Communication, 25*, 534–539.

Dutta, M.J., & King, A. (2008). Communication choices of the uninsured: Implications for health marketing. *Health Marketing Quarterly, 25*(1/2), 97–118. doi:10.1080/07359680802126160

Glaser, B., & Strauss, A. (1967). *The discovery of grounded theory: Strategies for qualitative research*. New York, NY: de Gruyter.

Heath, R.L. (2009). The rhetorical tradition: Wrangle in the marketplace. In R.L. Heath, E.L. Toth, & D. Waymer (Eds.), *Rhetorical and critical approaches to public relations II* (pp. 17–47). New York, NY: Routledge.

Landers, S.J., & Stover, G.N. (2011). Community health workers—Practice and promise. *American Journal of Public Health, 101*, 2198. doi:10.2105/AJPH.2011.300371

Lehmann, U., & Sanders, D. (2007, January). Community health workers: What do we know about them? *Evidence and Information for Policy, Department of Human Resources for Health Geneva, World Health Organization*. Retrieved on March 14, 2013, from http://www.who.int/hrh/documents/community_health_workers.pdf

Len-Ríos, M.E. (2012). The potential for communication scholars to set priorities that curb health disparities. *Howard Journal of Communications, 23*, 111–118. doi:10.1080/10646175.2012.667732

Lofstedt, R.E. (2004). Risk communication and management in the twenty-first century. *International Public Management Review, 5*(2), 36–51.

Love, M.B., Gardner, K., & Legion, V. (1997). Community health workers: Who they are and What they do. *Health Education Behavior, 24*, 510–522. doi:10.1177/109019819702400409

Lupton, D. (1994). Toward the development of critical health communication praxis. *Health Communication, 6*, 55–67.

Miles, M.B., & Huberman, M. (1994). *Qualitative data analysis: An expanded sourcebook* (2nd ed.). Thousand Oaks, CA: Sage.

Nedim, K. (2009). Social distance and affective orientations. *Sociological Forum, 23*, 538–562.

Palenchar, M.J. (2010). Risk communication. In R.L. Heath (Ed.), *The SAGE Handbook of Public Relations* (pp. 447–460). Thousand Oaks, CA: Sage.

Palenchar, M. J., & Heath, R. L. (2007). Strategic risk communication: Adding value to society. *Public Relations Review, 33*, 120–129.

Patsdaughter, C. A. (2005). Expanding definitions of cultural groups and under-served populations: Toward access to and quality healthcare for all. *Journal of Cultural Diversity, 12*(4): 123–125.

Potter, W. J. (1996). *An analysis of thinking and research about qualitative methods.* Mahwah, NJ: Lawrence Erlbaum Associates.

Reed, M. (2008). Stakeholder participation for environmental management: A literature review. *Biological Conservation, 141*(10), 2417–2431.

Rubin, H. J., & Rubin, I. S. (1995). *Qualitative interviewing: The art of hearing data.* Thousand Oaks, CA: Sage.

Vardeman-Winter, J. (2011). Confronting Whiteness in public relations campaigns and research with women. *Journal of Public Relations Research, 23*, 412–441.

Vardeman-Winter, J., & Tindall, N. (2010). "If it's a woman's issue, I pay attention to it": Gendered and intersectional complications in *The Heart Truth* media campaign. *PRism, 7*(4). Retrieved October 1, 2013, from http://www.prismjournal.org/fileadmin/Praxis/Files/Gender/VardemanWinter_Tindall.pdf

9 The Academy for Civic Professionalism

A Case Study in Relationship Management and Stakeholder Engagement

Brigitta R. Brunner and Giovanna Summerfield

The liberal arts have been the great hallmark of the elite and educated since the times of Greeks and Romans. However, in today's world many think that these areas of study are obsolete. After all, when was the last time you saw an employment ad for a philosopher? But, what people are forgetting is that the liberal arts are just as necessary today as they were in ancient times as much for how they teach as for what they teach. In fact, the liberal arts are very necessary for today's public relations student to succeed in the workplace. As the Commission on Public Relations Education (2006b) contends, "job prospects are brighter for those who have experienced a thoughtful, well-rounded curriculum that prepares them for what lies ahead" (p. 12). Research has identified characteristics common to successful public relations practitioners; one of these characteristics is "a high-quality liberal arts education" (Commission on Public Relations Education, 2012).

This chapter explores how both public relations and the liberal arts fit with the concept of civic professionalism as a means of engagement and public communication by examining the Academy for Civic Professionalism hosted by the Auburn University College of Liberal Arts. The Academy for Civic Professionalism is a three-day workshop for faculty who are interested in incorporating civic engagement/service learning practices into their courses, outreach scholarship, and promotion and tenure documentation. Sessions at the Academy explore and unpack the topic of civic professionalism, as well as ways to incorporate its tenets into research, teaching, and practice. Civic professionalism is a framework that incorporates the values of education with civic inquiry, reflection, and practical work. The authors of this chapter argue that civic professionalism may be a practical form of public relations that allows liberal arts educators to engage with community and explain higher education's contributions to society.

The liberal arts reach and develop students in many ways that other career-focused areas of studies may not. "I believe, and many believe, that a liberal arts education is the key to navigating the changes that come ahead" (A. Chan quoted in Dominus, 2013). While the liberal arts develop critical thinking skills, knowledge, and ethical reasoning, they are also necessary for personal growth and civic participation (Cohen, 2009). However, there is a caution—if higher education wants the liberal arts to remain relevant, higher education officials need to help liberal arts majors translate their knowledge into the skills employers seek (Dominus, 2013).

LITERATURE REVIEW

What Is the Purpose of a Liberal Arts Education? The liberal arts prepare students to think (Cronon, 1998). When students are exposed to new ideas, perspectives, and philosophies, they are forced to analyze them and evaluate them for their soundness. They cannot rely on what their parents might think, or what society might think, or what their professor might think. Instead, students have to stand on their own intellectually. Students learn to develop their own opinions, attitudes, values, and beliefs based on their own examination of logic, context, and evidence when they are immersed in the liberal arts. They learn to develop arguments, solutions, and sequence events. Students who study the liberal arts develop thinking habits and skills they can take to any employer and can use throughout life. Similarly, public relations students need to have both intellectual curiosity and the ability to think conceptually to be competent practitioners (Commission on Public Relations Education, 2006a). More and more employers are seeking graduates who have not only technical skills, but also a greater understanding of "research, problem-solving, strategic thinking, planning, and management and counseling skills" (Commission on Public Relations Education, 2006a, p. 14). Again, these sought-after skills are often developed through a combination of liberal arts and public relations-specific courses.

Students in the liberal arts learn how to learn (Cronon, 1998). Now we know that the preceding statement might seem trite, but it is true. When students are taking classes in the liberal arts they are engaged in the learning process. They aren't just memorizing facts and regurgitating them. Instead, they are processing these new ideas and concepts. They are synthesizing them, taking ideas from one subject area and mixing them with ideas from another subject area. They are building knowledge of their own and exercising creativity. PR educators and practitioners also call for such skills. They state that graduates with public relations degrees should have interdisciplinary knowledge and problem-solving skills, which come from the liberal arts (Commission on Public Relations Education, 2006a). These skills are deemed necessary so that today's public relations practitioners are able to understand societal trends, ethical issues, and political, historical, and economic frameworks and how these elements influence and affect their abilities to be effective public relations managers.

Studying the liberal arts can bring a student to a more complete understanding (Cronon, 1998). We are not saying that knowledge of a specific discipline is unnecessary or not valuable. What we are saying is that with an understanding of the liberal arts, a student broadens his/her perspective so that the skills needed to write, communicate, organize, persuade, and argue are also learned. With these additional tools, a student majoring in any field can better understand his/her given major and how it fits within the larger world. The student is able to make connections across many disciplines. As the Report of the Commission on Public Relations Education states,

> the undergraduate public relations curriculum must be strongly grounded in traditional liberal arts and social sciences. Coursework in public relations should be built on a foundation of liberal arts, social science, business and language courses. More than ever, this knowledge base must be interdisciplinary. Principles of public relations and management must be intertwined with and related to . . . other disciplines. Changes in the field of public relations demand integration of the knowledge and skills of these disciplines.
> (Commission on Public Relations Education, 2006b, p. 44)

Public relations graduates who have studied the liberal arts are better prepared to work through complexity, diversity, and change because they have broad knowledge of the world (Association of American Colleges & Universities, 2014).

Wisdom is also developed by the liberal arts (Cronon, 1998). This process transcends book smarts and knowledge and ultimately lends to discovery of identity and self. Studying the liberal arts often means that students get in touch with their inner selves. They gain a better understanding of how they see the world and why. Students also gain perspective for what they do not know or for where they could improve. In addition, they also learn how to change themselves to be more engaged citizens and human beings. Public relations graduates have to recognize that cultural identity, gender, sex roles, and physical traits affect how individuals perceive and interpret information because our society is more diverse and more globally connected than ever before in history (Commission on Public Relations Education, 2006a). By studying the liberal arts and by gaining self-awareness and wisdom, public relations students are better prepared for finding ways to build relationships, mutual understanding, and inclusion among publics and within public relations practice.

Liberal arts students are teachers (Cronon, 1998)—not teachers in a classroom per se, but teachers of life and experience. With a background in the liberal arts, a student is able to interact with others in more meaningful ways. This student is able to relate his/her life story to that of another. This student is better able to share his/her experience and also understand the experience of another. In addition, an appreciation for art, music, symbolism, personality, and so forth is also born from the study of the liberal arts. This knowledge helps to develop a person as a whole. Having a background in the liberal arts gives public relations practitioners the ability to listen to and to tell others' stories. It lets them appreciate difference and find inspiration in the arts. It allows them to "make sense of the world and act within it in creative ways" (Cronon, 1998, p. 78) so that they can articulate "what is in their minds and hearts so as to teach, persuade and move" those who read or listen to their words (Cronon, 1998, p. 76). This human appreciation and understanding then permits them to be critical and strategic thinkers who fulfill their professional responsibilities.

Finally, the liberal arts build citizens (Cronon, 1998). Students develop a sense of social responsibility. They are empowered to handle complex and changing times. They respect and understand the need for diversity. Not only do students who take classes in the liberal arts understand their major, but they also have a broader knowledge of the world. Students who study the liberal arts have the practical skills employers seek—communication, problem solving, critical thinking, and the ability to apply knowledge to real-world settings. As Cronon (1998) suggests, "liberally educated people understand that they belong to a community whose prosperity and well-being are crucial to their own, and they help that community flourish by making the success of others possible" (p. 77). Similarly, Grunig (1992) contends that public relations "should be practiced to serve the public interest, to develop mutual understanding between organizations and their publics, and to contribute to informed debate about issues in society" (p. 9). Therefore the ties among public relations, the liberal arts, community, and social responsibility seem permanent.

But alas, many students and parents are so focused on the end game—a career—that they lose sight of what the classics can do to enhance a career path beyond the entry level. This situation is one of the reasons why the liberal arts need public relations activities, such as the Academy for Civic Professionalism, to help community members better understand the purpose of higher education.

From Co-op Experience to Civic Professionalism. There are many ways in which experiential learning can be added into a curriculum. This way of learning is based on the concept that when given the opportunity to directly experience the issues that they are studying, students will learn how to analyze and solve community problems. Therefore, these learning experiences dovetail nicely with the goals of a liberal arts education.

Community-based learning often relies on field work and cooperative experience. Students in courses requiring community-based learning apply their skills and give something back to the community so that they learn what it means to be a citizen. Similarly, service-learning courses also require students to apply their skills to a community problem. However, there is an additional component: reflection. Students develop a deeper understanding of their career field and of civics through service-learning opportunities because they are asked to think about what they are learning, how they are learning, what they are doing to help their communities, and so forth. Service-learning makes learning a reciprocal relationship for students, faculty, and community partners. Each learns from the exchange with the other.

Another form of community-based learning is called civic engagement. Civic engagement uses a wide array of activities and skills to foster social change. At its most basic, civic engagement described the activities and interaction between citizens and society that form a partnership between higher education and community (Patrick, 1998). Students working in civic engagement develop solutions that make a difference in civic life and in communities. These students use their skills, values, and motivations to promote quality of life issues and may or may not involve political processes to do their work.

Finally, there is civic professionalism. Civic professionalism is a newer perspective, especially when applied to the liberal arts. Civic professionalism is based on the work of Sullivan (2004; 2005) and Saltmarsh (2005). To borrow from Sullivan, civic professionalism joins formal knowledge, professional inquiry, ethical exploration, and work for the public good. Civic professionalism asks students to think about the relationships among academic disciplines, the public good, character, intellect, and vocation. According to the tenets of civic professionalism, students should think about how they can have both a meaningful career while also developing citizenship. Therefore, students should think about not only what they will do in their career, but also how what they do in their career affects society and works toward a common good. Civic professionalism acknowledges that there is no separation between career and humanness.

While professionalism can be difficult to define, much like PR, it is typically thought of in terms of occupations with higher status such as doctors, lawyers, and clergy. Sullivan (2005) suggests that fields which characterize professionalism have some distinguishing features: specialized training, including formal education and apprenticeships; autonomy in terms of how the practice of the field is regulated; and a commitment to serve the public. Therefore, the discipline creates the ethical standards by which a field abides, but civic professionalism means that ethical responsibility is broadened to society at large.

Sullivan (2004) defines civic professionalism as a mutually beneficial relationship between the professional and the public that requires ethical responsibility on the part of the professional to better serve the public good. He calls upon the academy to develop three apprenticeship experiences for students so that they can find the connections between professional identity and public responsibility simultaneously.

The first apprenticeship calls for students to receive the theoretical and academic foundation necessary to succeed in their chosen fields. This apprenticeship is then one that exists in the classroom. Students receive formal instruction so as to build their skills and knowledge. This apprenticeship is one that every college student receives in some shape or form.

The second apprenticeship focuses on real-world application. In this apprenticeship, the student applies what he/she has learned in the classroom in a professional setting. This apprenticeship is very much like an internship.

The student has the book knowledge and the necessary skills, but now he/she must learn how to apply them.

The third apprenticeship takes the academic and practical knowledge that has been gained in the previous apprenticeships and marries that knowledge with ethics and public purpose. The goal of this apprenticeship is for students to learn how their profession serves society and the public good. Sullivan, Saltmarsh, and others argue that it is this third apprenticeship that has developed the least, as disciplines and professions have become more individualistic and as professional degrees have come to be valued more economically than socially. They argue that professionalism needs to be redefined to include the aspects of public purpose and civic responsibility within professional identity. A focus solely on the profession means that practitioners can separate their work and the society so that their skills are only available to those who can pay and those who can add to profit. The grander purpose of their work and their responsibility to society is lost. The concept of professionalism is enhanced with the integration of experience and engagement—therefore, higher education is the perfect place to bring all these elements (knowledge, practice, social responsibility, and ethics) together.

This discussion then leads us to one important research question, How can public relations activities, such as the Academy for Civic Professionalism, improve town–gown relationships?

METHOD

A case study is an especially good way to bridge theory and practice. Case studies "describe real-life events in such a way as to enhance our understanding and to bolster our insight" (Sypher, 1990, p. 4). Cases place theory in the context of reality, and case studies inform us about ways we can learn from an organization's mistakes, everyday procedure, best practices, or anything in between (Keyton & Shockley-Zalabak, 2004). In this paper, we use case study techniques to examine how the Academy for Civic Professionalism in Auburn University's College of Liberal Arts builds relationships and engagement with priority publics to further understanding of civic professionalism and its power to transform the liberal arts in the minds of constituents who may believe their liberal arts are irrelevant.

The Academy for Civic Professionalism has grown from the Summer Academy for Community and Civic Engagement in the College of Liberal Arts. The Summer Academy was designed to help College of Liberal Arts faculty who were interested in learning how to incorporate civic engagement into their teaching and research. Academy participants took part in workshops and also a community project. The academy ran for several days in between the spring and summer semesters and had anywhere from five to

15 participants. The following year, participants met monthly to talk about the challenges and successes they experienced after implementing their civic engagement plans. In addition, participants received materials including books about civic engagement and higher education, a binder with handouts and readings, and a stipend for their involvement.

With funding from the Teagle Foundation and Imagining America, the Summer Academy developed into the Academy for Civic Professionalism. Although the format is still similar—three days of workshop and lectures— much has changed in terms of content and mission. The Academy is now open to faculty not only at Auburn, but also interested faculty throughout the nation and the world. To be more sustainable, reading and handouts are now distributed via Dropbox and USB drives. Top keynote speakers in the field are invited to speak at the Academy and to spend time interacting with the participants. Previous speakers include Harry Boyte, founder of Public Achievement, a theory-based practice of citizens organizing to do public work for the common good that is used in schools, universities, and communities across the United States and in more than a dozen countries; Lorraine McIlrath, coordinator for the Community Knowledge Initiative at the National University of Ireland Galway, and principal investigator and cofounder of Campus Engage, a national Irish network to support civic engagement within higher education in Ireland; Julie A. Hatcher, Executive Director of the Center for Service and Learning and Associate Professor of Philanthropic Studies at Indiana University–Purdue University Indianapolis; Rick Battistoni, Professor of Political Science and Public and Community Service Studies and Director of the Feinstein Institute for Public Service at Providence College; and Timothy K. Eatman, Assistant Professor of Higher Education at Syracuse University and Director of Research for Imagining America: Artists and Scholars in Public Life. Students, faculty, and alumni also serve as presenters so that their opinions and perspectives can be learned. Some topics discussed at the Academy include: reinventing the concept of citizenship; developing civic-minded professionals; narrative and personal reflection; building engaged scholars; reconstructing undergraduate education; and citizen alums.

Community partners are invited to attend the sessions and to speak about their experiences. Participants visit local areas where faculty and students are working with community partners to demonstrate the power of their work. In addition, faculty and staff from across campus speak about topics such as research, funding, preparing syllabi, teaching tips, ethics/responsibility, careers, and so forth. The Academy has extended its reach by inviting K–12 faculty and administrators and also local government officials to the event for networking opportunities and as a way of sharing information with these publics. Finally, the Academy has an award for alumni of the program so they can share what they have learned through their civic professionalism work in the classroom and community.

FINDINGS AND DISCUSSION

The goals of the Academy are to build positive relationships and engagement among faculty, students, alumni, and the community so community members better understand the importance of the liberal arts and so faculty, students, and alumni better understand their responsibility to the community and society. More specifically, the purpose of the Academy is:

- To promote and develop civic professionalism knowledge and initiatives among faculty and colleges in the nation
- To encourage faculty to rethink their teaching strategies and goals as they develop courses with civic professionalism as a focus for students
- To develop an emphasis on ethics and responsibility as it pertains to knowledge and application
- To foster collaborative teaching, research, and outreach efforts among faculty and across universities
- To provide resources and support for engaged faculty.[1]

The Academy is publicized in several ways. Announcements about the keynote speakers, the purpose of the Academy, and application due dates are made and flyers with the same information are distributed at research conferences such as Imagining America and the Association of American Colleges and Universities. E-mail blasts to the listservs of organizations such as Imagining America, the Kettering Foundation, the Dave Matthews Center for Civic Life, the Talloires Network, and Campus Compact with content similar to the flyers are sent six months and then again three months in advance of the Academy.

Social media is also used as a means of promoting the Academy. There is an Academy for Civic Professionalism Facebook page.[2] This page is used to post information about the Academy, to post articles that might interest followers, and to provide a means of communication for past and current participants. In addition, past participants of the Academy and other faculty and staff who are involved in civic endeavors have been interviewed and videos of these interviews are available on the College of Liberal Arts' website. In addition, there is a blog devoted to civic involvement[3] and a Twitter account for the Academy.[4] Plans are in the works to hire a dedicated social media intern to expand the reach and impact of these efforts.

Much outreach is done on a personal level. Postcards are sent to the directors of university centers involved with civic work nationwide. These postcards detail the purpose of the Academy and list speakers and topics. Personal e-mails are used as a follow-up communication a few weeks later. E-mails are sent and phone calls are made to community partners, K-12 partners, local government officials, students, faculty, and staff to invite them to participate in the event as well. Finally, several luncheons are also held on campus so that interested faculty can come and learn more about the Academy in a relaxed and informal atmosphere.

According to Bruning, McGrew, and Cooper (2006), few institutions think of engagement in terms of opening the doors to the university and inviting the community in. However, by opening those doors, universities are better able to build relationships effectively and with little incurred costs other than listening and identifying common interests through dialogue. Community engagement for higher education should be seen "as a process of not only sending out, but also inviting in" (Bruning, et al., 2006, p. 130). In the next section, the authors will look to theory to explain how the Academy works for these stated goals.

How the Academy for Civic Professionalism Builds Relationships. Grunig and Huang (1998) have identified trust, control mutuality, relationship commitment, and relationship satisfaction as the most important outcome factors in an organization–public relationship. They identified these four features as the most pertinent because they appear consistently in both organizational and interpersonal communication literature (J. Grunig & Huang, 1998). They argue that most of these factors identified by other researchers are components of trust, control mutuality, satisfaction, and commitment.

Trust is widely accepted as a critical part of interpersonal, organizational, and organization–public relationships (J. Grunig & Huang, 1998). It is the cornerstone of successful relationships and can only be built with time (Davidson & Kapelianis, 1996; Dumoulin & Boyd, 1997). In fact, Vercic and J. Grunig (1995) go so far as to state that trust is the characteristic that allows an organization to exist (J. Grunig & Huang, 1998). Trust, however, is not necessarily an easily understood concept. As Hon and J. Grunig (1999) state, there are secondary components of trust. These underlying dimensions are integrity, dependability, and competence. If an organization has integrity, then publics believe that the organization is fair in its interactions. Dependability means that publics can rely on the organization to do what it says. Competence means that the organization has the resources and ability to follow through with what it says it will do. Because trust is so critical, it is foolish for an organization to compromise trust for a short-term payoff. The long-term reputation the organization will acquire by being trustworthy will better serve the organization and its publics (Hon & J. Grunig, 1999).

The Academy builds trust, and therefore relationships, on many levels. It is a venue in which the university can demonstrate to the community that it wants to be a partner. It is also a means by which the voices of many constituents can be heard—leaders, faculty, students, alumni, and community members. The Academy allows the university to open its doors and say, "let's share our knowledge, resources, and skills with each other and for the public good." Therefore, the Academy demonstrates the value of the liberal arts to the community through the integrity, dependability, and competence of its faculty, students, and alumni. This trust then allows faculty, students, and alumni further access to the community so that social responsibility is born and nurtured.

Control mutuality is similar to the concept of power (J. Grunig & Huang, 1998) and refers to the degree of agreement that exists between an organization and its publics about who has the power to influence the other (Hon & J. Grunig, 1999). J. Grunig and Huang (1998) state that some imbalance of power is unavoidable in many relationships and that control mutuality recognizes this asymmetry in power. However, if one party attempts to have unilateral control over the relationship, the other outcome factors—trust, satisfaction, and commitment—will suffer (Hon & J. Grunig, 1999). Therefore, it is more beneficial for parties to agree on the level of control mutuality in a relationship. Grunig also explains the difference between asymmetrical and symmetrical concepts of power: When used asymmetrically, power is used for control purposes, while symmetrical power is used to empower both parties so that collaboration and mutual benefit exist.

Through dialogue, the Academy serves as a means of creating a power balance between the university and community. Everyone has a contribution to make. Members of the university and of the community have expertise and experience to share. Everyone has the chance to be a part of the conversation. Members of the university and of the community have the opportunity to develop ideas, to make suggestions, and to state what simply is not working. Everyone has the ability to work toward a common goal: what is best for society. Through training and engagement in the liberal arts, faculty, students, and alumni are able to synthesize what is learned through these conversations to build solutions with community members.

Having satisfaction means that the organization and its publics feel positively toward each other. Satisfaction also may mean that the benefits of keeping the relationship outweigh the costs of maintaining it (Hon & J. Grunig, 1999). Commitment examines the degree to which both the organization and its publics believe that the relationship is worth spending time and resources on to maintain and promote (Hon & J. Grunig, 1999). Commitment therefore means that a long-lasting bond has been made between the organization and public.

By opening the channels of communication, the Academy helps to bring about important conversations—conversations that sometimes would not occur otherwise. By bringing all members to the table, satisfaction is grown so that there is positivity between town and gown. Additionally, all parties can see where and how they fit within these conversations. They see how and why these relationships are important and, therefore, commitment is secured. Both the university and community see how much they need each other. Through their work in the liberal arts, faculty, students, and alumni understand engagement. They understand what it means to be a citizen. They understand social responsibility, and they work with the community to solve the complex and compelling issues and problems it faces.

Civic Professionalism as a Means of Building Engagement. By encouraging faculty–student contact, developing cooperation, encouraging active learning and leadership, and respecting diversity of all types, institutions of higher learning can make a difference in their communities while also enhancing their mission to better society. In this time when the budgets and missions of institutions of higher learning are falling under greater scrutiny, it is important to remind society of the value of higher education. The Academy for Civic Professionalism is one way to do just that. In addition, colleges and universities that focus student efforts toward a purposeful engagement are deemed most effective because their efforts to work with the community are more apparent and visual (Hazeur, 2008). As noted by Beere, Votruba, & Wells (2011), universities can apply knowledge in a more impactful way than by merely publishing it in a journal; they can share knowledge to help communities solve problems.

To become a truly engaged campus, a university needs to be a part of the community and there needs to be collaboration among faculty and community partners (Beere et al., 2011). As collaboration between the university and community grows, so should the university's alignment of goals and objectives. New structures and policies should be in place to address how civic and community engagement are addressed in vision statements, institutional values, curricula, rewards, and resources (Beere et al., 2011). Once this alignment occurs, barriers will be torn down and support will be built up because leadership from all areas of campus will have consistent meanings and understanding (Beere et al., 2011). However, there is a caution. While faculty and students are often the strongest advocates for the need for engagement, and they are often the ones doing the work, such change cannot be done by an individual (Beere et al., 2011). Any program related to civic professionalism or engagement must have buy-in from many important members of the hierarchy for it to be transformative and not pushed to the side (Beere et al., 2011).

State legislators and constituents are increasingly asking for more accountability and transparency from higher education, while decreasing public support for it; this should push civic professionalism and engagement further into the spotlight because this work is visible and it demonstrates how higher education can provide solutions to society's problems (Jacoby & Hollander, 2009). Presidents must raise the visibility of their institutions' efforts to improve society among state legislators so that higher education's social value and role are better understood (Jacoby & Hollander, 2009). Such efforts could result in more state funding and support for civic professionalism and engagement efforts at both public and private institutions.

Presidents can also raise awareness among constituents by speaking about civic professionalism and engagement at civic organizations or writing op-ed pieces for local and national news sources (Jacoby & Hollander, 2009). Only administrators can garner the support necessary to sustain such important projects and initiatives and demonstrate their links to institutional and societal objectives and goals.

CONCLUSION

According to Alperovitz and Howard (2005) the engaged institution should meet the needs and expectations of not only today's students but also tomorrow's. It must solve community problems while enhancing students' learning by developing community partnerships that allow students to develop skills and that allow faculty to conduct meaningful research. The Academy for Civic Professionalism in Auburn University's College of Liberal Arts serves as a model of this kind of initiative. Although the goal may be lofty, the authors of this chapter ask readers to think about what they can do to be a part of this movement and through what changes they might continue such work at their home institution, so that the engaged institution is a reality at all colleges and universities and their surrounding communities, and it is no longer just an ideal written about in books.

Future Research and Limitations. As with any research project, there are limitations to be addressed. First, the Academy for Civic Professionalism is only in its second year. As of this writing, only 30 people have been in attendance. While much has been learned since its inception and many new ideas have been incorporated, their usefulness has yet to be determined. It will also be crucial to see how interest in the Academy builds. As the Academy matures, it will be important and interesting to see what new insights and what new directions it takes. Future research might include survey and in-depth interview data collected from participants to learn more about how the Academy has influenced teaching and research endeavors, as well as community partnership and mutual understanding, to increase positive town–gown relationships and interaction. Other research could look to see how efforts such as the Academy for Civic Professionalism are working to create culture change in higher education and how leaders with an interest in civic professionalism are developing and working for the good of society through higher education.

NOTES

1. Please see http://cla.auburn.edu/cla/cce/acp/ for more information.
2. See http://facebook.com/academyforcivicprofessionalism.
3. See http://academyforcivicprofessionalism.wordpress.com.
4. See http://twitter.com/ACP_AU (Twitter username @ACP_AU).

REFERENCES

Alperovitz, G., & Howard, T. (2005). The next wave: Building a university civic engagement service from the twenty-first century. *Journal of Higher Education Outreach and Engagement, 10*, 141–157.
Association of American Colleges & Universities (2014). What is a 21st century liberal education. Retrieved January 5, 2014, from https://www.aacu.org/leap/what-is-a-liberal-education

Beere, Votruba, & Wells, G. W. (2011). *Becoming an engaged campus: A practical guide for institutionalizing public engagement*. San Francisco, CA: Jossey-Bass.

Bruning, S.D., McGrew, S., & Cooper, M. (2006). Town-gown relationships: Exploring university-community engagement from the perspective of community members. *Public Relations Review, 32*, 125–130.

Cohen, P. (2009, February 25). In tough times, the humanities must justify their worth. *New York Times*. Retrieved October 31, 2013, from http://www.nytimes.com/2009/02/25/books/25human.html?pagewanted=all&_r=0

Commission on Public Relations Education. (2006a). Public relations education for the 21st century: The professional bond. Retrieved April 23, 2014, from http://www.commpred.org/_uploads/report2-full.pdf

Commission on Public Relations Education. (2006b). The professional bond report. Retrieved January 15, 2014, from http://www.commpred.org/theprofessionalbond/index.php

Commission on Public Relations Education. (2012). Standards for a master's degree in public relations: Educating for complexity. Retrieved April 23, 2014, from http://www.commpred.org/_uploads/report5-full.pdf

Cronon, W. (1998). "Only connect . . .": The goals of a liberal education. *American Scholar, 67*, 73–80.

Davidson, S., & Kapelianis, D. (1996). Towards an organizational theory of advertising: Agency-client relationships in South Africa. *International Journal of Advertising, 15*, 48–60.

Dominus, S. (2013, September 13). How to get a job with a philosophy degree. *New York Times*. Retrieved October 31, 2013, from http://www.nytimes.com/2013/09/15/magazine/how-to-get-a-job-with-a-philosophy-degree.html?_r=0

Dumoulin, C., & Boyd, K. (1997). Building a meaningful relationship: A direct marketing love story. *Direct Marketing, 60*, 32–33.

Grunig, J.E. (1992). *Excellence in public relations and communication management*. Hillsdale, NJ: Lawrence Erlbaum Associates.

Grunig, J.E., & Huang, Y. (1998). From organizational effectiveness to relationship indicators: Antecedents of relationships, public relations strategies and relationship outcomes. In J.A. Ledingham & S.D. Bruning (Eds.), *Relationship management: A relational approach to public relations*. Mahwah, NJ: Erlbaum.

Hazeur, C. (2008, March). *Purposeful co-curricular activities designed to increase engagement: A practice brief based on BEAMS project outcomes*. Washington, DC: Institute for Higher Education Policy.

Hon, L.C. & Grunig, J.E. (1999) *Measuring relationships in public relationships*. Draft of manuscript prepared for Relationship Task Force/Measurement Commission, Institute for Public Relations and Ketchum Public Relations.

Jacoby, B. & Hollander, E. (2009). Securing the future of civic engagement in higher education. In B. Jacoby & Associates (Eds.), *Civic engagement in higher education: Concepts and practices* (pp. 227–248). San Francisco, CA: Jossey-Bass.

Keyton, J., & Shockley-Zalabak, P. (2004). *Case studies for organizational communication*. Los Angeles, CA: Roxbury.

Patrick, J. J. (1998). *Building communities from the inside out: A path toward finding and mobilizing a community's assets*. Chicago, IL: ACTA.

Saltmarsh, J. (2005). The civic promise of service learning. *Liberal Education, 91*, 50–55.

Sullivan, W.M. (2004). Can professionalism still be a viable ethic? *Good Society, 13*, 15–20.

Sullivan, W.M. (2005). Markets vs. professions: Value added? *Daedalus, 134*, 19–26.

Sypher, B.D. (1990). *Case studies in organizational communication*. New York, NY: Guilford Press.

Vercic, D., & Grunig, J.E. (1995) *The origins of public relations theory in economics and strategic management*. Paper presented to the 2nd International Public Relations Research Symposium, Bled, Slovenia.

10 Building Mutually Beneficial Relationships
Recommended Best Practices for Online Grant Making Procedures

Giselle A. Auger

The Internet has provided a wealth of potential for organizations to build relationships with stakeholders. Recently, research has moved on from study of basic Internet applications such as organizational websites to that of social media interactions, yet for some types of organizations and their stakeholders a comprehensive and clear website continues to be of great value, perhaps even more so than that of social media. Among those organizations for which a comprehensive and clear website is paramount are foundation grantors.

A 2008 publication by Project Streamline, a collaboration initiative of the Grants Managers Network in partnership with organizations such as the Association of Small Foundations, the Foundation Center, and the National Council of Nonprofit Associations, highlighted the need for improved effectiveness in the grant making process (Project Streamline, 2008). With the current economic situation affecting organizations of all sizes, the need for improved efficiency of operation by both those nonprofit organizations that provide program services and their foundation grantors, is even more essential.

According to the U.S. tax code, both foundations (grantors) and the charitable organizations that they support (grantees) are classified as nonprofit organizations under Internal Revenue Service (IRS) section 501(c)(3). Although foundations come in several forms, notably corporate, community, or independent, for the purposes of this study "foundation" was used to refer to the independent foundations, while "nonprofit" was used to refer to what Fleishman (2007) referred to as operating nonprofits. Such operating nonprofits provide program services while the foundations provide some of the financial resources necessary for achievement of program goals.

Both independent foundations and operating nonprofits struggle with lack of administrative resources. Provision of clear, specific, grant making information in an online format can reduce administrative time for both foundations and their nonprofit grantees. As the Foundation Center (2011) indicated, there are approximately 76,545 independent foundations within the United States, yet according to their most recent report, the median number of employees held by such organizations ranges between 2.0 and 5.0

(FC Stats, 2011). Operating nonprofits are similarly hampered. According to Blackwood, Wing and Pollak (2008), approximately 44% of operating nonprofits had expenses less than $100,000, while just less than 4% had expenses of $10 million or more. Such administrative constraints may lead to less effective programming for both grantors and grantees. As Buchanan and Enright (2007) noted, the difficulty is determining the effectiveness of foundation grant making, given the fact that "Grant makers are only successful when their grantees achieve meaningful results" (p. 37).

In *Drowning in Paperwork, Distracted from Purpose* (Project Streamline, 2008), foundation grantors and their nonprofit grantees indicated that streamlining the grant process could reduce burdensome requirements on grantees while ensuring that grantors get the information that they most need. Of the six streamlining strategies adopted by foundations, posting requirements online scored highest. Fully 67% of respondents indicated that they were attempting to improve their grant making process through use of the Internet (p. 18).

Developing a streamlined grant making process lends itself to theories of organization–public relationships and also of collaboration where there is mutual benefit to participants: Grantors receive less inappropriate applications and questions, and grantees gain a clearer understanding of guidelines and procedures. Using a content analysis of independent foundation websites accessed through the Grantsmanship Center's (2009) online database,[1] this study analyzed the quality of grant information that is currently available online. As Project Streamline (2008) noted, the fact the foundations are placing information online does not necessarily make it less burdensome or complicated for nonprofit grantees.

LITERATURE REVIEW

Organization–Public Relationships: Grantor and Grantee. Two major streams of research have responded to the scholarly demand for measurement in organization–public relationships (OPRs). According to Yang and J.E. Grunig (2005), OPRs "have commonly been defined by focusing on either the processes of relationship formation or the outcomes of a relationship produced between an organization and its publics" (p. 307). Ledingham and Bruning (1998) defined such relationships as "the state which exists between an organization and its key publics in which the actions of either entity impact the economic, social, political and/or cultural well-being of the other entity" (p. 62).

The grantor–grantee relationship is a special form of OPR comprised of two different types of nonprofit organizations—one with the financial resources necessary for the other to succeed and the other providing program services that fulfill the broad mission of those that provide funds. This relationship is often been viewed as one of resource dependence, wherein "some organizations had more power than others because of the particulars of their interdependence and their location in social space" (Pfeffer & Salancik, 2003, p. xiii), particularly because one holds the financial strength required by the other; however, it is also possible to view the relationship as one of collaboration.

As Tsasis (2009) noted, rather than resource dependency, grantor–grantee OPR can be viewed "as a way to build capacity and leverage existing resources [enabling] organizations to address societal problems more effectively" (p. 5). Developing grantor–grantee collaboration is not a simple matter. According to Fairfield and Wing (2008), collaborative relationships are difficult to achieve and the quality of such relationships may vary greatly. Moreover, they suggest that the relationship is one of dependence or interdependence, which is necessary for each to obtain their respective goals.

Shaw and Allen (2006) described this type of relationship within the context of trust and control, arguing that "Funders and recipients must have confidence in each other" (p. 214). Through careful balance of trust and control between grantor and grantee, the authors contend that a situational fit will occur where "Both funders and nonprofit organizations have a greater understanding of each other's actions and needs. The levels of trust and control within the funding relationship are adapted to meet these needs" (p. 214).

Other authors have also noted the importance of grantor–grantee relationships. Among them, Zweibel and Golden (2007) suggested that:

> One of the most important and often overlooked aspects of working with funders is building and sustaining relationships. Strong relationships are mutually beneficial. Grant seekers receive necessary funding, authentication of programs, and reliability of organizational goals, while funders fulfill their missions by responding more effectively to needs within the community.
>
> (p. 45)

In addition to conceptions as resource dependent or collaborative, the grantor–grantee relationship can also be viewed as one of mixed motives, a type of relationship described by Fairfield and Wing (2008) as "requiring each party to confront the tension between its own interests and those of the other party" (p. 32). Alternately this type of mixed motives relationship could be described as one of mutual benefit. As Fairfield and Wing (2008) argued, the grantor–grantee relationship can be said to provide benefits to both parties, contending that nonprofits "depend on funds that cannot all come from service fees, government, or the public" (p. 32) and that receipt of such funds can provide a sense of legitimacy to nonprofit partners. On the grantor side, providing funds allows the organization to comply with the U.S. government-mandated payout of 5% per year of assets while also providing the societal benefit often demanded by boards and suggested by their mission.

Building Relationships Online. The Internet has provided vast opportunities for organizations to build relationships with stakeholders. Early research stressed the importance of good website design in the building and maintenance of organization–public relationships (Kent & Taylor, 1998; Vorvoreanu, 2006). As Vorvoreanu (2006) noted, "Organizations may engage in a variety of relationship building strategies and tactics, but one important site of relationship building and maintenance is the organizational website" (p. 395). Further, "a positive Web user experience is believed to hold the key to increased sales, return visits and good relationships with site visitors" (p. 396).

Later research explored the potential of the Internet and organizational websites as strategic tools in the development of relationships with donors and corporate sponsors (Waters, 2007; Ingenhoff & Koelling, 2009). These studies indicate that nonprofit organizations have not been using the Internet to develop two-way conversations with stakeholders and they have not been capitalizing on the Internet's potential to develop and cultivate relationships with new or existing stakeholders, particularly with regard to fundraising.

Based on theories of organization–public relationships and the opportunities for developing relationships online, the following research questions are posed:

RQ1: Is the quality of grant information provided online sufficient to encourage the development of positive grantor–grantee relationships?

RQ2: Are there foundations that provide exemplar sites that may be used to develop best practices for online grant making to encourage the development of positive grantor–grantee relationships?

RQ3: From the information analyzed, what best practices can be suggested that support the development of positive grantor–grantee relationships?

METHOD

Since the grantor–grantee relationship takes place primarily through the grant making process, the purpose of the study was to analyze grant making procedures on independent foundation websites to determine best practices for these procedures. Eighteen items were analyzed, including 14 features relating to the level of information provided in the grant making sections of foundation websites. Among these were eligibility requirements, focus areas, samples of prior grants, details of the application process and any screening process, deadlines, and details of notification. These items were considered as specific, general, or not present within the grant sections of the sites analyzed. Two items identified the extent to which the 501(c)(3) determination letter was required of grant seekers, as well as the extent to which IRS Form

990 was required. An additional two items considered demographic features: state of location and level of giving. Coders were also asked to make notations if they found a site to be an exemplar. The researcher plus an additional trained coder analyzed the websites with an intercoder reliability of 79% using Holsti's (1969) formula.

This study focused on the type and level of grant making information available on independent foundation websites. As such the Grantsmanship Center Institute website, which provides lists of the top 40 granters by state, was selected as the source of material. Because the Grantsmanship Center Institute ranks its foundations by levels of giving amounts, foundations were organized by five levels of giving: greater than $10 million; between $5 and $10 million; between $1.5 and $4.99 million; between $500,000 and $1.49 million; and less than $500,000.

Using the U.S. Census regional delineations (2000), 106 foundations from 12 states representing the East South Central and South Atlantic divisions, plus the District of Columbia, were chosen for study: Florida, Georgia, South Carolina, North Carolina, Tennessee, Alabama, Maryland, Virginia, Delaware, Washington, DC, West Virginia, Kentucky, and Mississippi. From the sample of 106, only independent foundations that had been identified as having grant application information online were needed (*n* = 36) and were analyzed for this study.

RESULTS

In *Drowning in Paperwork, Distracted from Purpose* (Project Streamline, 2008), the most cited technique to improve efficiency in the grant making process was to place information online. In addition, more than 50% of respondents in the Project Streamline study noted that they had "added a screening process, such as a letter of intent or a telephone conversation, to their application process" (p. 17).

Yet, of the 106 organizations analyzed, just 52 had organizational websites and only two-thirds (*n* = 36) of those included grant information. When viewed by size of foundation, the larger foundations were more likely to include grant information on their websites than the smallest organizations. As Table 10–1 illustrates, of those with websites, approximately 84% (*n* = 21) of the foundations in each of the two largest giving sizes had such information available online, while just more than 33% (*n* = 2) of the smallest organizations (< $500,000) had grant information available online.

Type of Information Available. The study analyzed 14 informational features that could be available on independent foundation websites. Table 10–2 illustrates the items analyzed and the extent to which the items were found to be specific, general, or not present within the sites analyzed. Included in this analysis were items relating to both eligibility and to criteria. Eligibility

Table 10–1   Number and Percentage of Independent Foundation Websites with Grant Information Found by Giving Amounts.

	Number of Independent Foundations Analyzed	Number of Websites Found	Number of Websites Containing Grant Information	Percentage of Websites That Contained Grant Information
> $10 million	19	13	11	84.6
$5 million to $10 million	23	12	10	83.3
$1.5 million to $4.99 million	22	11	8	72.7
$500,000 to $1.49 million	20	10	5	50.0
< 500,000	22	6	2	33.3
Total	106	52	36	69.2

was intended to apply to the type of organization the foundation would fund—for example, a 501(c)(3) nonprofit—while criteria indicated the type of programs supported. Of the sites with grant information, 94% ($n = 34$) included eligibility screening of some kind: Eight provided an eligibility quiz and six more required submission of a letter of intent, or inquiry (LOI).

While independent foundations appear to have a strong idea of the types of organizations they will fund, their criteria for programs are much less specific. Just 41.6% ($n = 15$) provided specific criteria information and nearly 28% ($n = 10$) included no criteria at all. Further, although specific, criteria could often be vague, for example, criteria from one foundation read as follows: "The general policy . . . is to make grants for innovative and creative projects, and to programs which are responsive to changing community needs in the areas of health, social service, education and cultural affairs" (The Abney Foundation, 2009). The words "innovative" and "creative" are specific, yet not very clear what types of programs would fall under those criteria. In contrast, another foundation provided clear and specific criteria on its site, "The Foundation will only consider funding requests from qualified nonprofit organizations that can effectively deliver emergency and basic support to citizens in Chester and Lancaster counties and a portion of York County" (Springs Close Foundation, 2009).

The researcher felt that examples of previously funded projects could provide additional information and clues to the meaning of specific although vague criteria as indicated above, therefore this study also searched for samples of prior grants. Nearly two-thirds of grant information included examples of prior grants ($n = 28$). However, just 25% ($n = 9$) of sites included a specific Frequently Asked Questions (FAQ) section, while 75% ($n = 27$) of sites contained no FAQ section at all.

Table 10–2   Usefulness of Grant Information Available on Foundation Websites and Percentage of Those with Specific Information.

n = 36	Specific	General	Not Present	Percent with Specific Information
Eligibility Requirements	28	6	2	77.7
Focus Areas	25	10	1	69.4
Project or Support Type	20	7	9	55.5
Criteria	15	11	10	41.6
What We Do Not Fund	26	2	8	72.2
Sample of Prior Grants	22	6	8	61.1
Frequently Asked Questions	9	0	27	25.0
Application Process	14	11	1	38.8
Screening Process	11	9	16	30.5
Deadlines	30	0	6	83.3
Details of Notification	10	4	22	27.7
Provides Multi-Year Funding	6	1	29	16.6
Provision for Return Applicants	5	1	30	13.8
Contact Information	12	23	1	33.3
Exemplar Sites	Harry and Jeanette Weinberg Foundation (MD) The Mary Reynolds Babcock Foundation (NC) The Quantum Foundation (FL) Sisters of Mercy of North Carolina Foundation (NC)			

Of the items researched, deadlines for submission of letters of inquiry or full proposals were the items most likely to be provided with specific detail. Fully 83% (*n* = 30) of independent foundations' grant information included specific deadlines. Unfortunately, just more than 27% (*n* = 10) also provided specific information regarding details of notification to grant seekers of the success or failure of their application.

Provision of information regarding the application process varied. If the organization provided a screening process, the application process was indicated as general and the screening process, if sufficiently detailed, was considered specific. Thirty-eight percent listed specific application information (*n* = 14) and 30% (*n* = 11) listed specific screening process information.

The independent foundations analyzed were fairly unified in their requests for specific information from grant seekers. Fully 80% (*n* = 29) of these foundations required the organization's IRS determinations letter, the 501(c)

(3), be included with either the letter or inquiry or the application proposal and 50% (*n* = 18) requested the organization's IRS Form 990.

Additional Information. While analyzing websites, both coders took note of those sites that appeared exemplar for the purposes of providing grant information online, as well as other unique or interesting categories, design, or other information. Of the websites analyzed, four sites were determined to contain exemplar features. All four sites came from the largest two categories of giving.

For unique or interesting items, the researcher found information for one foundation lodged within a law firm's website and another that had a heading for grant information that listed grants made with no additional information on either those grants indicated or how to apply for funding. Other sites required that visitors log in and set up an account before accessing information, and others that provided information in a ".docx" format inaccessible to those with earlier versions of Microsoft Word. Further, there were websites that provided adequate information on the grant process but did not indicate on the home page that they were no longer accepting applications. For example, the Blue Moon Fund (2009) had a well-designed site with detailed funding information; however it was not until the researcher clicked through two levels that the following notice was provided: "Due to current economic conditions, the [foundation] has temporarily suspended its consideration of unsolicited letters of inquiry" (Blue Moon Fund, 2009).

DISCUSSION

The purpose of this study was threefold. First, to investigate existing information on independent foundation websites to determine whether the available content provided adequate resources for building positive grantor–grantee relationships. Second, to determine whether there were exemplar websites among the independent foundation sites analyzed that could serve as the basis for development of best practices that would encourage positive organization–public relationships between grantors and grantees. Finally, to establish a set of best practices for independent foundations to determine the type, quantity, and design of grant information that could lead to more effective grant making practices beneficial to both the foundation and their nonprofit grantees.

Results of the study determined that the information provided on independent foundation websites was very site specific and varied greatly from one site to another. While there were a few exemplar sites, overall the websites lacked the specificity of information and directness of design that could facilitate mutually beneficial relationships.

Research has indicated the importance of well-designed websites to the development of positive organization–public relationships (Vorvoreanu,

2006). Research question one asked, "Is the quality of grant information provided online sufficient to encourage positive grantor-grantee relationships?" For the grantor–grantee relationship, a positive user experience is one in which key information for grant seekers, such as the application process, deadlines, types of projects funded, criteria, and types of organizations eligible for funding, are easily accessed, thereby eliminating unnecessary and time consuming queries to the foundation office.

Results of this study indicated that the quality of grant information provided online is not sufficiently robust to encourage positive OPR or provide mutually beneficial relationships between grantors and grantees. Less than 39% (n = 14) of the sites analyzed had specific application process details available and approximately 66% (n = 22) of the sites provided no indication of when applicants could expect to be notified of approval or denial.

The websites analyzed were also lacking in clarity about the types of projects they would or would not fund. While many sites indicated that they would not fund organizations outside of a specific geographic area, or would not fund religious organizations, or provide funds for individuals, the information provided was still lacking sufficient depth. For example, one foundation listed the following criteria: "The Foundation responds to a variety of charitable organizations serving the general welfare of the community, education, youth, Christian concerns and, to a limited extent, arts and cultural organizations" (J. Bulow Campbell Foundation, 2009).

Research question two asked whether there were exemplar sites that could be used to develop a set of best practices for the development of positive OPR and mutual benefit. Four sites achieved a score of 9 or 10 out of a possible 13 for provision of specific information and sufficient detail to support the specific information provided.

Within these websites information relating to the grant process was found clearly labeled, for example, "Guide for Grantseekers," "Grant Center," and "Apply for a Grant." Having followed the link for the grant process, all of the sites restated or provided a link to their mission, vision, and beliefs and/ or focus areas. All of the sites also provided a detailed step-by-step application process or a link to the process. Further, each of the four sites provided information on prior grantees, although they were inconsistent in the location and labeling of this information. For example, one site listed grants awarded under "Foundation News" while another listed it with potential confusion under "Grants."

In addition to detailed grant information, the exemplar sites were well designed and unique, ranging from simple backgrounds with clearly labeled navigation bars along the left or top of the screen, to those with multiple navigation bars, RSS feed links, rotating photo galleries, links to resources such as the organization's annual report, leadership and organizational development resources, and even a grantee perception survey.

Research question three questioned what best practices could be suggested to support the development of mutually beneficial outcomes for grantors and grantees. Results of this content analysis of independent foundation websites identified four broad best practices that could lead to mutually beneficial outcomes.

BEST PRACTICES

(1) Make It Easy to Find Information. It should be easy for grant seekers to find the information they need. Kent and Taylor (1998) advocated for use of table of contents and argued "Users/visitors should not have to follow seemingly 'random' links to discover what information a site contains and where links will lead" (p. 329). For the grantor–grantee relationship this suggests that grant information should be easy to find by those interested in applying for funding support.

To facilitate ease of use, each section relating to the grant process should be clearly labeled and provide links to additional information. These labels should be clearly identified in a standard navigation bar format, either along the left side of the home page or along the top. When links lead to a new page, it is helpful to retain the standard navigation bar for ease of use.

In addition the following content pages are recommended: About the Foundation; Focus areas (may also include project type such as capital campaigns); Eligibility of organizations; Criteria for program support; What We Do Not Fund (specifically what types of organizations and criteria the foundation will not fund); examples of Prior Grantees (preferably with description of the program supported); Application Procedures (including screening procedures, if any); Deadlines; expected Notification Date of success or failure of request; and Contact information.

(2) Provide Detailed and Clear Information. Research has demonstrated that provision of substantive information is the first step in building organization–public relationships (Kent & Taylor, 1998). In other words, the information provided must be such that it is of sufficient quality and value to visitors to warrant establishment of relationships. For grantors this means that the information should be extensive enough to answer sufficiently, most grant seekers' needs for information relating to requests for funding.

Foundations should be clear about the type of programs they support and also clear about the types of projects they do not support. Specifying "creative and innovative programs" does not provide adequate detail to grant seekers to determine if their proposed program is appropriate. By providing additional detail, the foundation could omit unwanted telephone and e-mail queries that deplete both organizations' valuable administrative time.

Detail should also include the deadlines for all stages of the application process as well as specific information regarding notification. Again, providing detail within the website may alleviate unwanted demands on administration. Grant seekers will be less apt to call or e-mail to seek the status of their proposal if it is made clear on the website that notification will be made, for example, within two weeks of the appropriate board meeting. If listing notification in this manner, the website should make certain to include the application/board meeting cycle and dates.

(3) **Provide Examples and FAQ.** Despite depth of information provided and ease of use, there will be grant seekers for whom provision of examples of prior grantees, and a list of FAQ will engender the greatest level of mutual benefit. As such, it is recommended that a clearly identified section that outlines in detail examples of prior grant making successes and/or failures is provided on the website. Such examples should be given not in mere linear name–amount given–location format but should include the story of the program, why it appealed to the foundation, and its impact on society.

Related to provision of examples is the provision of a set of FAQ. FAQ should have their own label from the home page and their own section. They should be general enough to answer questions and may direct viewers to additional information elsewhere on the site through provision of links.

(4) **Provide Contact Information and Opportunity for Feedback.** The development of positive organization–public relationships requires contact between the organization and its publics, in this case foundations and their grantees. Moreover, independent foundations are nonprofit organizations. As such, they should make themselves available to the public(s) with interest in their programs and operations. Yet, only 33% (n = 12) of the websites analyzed provided detailed contact information, in other words information that included a contact name as well as telephone number and/or e-mail address, and mailing address.

CONCLUSION

Results of this study indicated that independent foundation websites are not following the principles that could lead to the construction of positive organization–public relationships with their nonprofit grantees. Information on these sites was frequently site specific and general. Yet there were exemplar sites from which best practices could be drawn.

Building on established principles, four best practices for provision of grant making information were proposed that could encourage development of positive relationships between grantors and grantees. The first recommended that foundations strive for consistency in labeling, include 10 main sections with clear labels on a standard navigation bar located either to the left or top of the page, and maintain this navigation bar when viewers jump to a new page. The second recommendation asked that foundations provide the highest level of detail in their information to avoid confusion and inappropriate inquiries and applications. Third, the researcher recommended that websites include examples of prior grants funded, in detail and a list of FAQ. Finally, it was recommended that independent foundations provide sufficiently detailed contact information for those who required additional information and the opportunity for feedback.

Together, these recommendations for best practices could improve the grantor–grantee relationship, reducing frustration for both, as well as costly administrative time and resources. Further, easy-to-use websites with detailed information, examples, and contact information can facilitate the development of positive organization–public relationships, whereby grantees whose program services best match the focus areas and goals of the foundation, understand that they are the best match and apply, while those whose programs are outside those identified choose to allocate their administrative time to more likely grantors.

Limitations. This study examined just 36 websites of independent foundations located in the East South Central and South Atlantic divisions, plus the District of Columbia. Analysis of additional sites could result in different levels of specific and general information found, and would likely have identified additional exemplar sites.

NOTE

1. See http://www.tgci.com.

REFERENCES

Abney Foundation. (2009). Application guidelines. Retrieved November 14, 2009, from http://www.abneyfoundation.org/guideline.htm

Blackwood, A., Wing, K. T., & Pollak, T. H. (2008). The nonprofit sector in brief. Facts and figures from the *Nonprofit Almanac 2008*: Public charities, giving, and volunteering. *The Urban Institute*. Retrieved February 20, 2014, from http://nccsdataweb.urban.org/kbfiles/797/Almanac2008publicCharities.pdf

Blue Moon Fund. (2009). Eligibility quiz and letter of inquiry. Retrieved November 14, 2009 from http://www.bluemoonfund.org/grantmaking/grantmaking_show.htm?doc_id=447839&cat_id=1570

Buchanan, P., & Enright, K. (2007, February 8). What is an effective foundation? *Chronicle of Philanthropy, 19*(8), 37–37.

Fairfield, K. D., & Wing, K. T. (2008). Collaboration in foundation grantor-grantee relationships. *Nonprofit Management & Leadership, 19*(1), 27–44.

FC Stats: The Foundation Center's Statistical Information Service. (2011). Foundation staff positions by type of foundation. *The Foundation Center*. Retrieved February 20, 2014, from http://foundationcenter.org/gainknowledge/research/pdf/cof_salary_2011.pdf

Fleishman, J. L. (2007). *The Foundation: A great American secret*. New York, NY: PublicAffairs.

Foundation Center. (2011). Highlights of Foundation Yearbook. Retrieved February 20, 2014, from http://foundationcenter.org/gainknowledge/research/pdf/fy2011_highlights.pdf

Grantsmanship Center. (2009). Funding sources. Retrieved October 2009 from http://www.tgci.com/funding.shtml

Harry and Jeanette Weinberg Foundation. (2009). Grants. Retrieved November 2009 from http://www.hjweinbergfoundation.org/grants/

Holsti, O. (1969). *Content analysis for the social sciences and humanities*. Reading, MA: Addison Wesley.

Ingenhoff, D., & Koelling, A. M. (2009). The potential of web sites as a relationship building tool for charitable fundraising NPOs. *Public Relations Review, 35*, 66–73.

J. Bulow Campbell Foundation. (2009). Eligibility and grant criteria. Retrieved November 14, 2009, from http://www.jbcf.org/guidelines.html

Kent, M. L., & Taylor, M. (1998). Building dialogic relationships through the world wide web. *Public Relations Review, 24*(3), 321–334.

Ledingham, J. A., & Bruning, S. D. (1998). Relationship management in public relations: Dimensions of an organization–public relationship. *Public Relations Review, 24*(1), 55–65.

Mary Reynolds Babcock Foundation. (2009). Program description. Retrieved November 2009 from http://www.mrbf.org/program-description

Pfeffer, J., & Salancik, G. R. (2003). *The external control of organizations: A resource dependence perspective*. Stanford, CA: Stanford Business Books:

Project Streamline. (2008). *Drowning in paperwork, distracted from purpose*. Retrieved October 11, 2009, from http://www.projectstreamline.org/documents/PDF_Report_final.pdf

Quantum Foundation. (2009). Website. Retrieved November 2009 from http://www.quantumfnd.org/index.cfm?fuseaction=home.main&x=8326823

Shaw, S., & Allen, J. B. (2006). "We actually trust the community": Examining the dynamics of a nonprofit funding relationship in New Zealand. *Voluntas, 17*, 211–220.

Sisters of Mercy of North Carolina Foundation. (2009). Guide for grantseekers. Retrieved November 2009 from http://www.somncfdn.org/page.asp?urh=GuideForGrantseekers

Springs Close Foundation. (2009). What we do: The foundation's philosophy and interests. Retrieved November 14, 2009, from http://www.thespringsclosefoundation.org/home.htm

Tsasis, P. (2009). The social processes of interorganizational collaboration and conflict in nonprofit organizations. *Nonprofit Management & Leadership, 20*(1), 5–21.

Vorvoreanu, M. (2006). Online organization-public relationships: An experience-centered approach. *Public Relations Review, 32*, 395–401.

Waters, R. D. (2007). Nonprofit organizations' use of the Internet: A content analysis of communication trends on the Internet sites of the Philanthropy 400. *Nonprofit Management & Leadership, 18*(1), 59–76.

Yang, S.-U., & Grunig, J. E. (2005). Decomposing organisational reputation: The effects of organisation-public relationship outcomes on cognitive representations of organisations and evaluations of organisational performance. *Journal of Communication Management, 9*(4), 305–325.

Zweibel, N. R., & Golden, R. L. (2007, Summer). What foundations and nonprofits can do to foster productive relationships. *Generations, 31*(2), 41–46.

11 Disaster Public Affairs Training
A Test of the Crisis-Adaptive Public Information Model

J. Suzanne Horsley

On a stormy February afternoon in Atlanta, Georgia, I was preparing to do a live camera interview about a tornado that had just destroyed Georgia Tech's campus and surrounding neighborhoods. I reviewed my notes and silently rehearsed my key talking points. The producer motioned to me and said they were ready. Just as I stepped up to the camera to get my mic and earpiece, I heard a tornado siren. It was the first time I had ever heard one of these warning signals, and I wasn't exactly sure what it was.

I looked to my left to see the national public affairs director for the American Red Cross running down the convention center hallway, yelling, "This is not part of the exercise! Everyone to the basement!" About 120 Red Cross staff members, volunteers, media trainers, and camera operators made a hasty yet orderly exit down the stairs to the parking garage to wait out the warning. This was my first experience with the American Red Cross Advanced Public Affairs Team (APAT) Training Conference, and the impressively realistic scenario had just been ramped up a notch by an actual tornado warning in the area.

The four-day annual training conference is one of several ways the Red Cross trains its national team of elite disaster public affairs workers, a mix of volunteers and employees from the local, regional, and national levels of Red Cross. APAT members deploy to large-scale disasters throughout the United States and beyond to manage media relations and public information efforts. They bring skills and additional resources to local Red Cross chapters that may be overwhelmed by a disaster and need a higher level of expertise to work with the national and international media who are attracted to these events. My objective was to learn how the Red Cross prepares these team members for a wide variety of challenging disaster situations. I have been a volunteer with the Red Cross since 2005 and joined the national-level disaster public affairs team in 2009. Over the years, I have participated in training and been deployed to several natural disasters as a Red Cross spokesperson.

This study examines how the Red Cross public affairs department organizes, prepares, and trains staff and volunteers who respond to disasters throughout the United States. I used participant-observation methods to study the organization from its national headquarters over five weeks in 2009. The results of fieldwork and in-depth interviews are applied to an emerging model of crisis-adaptive public information (CAPI), which was developed after field studies with a state emergency management agency's public affairs unit (Horsley, 2010). The model is named for the way in which public information officers must adapt their job duties, areas of responsibility, geographic location, and lines of reporting to respond to a disaster or other major crisis. This study serves as the first attempt to test the model's fit with a nationwide nonprofit disaster response organization.

BACKGROUND AND LITERATURE REVIEW

Public relations, or public affairs, as it is often called in the nonprofit and government sectors, helps create a bridge to foster relationships between an organization and its publics. In stakeholder theory, positive relationships between an organization and its publics are necessary to manage crisis situations. While this is important for any organization that may experience crisis, it is vitally important for organizations that are mandated to respond to natural and manmade disasters. People who are affected by disasters rely on trusted organizations to give them the information they need to make decisions that may save lives, property, or livelihoods (Veil, Reynolds, Sellnow, & Seeger, 2008).

The American Red Cross network of chapters has employees and volunteers working in various communication positions with the goal to develop stakeholder relationships and disseminate vital public information. While some job titles include public affairs assistant, director of communications, or development director, smaller chapters may not have a designated communicator on staff. In this case, the chapter executive or a staff communicator in another location manages communications for that local office. However, the Red Cross has organized a group of more than 100 APAT members who are a mix of volunteers and employees from across the country. Originally known as the Rapid Response Team (RRT), which was first implemented in 1994 to work with national media in the first days after a major disaster, the group was renamed APAT in 2007 to better reflect the mission of the team and to improve communication with the media. APAT's primary goals are to work with national and international media to tell what the Red Cross is doing to help, explain who is getting help, describe how long the Red Cross will be providing assistance, and tell publics unaffected by disaster how they can help. While APAT members report directly to the Disaster Public Affairs office at headquarters in Washington, DC, the team coordinates with the local Red Cross chapter on public information efforts.

The American Red Cross has been the subject of several studies, most notably in the time since Hurricane Katrina. Of interest to this research are the studies that have examined the Red Cross in the context of communication and relationship management. Veil and Husted (2012) applied best practices analysis to a case study of the Red Cross's emergency communications after Hurricane Katrina in 2005. The authors identified several key best practices that the Red Cross performed well, but noted that the organization exhibited poor planning for a large-scale disaster, lacked strong partnerships with other organizations that could have helped with the response effort, had cases of misconduct among the largely untrained volunteer force, showed a lack of cultural awareness when dealing with certain publics, and had difficulty showing compassion and empathy. Likewise, Fussell, Collins, and Zoch (2010) found inadequacies in the Red Cross's response to organizational crises over a 10-year period. The authors found that the organization's spokesperson used responses from situational crisis communication theory in only one-third of the newspaper articles in their study and overused the "diminish" strategy, rendering it an ineffective response strategy. The authors noted that the use of a national-level spokesperson in nearly every news story indicated that the Red Cross took the accusations seriously, but suggested that the public and media reaction may have been more positive had spokespersons chosen the response strategies more carefully.

Red Cross's use of social media has been the subject of several studies. Liu, Yin, Briones and Kuch (2012) conducted interviews with 40 American Red Cross employees to develop their model of social-mediated crisis communication. The study found the Red Cross was proactive in communicating with its publics via social media channels and quickly addressed misinformation with corrective information. However, the interviews revealed that the system for responding to social media messages was inefficient, especially given their limitations in personnel and resources. The Red Cross has successfully used social media to build relationships with the media and its various stakeholders (Briones, Kuch, Liu, & Jin, 2011). However, the primary barriers to using social media have been a lack of staff time that was dedicated to monitoring and posting on the organization's various social media channels, making it difficult to foster relationships via this medium. In a similar vein, a study on 588 Red Cross chapter websites (Schmalzried, Fleming Fallon, & Harper, 2012) found inconsistencies in the type of information that was found on each chapter's webpage. While none of the websites had all nine emergency communication elements that the authors searched for, some had none and only seven sites had as many as seven of the elements.

Hamner (2008) offered a rare organizational perspective on the changes the Red Cross made to its disaster services human resource system in 2004. The case study examined the difficulties and ongoing problems that were caused by this major organizational change but did find that the changes would enhance organizational effectiveness and efficiencies.

While these studies inform the topics of crisis communication and organizational structure that are addressed by the present research, they do not specifically address the training, preparedness, and organizational structure of the public affairs function that may allow or impede Red Cross communication efforts and stakeholder relations during disasters.

Crisis-Adaptive Public Information Model. This study examines Red Cross public affairs training and preparedness through the lens of crisis-adaptive public information, a model informed by high reliability organizations (HROs) that routinely operate in a chaotic and uncertain environment (Horsley, 2010). HROs successfully operate under dangerous conditions on a daily basis, and this organizational trait applies well to a disaster-relief organization that regularly goes into destroyed cities and towns to help affected residents. However, the Red Cross does not constantly operate under disaster conditions, and the CAPI model takes into account the organizational change that occurs from routine public affairs to disaster public affairs.

CAPI was developed while studying the public affairs function of a state emergency management agency (Horsley, 2010). This study is the first test of the CAPI model with a nonprofit disaster relief organization. During routine operations, communicators in the agency focus on the first two phases of disaster: preparedness and mitigation. The members of the organization participate in training and simulated exercises to help prepare them to respond to a major disaster. During this time, they build up a library of response materials and develop relationships with the media and all stakeholders who may be involved in a future disaster response. In addition, communicators work to mitigate future disasters by educating stakeholders about personal, family, and organizational disaster preparedness. The purpose of mitigation is to prevent or reduce the amount of harm caused by a disaster that ultimately requires the resources of disaster response organizations (government, nongovernmental, and for-profit).

As the state emergency management agency responds to a disaster threat or event, the organization changes significantly. The CAPI organizational attributes increase as the situation becomes more complex and uncertain, and as the organization becomes more tightly coupled with other organizations that are involved in the event. The key attributes that the CAPI model borrows from HROs include a primary goal of safety, a flexible hierarchy, a culture of reliability, redundancy of critical jobs, tight coupling, and mindfulness. Tight coupling occurs when organizations must work together to bring their resources and abilities to a joint response effort (e.g., one organization may specialize in food preparation, while another has the vehicles and resources available to deliver the food to where it is needed). The point of morphogenesis, when the organization creates a new, ad hoc organization to respond to a specific disaster, occurs when a disaster is declared and the responding organization establishes an emergency operation center (EOC). For public affairs, the ultimate use of

CAPI attributes occurs when a joint information center (JIC) is activated. As the disaster is defused, the level of complexity and uncertainty declines, and the organization needs fewer CAPI attributes to function successfully. The organization may escalate or downgrade attributes as needed, but the changes are not necessarily linear. For example, a terrorist attack may have no warning, and the organization would escalate immediately to disaster mode. Eventually, the emergency management agency returns to the routine mode and applies what has been learned from the disaster to preparedness and mitigation efforts (Horsley, 2010). Figure 11–1 illustrates the attributes and levels of complexity for an emergency management agency during routine and disaster modes.

The existing literature on disaster communication in the American Red Cross has not examined how this organization trains and prepares its public affairs personnel to respond to a disaster. Therefore, this research asks the following questions:

RQ1: What formal training does the American Red Cross provide for its public affairs volunteers and staff who deploy to disaster settings?

RQ2: What attributes, if any, from the CAPI model are present in Red Cross disaster public affairs training and preparedness activities?

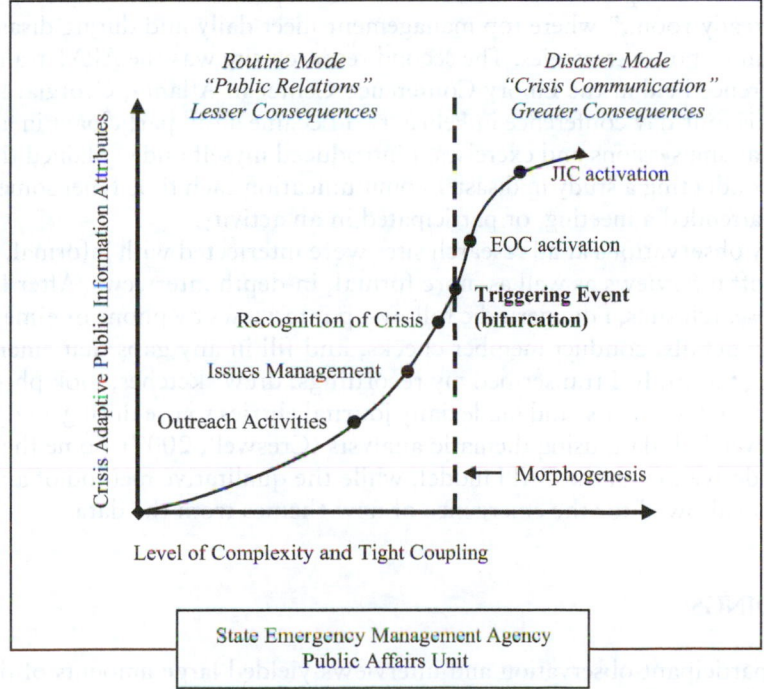

Figure 11–1   The Crisis-Adaptive Public Information Model.

METHOD

I conducted the participant-observation and field interviews for this study in January and February of 2009. Much of the preparation for my fieldwork involved taking courses offered by the American Red Cross and the Department of Homeland Security to familiarize myself with the role of public affairs in emergency management prior to entering the field (see Horsley, 2012). My method of observation was based on the work of Weick and Sutcliff (2007), who observed sailors aboard a U.S. military aircraft carrier to determine the attributes of a high reliability organization. My level of participation would be relatively low initially as I was an outsider to the American Red Cross National Headquarters and intended to be an open and flexible observer. I would adapt my inquiry and level of participation as I learned more information and as opportunities became available (Angrosino, 2007). As my experience with the Red Cross continued over the three-month period, I moved from being a primary observer in the public affairs department to a primary participant in training exercises, as will be explained in the results of my fieldwork. (A more detailed description of my fieldwork experience is discussed in Horsley, 2012.)

My first research site was the American Red Cross National Headquarters building in Washington, DC. The primary areas of interest included the public affairs department offices, the disaster operations center (DOC), and the "ready room," where top management meet daily and during disasters to plan response strategies. The second research site was the APAT training conference held at the Emory Conference Center in Atlanta, Georgia. During this four-day conference in February, I became a full participant in all of the training sessions and exercises. I introduced myself and explained that I was conducting a study in disaster communication each time I met someone new, attended a meeting, or participated in an activity.

My observations at all research sites were interjected with informal, off-the-cuff interviews as well as more formal, in-depth interviews. After I left the research sites, I did periodic follow-up interviews by phone or e-mail to clarify details, conduct member checks, and fill in any gaps that emerged during the study. I transcribed my recordings, drew sketches, took photos, collected documents, and made daily journal entries to use during analysis. I analyzed all data using thematic analysis (Creswell, 2007). Some themes were derived from the CAPI model, while the qualitative method of analysis also allowed for the emergence of new themes from the data.

FINDINGS

The participant-observation and interviews yielded large amounts of data, but I limited the results of this study to data related to the organization of the Red Cross public affairs training function that would inform the crisis-adaptive public information (CAPI) model. As the model is divided into "routine mode public relations" and "disaster mode crisis communication," most of the findings from this study specifically inform the "routine mode." However, the policies and procedures that are integrated in the training give insight into what would transpire during "disaster mode." The prevailing theme from the two research sites (the Red Cross headquarters and the APAT conference) was that the Red Cross invested heavily in both time and effort to train public affairs staff.

Disaster Public Affairs Training. The American Red Cross has formalized training that it offers to employees and volunteers who wish to work in the public affairs function during disaster. At the time of this study, the organization offered a basic online course in disaster public affairs; an on-site class on conducting public affairs during a smaller, localized disaster; an on-site class on conducting public affairs during a larger disaster of national concern; and an invitation-only annual training conference for advanced public affairs disaster personnel. Of most concern to the public affairs staff at the national headquarters is the annual training conference known as the APAT conference. There are approximately 100 men and women nationwide who are selected for the APAT team based on experience, public relations, or media skills, and the need for that position in particular regions of the country. These individuals not only deploy to large-scale disasters that attract national and international media, but also become disaster communication experts in their home communities. All APAT members must be willing to be on call for a minimum of two weeks per year, during which they can deploy to a disaster in less than 24 hours.

I participated in the four-day APAT training conference held in Atlanta, Georgia, in February 2009. As a full participant, I was evaluated and given feedback on all phases of the training. In addition, because of my ongoing field study, conference organizers gave me small roles to play in simulations and included me in the planning sessions prior to the conference. For example, I helped the disaster public affairs manager develop the training scenario while I was visiting the national headquarters, and I played the role of a "reporter" during ambush media interviews as conference attendees arrived at the conference hotel.

Conference participants received information about the evolving disaster scenario prior to arriving onsite, and the organizers staged their arrival to mimic arriving at a disaster site with limited details on the relief efforts. As participants entered the conference center with luggage in tow, "reporters," including myself, met the travel-weary team members at the door with an audio recorder in one hand and multiple questions about the Red Cross's response to the disaster scenario, which was a tornado that struck downtown Atlanta. The responses by the participants varied greatly. Many stated that they had not received the scenario details prior to traveling, while others complained that they were tired and just wanted to check in at the hotel. Some participants easily engaged in the role play and demonstrated their past experience communicating during uncertain situations. The senior director of public affairs, who oversees the conference, told me that it was not uncommon for public affairs officers to arrive on scene and immediately respond to reporter inquiries with little or no details about the operation. She and her conference organizers wanted to reinforce the realities of disaster deployments and remind APAT members of the basic Red Cross messaging that they can always use in the first few hours of a disaster response while there are still many unknown facts. This exercise set the tone for the rest of the conference as attendees worked through a complicated, evolving scenario and attended a variety of classroom sessions.

All participants were given two documents during the first general session. The first was an APAT Conference Onsite Information book with the agenda, workshop descriptions, a schedule of individual media training exercises, biographies of presenters, the APAT manual, a disaster services glossary, social media information, fundraising language, and Federal Emergency Management Agency (FEMA) protocol and acronyms. The second document was titled "Messaging" and included sample disaster messaging in English and Spanish; hot topics (e.g., talking points for specific issues such as working with undocumented clients or policies regarding sex offenders in shelters); and disaster services guidance related to core organizational values and working with the media. Participants received daily updates to the evolving scenario to use in their media exercises. The Red Cross hired media professionals from television, radio, and newspapers to conduct live interviews, edited interviews, and remote IFB (interruptible feedback) interviews with anchors in the "studio." These interviews took place in between classroom activities and discussions in social media, critical thinking and storytelling, developing relationships with stakeholders, and photography and videography.

Although some APAT conference attendees were surprised by their sudden immersion into the disaster scenario upon arrival, it was evident that most participants quickly transitioned into a disaster mode of thought and participated fully. The realism of the scenario kept the participants on edge. Many of them commented that they were terrified of being interviewed by the "real" reporters. One participant who was new to APAT said, "I don't want to mess up in front of the real reporters. I don't want them to trip me up on questions, especially when we have just a few facts in the scenario." Several wanted to do well so they would be considered for a deployment but also wondered if they would be prepared when the time came to work at their first disaster. On the other hand, more veteran communicators took the exercise in stride knowing it was just that: an exercise. One woman, a Red Cross employee from Indiana, commented that the media training was harder than an actual disaster:

It's easier to talk about a real disaster because you have tangible details you can talk about and describe. It's hard to be empathetic on camera when all you have is a scenario update and you have to make up the details.

Throughout the four-day conference, participants, leaders, and trainers shared meals and nightly social time at the conference center lounge or at local area restaurants. The energy and enthusiasm displayed during the sessions and exercises carried over after classes were done. Many of these people had worked together before and become good friends; however, the new members, or "green dots" as they affectionately were called because of the stickers on their name badges, were welcomed into the more veteran groups. As a green dot myself, I felt welcomed and part of the entire experience. Teamwork is highly valued because APAT members rarely deploy alone. Depending upon the magnitude of the disaster and the amount of media attention, APAT teams of two or more work together during a disaster. Long-term disasters require that additional teams come in to relieve the first wave of workers. The teamwork required for the deployments was reinforced not only during most of the training sessions, but also during downtime. Even though APAT members had to complete the media interviews individually, it was common to see members coaching each other before an interview, just as they would in the field.

CAPI Model Attributes Found in Disaster Public Affairs Training. Many of the attributes from HROs and the CAPI model were evident in the Red Cross training. Redundancy of personnel is a major premise of the APAT organization. The APAT members have their day jobs. They may be Red Cross employees working in various functions at national headquarters (NHQ) or in chapter offices around the country, or they may be volunteers who are retired, not employed, or respond to disasters during their vacation time from other jobs. The disaster public affairs manager responsible for deploying team members explained that about 15% of APAT members were retired (from Red Cross or other occupations), about 50% were Red Cross employees, and about 35% were volunteers who make time for APAT responsibilities. All have communication, PR, and journalism backgrounds. However, once they deploy as public affairs officers, they dramatically increase the number of public affairs experts on the scene. No single Red Cross chapter could sustain this number of trained public affairs staff on a regular basis, but when this pool of resources is gathered and brought to a disaster site, the sudden redundancy of personnel creates reliability in media relations and public information efforts. Redundancy does not occur during "routine mode," which would be considered inefficient, but becomes an efficient method of operation during "disaster mode" when there is heightened media interest and a need to communicate quickly and accurately with the public.

A flexible hierarchy is another hallmark of HROs and CAPI that was evident in Red Cross disaster public affairs. The disaster public affairs manager explained that she uses a "battle org chart" that "can be scaled up or down" depending upon the disaster. In addition, all APAT members, including Red Cross employees from other areas of the organization, report to her and leave behind their routine responsibilities. This flexible hierarchy ensures that all deployed APAT members take their instructions from and get evaluated by the head of disaster public affairs, avoiding confusion and divided chains of command. With long, stressful days working on the disaster operation, APAT members need to be able to focus on the task at hand.

"I will talk to their supervisors to make sure that they understand DOC (disaster operations center) policies and procedures, but make sure that the APATers still communicate with their supervisors," she explained. The manager added that, for Red Cross employees, it is important to educate supervisors so that they will continue to support their employees' involvement in APAT. Disaster deployments for APAT team members typically last 2–5 days and end once the national media attention wanes. However, it is not unusual to have a longer deployment for larger disasters, such as Hurricane Katrina in 2005, the Alabama tornadoes in 2011, or Hurricane Sandy in 2012. APAT members were on deployment for several weeks during these prolonged disaster response and recovery efforts.

A shared goal is another key attribute that is apparent from disaster public affairs training. While HROs focus on the goal of safety, "the American Red Cross prevents and alleviates human suffering in the face of emergencies by mobilizing the power of volunteers and the generosity of donors" ("Mission, Vision, and Fundamental Principles," 2012). The vice president of communications explained that the goal of the APAT is to focus on stakeholders' communication needs to include that of the media, disaster victims, donors (of time, money, and blood), partners in the disaster response, Red Cross personnel, and the general public. However, the disaster public affairs manager explained goals in terms of organizational levels, saying, "The role of the DOC is to protect the Red Cross reputation and to think 'corporate.' In the field, we need to think about clients and the media. But helping clients is our first priority." While APAT members receive direction from the DOC, their priorities are localized to the disaster and those who have been affected. While my participant-observation activities revealed a shared goal among the APAT training participants, the interviews suggested there may be a disconnect between the goals of the national organization and those of the local chapters during a disaster.

A culture of reliability is perpetuated not only by the APAT training program, but also by the vision of the American Red Cross: to "turn compassion into action" ("Mission, Vision, and Fundamental Principles,"

2012). Reliability is generated through training, rehearsal, and organizational learning. The disaster public affairs lead spends all of her time during "routine mode" preparing for the next disaster by communicating regularly with APAT team members, collecting members' deployment availability on a quarterly basis, and assisting with messaging and training for annual conferences. During disasters, she recruits and deploys APAT members, counsels them in the field, and communicates with the affected chapters' communication staffs or directors so that they understand the type of support they will get from the APAT members. "In training, we want them to know how to give one corporate message and how to put on their best face without giving up ethics," she said. "We want them to be the best spokespeople and critical thinkers with a strong messaging foundation." The APAT training conference provides current key messages, refreshes old skills while teaching new ones, and gives attendees opportunities to rehearse what they have learned through intensive media interview exercises. The training they receive during the conference is reinforced throughout the year with topical webinars, e-mail messages, and a monthly e-mail newsletter, "The Rapid Responder."

Throughout all of the training, the APAT members practice mindfulness: the art of paying attention to signals that may indicate a problem or an opportunity. They learn not to ignore misinformation or rumors in media reports or on social media, and they learn to notice activity in the disaster area that may spur a human-interest story, a video for the online newsroom, or a photo that captures the essence of the relief effort. While the team members' primary focus is learning how to work with national media and develop proactive communications, the vice president of communications said they also serve as "the eyes and the ears" of the Red Cross to monitor local media reports, assess public reaction, and look for potential problems. Because APAT members have access to all Red Cross disaster operations and facilities, they also can use an objective eye to look for issues throughout the organization, including the local disaster headquarters, client relief shelters, client casework centers, and mobile feeding stations. The mindfulness of APAT team members can allow the organization to preempt problems as well as be proactive about pitching new stories or generating online content.

All APAT activities are conducted in a system of tight coupling, a final attribute of HROs and CAPI. APAT members cannot operate in isolation during a disaster response. They must seek out and coordinate their efforts with all aspects of the Red Cross operation, including the local chapter management, sheltering, feeding, supply distribution, donations, and blood drives, among others. In addition, APAT members may be working in a joint information center with officials from state, local, or federal emergency management agencies. They rely on leaders within the disaster relief operation to supply them with current statistics, such as the number of open shelters, how many people received assistance, how many meals were served, and where the food distribution locations will be on any given day so that the information can be shared with the media and public. They are also tightly coupled with reporters whom they rely on to disseminate important information in an accurate and timely manner. As the disaster operation intensifies, the level of cooperation and reliance increases, but as the operation dies down, the level decreases. Once tight coupling has reduced significantly, often signified by national media moving on to other stories and leaving town, the APAT team member's job ends.

DISCUSSION AND CONCLUSIONS

The Crisis-Adaptive Public Information model appears to inform Red Cross disaster public affairs training on all of its key attributes: a commonly shared goal, a flexible hierarchy, a culture of reliability, redundancy of key jobs, tight coupling, and a practice of mindfulness. However, the observations and interviews revealed several key points that should be considered further. The attribute of a commonly shared goal was problematic because there appeared to be two goals: a corporate goal of reputation management and a localized goal of serving disaster clients and other stakeholders. Although the Red Cross is a nonprofit organization, the leaders often referred to NHQ as "corporate" as opposed to "chapters" or "regions," suggesting that this apparent disconnect between NHQ and field offices was not an oversight. While I did not observe any direct consequences of this during my fieldwork, many NHQ leaders mentioned communication challenges with chapters during disaster preparedness and response efforts. For example, the vice president of communications said, "NHQ would promote the Red Cross role (in a disaster response), while the state or region would promote public information for clients." The disaster public affairs manager noted, "issues with chapters are fairly common. You have to pick your fights. Our goal with chapter communicators is to get them to know us before they need us. We need to do more education with chapters." She extended the differences in goals to roles, saying, "The difference is the DOC has an advising role, but the field is doing it." Part of the advising is the consideration of the whole organization's reputation, while the APAT members have to affirm that reputation in their actions. One example of opposing goals came up during a commercial airplane crash while I was visiting the national offices. The Red Cross responded by supporting the families of those who lost loved ones, but the cost was minimal because the Red Cross did not need to feed and shelter people as it does during a natural disaster. The local chapter executive wanted to use the increased publicity to solicit donations, but the NHQ public affairs staff believed that was the wrong approach. The senior director of public affairs described their strategy:

We talked to the chapter and told them that we don't fundraise for mass casualty events because these are sensitive events with loss of life, and it doesn't cost us that much to respond. The airlines took care of them (the families) and spent money on the response. The Red Cross mainly provided emotional support and served as a buffer between the families and the media. It's not fair to solicit when we don't spend a lot of money.

While the local chapter was directly involved in the airplane crash response and saw the increased visibility as an opportunity to raise money, NHQ thought it would send the wrong message and potentially damage the Red Cross reputation.

The differences in communication goals between corporate and non-profit organizations have been established (Liu & Horsley, 2007; Liu, Horsley, & Levenshus, 2010), but this phenomenon has not been examined within the context of a parent/national nonprofit organization and its chapters/field offices. The hierarchy of a national organization with localized offices suggests that the CAPI model would need to consider these organizational disparities. As the situation escalates and becomes more complex and tightly coupled (see Figure 11–1), the CAPI attributes, including common goals, must increase. An organization such as the Red Cross would need to reach an agreement on organizational goals to effectively enact CAPI attributes.

Training and rehearsal consumes a majority of the "routine mode" for Red Cross public affairs personnel. Currently, outreach activities and issues management are depicted on the CAPI model, but this research suggests that training and rehearsal also merit inclusion under "public relations" activities. While the attribute of a reliable culture is an important component of CAPI, the training programs and simulations are essential to accomplishing and perpetuating that culture. The training establishes clear expectations for all areas of reliability, including promoting a common goal, educating participants on the hierarchical changes that occur when activating the disaster response, producing trained individuals who can contribute to the redundant resource pool, reinforcing mindful practices, and understanding how to work with partners with which the Red Cross is tightly coupled. The investment in time and resources for training and rehearsal is essential for following the CAPI model; therefore, I suggest adding that to the model rather than simply inferring it (see Figure 11–2).

While there were some areas of CAPI that did not form a complete fit with Red Cross disaster public affairs training and preparedness, the organizational complications from these omissions suggest that the model is still a good representation of organizations with high reliability attributes that transition from routine to disaster mode to communicate during public crises. More research must be done, however, on the effectiveness of this model, as is described in the final section.

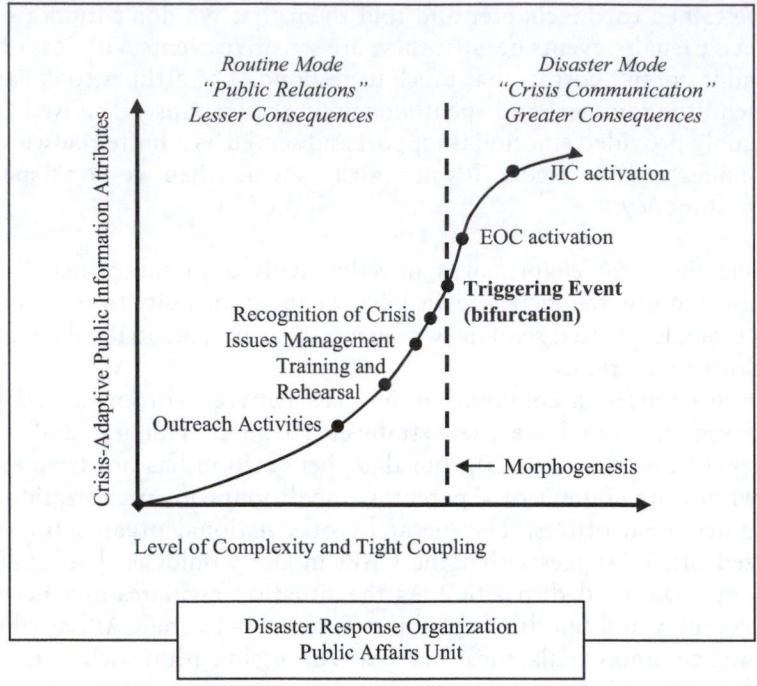

Figure 11–2   Revised Crisis-Adaptive Public Information Model.

LIMITATIONS AND FUTURE RESEARCH

As in any qualitative field study, this research was limited by my ability to be on location for an adequate amount of time and to observe Red Cross public affairs personnel participating in all aspects of training and preparedness. While I attempted to observe a significant cross section of training and exercises at two sites, the data collection and analysis would have been improved by the addition of more researchers. Future research will examine how well the training and preparedness activities correlate with an actual disaster response through additional participant-observation of Red Cross public affairs workers in an active disaster setting. In addition, the effectiveness of the disaster response should be evaluated based upon the CAPI model's assumptions. The CAPI model also should be tested further with other types of disaster response organizations, such as federal disaster management or other nongovernmental organizations. The field of disaster communication research presents ample opportunities to apply the CAPI model under varying conditions and operating environments.

REFERENCES

Angrosino, M. (2007). *Doing qualitative ethnographic and observational research*. London: Sage.

Briones, R. L., Kuch, B., Liu, B. F., & Jin, Y. (2011). Keeping up with the digital age: How the American Red Cross uses social media to build relationships. *Public Relations Review, 37*(1), 37–43. doi:10.1016/j.pubrev.2010.12.006

Creswell, J. W. (2007). *Qualitative inquiry and research design: Choosing among five approaches*. Thousand Oaks, CA: Sage.

Fussell Sisco, H., Collins, E. L., & Zoch, L. M. (2010). Through the looking glass: A decade of Red Cross crisis response and situational crisis communication theory. *Public Relations Review, 36*(1), 21–27. doi:10.1016/j.pubrev.2009.08.018

Hamner, M. P. (2008). Organizational transformation: Impact of redesigning the American Red Cross disaster services human resource system. *Journal of Homeland Security & Emergency Management, 5*(1), 1–19. Retrieved March 16, 2014, from http://search.ebscohost.com/login.aspx?direct=true&db=i3h&AN=32963439&site=ehost-live

Horsley, J. S. (2012). Planning for spontaneity: The challenges of disaster communication fieldwork. *International Journal of Qualitative Methods, 11*(3), 180–194.

Horsley, S. (2010). Crisis-adaptive public information: A model for reliability in chaos. In W. T. Coombs & S. J. Holladay (Eds.), *The handbook of crisis communication* (pp. 550–567). Chichester, UK: Wiley-Blackwell.

Liu, B. F., & Horsley, J. S. (2007). The government communication decision wheel: Toward a public relations model for the public sector. *Journal of Public Relations Research, 19*(4), 377–393.

Liu, B. F., Horsley, J. S., & Levenshus, A. B. (2010). Government and corporate communication practices: Do the differences matter? *Journal of Applied Communication Research, 38*(2), 189–213.

Liu, B. F., Jin, Y., Briones, R., & Kuch, B. (2012). Managing turbulence in the blogosphere: Evaluating the blog-mediated crisis communication model with the American Red Cross. *Journal of Public Relations Research, 24*(4), 353.

Mission, Vision, and Fundamental Principles. (2012). American Red Cross. Retrieved September 1, 2012, from http://www.redcross.org/about-us/mission

Schmalzried, H. D., Fleming Fallon, L., & Harper, E. A. (2012). Assessing informational website communications during emergencies and disasters. *International Journal of Nonprofit and Voluntary Sector Marketing, 17*(3), 199–207. doi:10.1002/nvsm.1423

Veil, S., Reynolds, B., Sellnow, T. L., & Seeger, M. W. (2008). CERC as a theoretical framework for research and practice. *Health Promotion Practice, 9*(4), 26S–34S. doi:10.1177/1524839908322113

Veil, S. R., & Husted, R. A. (2012). Best practices as an assessment for crisis communication. *Journal of Communication Management, 16*(2), 131–145. doi:10.1108/13632541211217560

Weick, K. E., & Sutcliffe, K. M. (2007). *Managing the unexpected: Resilient performance in an age of uncertainty* (2nd ed.). San Francisco, CA: Jossey-Bass.

Part III

Public Awareness and Advocacy

12 Legitimation Strategies in Radical Activist Issues Management
Congressional Testimony of the AIDS Coalition to Unleash Power (ACT UP)

Erich J. Sommerfeldt and Sifan Xu

Public relations research on activism has become increasingly associated with nonprofit public relations scholarship, as the difference between activist and nonprofit advocacy organizations may often be in name only (Sommerfeldt, 2013). Like nonprofits, activist groups are highly dependent on public support and must struggle to position their issue as a legitimate public concern and their organization as a legitimate spokesperson on that issue to attract future members and resources (Heath & Palenchar, 2009). As Sommerfeldt (2013) noted, "As issues gain legitimacy and mature, so too must the successful activist group legitimate itself if it is to endure" (p. 363). Maintaining organizational legitimacy is among the most important functions of public relations practice (Metzler, 2001) and legitimacy is a foundational principle of issues management (Heath & Palenchar, 2009), yet the concept has received relatively scant attention in the literature. For an organization to be perceived as legitimate, it must seek to appear in congruence with the social values and norms of the larger social system of which they are a part (Dowling & Pfeffer, 1975). Yet, if the prerequisite of organizational legitimacy is engaging in actions and behaviors that are consistent with societal values and norms, it begs the question: How do groups that engage in what are perceived to be illegitimate actions establish legitimacy for themselves and for their issues of concern?

Just as more "traditional" organizations, activist groups require legitimacy to achieve their goals. However, for radical activist groups whose behavior often flouts social norms and values, legitimacy becomes an especially important consideration. Engaging in socially illegitimate activities creates "legitimacy dilemmas" for activist groups (Elsbach & Sutton, 1992). Illegitimacy may hamper activist efforts to affect public policy—a common goal of activist activity and issues management practice (Heath & Palenchar, 2009). The rhetorical strategies that activist groups use to (re)gain legitimacy are thus of particular interest for research interrogating the nexus of activism, public relations, and issues management. This chapter situates itself within this nexus by examining how a radical activist group, ACT UP (the AIDS Coalition to Unleash Power), enacted legitimacy for themselves, their issues, and their policy recommendations in testimony before Congress.

LITERATURE REVIEW

Legitimacy and Public Relations. Legitimacy has been defined in a number of ways, suggesting the concept has multiple dimensions. Work by Shoemaker (1982) proposed that legitimacy may be based on the organization's legality, the capacity of the organization to achieve its goals, and the perceived stability and credibility of the organization. Shoemaker thus positioned organizational legitimacy as contingent on differing sets of norms and values: legal, moral, and power based. While organizations must work to appear in congruence with such norms and values, organizational theorists recognize that publics alone award organizations with legitimacy (Pfeffer & Salancik, 1978), and that legitimacy is gauged by the utility and responsibility of the organization within the larger social system (Epstein, 1972). In this vein, Suchman (1995) offered a popular definition of legitimacy as the "generalized perception or assumption that the actions of an entity are desirable, proper, or appropriate within some socially constructed system of norms, values, beliefs and definitions" (p. 574). While scholars have framed legitimacy in many ways (cf. Boyd, 2000; Metzler, 2001), the common thread running through such definitions is that legitimacy is awarded by publics to organizations that act in a fashion commensurate with social norms and values.

Gower (2006) framed legitimacy as public relations' reason for being, writing that all types of organizations "must be seen as legitimate in the eyes of at least a portion of society if they wish to achieve their goals" (p. 181). For Hearit (1995), legitimacy is a concept that helps to explain the public relations tactics organizations use to convince publics they are useful, responsible, and deserving of support. Thus, organizations can suffer from a "legitimacy gap" when there is a disparity between what the organization does and what their publics expects the organization to do (Sethi, 1977). This "gap" can result in consequences including "conflicting attitudes and behaviors between organizations and those of the persons whose goodwill they need" (Heath, 2006, p. 57). Indeed, as legitimacy often only comes to the forefront of organizational concerns when it is questioned (Habermas, 1979), legitimacy has most often been studied in connection with organizational crises. Innumerable studies have examined how organizations use rhetorical strategies to repair their image when it is damaged by crisis and restore legitimacy (e.g., Liu, 2007).

Legitimacy, however, is not a subject germane only to crisis research. Legitimacy has also been viewed as a symbolic communication tool (Coombs, 1992; Grunig & Huang, 2000), a measure of the quality of organization–public relationships (Bruning & Ledingham, 1999), and a means to gain support for organizational actions (Boyd, 2000). Boyd argued that efforts to (re)establish legitimacy are not necessarily connected to organizational image or reputation. Instead, legitimation—the act of asserting legitimacy—can be equated with "gaining the support or approval of various publics for a specific action" (p. 348). From this perspective, legitimation is a strategic communication function of organizations to achieve particular goals and gain social acceptance. As de Bussy (2007) has suggested, "many public relations activities can be construed as strategic legitimation efforts by managers attempting to control often-symbolic resources" (p. 290). Legitimacy can thus be studied as a rhetorical tool used to gain support for an organization, its actions, and its issues (Coombs, 1992).

Legitimacy in Issues Management. Pratt (2001) summarized issues management as a function that helps "organizations to anticipate issues, project and communicate their probable impacts on the organizations, formulate policies and actions that implement their strategic thinking, and influence public policy debates" (p. 336). Issues management was first premised on the idea that corporations, like activist groups, can and should participate in the public policy process (Jones & Chase, 1979). While issues management has taken on broader usage within public relations scholarship (cf. Heath & Palenchar, 2009), shaping public policy is the "dominant and original objective" of issues management (Coombs, 1992, p. 103). Coombs suggested that legitimacy is a "valuable resource when one is involved in a struggle of how an issue is to be resolved" (p. 102). Indeed, Heath and Palenchar (2009) argued that legitimacy is perhaps the central theme in issues management, claiming "issues management is a clash for legitimacy" (p. 10).

Coombs (1992) posited that legitimacy affects participation in public policy formation in three ways: public acceptance of the issue, public acceptance of the issue manager, and public acceptance of the policy proposal. First, as Crable and Vibbert (1985) have defined them, issues are created when "one or more humans attaches significance to a situation or perceived problem" (p. 5). Coombs argued that an issue has legitimacy when relevant publics accept it as worthy of concern. Second, the issue manager—any person or group that attempts to affect public policy formation—is deemed legitimate when publics accept that the issue manager has the right or authority to speak on the issue. Third, the public policy proposal has legitimacy when publics accept it as a "workable resolution for the issue" (p. 105). Policies are thus answers to the questions posed by issues (Crable & Vibbert, 1985). Policy discussions are among the last phases of an issue's life cycle, and are often contentious as different proposals are put forward to resolve the issue. In Coombs's view, the issue manager must work to concurrently bolster legitimacy claims for the organization, for the issue, and the policy proposal using different forms of support.

Rhetorical Strategies for "Bolstering" Legitimacy. Heath (2006) wrote that the "rhetorical enactment of issues management entails multiple and varied voices who advocate various issues and policy positions" (p. 58). Drawing on literature from sociology, social movements, and persuasion, Coombs (1992) outlined a typology of 10 strategies, or bases, for rhetorically bolstering legitimacy in issues management (pp. 106–107). Issue managers can draw upon bases such as *tradition,* where the rhetor states that things have always been done in a particular way and thus should remain so, or *de-legitimacy,* where the rhetor's legitimacy is bolstered by attacking the legitimacy of an opponent. Rhetors can also draw upon Aristotle's three modes of persuasion: ethos, logos, and pathos—or, as Coombs named them, credibility (expertise and trustworthiness), rationality (the use of empirical and logical evidence), and emotionality (use of emotions). These and other bases (presented in Table 12–1) can be combined with presentational tactics, such as an endorsement from another legitimate party; establishing an association between the issue, issue manager, or policy proposal to some base of legitimacy; or self-evidence, which relies on some innate attribute of the issue or proposal to establish legitimacy. Legitimacy bases can be combined with presentation tactics to create strategies for enacting legitimacy; the "arguments for the acceptance of a legitimacy claim" (p. 107).

Table 12–1   Legitimacy Bases and Tactics.

Bases of Legitimacy	
Tradition	Draws legitimacy from history (e.g., things have always been done in a certain way and should remain that way).
Charisma	Draws legitimacy from the extraordinary characteristics of a person, characteristics that set them apart from and above others.
Bureaucracy	Draws legitimacy from accepted rules, laws, and statutes.
Values	Absolute values are values accepted by all peoples as just and right, such as natural laws; societal values represent the norms of a specific social system, such as the United States.
Symbols	Things that stand for something else, and these symbols can act as a source of legitimacy.
De-legitimacy	Bolstering one's legitimacy by eroding the legitimacy of the opposition.
Credibility	A speaker's personal characteristics and centers on expertise and trustworthiness.
Rationality	The use of empirical and logical arguments.
Emotionality	The use of emotions.
Entitlements	Direct experience with the subject.
Legitimacy Tactics	
Endorsement	The approval or support of some legitimate actor.
Association	Establishes a relationship between the organization, issue, or individual by some bases of legitimacy.
Self-evidence	Elements intrinsic to the issue to create legitimacy.

Note: Cf. Coombs (1992, pp. 106–107).

Coombs further argued that not all strategies are appropriate for each form of legitimacy claim and provided a list of strategies and their proper uses (see Table 12–2).

An organization is deemed legitimate if the public evaluates and accepts its actions as congruent with social norms and values. If this definition is to be accepted, an organization (or the issue manager) that engages in illegitimate actions will face difficulty in gaining public acceptance for its issues and policy proposals. Legitimacy is thus an immediate and pressing concern for activist groups, particularly those who engage in radical behaviors.

Legitimacy and Activist Issues Management. Activists typically direct their activities at questioning the legitimacy of other institutions or organizational practices (Metzler, 2001). However, as a consequence of questioning the legitimacy of other entities or actions, activists themselves are in need of legitimation. Activists thus face a "dual legitimacy challenge"—establishing legitimacy for themselves while at the same time undermining the legitimacy of others (Smith & Ferguson, 2010, p. 401). Quite simply, activist organizations are as much subject to the question of legitimacy as they are instigators of questioning another entity's legitimacy.

Activist groups vary widely in form and behavior and recognizing the differences among activists is important to theorizing about them (Derville, 2005). While many activist groups exhibit structural characteristics and practices

Table 12–2   Strategies for Legitimacy and Appropriate Usage.

Strategy	Appropriate Use
Endorsement by credibility	Issues, issue managers, policy proposals
Endorsement by charisma	Issues, issue managers, policy proposals
Endorsement by tradition	Issues, issue managers, policy proposals
Endorsement by bureaucracy	Issues, issue managers, policy proposals
Association with values	Issues, policy proposals
Association with symbols	Issues
Association with entitlement	Issue managers
Self-evidence of rationality	Issues, policy proposals
Self-evidence of emotionality	Issues, policy proposals
Self-evidence of tradition	Issues, issue managers, policy proposals
Self-evidence of credibility	Issue managers
Self-evidence of bureaucracy	Issue managers
Self-evidence of charisma	Issue managers
Self-evidence of de-legitimacy	Issue managers

Note: Table recreated from Coombs (1992, p. 108).

typical of established nonprofit organizations (Sommerfeldt, 2013), activists who engage in actions largely counter to existing norms about how organizations should behave are particularly vulnerable to perceptions of illegitimacy. In calling for fundamental social change, radical activists use tactics that are "widely viewed as unconventional, inappropriate, or illegitimate" (Haines, 1988, p. 197). Controversial behaviors may have the effect of driving away current and potential members, jeopardizing endorsements from outside constituencies, and providing ammunition for adversaries (Elsbach & Sutton, 1992). However, just as vitriolic rhetoric can work to delegitimize activist groups, the ways in which activists may seek to gain legitimacy for themselves, their issues, and their actions are rhetorical. For example, Elsbach and Sutton explained that engaging in illegitimate activities may often be but the first step in radical activists' endeavors to convince publics that their issue, and thereby their illegitimate actions, are of public concern and are therefore actually legitimate. They do so by "portraying the event and the organization in a positive light" (p. 717). In articulating the issue and demonstrating how it affects others, activists are able to win legitimation and successfully manage their issues (Heath & Palenchar, 2009).

Activist groups, as part of the larger nonprofit sector, are "dedicated to the management of issues to a resolution satisfactory to the group's stakeholders" (Sommerfeldt, 2013, p. 347). While issues management was, in part, formulated as a means to deal with activist group pressures (Jones & Chase, 1979), Crable and Vibbert (1985) suggested that activists themselves are particularly skilled issues management practitioners, utilizing issues management strategy with greater dexterity than "traditional" organizations (p. 10). Indeed, the primary purpose and ultimate aim of many activist organizations is to influence public policy. However, Smith and Ferguson (2010) would comment that activists face challenges in affecting public policy—challenges that are usually tied to legitimation. Thus, to be efficacious in issues management practice and policy formation, activists must establish legitimacy for themselves, for their issues, and for their policy recommendations.

As noted previously, the final function of issues management is advocacy (Heath & Palenchar, 2009). One such mode of advocacy is, as Heath and Palenchar described, "to engage in actions designed to create, change, or defeat legislation or regulation" (p. 36). Given that Congress is the ultimate forum for shaping public policy, Congress is often the target of activist group communication efforts (Brouwer, 2001). Being selected as a witness to testify before Congress not only provides the opportunity to potentially shape legislation, but hearings are also a powerful form of publicity given the presence of national media. In many ways, congressional hearings represent the ideal platform for issue managers, particularly for activists who are rarely granted access to such a powerful forum for decision making. Such was the case for the radical activist group ACT UP.

The Case of ACT UP. The AIDS Coalition to Unleash Power (ACT UP) is an activist group that formed in New York City in 1987. From its inception,

ACT UP was vociferously critical of federal government's slow and apathetic response to the AIDS epidemic and organized dozens of protests around the nation. ACT UP staged its first demonstration on Wall Street only 12 days after forming, protesting the relationship between the FDA and the pharmaceutical company Burroughs Wellcome—which at the time was the sole maker of azidothymidine (AZT), the first drug treatment for HIV/AIDS. Over the next several years, ACT UP became known for highly disruptive, unruly, and "performative" modes of protest in public spaces (Brouwer, 2001). Brouwer has called ACT UP the "radical wing of the AIDS social movement" (p. 97), and Elsbach and Sutton (1992) characterized the actions of ACT UP during the late 1980s and early 1990s as often unlawful and illegitimate.

While ACT UP representatives were not the first to testify on AIDS issues before Congress, ACT UP was certainly the most controversial group to do so. The purpose of this study was thus to determine how ACT UP representatives used rhetorical legitimation strategies in their testimony to Congress as part of their larger issues management goal of shaping public policy. As Coombs (1992) argued, issue managers must first establish legitimacy for themselves to gain a right to speak about their issues. Second, the issue must be positioned as a problem of public concern. Finally, issue managers must also work to establish legitimacy for their policy proposals if they want to affect the resolution of the issue (Crable & Vibbert, 1985; Coombs, 1992). Given the "illegitimate" behaviors of ACT UP, the testimony of ACT UP before Congress provides an interesting vantage point from which to examine their legitimation strategies. Thus, the study was guided by the following question:

RQ: How did ACT UP issue managers bolster legitimacy for themselves as issue managers, for their issues, and for their public policy proposals in testimony before Congress?

METHOD

Given the particular importance of legitimacy for activist groups, a better understanding of how radical activists use legitimacy claims are needed. While more than two decades old, ACT UP's congressional testimony provides a unique case in which to examine how radical activists legitimated themselves and participated in public policy formation.

Sample. A search of the LexisNexis Congressional Hearings Digital Collection from 1987 to 2009 revealed that between 1987 and 1990, five individuals explicitly affiliated with ACT UP testified before Congress. Dr. Iris Long, founder of ACT UP's Treatment and Data Committee, testified on April 28, 1988, on the issues of development, testing, and availability of therapeutic drugs for AIDS. On July 20, 1989, two representatives of ACT UP, Martin Delaney and Jim Eigo, testified on HIV/AIDS drug development research. On March 21, 1990, Jim Davis testified on housing needs for people with AIDS, and on August 1, 1990, Tony Davis testified before a House subcommittee on drug availability and research for AIDS infections. The transcripts of their testimony served as the corpus to be examined.

Analysis. The analytic method employed in this study was modeled after Coombs (1992). Coombs suggested that legitimacy bases and tactics can be combined in various ways to create legitimacy strategies, or arguments for the acceptance of a legitimacy claim. The specific method used to examine the testimony of ACT UP was idea analysis. According to Coombs, idea analysis involves identifying what topics are present and what topics are absent in the discourse. The presence and absence of various topics is then used to inform the criticism. Hart and Daughton (2005) posit that idea analysis demands a list of possible topics from which rhetors may choose. Hart and Daughton asserted that idea analysis can help the researcher to: (1) identify what is present in the text and what is not, (2) find rhetorical patterns in the text, and (3) explain the rhetorical "tone" of the text (p. 60). Coombs's typology of legitimacy bases and tactics (see Tables 12–1 and 12–2) represented the possible topics from which issue managers can choose when constructing their legitimacy claims. Idea analysis was used to examine the testimony of ACT UP representatives attempting to establish issue manager, issue, and policy proposal legitimacy.

RESULTS

Despite ACT UP's publicly avowed dedication to extreme tactics and unwillingness to work through "standard channels" (Asen, 2004), by all accounts the behavior of the five who testified before Congress was calm, if occasionally pointed. What follows is a discussion of the legitimation strategies ACT UP used to bolster legitimacy for themselves as issue managers, their issues, and their policy proposals. While a discussion of all of the strategies used by ACT UP is not possible, the subsequent sections highlight the most prominent strategies used in the examined testimony.

ACT UP as an Issue Manager. Coombs (1992) characterized issue manager legitimacy as when "publics perceive the issue manager as having a right to speak on the issue" (p. 105). As ACT UP had engaged in "illegitimate" activities, establishing legitimacy as issue managers before Congress was an important consideration if the group was to have meaningful consequences on policy formation.

Association of Entitlement and Self-Evidence of De-legitimacy. The most common way in which ACT UP legitimated themselves was via establishing a relationship between themselves as the issue manager and the issue itself. Coombs (1992) conceived of entitlement as direct experience with an issue. Tony Davis bolstered legitimacy for ACT UP as an issue manager by repeatedly citing examples of the protests in which the group had engaged. He mentioned protests at the Centers for Disease Control (CDC) and the National Institutes of Health (NIH) to "demand a comprehensive study of the natural history of the syndrome of diseases called AIDS" (U.S. House, 1990, p. 26). On both occasions the group demanded further AIDS research. He cited the reports ACT UP created and submitted to government agencies on AIDS issues. Davis thus made a case for the legitimacy of ACT UP as issue managers through the expertise ACT UP had with the issue. Jim Eigo similarly highlighted the legitimacy of ACT UP by calling attention to ACT UP's status as the nation's "oldest, largest AIDS activist group," which had gained national prominence through its publications, actions and public testimony (U.S. House, 1989, p. 39). Martin Delaney further legitimized ACT UP as an issue manager when he stated that much of the information used by Congress on AIDS "originally came from documents submitted by activists" (U.S. House, 1989, p. 30). Thus, ACT UP's legitimacy as an issue manager stems not only from association with others that have legitimacy (to be addressed shortly), ACT UP's credibility was self-evident. Experience and dedication made ACT UP a legitimate issue manager.

The government and medical community were repeatedly framed as opponents of ACT UP because of their failure to effectively manage the AIDS issue. Coombs (1992) defined de-legitimacy as the "process of bolstering one's own legitimacy by eroding the legitimacy of the opposition" (p. 107). In testimony from Dr. Iris Long, attempts to delegitimize government were complemented by simultaneously bolstering the legitimacy of ACT UP via entitlement. Long bolstered legitimacy for ACT UP as an issue manager by discussing the group's extensive experience with AIDS and ACT UP's history of public advocacy. As an example, Long delegitimized the government by saying "We are outraged at the both the government and medical establishment's handling of the AIDS crisis," and followed with an entitlement statement, "ACT UP's goal is to bring the medical and political issues surrounding AIDS before the public and government officials for dialogue and resolution" (U.S. House, 1988, p. 198).

Both Iris Long and Jim Eigo bolstered legitimacy for ACT UP and simultaneously delegitimized the government by claiming it was government that is being watched by ACT UP, and not vice versa. For example, Long highlighted ACT UP's watchdog status in another de-legitimacy/entitlement strategy, beginning with an entitlement claim, "ACT UP was the first organization to monitor the status of the AIDS treatment program of NIAID (National Institute of Allergies and Infectious Diseases)," and followed with an entitlement/de-legitimacy claim "We've focused media attention on the government's mismanagement of the AIDS crises" (U.S. House, 1988, p. 198). She further stated "ACT UP is the only organization that has consistently monitored the Presidential Commission on the HIV epidemic and advised the Commission on the problems with the clinical trials and other issues" (p. 198). Via these instances of legitimation, Long established ACT UP as an experienced issue manager, and also delegitimized government and its handling of the issue. As such, Long positioned ACT UP as entitled to participate in shaping policy regarding government handling of the epidemic.

Endorsement by Credibility. Coombs (1992) argued that legitimacy for issue managers could be bolstered through association with entities that have credibility. While present in the testimony, this strategy was used with noticeably less frequency. Long associated ACT UP with the AmFAR (the Foundation for AIDS Research) Directory of Experimental Research for AIDS, saying, "we have recently acted as consultants for the AmFAR directory . . . advising them to list trials for opportunistic infections" (U.S. House, 1988, p. 193). At the time, AmFAR was the largest nonprofit research foundation for the study of AIDS. Long thereby bolstered legitimacy for ACT UP via association with a credible research institution. As another example, Tony Davis stated that the Treatment and Data Committee of ACT UP, on which he sat at the time, had "met with researchers, clinicians, and pharmaceutical companies" (U.S. House, 1990, p. 26). Davis thus attempted to position ACT UP's meetings with other institutions as a tacit form of endorsement.

Legitimizing Issues. Coombs (1992) posited that an issue has legitimacy when it is accepted as a public concern. The HIV/AIDS epidemic was nearing its zenith in 1987, the year that ACT UP formed. No member of Congress questioned the legitimacy of AIDS in the testimony as a national issue. The individual testimony of ACT UP representatives, however, was targeted at four different issues, all related to the larger AIDS issue. Accordingly, a significant goal for the issue managers was to establish the individual issues as a matter of concern so as to facilitate their policy recommendations. They did so through use of the legitimacy bases of emotionality and rationality.

Self-Evidence of Emotionality. Coombs (1992) identified emotionality as the "use of emotions to persuade an audience" (p. 107). Given the emotions inherent in the AIDS issue, ACT UP representatives frequently drew upon self-evidence of emotionality to support the claim of legitimacy for their issues. Delaney and Eigo appeared together before Congress to urge the development of parallel-track research designs for clinical drug testing. At the time, AZT was the only FDA approved drug for treatment of HIV/AIDS, and many patients were beginning to outlive the usefulness of the drug only to find that other drugs were still being tested and not publicly available. Delaney used appeals to emotionality for the issue of alternative drug development in parallel-track research, commenting that "Currently, patients are dying every day of the week because they're not permitted access to an anti-infective or antifungal drug that's on the shelf because it hasn't reached licensing" (U.S. House, 1989, p. 29). Eigo recited the names of personal friends who had died either because AZT had ceased to be effective or because they did not have access to drug trials.

Self-Evidence of Rationality. Rationality as a basis for legitimacy entails the use of empirical or logical evidence to persuade (Coombs, 1992). Jim Davis also relied on self-evidence of rationality when he talked about the degrading living conditions at homeless shelters. In his testimony to argue for housing development specific to people with HIV/AIDS, Davis claimed that 80% of men at homeless shelters in New York City were HIV positive, and that there were between 9,000 to 11,000 people in the city with AIDS. Further, he recounted the number of people infected in the United States and how many had died since the disease's outbreak to heighten the importance of the issue.

Tony Davis focused on the problem of only studying White, gay men in AIDS research, when other groups infected with HIV/AIDS were likely to experience opportunistic infections of different types. He talked about the exclusion of women from drug trials: "The trials, as they have been designed, often excluded women of childbearing age as a group, and of course, that is the largest group of women infected by AIDS. So the de facto situation is, women are excluded" (U.S. House, 1990, p. 149). He positioned the need for examination of other populations infected with AIDS, discussing the figures of opportunistic infections in African Americans, women, and children, and the differing rates of AIDS progression within such groups.

Legitimizing Policy Proposals. The ultimate goal of issues management is to affect policy formation in an organization's favor (Crable & Vibbert, 1985). Issue managers must therefore establish legitimacy for their policy recommendations. ACT UP's efforts to legitimate their policy proposals—like efforts to bolster legitimacy for their issues—largely relied upon emotionality and values.

Self-Evidence of Emotionality. Delaney said that many people with AIDS were in a crisis as of July of 1989, given that they have "outlived the usefulness of AZT" (U.S. House, 1989, p. 27) and that there was a drastic shortage of alternative drugs available to them at the time. He bolstered legitimacy for his policy recommendations using the tactic of appeals to emotionality and social values by saying "unless we move rapidly on this parallel track, or the concepts put here today, thousands of people are going to die needlessly" (p. 27). Delaney further noted that ACT UP would not accept a resolution of the issue that "forces patients to treat with AZT until they get sick from the drug itself to qualify for DDI [didanosine, a drug that was used for severe cases]" (p. 29). In other words, Delaney explained that unless the policy recommendations were adopted, those infected with AIDS would be forced to wait until they became seriously ill before receiving treatment. Delaney called for more compassion from government and drug companies in dealing with people who have AIDS-related infections. Compassion and empathy thereby became a substantial portion of the evidence offered to establish parallel-track research on AIDS treatments.

Association with Values. Coombs (1992) suggested that values can be subdivided as *absolute*, "accepted by all people as just and right" (p. 106); or *social*, accepted by the norms of a particular social system. Long, in her testimony against the use of placebos in clinical drug trials for AIDS patients, drew upon widely held social values within the medical community that patients are not to be harmed in scientific research, as well as an absolute social value that children are to be protected at all costs. Long cited the abuse of patients in clinical trials of AIDS medication, saying it is "unethical to introduce bacterial infections in the control group, in a trial which proposes to prevent bacterial infections in a treatment group" (U.S. House, 1988, p. 194). She called the use of placebos unethical and cruel, highlighting the fact that those being treated with placebos are often seriously ill and, in one drug trial, involved mortally ill children, and stated "When AIDS-related complex is a life-threatening condition, a placebo should not be used" (p. 193).

Self-Evidence of Rationality. Long called into question the use of placebos in clinical trials, asking if such behavior is ethically and experimentally justified. She cited repeated examples of studies analyzing the effects of placebos and AZT on AIDS patients failing to produce timely results. She further claimed that information on such trials has not been made available; the results of the drug trials were therefore "not evaluable" (U.S. House, 1988, p. 195). And because the information on drug trials was not available to the public, Long stated that ACT UP had a plan to establish a directory of all the clinical trials going on at the time, with plans to disseminate the information to members of the AIDS community. She argued for the establishment of a national registry, referencing a proposal from ACT UP submitted earlier in 1988 to the Presidential Commission on HIV, and cites research that claimed "informed patients live longer while uninformed patients die" (U.S. House, 1988, p. 195), making a final plea for ACT UP's policy proposal using the legitimacy basis of rationality.

Delaney pointed out that other drugs had been shown to be effective in treating people with AIDS, yet the FDA was unwilling or unable to allow such drugs to become available to the public. Delaney delegitimized the FDA via the tactic of rationality, positioning the FDA as not willing to act on viable drug treatments and criticizing the communication strategies of the agency. He blamed the FDA for sending mixed signals to pharmaceutical companies on the development of parallel-track research. Eigo, advocating for the same proposal, suggested that a parallel track would help researchers gain cleaner data. He further argued the development of a parallel track would also help drug companies through shorter trials, cleaner data, good community relations, and even free publicity.

DISCUSSION

Just as corporations, activist groups must strive to be "the good organization communicating well" (Heath & Palenchar, 2009, p. 2010). Considerably more research is required to further public relations' understanding of how activists legitimate themselves in different forums. While this study focused on but one organization's legitimation strategies in an isolated set of inter-related incidents, there are nonetheless implications that can be derived from this study that may serve as heuristics for future research.

The Dual Challenge of Legitimacy. The strains that lead to the formation of activist groups results in confrontations between activists and their targets as to who has the better definition of a problem and recommended solutions (Heath & Palenchar, 2009). Activists and their targets perform the "legitimacy dance" (Smith & Ferguson, 2010, p. 401), where each party struggles to be recognized as the authoritative spokesperson on the issue. This "dance" becomes all the more complex when organizations risk developing an unfavorable public image as a consequence of illegitimate behavior. Illegitimate actions lead to media coverage—an essential power resource for grassroots activist groups (Sommerfeldt, 2013). But media coverage of illegitimate actions has the dual effect of gaining support from some publics while simultaneously alienating others. Given this, activists must work to "accentuate the benefits of illegitimate actions" (Elsbach & Sutton, 1992, p. 712) in future communications.

Questioning the legitimacy of other organizations or institutions is the raison d'être of activist groups, but in so doing the group must concurrently seek to bolster legitimacy for itself, which in this case was accomplished via entitlement strategies. The pairing of entitlement with delegitimization strategies makes intuitive sense. Rhetors like Iris Long called the legitimacy of government into question and grounded ACT UP as an entitled, and therefore legitimate, issue manager. Activists have the "power of exposé," or the strategy of calling some attribute of their target into question (Heath & Palenchar, 2009, p. 167). In this case, ACT UP representatives called into question the legitimacy of the very body before which they were testifying.

This analysis thus not only provides insight into what ACT UP as the rhetor attempted to convey of ACT UP's credibility and character, but also revealed ACT UP's view of their audience—the "second persona" (cf. Black, 1970) in rhetorical discourse. While rhetors speak about their own persona in the process of addressing an issue, we must also consider how rhetors think about and portray their audiences in legitimation discourses. How legitimation efforts are interpreted and acted upon are likely the result of what "receivers see as the intended second persona and whether they are willing or able to accept that persona" (Heath, 1994, p. 164). Whether members of the House accepted the persona of deficient issue managers is unknown, but if radical activists—or other organizations—are not effective in crafting an accurate second persona for targets in issue management efforts (in this case a delegitimized persona for government), we could expect a less successful outcome than that was achieved by the strategies used by ACT UP in particular and the AIDS movement at large.

Despite the fact that many at the time deemed ACT UP's behavior to be illegitimate, the testimony suggests that ACT UP representatives saw ACT UP's investment in the issue and their attempts to bring public attention to it as self-evidence of their legitimacy as issue managers. Whereas most organizations seek to acquire and maintain legitimacy via adopting structures and practices consistent with social expectations (Metzler, 2001), ACT UP built its reputation as a group unwilling to adopt "legitimate tactics." Asen (2004) called their dedication to extreme tactics as a "principled refusal to accept as settled standard ways of debating health issues" (p. 192). Asen partly attributed ACT UP's success in achieving policy reforms to their illegitimate behaviors, and suggested they might not have been as effective should they have "sought redress through standard channels" (p. 192). Indeed, Asen went so far as to suggest that the act of participating in congressional testimony approached co-optation, as testifying before Congress meant ACT UP had to abide by the rules of the institution. That said, ACT UP representatives themselves appeared to appreciate the irony of their testimony. In an article published shortly after his testimony, Eigo (1990) wrote, "several [ACT UP] members have become players in the AIDS bureaucracy—an odd position for people who consider themselves radicals" (p. 378).

The adoption of visible structures and practices that conform to social norms can serve to "mask or distract attention from controversial activities" (Elsbach & Sutton, 1992, p. 700). Consequently, ACT UP could have attempted to decouple its past behavior from its testimony within the highly visible and socially legitimate forum of the House of Representatives. Yet on several occasions ACT UP issue managers drew upon the organization's past activities (illegitimate or not) and stated the organization deserved credit for their actions because of the goals achieved. In the eyes of ACT UP, consistently demanding change positioned the group as a legitimate issue manager whose policy recommendations deserved to be heard—irrespective of the organization's past behavior.

Recent work has questioned whether communicative ideals like symmetry and collaboration should be considered core values or best practices in public relations, suggesting that concepts like "agonism" (Ganesh & Zoller, 2012) should be considered as ethical and normative forms of public relations. While the ethicality of some of ACT UP's actions is debatable, ACT UP's frequent references to past illegitimate behaviors pose an interesting dichotomy for praxis. Publics external to radical activist groups may evaluate their actions as illegitimate, thereby resulting in a "legitimacy gap" between the group and the publics from whom activists require support. Yet, for radical activist groups extreme tactics are simultaneously indicative of proactive attempts to gain support from publics for particular courses of action and for their organization. However, instead of using rhetorical strategies to rebuild organizational legitimacy following illegitimate actions, activists may instead try to rhetorically legitimate their actions by explaining that such actions were actually responsible (a focus of actional legitimation, cf. Boyd, 2000) despite prevailing attitudes to the contrary. Illegitimate actions may actually serve as a rhetorical resource in future legitimation efforts. Yet, as Ashforth and Gibbs (1990) noted, "The protestation of legitimacy will be greatest for organizations with low legitimacy (as perceived by constituents)" (p. 185). ACT UP's repeated attempts to legitimate past activities may then be interpreted as efforts to position those activities as points of pride and to (re) build a damaged reputation. Activist legitimation can perhaps be understood through the lenses of both proactive actional legitimation (Boyd, 2000) and reactive, post-crisis image restoration (Benoit, 1997).

Legitimation Strategies Reveal Rhetorical Resources. According to Black (1970), "discourses contain tokens of their authors . . . [and] are, directly or in transmuted form, the external signs of internal states" (p. 110). Examination of the strategies used to bolster legitimacy for ACT UP and its issues reveal the resources available to issue managers in the legitimation process. Indeed, as Coombs (1992) found in his own study of the congressional testimony of a hunger task force, the issue managers in question relied almost exclusively on the strategy of self-evidence of credibility to bolster their legitimacy. In the present case, ACT UP's representatives generally did not seek to bolster their personal credibility as issue managers. More commonly, the accomplishments, entitlements, credibility, and charisma of ACT UP as a whole were used to bolster the legitimacy of issue managers, which buttressed their arguments for ACT UP's right to have a seat at the decision-making table. Coombs (1992) claimed the issue managers in his study failed at establishing legitimacy for themselves due to overreliance on the strategy of credibility. If the issue managers had more available resources from which to legitimate themselves, Coombs claimed the outcome may have been different. While it is difficult to assess precisely how successful ACT UP was in legitimating themselves as issue managers, all of the policies for which they advocated were eventually adopted. For activist groups and nonprofits, the implication of this may be to rely less on the personal credibility of individual rhetors (although the ethos of individual rhetors is certainly not without import in legitimation discourse) and more on the entitlement of the organization to speak on the issue.

Some of the legitimation strategies used by ACT UP are tried and true ways of effective rhetorical persuasion. To legitimate their issues and policy recommendations, ACT UP drew upon bases of emotion and rationality. The pairing is a classic one: "Emotion gains attention; evidence and reasoning give an issue permanence" (Heath & Palenchar, 2009, p. 176). The use facts to support the legitimacy of the issues for which they advocated were natural extensions of the emotionality bases. As the larger AIDS issue was a legitimate national concern, the issue managers needed to provide support for the subsidiary issues of drug development and housing for AIDS patients. Rational argument about how these ancillary issues were symptomatic of larger issue imbued them with some level of legitimacy. Statistics and verifiable information that supported the anecdotal use of emotionality in stories of human suffering and death worked well to establish the issues and proposed resolutions to those issues as legitimate.

However, the absence of the other legitimation strategies is notable. The various AIDS issues for which these representatives were testifying were well developed given the issues had reached critical status and entered the policy development phase (cf. Crable & Vibbert, 1985). Emotions and values thus served to strengthen proposed policy solutions. However, absent from the legitimacy bases used to support ACT UP as issue managers, their issues, or policies, were tradition, bureaucracy, and symbols. The absence of these bases makes intuitive sense given the nature of ACT UP as an organization. An activist group with radical tendencies like ACT UP could make no claims of tradition, nor could bureaucracy or symbols be used as forms of support. ACT UP earned its stripes publicly abjuring accepted rules, laws, and statues, and had violated public and religious symbols such as desecrating communion wafers during a mass at St. Patrick's Cathedral. Further, the group had few public endorsements on which to draw. The omission of these legitimacy bases may be attributed to the type of organization, their mission, and past behaviors, and therefore suggests viable strategies for organizations other than activists. Like activists, nonprofit and civil society organizations must compete for a limited pool of resources, and therefore must position themselves as the most effective manager of the issue they support (Sommerfeldt, 2013). Drawing on bases such as tradition and symbols may be effective legitimation strategies for organizations without ACT UP's "illegitimacy baggage" of radical activist groups.

CONCLUSION

A goal of this chapter was to make the relationship between legitimacy and issues management clearer. Public relations scholars have for too long restricted the study of organizational legitimacy to crisis communication. Interpretive frameworks such as the image restoration typology (Benoit, 1997) have been applied in countless studies of organizational reactions to crises, yet we know very little about the legitimation strategies used by organizations—corporate and activist, for-profit, and nonprofit—as they engage in proactive issues management. Common sense dictates that public relations scholars should be just as concerned with how organizations build support for issues and prevent crises as with how organizations recover from legitimacy gaps. It is important to study the range of legitimation messages offered by activists and their target organizations as these messages will potentially shape public perceptions of issues as they progress through their lifecycle. Moreover, as the study outlined in this chapter has demonstrated, for radical activists the line between legitimizing issues and recovering from legitimacy crises is a blurred one worthy of further explication. If establishing and maintaining organizational legitimacy is indeed at the center of public relations practice, scholars and practitioners should have a better grasp of the intricacies of legitimacy as a theoretical construct and what it means for successful public relations and issues management practice. This need is further heightened for activist and nonprofit organizations that rely on the salience of their issue for continued viability.

REFERENCES

Asen, R. (2004). A discourse theory of citizenship. *Quarterly Journal of Speech, 90*(2), 189–211.

Ashforth, B. E., & Gibbs, B. W. (1990). The double-edge of organizational legitimation. *Organization Science, 1*(2), 177–194.

Benoit, W. L. (1997). Image repair discourse and crisis communication. *Public Relations Review, 23*(2), 177–186.

Black, E. (1970). The second persona. *Quarterly Journal of Speech, 56*, 109–118.

Boyd, J. (2000). Actional legitimation: No crisis necessary. *Journal of Public Relations Research, 12*, 341–353.

Brouwer, D. C. (2001). ACT-ing UP in Congressional hearings. In R. Asen & D. C. Brouwer (Eds.), *Counterpublics and the state* (pp. 87–109). Albany: State University of New York Press.

Bruning, S. D., & Ledingham, J. A. (1999). Relationships between organizations and publics: Development of a multi-dimensional organization–public relationship scale. *Public Relations Review, 25*(2), 157–170.

Coombs, W. T. (1992). The failure of the task force on food assistance: A case study of the role of legitimacy in issue management. *Journal of Public Relations Research, 4*(2), 101–122.

Crable, R. E., & Vibbert, S. L. (1985). Managing issues and influencing public policy. *Public Relations Review, 11*(2), 3–16.

de Bussy, N. (2008). Applying stakeholder thinking to public relations: An integrated approach to identifying relationships that matter. In B. Ruler, A. T. Vercic, & D. Vercic (Eds.), *Public relations metrics: Research and evaluation* (pp. 282–300). New York, NY: Taylor & Francis.

Derville, T. (2005). Radical activist tactics: Overturning public relations conceptualizations. *Public Relations Review, 31*(4), 527–533.

Dowling, J., & Pfeffer, J. (1975). Organizational legitimacy: Social values and organizational behavior. *Pacific Sociological Review, 18*(1), 122–136.

Eigo, J. J. (1990). Expedited drug approval procedures: Perspective from an AIDS activist. *Food Drug Cosmetic Law Journal, 45*, 377–384.

Elsbach, K. D., & Sutton, R. I. (1992). Acquiring organizational legitimacy through illegitimate actions: A marriage of institutional and impression management theories. *Academy of Management Journal, 35*(4), 699–738.

Epstein, E. M. (1972). The historical enigma of corporate legitimacy. *California Law Review, 60*, 1701–1717.

Ganesh, S., & Zoller, H. M. (2012). Dialogue, activism, and democratic social change. *Communication Theory, 22*(1), 66–91.

Gower, K. K. (2006). Public relations research at the crossroads. *Journal of Public Relations Research, 18*(2), 177–190.

Grunig, J.E., & Huang, Y. (2000). From organizational effectiveness to relationship indicators: Antecedents of relationships, public relations strategies, and relationship outcomes. In J.A. Ledingham & S.D. Bruning (Eds.), *Public relations as relationship management* (pp. 23–54). Mahwah, NJ: Lawrence Erlbaum Associates.

Habermas, J. (1979). *Communication and the evolution of society.* Boston. MA: Beacon Press.

Haines, H.H. (1988). *Black radicals and the civil rights mainstream, 1954–1970.* Knoxville: University of Tennessee Press.

Hart, R.P., & Daughton, S. M. (2005). *Modern rhetorical criticism* (3rd ed.). Boston, MA: Allyn and Bacon.

Hearit, K.M. (1995). "Mistakes were made": Organizations, apologia, and crises of social legitimacy. *Communication Studies, 46*(1), 1–17.

Heath, R.L. (1994). *Management of corporate communication: From interpersonal contacts to external affairs.* Hillsdale, NJ: Lawrence Erlbaum Associates.

Heath, R.L. (2006). A rhetorical theory approach to issues management. In C.H. Botan & V. Hazleton (Eds.), *Public relations theory II* (pp. 31–50). Mahwah, NJ: Lawrence Erlbaum Associates.

Heath, R.L., & Palenchar, M.J. (2009). *Strategic issues management: Organizations and public policy challenges* (2nd ed.). Thousand Oaks, CA: Sage.

Jones, B.L., & Chase, W.H. (1979). Managing public issues. *Public Relations Review, 5*(2), 3–23.

Liu, B.F. (2007). President Bush's major post-Katrina speeches: Enhancing image repair discourse theory applied to the public sector. *Public Relations Review, 33*(1), 40–48.

Metzler, M.S. (2001). The centrality of organizational legitimacy to public relations practice. In R.L. Heath (Ed.), *Handbook of public relations* (pp. 321–333). Thousand Oaks, CA: Sage.

Pfeffer, J., & Salancik, G. (1978). *The external control of organizations: A resource dependence perspective.* New York, NY: Harper & Row.

Pratt, C.B. (2001). Issues management: The paradox of the 40-year U.S. tobacco wars. In R.L. Heath (Ed.), *Handbook of public relations* (pp. 335–346). Thousand Oaks, CA: Sage.

Sethi, S.P. (1977). *Advocacy advertising and large corporations: Social conflict, big business image, the news media, and public policy.* Lexington, MA: Lexington Books.

Shoemaker, P.J. (1982). The perceived legitimacy of deviant political groups: Two experiments on media effects. *Communication Research, 9*(2), 249–286.

Smith, M.F., & Ferguson, D.P. (2010). Activism 2.0. In R.L. Heath (Ed.), *The SAGE handbook of public relations* (pp. 395–408). Thousand Oaks, CA: Sage.

Suchman, M.C. (1995). Managing legitimacy: Strategic and institutional approaches. *Academy of Management Review, 20*(3), 571–610.

Sommerfeldt, E.J. (2013). Online power resource management: Activist resource mobilization, communication strategy, and organizational structure. *Journal of Public Relations Research, 25*(4), 347–367.

U.S. House. (1988). Subcommittee on Human Resources and Intergovernmental Relations of the Committee on Government Operations. *Therapeutic drugs for AIDS: Development, testing, and availability.* 100th Cong., 2nd sess., 28 and 29 April.

U.S. House. (1989). Subcommittee on Health and the Environment of the Committee on Energy and Commerce. *AIDS issues (Part 2).* 101st Cong., 1st sess., 20 July and 18 September.

U.S. House. (1990). Subcommittee on Human Resources and Intergovernmental Relations of the Committee on Government Operations. *Drugs for opportunistic infections in persons with HIV disease.* 101st Cong., 2nd sess., 1 August.

13 The Cape Wind Debate

Framing by Energy Activist Groups and Frame Salience for Active Online Audiences

Ben Benson and Bryan H. Reber

Energy independence, foreign oil supplies, and sustainable energy are routine news topics. In the past decade, the mere mention of "sustainability" has increased tenfold in the *New York Times* (Tolland, 2010). Businesses are designing products and energy projects that appeal to environmental consumer values (Peattie, 1999).

The value behind energy proposals, legislation, or feel-good thinking, however, depends on its effectiveness. Public opinion polling has shown American citizens value clean energy and believe the government and businesses should invest in renewable energy technology (Bolsen & Cook, 2008). Politicians have called for energy independence since the global energy crisis in the 1970s caused major structural changes in our energy consumption (Donavan, 2009). Solar, wind, biomass, and geothermal energy are all of growing importance to the American electrical grid. According to the U.S. Department of Energy, 24 states set binding goals for a certain percentage of energy to come from renewable sources; several more states have passed nonbinding renewable energy targets. Global competition has further encouraged American policymakers and businesses to promote growth in sustainable energy sectors, before other nations outpace the United States in clean energy capabilities. However, past research has shown our willingness to engage in environmental behavior depends on our surrounding social context (Haller & Hadler, 2008), and Americans may differ from citizens of other countries by being less likely to engage in pro-environmental behavior (Cordano, Welcomer, Scherer, Pradenas, & Parada, 2010). In addition, people can feel involved in environmental behavior without actually acting upon their beliefs (Lubell, 2004).

Frequently, renewable energy projects face significant opposition when they are proposed in a community. Opponents of such projects are often-times labeled NIMBYs, an acronym for not-in-my-backyard. NIMBYs are people who support renewable energy projects, with the caveat that those projects are not installed near them.

This chapter examines communication surrounding the Cape Wind Energy Project, a proposed offshore wind farm in Massachusetts. In 2001, after the project's inception, the Alliance to Protect Nantucket Sound formed to halt the construction of Cape Wind. Clean Power Now, a Massachusetts-based group, began in 2003 to support Cape Wind's passage. These groups engaged in almost a decade of public debate with state policymakers, Massachusetts residents, businesses, utility companies, lawyers, and federal officials.

This research examined online news comments and compared them to the activist groups' messaging to measure public opinion about the Cape Wind Energy Project.

LITERATURE REVIEW

Activist Groups, Public Opinion, and Social Movements. Activist groups play important roles in opposing and advocating for public projects and shaping public discourse. According to Coombs and Holladay (2010), activist groups are motivated by their members who perceive themselves to hold the moral high ground by taking a stand (Heath & Palenchar, 2009).

Activist groups have the ability to work with businesses and government or stand fully against them (Dozier & Lauzen, 2000; Stokes & Rubin, 2010). However, activist groups have been criticized for colluding with businesses or governments, spurring stakeholders to say the groups have betrayed their mission (Coombs & Holladay, 2010).

In opposition to Grunig's excellence theory (Dozier, Grunig, & Grunig, 2001), which proposes two-way symmetrical communication as normative, activist groups may best achieve their goals by avoiding symmetrical communication. Symmetrical communication purportedly leads to a win-win situation for both the public and organization (Grunig, 1993; Grunig, 2006). Critical theory suggests, however, a symmetrical worldview does not adequately offset the resource disparity between corporations and activist publics, and, instead, may lead to corporations exerting a hegemonic effect over their constituencies (Dozier & Lauzen, 2000; Roper, 2005).

Dozier and Lauzen (2000) say a paradox exists in understanding the normative practice of public relations between organizations and activist groups. Activist groups often do not have the resources to undertake two-way symmetrical public relations, and organizations have trained public relations professionals whose role is to overcome activists. The win-win zone may not exist in this case, and irreconcilable differences are not accommodated. Coombs and Holladay (2010) say corporations tend to favor only their primary stakeholders and activist organizations have to be mindful of all their members. A basic difference is that activist groups view their cause as noble, and corporations view activists as obstacles.

Public relations scholarship has room to expand its research on social movements, examining how ideas begin at the micro-level and grow to the macro-level. Sine and Lee (2009) explain that social movements can change and create markets and foster entrepreneurial activity. Social movements challenge the status quo and promote a new set of assumptions, norms, values, and regulations that shape the opportunities available for entrepreneurs. Based on a state-by-state wind energy study from 1978 to 1992, environmental group membership and activism played a large part in determining the development of a viable wind energy sector. Activist groups framed the issue as the moral high ground and vilified traditional energy sources. The environmental social movement also lobbied state governments and advocated for increased wind energy economic activity. Through this, the social movements changed the normative entrepreneurial activity for a state's energy production.

Renewable Energy Is Great, But Not in My Backyard. Gallup polls show that a majority of Americans want more renewable energy projects pursued at a national level (Jones, 2009); however, these projects often conflict with people at a local or regional level. Researchers and journalists define this situation as the "Not In My Backyard" (NIMBY) effect. NIMBY projects have high public approval ratings from the overall population, but face staunch local opposition. Robert Cialdini cites two major reasons for NIMBY effects (Rosenthal, 2011). Public projects tend to encounter tough local opposition when the project is at odds with that publics' normative environment and behavior. Further, people respond more actively to immediate rewards or consequences than those that are deferred.

Previous research has shown that opposition to local wind farms is related to governance, technology, landscape aesthetics, issues of participation, and power inequalities (Ellis, Barry, & Robinson, 2007). Devine-Wright's (2005) research has shown that people and communities exhibit better attitudes toward wind farms when they are involved in the project or have part ownership. Local involvement, in either political or economic terms, has a positive effect on public perceptions (Ellis, Barry, & Robinson, 2007). Robert Thayer and Carla Freeman (1987) found that supporters of wind energy who lived further away from wind turbines identified with the pro-environment symbolism of wind turbines. However, people who lived closer to wind farms found them to appear more unnatural and less aesthetically pleasing on the landscape.

Framing Theory and Public Relations. Framing theory expands upon psychological and sociological concepts and theories, combining them with communication research. It introduces a psychological component to agenda setting, especially second-level agenda setting. Second-level agenda setting asserts that the news media can influence how people think about a topic by selecting and highlighting salient attributes of an issue, while ignoring other attributes (Kiousis, Mitrook, Wu, & Seltzer, 2006). Gamson and Modigliani (1989) defined a frame as a central organizing idea that makes sense of an issue and suggests the involved stakes. Goffman (1974) defined a frame as a "schemata of interpretation." Pan and Kosicki (1993) stated that news media frames are a "cognitive device used in information encoding, interpreting, and retrieving. . . . Framing, therefore, may be studied as a strategy of constructing and processing news discourse as a characteristic of the discourse itself" (p. 57). Participation in the public discussion precipitates framing; simply by being involved in a discussion, people and organizations frame issues (Pan & Kosicki, 2003).

Public relations practitioners frame messages by either highlighting certain aspects of information or withholding certain points (Zoch & Molleda, 2006). Entman (1993) explained how public relations uses frames: "Frames select and call attention to particular aspects of the reality described, which logically means that frames simultaneously direct attention away from other aspects" (p. 54). Framing involves specific selection and salience of an issue. Framing highlights a particular attribute of a problem or solution, a recommendation, and tries to create a causal relationship among problems (Entman, 1993).

Hallahan (1999) identified seven models of framing used in public relations, including situations, attributes, choices, actions, issues, responsibility, and news. The framing choices of attributes, issues, and news are most relevant to this Cape Wind research. Attribute framing involves accentuating objects and information and focusing a frame on a central position. Issues framing explains how groups and stakeholders vie with one another to explain the same situation in their own terms. News framing can measure how successful public relations practitioners or activist groups are at communicating their preferred frames to the news media and the public. News framing that reaches a news outlet or reporter has an increased chance to reach a larger audience (Hallahan, 1999).

Activist groups inherently frame issues by participating in public discourse and communicating with the media, their members, policymakers, and other publics. According to Snow and Benford (2000), activist groups engage in framing with collective action frames. Collective action frames provide an interpretive frame for events and problems and seek to mobilize stakeholders (Snow & Benford, 1988). Snow and Benford (1988) said activists' collective action frames encompass three "framing tasks" to resolve an issue.

Collective action frames can be broadly organized into a "master algorithm" (Snow & Benford, 2000). Master frames are broad enough to connect social movements (Snow & Benford, 2000; Luther & Miller, 2005). Master frames are supported by sub frames, which are claims that support the master frames (Reber & Berger, 2005). The effectiveness of master frames can be evaluated by how well the frames resonate with and help motivate specific publics (Snow & Benford, 2000). The ability for a frame to resonate with an audience depends upon the frame's credibility and relative salience. Snow and Benford (2000) said an activist movement's ability to mobilize stakeholders depends on how well it aligns its beliefs, ideas, and values with its stakeholders.

News media help activist groups communicate their goals to the public. By supporting activist groups and amplifying their message to a larger audience, news media increase the possibility of changing social structure or public policy (McCluskey, 2008). Additionally, news media tend to give more positive coverage to activist groups that lack significant media or personnel resources (McCluskey, 2008). Under increasing media clutter, activist groups have turned to online strategies as well to communicate directly with their publics. Online communication can reflect the nature of the group as a whole (Mabry, 2003).

This study posed three research questions:

RQ1: What are the pro- (Clean Power Now) and anti- (Alliance to Protect Nantucket Sound) wind energy activist groups' frames?

RQ2: What pro- and anti-wind energy activist frames are most repeated by active publics?

RQ3: Are any frames found within news comments recommended significantly more or less by online readers?

METHOD

When this research began, Clean Power Now had more than 70 news releases on its website, while the Alliance to Protect Nantucket Sound website contained nearly 300. These releases dated back to Clean Power Now's and the Alliance to Protect Nantucket Sound's beginnings in 2003 and 2001, respectively. News releases were chosen to create a master coding mechanism. News releases were selected because they are distributed to media outlets with the intent to garner media attention and frame the resulting news story (Zoch & Molleda, 2006). Organizations strategically craft information subsidies in a manner to guide public perception and achieve a certain outcome (Hallahan, 1999).

Only the most recent news releases were coded to ensure relevance and salience to activists and to maintain a similar sample size between organizations. Twenty news releases from March 2008 to June 2010 were downloaded from the Clean Power Now website. Twenty-six news releases from February 2009 to June 2010 were downloaded from the Alliance to Protect Nantucket Sound website. These date ranges also aligned with the content analysis in the second part of the study. The master code sheet was then developed from this sample of news releases based on a qualitative analysis. The code sheet was designed to capture the activist groups' master frames about the Cape Wind Energy Project and wind energy. The master frames were identified from collected news releases and sorted according to the framing categories developed by Stephens, Rand and Melnick (2009). Stephens and colleagues constructed the wind energy frames based on Luhmann's social theory of ecological communication (Luhmann, 1989).

The six risk and benefit categories include economic, environmental, technical, political, aesthetic, and health and safety (Stephens et al., 2009). Within each of the six categories, the supporting sub frames were qualitatively identified and added to the master coding sheet. Frequency of master frames and sub frames was not considered; every master frame and sub frame found within the news releases was added to the master coding mechanism.

Clean Power Now's wind master frames highlight Cape Wind's benefits, whereas the Alliance to Protect Nantucket Sound's master frames highlight the risks. The resulting coding mechanism organized the activist groups' master frames according to the six risk and benefit categories.

In the second phase of research, news comments from the *Boston Globe* website were content analyzed. The analysis used the coding mechanism developed from the activist groups' news releases.

The *Boston Globe* was chosen because it has the highest online readership of any Massachusetts newspaper and archives its comments along with its online news articles. According to the 2008 Newspaper Audience Ratings Report (Meo, 2008), the *Boston Globe* had 759,000 unique online readers each week. Including both print and online newspaper editions, the *Boston Globe* reached 44% of the designated market audience. Based on the reports in its media kit, the *Boston Globe* had more than 200 million page views each month.

A sample of news articles was drawn by searching for the *Boston Globe*'s online archives between January 2010 and June 2010. This encompasses the most salient news coverage. A search of "Cape Wind" yielded 140 results. A secondary search of "wind energy" and "Nantucket Sound" yielded 58 results, all were duplicated from the first search. Out of the 140 articles, 34 news articles and 4 opinion pieces were selected to gather the entire sample of news comments after duplicates and irrelevant articles were discarded.

The 38 selected news articles and their corresponding comments were downloaded. The first article in the sample, "A decision in sight on Cape Wind dispute," was published on Jan. 5, 2010, and the last article, "Six groups file first suit to halt wind farm," was published on June 26, 2010. Comments published to these articles after November 24, 2010, were not included in the sample. The quantity of comments on news articles ranged from only three to 305. In total, 38 news articles and editorials generated 1,665 comments. Each article averaged 44 comments.

The *Boston Globe* deletes comments with swear words, hate speech, spam, personal attacks, libel, and advertisements. The *Boston Globe* reserves the right to edit or delete comments, or ban the author of the comment altogether. This comment policy should make online comments less toxic and combative compared to a fully open, anonymous comment policy (Gsell, 2009). The final sample of 1,665 comments does not include comments that violated the newspaper's comment policy.

Online comments were then coded and assigned categories based on the master coding mechanism. The arguments identified in the news comment section were matched to the frames developed by the activist groups. Comments from supporters of Cape Wind were coded according to Clean Power

Now's coding mechanism. Opposition comments were coded according to the Alliance to Protect Nantucket Sound's coding mechanism.

The *Boston Globe* allows readers to "recommend" a news comment. The number of recommendations to a comment was recorded. Online readers do not have to be an active commenter or registered on the *Boston Globe* website to recommend a comment, so recommendations can measure latent public opinion about a specific comment.

The entire sample of online comments was coded using the coding mechanisms developed from the activist group frames. Master and sub frames used by the activist groups were found in 493 comments. Comments with frames made up 29.6% of the total sample of 1,665 comments.

To ensure the reliability of the coding mechanism, a trained coder separately coded 396 comments from nine articles, corresponding to 23.7% of the total comments. An intercoder reliability measurement was used on each of the six categories, similar to Stephens et al. (2009). The indices used to measure intercoder reliability were simple agreement and Scott's pi index. An acceptable Scott's pi value is above 0.50 (Scott, 1955) or as low as 0.45 (Riffe, Lacy, & Fico, 1998). The lowest reliability measurement had a Scott's pi index of 0.75. All other Scott's pi values were above 0.80.

RESULTS

Identifying Activist Groups' Master Frames. Clean Power Now's and the Alliance to Protect Nantucket Sound's master and sub frames were qualitatively coded according to the six benefit and risk categories defined by Stephens and colleagues (2006). Supporting sub frames were sorted based on these categories, or master frames. Frequency of master frames and sub frames was not taken into account to answer this research question. Every identified master frame and sub frame was included in the analysis.

Frames Clean Power Now Used in Its News Releases. Clean Power Now's economic master frames concerned *long-term cost savings* and the *creation of jobs*. Environmental master frames related to *Cape Wind's clean energy production*. Health and safety frames claimed *Cape Wind would not disrupt navigation* and *promotes a healthier living environment*. Beneficial political master frames were about *energy independence*, especially in regard to *reducing consumption of foreign oil*. Finally, the technical benefits were about *wind energy promoting a clean energy future*. Clean Power Now did not use aesthetic frames.

Frames the Alliance to Protect Nantucket Sound Used in Its News Releases. The Alliance to Protect Nantucket Sound's economic master frames claimed *Cape Wind will increase electricity prices* and *result in a loss of jobs*. Environmental risk frames said the *project would harm wildlife* and *destroy the* *natural environment.* Health and safety risk master frames claimed *the project would disrupt naval and aerial navigation.* Political risk master frames claimed *Cape Wind received excessive public subsidies* and *would privatize Nantucket Sound.* Aesthetic master frames concerned *Cape Wind negatively affecting the scenery and "natural beauty" of Nantucket Sound.* The Alliance reinforced its aesthetic risk frame by often referring to Nantucket Sound as a *"national treasure."* The Alliance did not use any technical risk frames.

Identifying Frames from the *Boston Globe*'s Online Comments. The content analysis of the 1,665 online comments resulted in a final sample of 493 (29.6%) comments containing frames. Comments were split between Clean Power Now, 41.4% (*n* = 204) and the Alliance to Protect Nantucket Sound 58.6% (*n* = 289). The final sample included comments written by 293 *Boston Globe* users with an average of 1.66 comments each. Most *Boston Globe* users wrote only one comment; 63 had more than one comment in the sample. Only four users exceeded 10 comments. Of those four users, three opposed and one supported Cape Wind.

Analysis of Activist Group Frames Found in Online Comments. The Alliance to Protect Nantucket Sound opposition frames had 289 comments. Nearly half contained frames relating to economic risk (47.4%; *n* = 137). Within the total sample of opposition frames, 44.3% (*n* = 128) contained the master frame "Cape Wind increases electrical costs" and 20.8% (*n* = 60) argued Cape Wind could more than double electricity costs. Fewer comments (9.0%; *n* = 26) said that wind energy was more expensive than other energies. The topic of jobs was less salient than electricity costs in the economic risk category; few comments said Cape Wind would result in a loss of jobs (3.1%, *n* = 9), of tourism jobs (0.3%, *n* = 1), or of fishing industry jobs (0.3%; *n* = 1).

Nearly one-fifth of the opposition comments contained an environmental risk frame (19.7%; *n* = 57). However, only 10.0% (*n* = 29) of the comments said Cape Wind would damage the environment. Few comments said Cape Wind would destroy the sea floor (0.7%; *n* = 2) or that dredging would have a negative impact on wildlife. More environmental risk frames pointed out that Cape Wind poses the risk of an oil spill (4.2%; *n* = 12) and could endanger wildlife (11.4%; *n* = 33). Only one comment (0.3%) said Cape Wind is a risk to whales, while more comments (6.6%; *n* = 19) said it is a risk to birds. Only two comments (0.7%) said Cape Wind may not comply with the Migratory Bird Treaty Act.

The health and safety risk frames were found in 14.2% (*n* = 41) of the sample. Most comments in this category said that Cape Wind would be a navigation hazard (13.8%; *n* = 40), and they often specified the risk to ships and ferries (5.2%; *n* = 15) or aircraft (9.3%; *n* =27).

The political risk category consisted of 36.0% (*n* = 104) of the sample. Many of the political risk comments (27.0%; *n* = 78) concerned the public subsidies for Cape Wind. Fewer political comments (12.5%; n = 36) indicated that Cape Wind privatizes Nantucket Sound or a private developer is using Nantucket Sound at the public's expense (6.6%; n = 19).

One-quarter of the comments (25.6%; n = 74) contained frames in the aesthetic risk category. Many of these said that Cape Wind threatened the beauty and scenery of Cape Cod (18.7%; n = 54). A few comments (2.8%; n = 8) said Cape Wind would be larger than Manhattan. Eight percent (n = 23) of the comments claimed Cape Wind would negatively affect Native American tribes and interfere with their cultural and religious ceremonies (4.5%; n =13).

The Clean Power Now advocacy frames had a final sample size of 204 comments. Almost one-fifth (18.6%; n = 38) of the frames were within the technical benefit category. Most of these frames (15.2%; n = 31) said Cape Wind establishes a clean energy future, while 4.4% (n = 9) said Cape Wind establishes Massachusetts as a national wind energy leader.

More than one-tenth (13.7%; n = 28) of the advocacy comments noted economic benefits. A few mentioned the long-term cost savings (7.4%; n = 15), and several comments said Cape Wind would ensure price stability (1.5%; n = 3) or that wind energy used "free" fuel (1.0%; n = 2). About the same number of comments claimed Cape Wind would create jobs (6.4%; n = 13); a few referred specifically to wind energy jobs (1.5%; n = 3).

The most common advocacy frames concerned environmental benefits (62.7%; n = 128). More than half noted wind energy produces clean or sustainable energy (50.5%; n = 103) and 19.1% (n = 39) said Cape Wind avoids the risk of oil spills. Fewer comments claimed wind energy reduces carbon emissions (6.9%; n = 14) or addresses global climate change (3.4%; n = 7).

Fewer than one-tenth (9.3%; n = 19) of the comments were in the health and safety benefit category. Most of these (7.4%; n = 15) said Cape Wind would not be a navigation hazard to airplanes or ships. Fewer (2.9%; n = 6) said Cape Wind could decrease health problems, mainly related to respiratory problems, or that it would lead to a healthier environment (2.5%; n = 5).

Political benefit frames were the second largest category (23.5%; n = 48) within advocacy comments. Every comment in the political benefit category related to energy independence (23.5%; n = 48). About half of these specifically mentioned reducing America's dependence on foreign oil (13.2%; n = 27), but only 2.5% (n = 5) said Cape Wind would alleviate the price volatility of foreign fossil fuels.

In the entire sample of 493 comments, the debate over Cape Wind was largely framed by two categories. Even though opposition comments outnumbered supporter comments, the environmental benefit (26.0%; n = 128) and economic risk (27.8%; n = 137) categories were practically equal in the combined sample. The environmental benefit category was dominated by the production of clean energy (20.9%; n = 103), while most economic risk frames addressed increased electrical costs (26.0%; n = 128). People used economic benefit (5.7%; $n = 28$) and environmental risk (11.6%; $n = 57$) categories less often than their counterparts. Although political frames were the second most used category in both groups, political risk frames (21.1%; $n = 104$) had twice the presence compared to political benefit frames (9.7%; $n = 48$). Health and safety frames were used the least by both supporters (3.9%; $n = 19$) and opponents (8.3%; $n = 41$).

Measuring Influence in Public Opinion via Comment Recommendations. The *Boston Globe*'s policies allow any online reader to recommend a comment. Instead of comparing the means of the two samples, the non-parametric Mann-Whitney U test was used to compare the medians of recommendations.

A Mann-Whitney U test was conducted to evaluate whether the number of recommendations differed between advocacy comments and opposition comments. The results of the test were significant, $z = -3.099$, $p < .01$. The Alliance to Protect Nantucket Sound comments had an average rank of 230.43, while Clean Power Now had an average rank of 270.48. The comments of Cape Wind advocates were recommended significantly more often than were the comments of opponents.

The number of recommendations attributed to news comments was then compared within each respective sample, advocacy, and opposition comments. The sample was separated based on Clean Power Now frames and the Alliance to Protect Nantucket Sound frames. The goal was to determine whether supporters or opponents of the project preferred one type of frame over another.

Significant results were found in the aesthetic risk category. Comments that addressed Cape Wind's aesthetic risks had significantly more recommendations than other opposition comments, $z = -3.083$, $p < .01$. Aesthetic risk comments had a mean rank of 170.57, whereas other opposition comments had a mean rank of 136.20. Within this category, the frame "Cape Wind threatens the beauty and scenery of Cape Cod" also had significantly more recommendations than other opposition comments, $z = -3.120$, $p < .01$. Comments within the aesthetic risk frame had a mean rank of 176.68, while other opposition comments had a mean rank of 137.72. Therefore, aesthetic risk frames about the scenery and beauty of Cape Cod were recommended significantly more often than other opposition comments.

In contrast to the opposition frames, not a single frame differed significantly among advocacy supporters in recommendations.

DISCUSSION

Despite the differences among active audiences, both activist groups use the "moral high ground" in their communications (Heath & Palenchar, 2009). The Alliance to Protect Nantucket Sound identified itself as an environmental group on its website and touted moral reasons to oppose the Cape Wind

Energy Project. For example, the Alliance claimed Cape Wind would violate the rights of Native Americans, ruin the livelihoods of Cape Cod residents, and destroy a national treasure. However, these morally grounded arguments nearly disappeared among supporters' framing in the *Boston Globe* comments. Active publics focused on economic reasons to argue against Cape Wind. The Alliance's often-used argument that electricity from Cape Wind costs double was a particularly salient point; half of the people who said Cape Wind would increase electrical costs also said that electricity produced by Cape Wind would cost twice as much. Even though the activist group uses value framing to achieve a moral high ground, the dominant frame used as an argument among active publics related to material framing. Furthermore, the economic reasons against Cape Wind regarding electrical costs were the go-to arguments in news comments. The economic risks based on cost were a salient and immediate argument since all Massachusetts residents pay for electricity. On the other hand, Clean Power Now's economic arguments stressed long-term cost savings, which isn't as salient an argument (Rosenthal, 2011).

Like the opposition group, Clean Power Now stresses a moral high ground, albeit in the form of building a renewable, clean energy source. Unlike the Alliance to Protect Nantucket Sound, Clean Power Now used broader master frames in its news releases. While the Alliance to Protect Nantucket Sound would make specific claims such as "Cape Wind would be larger than Manhattan," Clean Power Now avoided analogies and narrow claims. However, it is important to recognize that during this study's time frame, Clean Power Now had state and federal government support. Cape Wind had politicians advocating for its approval and encouraging the adoption of wind energy in Massachusetts. The support of politicians may have affected Clean Power Now's messaging strategies, while the Alliance to Protect Nantucket Sound likely changed its messaging in a similar manner to compensate for the political environment. Previous research has shown that opposition to wind farms can be influenced by power inequalities and governance (Ellis et al., 2007).

Among the supporters of Cape Wind, the most salient frames concerned energy independence, decreasing the use of foreign oil, and avoiding oil spills. The reasons supporting energy independence and decreased usage of fossil fuels should resonate with active publics. In this manner, activist groups shape new possibilities and opportunities for businesses (Sine & Lee, 2009).

Looking at the results as a whole, the content analysis shows the disparities between how activist groups portray the Cape Wind Energy Project compared to how active audiences think of the project. Using "diagnostic framing" (Snow & Benford, 2000), Clean Power Now and the Alliance to Protect Nantucket Sound attributed a variety of characteristics to Cape Wind in their messaging. However, the public perceptions regarding Cape Wind were primarily about economic risks versus environmental benefits. Even though opposition comments outnumbered advocacy comments, the quantity of economic risk and environmental benefit frames was nearly identical. The basis for these two dominant arguments reflects the nature of the opposing viewpoints. Opponents citing economic risks used a material appeal to persuade people that Cape Wind costs too much, while the environmental benefits used by supporters appealed to a person's ethics.

A Different Way to Measure Public Opinion. In addition to the descriptive nature of the methodology, this project measured the public opinions of audiences who may not participate in writing news comments. This information was measured by recording the number of recommendations given to a particular comment. By recommending one comment over another, latent publics chose which frames resonate most with them.

Previous polling measurements showed the majority of Massachusetts residents favored Cape Wind's construction (Fulham, 2010). In line with this, the advocacy frames in the comments were recommended more often than opposition frames. While more opponents wrote arguments against Cape Wind, overall the *Boston Globe* readership significantly rated supporter comments higher.

Latent publics may have been able to identify best with aesthetic reasons for not building Cape Wind. The Alliance to Protect Nantucket Sound's consistent labeling of Nantucket Sound as a national treasure was salient, since this frame was repeated often and highly rated during the online discussions. Although NIMBY-type responses are not necessarily present in communities familiar with a specific type of project (Wolsink, 2000; Devine-Wright, 2005), they can occur in places where people are unfamiliar with the project (Thayer & Freeman, 1987). Massachusetts citizens would be unaccustomed to large-scale wind projects, and all U.S. citizens would be unaccustomed to offshore wind turbines. The nature of Cape Wind being the first offshore wind farm in the nation lent itself to a NIMBY perfect storm.

Aesthetic risks make a strong, tangible argument for opponents despite not being the most common argument against Cape Wind. In the same manner that supporters symbolize wind turbines with clean energy (Warren, Lumsden, O'Dowd, & Birnie, 2005), opponents may symbolize wind turbines with the negative effects of clean energy generation such as increased electrical costs, excessive subsidies, damaged views, environmental destruction, and safety risks. In essence, aesthetic risks combine all frames into one argument, creating a more concrete message.

Creating Salient Activist Messages. Aside from this project's theoretical and methodological contributions, the results show how public relations practitioners can create salient messages for their audiences and have their members carry their activism into the public sphere. The results revealed the most salient messages among active publics, which may help activist groups create "motivational frames" for future campaigns (Snow & Benford, 2000).

Clean energy campaigns may be able to enhance their messages by connecting clean energy to decreased oil consumption. Clean Power Now's main messages that resonated with online publics related to oil; these two salient points concerned avoiding oil spills and reducing the consumption of foreign oil. Although oil-related messages were salient, wind energy does not typically replace oil consumption. Instead, wind energy primarily replaces coal and natural gas, which are the usual fossil fuels burned for electricity. Cape Wind most likely represents a forward-looking path toward energy independence and a clean energy future. However, the clean energy movement can create its salient messages framed around the adverse effects of oil consumption.

Activist groups opposing renewable energy projects should emphasize cost and aesthetic arguments in their messaging. Far and away, economic reasons concerning cost were the most frequently used frames. Since energy costs affect everyone, framing an argument around increased energy costs creates a salient message.

Likewise, arguments based on aesthetic risks are salient messages, despite these arguments representing a NIMBY response. Messages based on aesthetics can be crafted into a condensed and targeted frame. The Alliance to Protect Nantucket Sound successfully created an aesthetic frame against Cape Wind by labeling Nantucket Sound a national treasure. This frame gave the Alliance a morally based argument against Cape Wind. Opposing Cape Wind on the basis of refusing to harm a national treasure transcends resisting the project solely on economic grounds.

CONCLUSION

In summary, this study developed a content analysis method to understand public opinion about one renewable energy project. Over the course of a decade, activist groups for and against the Cape Wind Energy Project used many types of appeals in their news releases and communication materials to influence the media and public. Each activist group strove to garner public support by portraying the project in a particular light. Certain appeals most effectively resonated with active publics. Opponents primarily cited economic and political reasons against Cape Wind, although aesthetic arguments may best symbolize their concerns. Supporters largely identified with environmental reasons to argue for local wind energy. Opponents were more vocal than supporters, but, based on comment recommendations, more Cape Wind supporters read the online comments. Finally, this research, methodology, and results could be used by public relations practitioners to develop energy messaging or expanded upon into other energy, social, political, and environmental contexts.

As for limitations, this study looked at only one renewable energy project during a six-month time span. Results may change depending on the type of energy project, the location, political factors, economic factors, news con-text, and other variables. Given these possible variables, the results in this study may be unique to the *Boston Globe*, Cape Wind, these online audi-ences, and this specific time frame. Public opinion can be also influenced by external events unrelated to Cape Wind. Furthermore, this study did not examine the frequency of frames in activist group messaging or account for arguments outside of the identified frames. For example, one notable frame found in the comments concerned aesthetic benefits of wind turbines, but Clean Power Now did not emphasize these benefits in its messaging. Previ-ous research has shown that people who relate to wind turbines' symbolic features enjoy seeing them (Thayer & Freeman, 1987).

REFERENCES

Bolsen, T., & Cook, F. L. (2008). The polls—Trends: Public opinion on energy policy: 1974–2006. *Public Opinion Quarterly, 72*(2), 364–388.

Coombs, W. T., & Holladay, S. J. (2010). *PR strategy and application: Managing influence*. Malden, MA: Wiley-Blackwell.

Cordano, M., Welcomer, S., Scherer, R., Pradenas, L., & Parada, V. (2010). Under-standing cultural differences in the antecedents of pro-environmental behavior: A comparative analysis of business students in the United States and Chile. *Journal of Environmental Education, 41*(4), 224–237.

Devine-Wright, P. (2005). Beyond NIMBYism: Towards an integrated framework for understanding public perception of wind energy. *Wind Energy, 8*, 125–139.

Donavan, J. (2009). Energy policy, presidential agenda setting and the public: From Jimmy Carter to George W. Bush. *Conference Papers—Western Political Science Association*, 1–17. AllAcademic Research database. Retrieved April 1, 2013, from http://citation.allacademic.com/meta/p_mla_apa_research_citation/3/1/7/6/8/pages317689/p317689-1.php

Dozier, D. M., Grunig, L. A., & Grunig, J. E. (2001). Public relations as commu-nication campaign. In R. E. Rice & C. K. Atkin (Eds.), *Public communication campaigns* (pp. 231–248). Thousand Oaks, CA: Sage.

Dozier, D. M., & Lauzen, M. (2000). Liberating the intellectual domain from the practice: Public relations, activism, and the role of the scholar. *Journal of Public Relations Research, 12*(1), 3–22.

Ellis, G., Barry, J., & Robinson, C. (2007). Many ways to say "no", different ways to say "yes": Applying Q-methodology to understand public acceptance of wind farm proposals. *Journal of Environmental Planning and Management, 50*(4), 517–551.

Entman, R. (1993). Framing: Toward a clarification of a fractured paradigm. *Journal of Communication, 43*, 51–58.

Fulham, P. W. (2010, June 4). Cape Cod wind farm controversy still roiling Nantucket Sound. *Politics Daily*. Retrieved October 2, 2014, from http://www.politicsdaily.com/2010/06/04/cape-cod-wind-farm-controversy-still-roiling-nantucket-sound/

Gamson, W. A., & Modigliani, A. (1989). Media discourse and public opinion on nuclear power: A constructionist approach. *American Journal of Sociology, 95*, 1–37.

Goffman, E. (1974). *Frame analysis: An essay on the organization of experience*. Cambridge, MA: Harvard University Press.

Grunig, J. E. (2006). Furnishing the edifice: Ongoing research on public relations as a strategic management function. *Journal of Public Relations Research, 18*(2), 151–176.

Grunig, L. A. (1993). Image and symbolic leadership: Using focus group research to bridge the gaps. *Journal of Public Relations Research, 5*(2), 95–125.

Gsell, L. (2009). Comments anonymous. *American Journalism Review, 31*(1), 16–17.

Hallahan, K. (1999). Seven models of framing: Implications for public relations. *Journal of Public Relations Research, 11*(3), 205–242.

Haller, M., & Hadler, M. (2008). Dispositions to act in favor of the environment: Fatalism and readiness to make sacrifices in a cross-national perspective. *Sociological Forum, 23*(2), 281–311.

Heath, R. L., & Palenchar, M. J. (2009). *Strategic issues management.* Thousand Oaks, CA: SAGE.

Jones, J. M. (2009, March 13). Americans on energy: Promote both new sources and old [Press release]. Gallup News Service.

Kiousis, S., Mitrook, M., Wu, X., & Seltzer, T. (2006) First-and second-level agenda-building and agenda-setting effects: Exploring the linkages among candidate news releases, media coverage, and public opinion during the 2002 Florida gubernatorial election. *Journal of Public Relations Research, 18*(3), 265–285.

Lubell, M. (2004). Collaborative environmental institutions: All talk and no action? *Journal of Policy Analysis & Management, 23*(3), 549–573.

Luhmann, N. (1989). *Ecological communication.* Chicago, IL: University of Chicago Press.

Luther, C., & Miller, M. (2005). Manifestations of U.S.-Iraq War demonstration groups' pro and anti-war master frames in the U.S. mainstream press. *Conference Papers—International Communication Association,* 1–39.

Mabry, E. A. (2003). Textual framing as a communication climate factor in online groups. In S. Reese, O. Gandy, Jr., & A. Grant (Eds.), *Framing public life* (pp. 323–336). Mahwah, NJ: Lawrence Erlbaum.

McCluskey, M. (2008). Activist group attributes and their influences on news portrayal. *Journalism and Mass Communication Quarterly, 85*(4), 769–784.

Meo, G. A. (2008). Scarborough newspaper audience ratings report 2008. *Scarborough Research.* Retrieved February 10, 2011, from http://www.wan-press.org/MMITF/download.php?type=pdf&file_name=MMITF_Scarborough_2008_final

Pan, Z., & Kosicki, G. M. (1993). Framing analysis: An approach to news discourse. *Political Communication, 30,* 55–75.

Pan, Z., & Kosicki, G. M. (2003). Framing as a strategic action in public deliberation. In S. Reese, O. Gandy, Jr., & A. Grant (Eds.), *Framing public life* (pp. 35–66). Mahwah, NJ: Lawrence Erlbaum.

Peattie, K. (1999). Trappings versus substance in the greening of marketing planning. *Journal of Strategic Marketing, 7*(2), 131–148.

Reber, B., & Berger, B. (2005). Framing analysis of activist rhetoric: How the Sierra Club succeeds or fails at creating salient messages. *Public Relations Review, 31*(2), 185–195.

Riffe, D., Lacy, S., & Fico, F. G. (1998). *Analyzing media messages: Using quantitative content analysis in research.* Mahwah, NJ: Lawrence Erlbaum.

Roper, J. (2005). Symmetrical communication: Excellent public relations or a strategy for hegemony? *Journal of Public Relations Research, 17*(1), 69–86.

Rosenthal, E. (2011, March 12). Green development? Not in my (liberal) backyard. *New York Times.* Retrieved April 1, 2013, from http://www.nytimes.com/2011/03/13/weekinreview/13nimby.html?pagewanted=all&_r=0

Scott, W. A. (1955). Reliability of content analysis: The case of nominal scale coding. *Public Opinion Quarterly, 19*(3), 323–325.

Sine, W.D., & Lee, B.H. (2009). Tilting at windmills? The environmental movement and the emergence of the U.S. wind energy sector. *Administrative Science Quarterly, 54,* 123–155.

Snow, D.A., & Benford, R.D. (1988). Ideology, frame resonance, and participant mobilization. In B. Klandermans, H. Kriesi, & S. Tarrow (Eds.), *International social movement research* (pp. 197–217). Greenwich, CT: JAI Press.

Snow, D.A., & Benford, R.D. (2000). Framing processes and social movements: An overview and assessment. *Annual Review of Sociology 2000, 26,* 611–639.

Stephens, J.C., Rand, G.M., & Melnick, L.L. (2009). Wind energy in U.S. media: A comparative state-level analysis of a critical climate change mitigation technology. *Environmental Communication, 3*(2), 168–190.

Stokes, A.Q., & Rubin, D. (2010). Activism and the limits of symmetry: The public relations battle between Colorado GASP and Philip Morris. *Journal of Public Relations Research, 22*(1), 26–48.

Thayer, R.L., & Freeman, C.M. (1987). Altamont: Public perceptions of a wind energy landscape. *Landscape and Urban Planning, 14,* 379–398.

Toland, B. (2010, March 16). Cities have been embracing sustainability movement. *Pittsburgh Post-Gazette (PA).*

Warren, C.R., Lumsden, C., O'Dowd, S., & Birnie, R.V. (2005). "Green on green": Public perceptions of wind power in Scotland and Ireland. *Journal of Environmental Planning & Management, 48*(6), 853–875.

Wolsink, M. (2000). Wind power and the NIMBY-myth: Institutional capacity and the limited significance of public support. *Renewable Energy, 21,* 49–64.

Zoch, L.M., & Molleda, J. (2006) Building a theoretical model of media relations using framing, information subsidies, and agenda-building. In C.H. Botan & V. Hazleton (Eds.), *Public relations theory II* (pp. 279–309). Mahwah, NJ: Erlbaum.

14 The Influence of Message Source and Cultivation Strategies in a Nonprofit Public Relations Context

Liz Gardner, Trent Seltzer, Andrea L. Phillips, and Rachel E. Page

Public relations research has examined the creation and impact of different communication strategies by the press and by public relations practitioners, but a need exists to bring more ideas from classic persuasion theories, such as source credibility and message appeal strategies, into the current public relations literature. This study attempts to do so by looking at the influence of two variables in public communication design: message source, operationalized as messages provided by the organization itself (e.g., on an nonprofit organization's website or blog) as opposed to the same messages provided by a news media source (e.g., a local newspaper on its website or blog), and the use of cultivation strategies, specifically openness and networking, operationalized as providing specific details, information about organizational expenses, and mentions of community partnerships.

An online experiment with a nationwide, nonstudent adult sample examined whether source type and use of cultivation strategies in news stories about a hypothetical nonprofit organization influenced outcomes and indicators of relationship strength: perceived communication symmetry, relational trust with the nonprofit, attitude toward the message, and intentions to volunteer with and donate to the nonprofit.

Findings both enhance our theoretical understanding of how nonprofit public relations drive prosocial behavior and inform efforts for nonprofit organizations looking to expand their volunteer and donor bases. The purposes of this chapter, therefore, are to apply public relations theory in a nonprofit context and test strategies for practitioners in public relations, and to do so simultaneously.

LITERATURE REVIEW

Organization–Public Relationships. The field of public relations has focused on the development and measurement of organization–public relationships (OPRs) for the past several decades, as discussed in several chapters throughout this book. Briefly, the relational paradigm positions public relations as a management function that cultivates relationships between organizations and publics to generate understanding and mutual benefit for both parties (e.g., Broom, Casey & Ritchey, 1997; Ferguson, 1984).

Current research draws on a variety of OPR models and related scales to understand relationships states and outcomes. Hon and Grunig (1999)'s widely used scale for measuring OPRs, for example, examines four dimensions of relationship state: trust, satisfaction, degree of mutual control, and commitment. Taken together, the various models of OPR (e.g., Broom et al., 1997; Ledingham & Bruning, 1998; Jo, 2006; Ki & Hon, 2007) generally propose four common tenets: (1) antecedents such as preexisting needs and behaviors impact relationship development; (2) relationships can be managed via maintenance/cultivation strategies; (3) the use of these strategies influences the state of the relationship as measured along the dimensions stated previously; and (4) the relational state has consequences for the organization, the public, and the organization's environment, including attitudes and behavioral intentions.

Organization–Public Relationships in a Nonprofit Context. Nonprofit organizations provide an excellent context for study of cultivation strategies and OPR outcomes. For-profit organizations' key relationships, those with customers and employees, are based largely on an exchange relationship, and the value of that exchange may hold an otherwise unhealthy relationship together. In contrast, nonprofits' key relationships, those with clients, donors, and volunteers, are based on more communal relationships, which are rooted in common interest and rarely hold together in the absence of some relational satisfaction (Hon & Grunig, 1999). Examining the impact of cultivation strategies on OPR outcomes without including this value exchange may produce more clear results. Moreover, both the consistent growth in the nonprofit sector and the increasing value of volunteerism (Wymer & Starnes, 2001) call for research examining recruitment, cultivation, and retention practices at nonprofits.

The volunteer/donor roles in nonprofit organizations are a particularly important ones, but research examining volunteer/donor attitudes, motivations, and relationship-building strategies is rarely undertaken—particularly in the PR literature. In regard to donor and volunteer relationships, specifically, the relational approach focuses on the satisfaction that these constituents receive as a result of their interaction with the organization (Waters, 2009). Data have shown that volunteerism correlates with charitable giving, illustrating the tendency of those who volunteer for an organization to support it financially as well (Wymer & Starnes, 2001). In a survey of donors to a nonprofit healthcare organization, Waters (2008) found that major gift and repeated donors reported a stronger relationship with the organization than those who gave smaller or one-time gifts. Moreover, donors reporting stronger feelings of trust, satisfaction, commitment, and control mutuality with the organization were more likely to give larger gifts and to give more often, underscoring the link between cultivating organization–donor relationships and fostering positive giving behavior.

In a later study, Waters (2009) used a co-orientation approach to examine how nonprofit fundraisers and donors each valued cultivation strategies in the development of the organization–donor relationship. Although both fundraisers and donors had only positive attitudes toward cultivation strategies, fundraisers valued them more highly than donors, and the two groups prioritized cultivation strategies differently. Openness was most important for both groups, but fundraisers rated networking as second in importance and assurances as fifth, while donors rated assurances as second and networking last. Herman and Rendina (2001) also illustrated the importance of openness to donors in their study of donor reactions to nonprofits who engage in commercial enterprises; they found that donors cared little about a nonprofit's non-gift income—unless the organization's commercial activity in some way violated or obstructed the organizational mission. This finding points to the value of transparent reporting combined with assurances in building donor confidence: Donors who are fully apprised of the financial activities of the organization are likely to continue support for the organization provided there is assurance that the organizational mission is not compromised.

Like donors, volunteers commonly engage with a nonprofit because of the organization's mission. Unlike donors, whose gift-giving is normally a momentary action, volunteers invest an arguably greater degree of time and effort in their volunteer activity, which is often a multifaceted experience. Recruiting and retention strategies, including efforts to understand what factors influence the decision to volunteer, are, therefore, key to developing strong organization–volunteer relationships (Wymer & Starnes, 2001). Wymer and Starnes (2001) proposed a model of factors determining volunteerism, including personal influences (such as personality and values), interpersonal influences (such as social norms and social ties), and attitudes toward the organization and/or its components. Clary and colleagues (1998) identified six classes of functional motivation that describe what people hope to gain by volunteering, including a values function (expressing one's values) and a social function (affirming social norms), among others. Greenslade and White (2005) investigated the efficacy of both the functional approach and the theory of planned behavior (TPB) to predict volunteerism; they found that while both are effective, TPB—which considers the influence of attitudes, perceived behavioral control, and subjective norms—was a better predictor of volunteer intentions and behavior. Each of these proposed approaches toward volunteerism acknowledges the influence of multiple factors, identifies a role for individual values, and points to the probable impact of social norms on volunteering decisions. With these models in mind, we see that cultivation strategies can enhance or deter volunteer recruitment and retention, as cultivation strategies can make organizational values more apparent and attractive to prospects, highlight social norms enacted through volunteering, and help prevent and/or resolve conflicts that might alter favorable attitudes toward the organization (Starnes & Wymer, 2001; Wymer & Starnes, 2001).

Cultivation Strategies in Relationship Management. The current study is specifically interested in examining the effectiveness of strategies employed by an organization for relationship cultivation and maintenance. Ki and Hon (2009) define cultivation strategies as "any organizational behavioral efforts that attempt to establish, cultivate, and sustain relationships with strategic publics" (p. 5). These efforts, or strategies, can be classified into two major groups (Hon & Grunig, 1999). Symmetrical strategies, which seek to balance organizational interests with the public's interests, include approaches such as providing access to organizational decision-making processes, practicing transparency and accountability, making publics feel that their opinions are legitimate and important, and networking with groups that also share relationships with the organization's stakeholders, among others. Conversely, asymmetrical strategies, which seek to provide benefit to one party often at the expense of the other, include approaches such as exercising dominance, placing blame, making threats, and forms of compromise that leave one or both parties dissatisfied with the outcome. The various public relations scholars who have examined cultivations strategies (e.g., Kelleher & Miller, 2006; Ki & Hon, 2006) generally agree that the use of symmetrical strategies engenders a healthier OPR state and produces healthier relational outcomes.

The current study seeks to assess this claim by examining the use of symmetrical cultivation strategies by a nonprofit organization at the tactical, message design level. Given that cultivation strategies are implemented through media channels, we also examined the impact of cultivation strategies on source credibility and message-related attitudes. Finally, with an interest in nonprofits' specific needs, we assessed the impact of cultivation strategies on intentions to volunteer and donate. Accordingly, the following hypotheses were proposed:

H1: Use of cultivation strategies in nonprofit communication will predict greater relational trust and perceived communication symmetry.

H2: Use of cultivation strategies in nonprofit communication will predict greater perceived source credibility.

H3: Use of cultivation strategies in nonprofit communication will predict more positive attitudes toward the message.

H4: Use of cultivation strategies in nonprofit communication will predict greater likelihood to volunteer for and donate to the nonprofit.

Source Credibility in Public Relations. In public relations, source credibility is arguably one of the most important components of messaging, as perceptions about a message source can drive acceptance or rejection of the message content. Credibility can best be defined as "the judgments made by a message recipient concerning the believability of a communicator" (Callison, 2001, p. 220). The general consensus from the wealth of research on credibility in the field of public relations is that highly credible sources are perceived as having more expertise and being more honest than low-credibility sources communicating the same message, and that these perceptions often imbue their positive influence into the message itself (e.g., Hovland & Weiss, 1952; Lafferty & Goldsmith, 1999; Callison, 2001). In Hovland and Weiss (1952), for example, communicator credibility significantly impacted perceptions of fairness and trustworthiness, as well as opinions regarding the topic debated by the communicator. McCroskey and Young (1981) identified eight dimensions of perceived source credibility: sociability, competence, composure, extroversion, character, size, weight, and time. Looking specifically at health messages, Avery (2010) found three leading factors influenced recipients' evaluations of source credibility: transparency, expertise, and knowledge of the source.

Callison (2001) identified two primary components of credibility—source competence and source trustworthiness—when comparing perceptions of messages from public relations and generic sources. Callison found that the public relations source was perceived as less credible, honest, and trustworthy than the generic source, yet a study by Avery (2010) of sources for health messages found that PR practitioners were rated third in trustworthiness, behind only doctors and scientists, and ahead of government officials and private corporations' spokespeople.

Avery suggested that the contradiction between her findings and Callison's (2001) may be attributed to the nature of the message content: health communicators may be seen as more sincere in seeking public interests than practitioners communicating corporate messages. It may be, then, that nonprofit communicators perceived as serving the needs of others similarly will be met with less skepticism as message sources. Accordingly, we examined whether the type of message source, that is, whether it was attributed to the nonprofit organization or a news source, had an impact on message and relational outcomes through the following research questions:

RQ1: What impact does source type (organization vs. news) have on relational trust and relational perceived communication symmetry?

RQ2: Will a news source or the nonprofit organization itself be rated as a more credible source of nonprofit communication?

RQ3: What impact does source type have on attitudes toward the message?

RQ4: What impact does source type have on likelihood to volunteer for and donate to the nonprofit?

METHOD

A 2 (source) × 2 (cultivation) × 2 (message) experimental design was employed to test the influence of a nonprofit communication's source (news, organization) and use of cultivation strategies (openness and networking;

present, not present) on indicators of the organization-public relationship and message persuasiveness. A message repetition factor (2) was included in the design to control for idiosyncratic effects of a single message. Message was the only within-subjects variable; all other variables, including order (8), were manipulated between subjects.

Participants. Participants included 284 adult participants in Amazon's Mechanical Turk (mTurk), an online "crowdsourcing Internet marketplace" that offers researchers access to individuals willing to complete brief online tasks (including research studies) for monetary incentives. The participant pool for this study was restricted to adult U.S. residents.

Participants who chose to complete the online study received $2.00, which they could redeem as an Amazon gift card or as a monetary transfer to their bank account. All recruitment and incentive distribution was managed by the mTurk system, maintaining complete anonymity of the participants in regards to the researchers.

Stimulus Messages. Stimulus messages for this study were short print messages purportedly from the website of either a hypothetical nonprofit organization or a hypothetical news organization. The messages were soft news pieces that reported either a holiday drive for local families in need or a summer reading camp for local elementary students. Average message length was 244 words.

For the source manipulation, the message was preempted by instructions that labeled it with either, "This story is copied from the website of a nonprofit organization, [NPO name]." or "This story is copied from the website of a daily newspaper, [paper name]." Additionally, the byline for the stories was either a reporter (e.g., Kris Johnson, Staff Writer, the *Winston Observer*) or a public relations representative for the nonprofit (e.g., Kris Johnson, Communication Director, Winston Community Action).

The cultivation manipulation incorporated two cultivation strategies: openness and networking. Openness was operationalized by disclosing specific information for details such as the amount of money raised for or given to a cause, the percentage of administrative/personnel expenses relative to programming expenses, and the specific number of families helped or volunteers involved, and so forth. The networking strategy was operationalized by stating explicitly the presence of partnerships between the nonprofit and community organizations (e.g., a local community college) to accomplish the event's goals.

The design also incorporated a message factor, purely to guard against idiosyncratic effects of a single message. Each participant read two messages, one for hypothetical nonprofit Winston Community Action ("Annual 'Help for the Holidays' drive makes the season bright for local families") and one for hypothetical nonprofit KidsKamp ("KidsKamp brings together local students for learning and mentoring").

Pretest. A pretest to check the cultivation manipulation was conducted with 16 adults who did not participate in the full study. The pretest confirmed the manipulation was valid: cultivation messages were rated as more specific ($p < .001$, $M_{cul} = 6.00$ ($se = 0.872$), $M_{non} = 3.78$ (1.437)), less vague ($p < .001$, $M_{cul} = 2.06$ (0.896), $M_{non} = 3.97$ (1.845)), and as displaying more teamwork ($p < .001$, $M_{cul} = 5.97$ (1.233), $M_{non} = 4.25$ (1.728)). Interestingly, there was no difference between conditions for transparency, suggesting that this may be a more implicit concept. As expected, there was no difference between conditions for message clarity or message liking, nor were there any differences between the two different nonprofits' messages.

Measures. A series of multiple-item scales measured outcomes for this study including relational trust, perceived communication symmetry, source credibility, attitudes toward the message, and intentions to donate or volunteer. Several participant characteristics were also assessed.

Relational trust ($\alpha = .888$) was measured with an index from Hon and Grunig (1999) that includes six 7-point Likert items, such as "This organization treats people like me fairly and justly" and "This organization has the ability to accomplish what is says it will do."

Perceived communication symmetry ($\alpha = .797$) was measured with an index from Huang (2004) that includes four 7-point Likert items, such as "The organization consulted those influenced by their policies and opinions during decision making" and "The organization considered how their public relations activities influenced the public."

Source credibility ($\alpha = .846$) (trustworthiness and expertise dimensions) was measured with a 5-item index adapted from Callison (2001). The stem "the source of the message is" was followed by anchors such as informed/uninformed and honest/dishonest on 7-point semantic differentials.

Attitude toward the message ($\alpha = .791$) was measured with a 3-item index from Mackenzie and Lutz (1989). Participants rated their impressions of the message on three 7-point semantic differentials: good/bad, favorable/unfavorable, positive/negative.

Intentions to volunteer/donate were measured with a 2-item index. Participants rated the likelihood that they would consider volunteering for or donating to the hypothetical nonprofit on 7-point semantic differentials: not at all probable/very probable, not at all possible/very possible. Participants were also asked a ratio-level question to measure intention: If they had $50 to donate or 5 hours to volunteer for any number of nonprofits, how much money/time would they give to this nonprofit? The index and ratio-level item combined into a volunteering intention index ($\alpha = .852$). For donations, the ratio item did not combine with the other intention items and was not retained in the donation intention index ($r = .750$).

Participant characteristics measured for this study included sex, race, ethnicity, household type, average hours volunteered with a nonprofit organization (NPO) in a week/month, number of NPOs volunteered for annually, average donation to an NPO in a month/year, number of NPOs donated to annually, and political ideology (general, social, financial).

Procedure. Participants found a link to the study via the Amazon Mechanical Turk system and completed the study online and individually via Qualtrics online survey software. The first page of the questionnaire included a recruitment script and consent statement. After granting consent, each participant read two short print messages in one of four conditions: (1) news source, noncultivation, (2) news source, cultivation, (3) organizational source, noncultivation, and (4) organizational source, cultivation. After reading each message, participants answered questions measuring the dependent variables. Finally, participants completed a series of demographic and control measures. Upon completing the study, participants received a code to enter into the Amazon system and receive their payment.

This study took participants an average of 15.1 minutes to complete. To guard against nonthoughtful responses, two questions were included in each condition that asked participants to click a particular answer (e.g., "To indicate that you are paying attention, click 'Disagree' below"). Participants who did not answer these questions correctly were removed from the sample. Additionally, participants who took less than 4 minutes to complete or did not complete the questionnaire were dropped from analyses, for a total of 17 invalid responses and 267 participants retained for analyses reported here.

FINDINGS

Data were cleaned and analyzed using SPSS version 20. Repeated-measures analyses of variance (with Message as the repeated measure and Source and Cultivation as between-subjects factors) were run to test for main effects and interactions of the independent variables.

Looking briefly at the makeup of our participant pool, the average participant age was 30 years old (range: 18–65, $SD = 9.97$), and the pool included 56% men and 44% women. Participants reported moderate involvement with nonprofits. Participants reported currently volunteering approximately five hours a month ($SD = 11.55$), 1.3 hours a week ($SD = 3.24$), and for an average of 1.4 nonprofit organizations in a year. Participants reported currently donation practices of approximately $24 given to nonprofits in an average month ($SD = 132.14$), $384 in an average year ($SD = 2042.74$), and to an average of two organizations in a year.

H1 predicted that the use of cultivation strategies would predict an enhanced relational state, specifically greater (a) relational trust and (b) perceived communication symmetry. RQ2 asked whether source would have the same impact. Use of cultivation strategies significantly predicted greater trust ($F(1, 263) = 4.942$, $p = .027$, $\eta^2_{part} = .018$; $M_{cul} = 5.86$ ($se = .059$), $M_{non} = 5.68$ (.060)), but not perceived communication symmetry ($p = .190$), although mean difference was in the predicted direction (M_{cul} = 5.45 (*se* = .067); M_{non} = 5.32 (.067)). The influence of source was significant for neither trust (*p* = .526) nor symmetry (*p* = .391). H1 was partially supported.

H2 predicted that using cultivation strategies would increase perceived source credibility, and RQ2 asked whether credibility would be higher for news or organization sources. H2 was not supported. Source, however, significantly predicted source credibility ($F(1, 263)$ = 4.767, *p* = .030, η^2_{part} = .018), such that stories from the nonprofit (M = 5.84, *se* = .067) were rated as more credible than the news stories were (M = 5.64, *se* = .067). The use of cultivation strategies was not a significant predictor (*p* = .148), but mean differences demonstrate a trend toward higher credibility for messages that use cultivation strategies (M = 5.87, *se* = .066) compared to those that do not (M = 5.61, *se* = .068).

H3 predicted that the use of cultivation strategies would foster more positive attitudes toward the message, and RQ3 asked whether source would have the same impact. The use of cultivation strategies was nearly significant in predicting more positive attitudes ($F(1, 263)$ = 3.611, *p* = .058; M_{cul} = 6.39 (.059), M_{non} = 6.27 (.060)), thus finding partial support for H3. The influence of source was not significant for attitude toward the message (*p* = .682).

H4 predicted that the use of cultivation strategies would predict (a) volunteer and (b) intentions, and RQ4 asked whether source would do so as well. H4 was not supported. For volunteering, neither source (*p* = .159) nor use of cultivation strategies (*p* = .488) was a significant predictor, with an identical pattern for donation (source: *p* = .160; cultivation: *p* = .442). Again, however, mean differences were in the predicted direction for both volunteering (M_{cul} = 3.94, *se* = .122; M_{non} = 3.82, *se* = .124) and donation (M_{cul} = 10.12, *se* = .443, M_{non} = 9.63, *se* = .452).

There were no significant interactions between any of the factors for any of the tests reported.

Message Effects. The effect of message was significant for trust ($F(1, 263)$ = 5.508, *p* = .020, η^2_{part} = .021), with a slight preference for the Winston Community Action story (M = 5.81 (*se* = .047) vs. 5.73 (.045)). Message was also significant for donation likelihood ($F(1, 263)$ = 5.484, *p* = .020, η^2_{part} = .020), with a slight preference for the Winston Community Action story (M = 10.19 (.354) vs. 9.56 (.333)). Message was not a significant predictor for any of the other tests reported.

DISCUSSION

This study examined the influence of message source and cultivation strategies in reception of and reaction to nonprofit communication. Although some predictions were unsupported, several findings advance public relations theory and inform nonprofit public relations practice.

The first key finding was the significant link from the use of openness and networking strategies to increased relational trust, as well as a nearly significant link to more positive impressions of the message. Moreover, although cultivation strategies did not significantly predict the other dependent variables, mean differences universally favored the cultivation messages over the noncultivation messages. These findings support existing OPR models and assertions regarding the use of symmetrical cultivation strategies to enhance positive perceptions of dimensions of organization–public relationships (Hon & Grunig, 1999). It is curious, however, that these strategies, while effective in moving the dependent variables in the predicted direction, were not perceived as symmetrical by these participants. Further research is needed to examine the application of the strategies independently to determine whether some symmetrical strategies are more likely to be perceived as symmetrical by publics targeted by communication tactics implementing those strategies. It is possible that while the strategy behind the tactics is intended to be symmetrical from the organization's standpoint, message receivers may not be able to discern this symmetrical intent at the tactical level. Depending on the context for communication and relationship building, message receivers may be more or less inclined to perceive the dialogic nature of these exchanges. For subsequent studies, we will enhance the cultivation manipulation by incorporating more cultivation strategies into the messages.

We also found that organizational stories were rated as more credible than news stories were. This finding indicates that public relations practitioners may save time and resources—often in short supply at nonprofits—without losing credibility by posting messages about their activities and accomplishments in organizational media, such as blogs or newsletters. Source did not have any other effects, however; returning to the literature and considering the sheer volume of messages that people receive (and the growing murkiness about the source of those messages), this finding is not as surprising. Our plan, accordingly, is to replace this predictor with a different persuasion variable or cultivation strategy for follow-up research.

The lack of support for other tests involving the use of cultivation strategies on source credibility, intention to volunteer, and intention to donate is troubling at first glance. When one considers the existing OPR models, however, cultivation strategies are hypothesized to influence perceptions of the OPR; it is positive OPR perceptions that, in turn, lead to favorable outcomes, such as attitude and behavioral intent. In the current study, we only included measures of relational trust and perceived symmetry as indicators of participants' perceptions of OPR; follow-up studies could include the full OPR scale (i.e., also satisfaction, control mutuality, and commitment), and then examine the influence of those dimensions on nonprofit-related outcomes such as intention to volunteer and donate. Another possible explanation for the lack of significant findings regarding the link between symmetrical cultivation strategy use and positive OPR outcomes could be related to the experimental context and the use of hypothetical organizations. One of the primary axioms of relationship management is that relationships take time to develop (Ledingham, 2006); here, given the hypothetical nature of the organizations used in the study, it was impossible for the participants to have a long-term relationship with either organization.

The online experimental design also introduces a limiting degree of artificiality that may lead to augmented effects outside of a "lab" setting; we feel confident, however, that the method's ability to control for potential confounds, combined with our efforts to create realistic stimulus messages, enhances the ecological validity of this study. Additionally, some may question the use of Mechanical Turk as a valid participant recruitment pool, but multiple published studies at this point illustrate the usefulness of this resource for social scientific researchers. We also built question timing and multiple attention checks into the online instrument to scan for non-thoughtful responses. Mechanical Turk provides a rare opportunity to collect data from a national, all-adult sample for a relatively low cost; given distinct differences in both volunteering and donation patterns between college students and adults, we considered it strategic to choose adults as participants for this study.

Despite these limitations, the current study does have both theoretical and practical implications. First, it provides an empirical test of existing OPR models; more research in public relations should strive to incorporate rigorous testing of assumptions made in the literature. Second, it makes additional contributions to the research on OPRs within a nonprofit context by examining the use of cultivation strategies on perceptions of OPRs with nonprofits, as well as considering intentions to donate and to volunteer as possible outcomes of effective relationship management. Third, practitioners working in nonprofit contexts should make note of the findings when designing messages intended to raise funds or recruit volunteers; although the current study did not find *significant* direct effects of symmetrical cultivation strategies on behavioral intentions, it did demonstrate that the use of symmetrical strategies did have a significant effect on perceptions of relational trust, a necessary first step in building long-term health relationships that—*over time*—may result in increased likelihood to make a donation or volunteer. In particular, the success of the specific cultivation strategies employed—openness and networking—in driving positive perceptions of relational trust should not only encourage practitioners to be more transparent in their communication, but should guide practitioners regarding what type of information to include—and how best to frame that information—in fundraising and recruiting messages.

CONCLUSION

The current study provides a critical first step in the empirical testing of the use of cultivation strategies within nonprofit messaging. Future research can build off this initial study by examining the full gamut of cultivation strategies under a variety of conditions to foster stronger organization–public relationships between nonprofit organizations and their stakeholders. While this study demonstrates the effectiveness of incorporating openness and networking strategies into communication with target publics for building relational trust, much work remains to determine boundary conditions under which relationship management strategies predict organizational success, particularly for nonprofit organizations.

REFERENCES

Avery, E. J. (2010). The role of source and the factors audiences rely on in evaluating credibility of health information. *Public Relations Review, 36*, 81–83.

Broom, G. M., Casey, S., & Ritchey, J. (1997). Toward a concept and theory of organization-public relationships. *Journal of Public Relations Research, 9*, 83–98.

Callison, C. (2001). Do PR practitioners have a PR problem?: The effect of associating a source with public relations and client-negative news on audience perception of credibility. *Journal of Public Relations Research, 13*(3), 219–234.

Clary, E. G., Snyder, M., Ridge, R. D., Copeland, J., Stukas, A. A., Haugen, J., & Miene, P. (1998). Understanding and assessing the motivations of volunteers: a functional approach. *Journal of Personality and Social Psychology, 74*(6), 1516–1530.

Ferguson, M. A. (1984, August). *Building theory in public relations: Interorganizational relationships as a public relations paradigm.* Paper presented at the annual conference of the Association for Education in Journalism and Mass Communication, Gainesville, FL.

Greenslade, J. H., & White, K. M. (2005). The prediction of above-average participation in volunteerism: A test of the theory of planned behavior and the volunteer functions inventory in older Australian adults. *Journal of Social Psychology, 145*(2), 155–172.

Herman, R. D., & Rendina, D. (2001). Donor reactions to commercial activities of nonprofit organizations: An American case study. *Voluntas: International Journal of Voluntary and Nonprofit Organizations, 12*(2), 157–169.

Hon, L. C., & Grunig, J. E. (1999). *Guidelines for measuring relationships in public relations.* Gainesville, FL: Institute for Public Relations.

Hovland, C. I., & Weiss, W. (1952). The influence of source credibility on communication effectiveness. *Public Opinion Quarterly, 15*(4), 635–650.

Huang, Y. (2004). PRSA: Scale development for exploring the impetus of public relations strategies. *Journalism & Mass Communication Quarterly, 81*, 307–326.

Jo, S. (2006). Measurement of organization-public relationships: Validation of measurement using a manufacturer-retailer relationship. *Journal of Public Relations Research, 18*(3), 225–248.

Kelleher, T., & Miller, B. M. (2006). Organizational blogs and the human voice: Relational strategies and relational outcomes. *Journal of Computer-Mediated Communication, 11*(2), 395–414.

Ki, E., & Hon, L. C. (2006). Relationship maintenance strategies on *Fortune 500* company web sites. *Journal of Communication Management, 10*(1), 27–43.

Ki, E., & Hon, L. C. (2007). Testing the linkages among the organization-public relationship and attitude and behavioral intentions. *Journal of Public Relations Research, 19*, 1–23.

Ki, E., & Hon, L. C. (2009). A measure of relationship cultivation strategies. *Journal of Public Relations Research, 21*, 1–24.

Lafferty, B. A., & Goldsmith, R. E. (1999). Corporate credibility's role in consumers' attitudes and purchase intentions when a high versus a low credibility endorser is used in the ad. *Journal of Business Research, 44*, 109–116.

Ledingham, J. A. (2006). Relationship management: A general theory of public relations. In C. Botan & V. Hazleton (Eds.), *Public relations theory II* (pp. 465–483). Mahwah, NJ: Lawrence Erlbaum, Inc.

Ledingham, J.A., & Bruning, S.D. (1998). Relationship management and public relations: Dimensions of an organization-public relationship. *Public Relations Review, 24*, 55–65.

MacKenzie, S.B., & Lutz, R.J. (1989). An empirical examination of the structural antecedents of attitude toward the ad in an advertising pretesting context. *Journal of Marketing, 53*, 48–65.

McCroskey, J.C., & Young, T.J. (1981). Ethos and credibility: The construct and its measurement after three decades. *Central States Speech Journal, 32*, 24–34.

Starnes, B.J., & Wymer, W.W. (2001). Conceptual foundations and practical guidelines for recruiting volunteers to serve in local nonprofit organizations: Part II. *Journal of Nonprofit & Public Sector Marketing, 9*(2), 97–118.

Waters, R.D. (2008). Applying relationship management theory to the fundraising process for individual donors. *Journal of Communication Management, 12*(1), 73–87.

Waters, R.D. (2009). The importance of understanding donor preference and relationship cultivation strategies. *Journal of Nonprofit & Public Sector Marketing, 21*, 327–346.

Wymer, W.W., & Starnes, B.J. (2001). Conceptual foundations and practical guidelines for recruiting volunteers to serve in local nonprofit organizations: Part I. *Journal of Nonprofit & Public Sector Marketing, 9*(1), 63–96.

15 Public Relations for the Next Generation

An Historical Perspective on Activism on Behalf of Children's Broadcasting Initiatives

Rachel Kovacs

Serving the public interest is a responsibility of broadcasting institutions in a democratic society, but children's television programming might not top the "public interest" list. In the late 1920s, when the Reithian public service broadcasting remit was first conceptualized (Crawford Committee, 1926), the BBC's mandate was to "inform, educate, and entertain" (BBC, 1992) and prepare citizens for participation in civil society. Children were not, nor are they now, at the core of broadcasting discourse. This complicates public relations' and children's broadcasters' tasks, as issues perceived as less significant than others may bypass the "radar screen" of policymakers and the media agenda.

Activists and "fellow travelers" have proposed that children's television's future as an indigenous U.K. genre, given industry and environmental stresses, is questionable. Their view is that convergence and commercial pressures have so reduced and morphed children's content that it is barely indigenous, with cheap, imported programming leaving few quality alternatives.

Activists strive to get their messages across multiple channels to disseminate information and provide feedback mechanisms for discourse around kids' TV. The well resourced, however, have greater access to media than those who lack resources and power. Hiebert (2005) said:

> Civil society, or democracy, requires a level playing field in the public sphere, meaning that competing interests must have more or less equal access to the marketplace . . . We know now that mass media . . . are no longer likely to provide equal access . . . The only possible solution is public relations . . . in terms of developing real public relationships in the public sphere.
>
> (p. 3)

This chapter focuses on public relations, which has been much maligned for allegedly putting corporate above public interests. The author posits that as implemented by U.K. broadcasting activists, public relations generates public discourse about children's broadcasting such that it may affect policy. The chapter explores cross-disciplinary scholarship on activism and identifies multiple strategies (e.g., media advocacy, relationship building) that create a public sphere placing children's television issues on the public agenda.

LITERATURE REVIEW

The Public Sphere, Public Relations' Function, and Its Appropriate Relationship with Public Service Broadcasting. Broadcasting's fundamental public service roles (e.g., civic engagement, social cohesion, perspectives reflecting a diverse U.K. society), as germane to children's TV, are appropriate issues for public relations practitioners and activists to bring to the public sphere (Habermas, 1991) and to the media (Garnham, 1992; see Jakubowicz, 1991 re: post-communist Europe). In this chapter, public relations' creation of a public sphere for democratic dialogue around children's television is explicated.

Activists are not monolithic and in employing public relations to position issues at the center of broadcasting debate, they play to their respective strengths. Voice of the Listener and Viewer (VLV) has conducted, commissioned, and notably, responded to credible research—consultations and testimony in political venues. VLV and other activist groups have excelled in networking with influential professionals and politicians, staying informed, and informing others about salient issues. According to Pimlott (1951):

> One of the reasons for their existence is the gulf between "big" institutions and their "publics." Secondly, the measure of their success is their ability to communicate effectively. . . . Thirdly, public relations is being used by those who deliberately set out to raise the level of information and interest in serious topics."
>
> (p. 140)

This subset of activists represents those for whom public service broadcasting (PSB) is an imperative for a diverse British society and the link between the public sector and a public-interest mandate is clear. It is considerably less clear as regards the private sector. Arthur Page's conviction that AT&T's tech contributions were in the public interest (Russell, 2007) has seemed implausible to some. Yet Page saw corporate public relations' work in the interests of democracy. Similarly, the U.K. commercial sector's (i.e., ITV and, somewhat, Channel 4) managers and executives have understood their organizations' PSB obligations and their connection to democratic engagement in society (Kovacs, 2003). U.K. activists are fairly diverse but overall better educated and more elite than most citizens. Yet, they exemplify how public relations can help bridge the "gulf which, despite advances in education and communication, exists between: 'we'—the millions of plain men and women—and 'they' . . . who constitute the effective ruling class" (Pimlott, 1951, p. 140).

Sir John Reith's (Crawford Committee, 1926) conceptual framework for the BBC had at its center an informed citizenry for whom broadcasting enhanced participation in civil society. The well-embedded concept of public service obligations pervaded even commercial television when it was established (Wilson, 1954). As part of the larger Reithian ethos, U.K. children's television, and notably, drama, flourished financially and creatively for many years, although financial reins tightened during the Thatcherite years. Yet pockets of dissatisfaction with available programming existed, as Mary Whitehouse's National Viewers and Listeners Association's (NVALA, renamed MediawatchUK in the 1990s) campaigns and others found children's viewing on some channels and in other "adult" time slots concerning. If broadcasting was obliged to nourish children's minds and spirits as preparation for responsible citizenship, then it seemed axiomatic that new media technologies should design and deliver arts, science, technology, and education in innovative ways (e.g., activists attempted to get *BBC Jam*'s digital children's archive available online). This study focuses on those issues that activists claim fall under broadcasters' public service obligations to children and how the former showcase those issues using public relations strategies.

Historical Overview of Activists and Activism. In the 1960s, activism around television issues came of age. Mary Whitehouse perceived a lack of taste and decency in the U.K. media and created NVALA. She mobilized coalitions of voluntary and church groups, politicians, and others because she felt "adult" television could morally bankrupt the British nation, including children. "Blasphemous" publications also raised her ire. NVALA's campaigns for taste and decency (Whitehouse, 1967; 1993; Horrie & Clarke, 1994) preceded, by about four decades, campaigns around public service obligations for funding and content (Kovacs, 2006; 2013; Kovacs & Tongue, 2008). NVALA's "Clean Up TV" campaigns were followed by the Campaign for Quality Television's (CQT) lobbying for a "quality threshold" in the Broadcasting Act, which raised the bar for commercial bids for TV companies (U.K. Parliament, 1990; Horrie & Clarke, 1994; Albury, personal communication, January 14, 1997) and transcended any one genre, even children's.

Independent Television (ITV) rationalized pullback from public service obligations to children's television due to reduced funding for original content, compounded by reduced ad revenue (Childs, personal communication, June 3, 2009). Thus it dropped kids' TV production almost concurrent with the junk food ad ban. The result: "despite a continuing commitment to range . . . more . . . animation . . . and . . . licensing products from program spin-offs" (Museum of Broadcast Communications, 2013).

It was noted earlier that children's TV issues often are not perceived as compelling. Thus, activists "upped the stakes" and contextualized them within the future of PSB, and the skills and knowledge needed for participation in civil society (see Ofcom, 2011). VLV (2010b) posted that "children's television in Britain is in crisis and only one broadcaster—the BBC—is now producing original children's programming in any volume." The quotation is in paragraph 1 of the web document.

Palmer (2006) had already underscored the negative impact of contemporary culture and technologies on child development and learning, and this supported activists' case for purposeful, quality, indigenous programming. Pullman (2006) further reinforced broadcasters' accountability:

> There used to be . . . a sense of responsibility among broadcasters . . . this extraordinary medium . . . should make things better . . . especially for children. But . . . "profit before everything" shows itself . . . toxic . . . children are regarded as a marketing opportunity . . . This social poison goes much deeper than broadcasting . . . but it's particularly visible there.
>
> (para. 3)

"Social poison," "sense of responsibility," and other terms fall within rhetorical framing, which will be discussed later.

Rhetoric and Advocacy. British broadcasting advocacy was evident even prior to ITV's birth (Wilson, 1954), but Mary Whitehouse's strategic use of coalitions and prominent individuals established NVALA as a conservative watchdog relying heavily on rhetoric. Its approach resembled media advocacy, which employs rhetoric in public interest campaigns. It frames social and public health problems as stemming from flawed policies warranting change, rather than from individual failure. Broadcasting activists (e.g., NVALA) used similar strategies to show the broader impact of broadcasting policies. For instance, Whitehouse (1967) pointed to the dangers of media to the moral fiber of Britain. Other PSB advocates also used rhetorical appeals to identify potentially harmful changes to the status quo. Sometimes appeals for policy change or stasis are more effective when nongovernmental organization (NGO) activists work in tandem with the government or in coalitions.

Issues That Transcend Borders, Regions, Communities, and Generations and Put Children at Risk. VLV (2010a) and the European Alliance of Viewer and Listeners (EURALVA, 2010) operate in the U.K. and Brussels, respectively. Each raised concerns about children's TV and junk food ads. With support from others, they succeeded in having junk food TV ads banned.

Palmer's (2006) indictment of contemporary culture's and new technologies' impact on children and their learning was echoed by Tongue (2007), and later in the U.K. by Children's Charities' Coalition on Internet Safety (CHIS) (2013), which promoted quality, indigenous programming and the filtering by Internet providers of potentially harmful sites for children. Its European Commission submission extended its agenda to pan-European audiences. Converging platforms for kids' content today underscore this issue's relevance.

NGOs and Coalitions. Castells (2000) posited that NGOs take up the mantle where the nation-state fails to do so. Doh and Teegan (2003) identified a triangular NGO relationship with business and government, with NGOs' power ascending. This study's NGOs sought broadcasters' fulfillment of public service obligations, increased corporate social responsibility (CSR), and preservation of cultural diversity.

Scholarship on coalitions has been more prevalent in politics/social sciences (Gamson, 1961) and social psychology, particularly in Europe (Van Beest, Van Dijk, and Wilke, 2004a; 2004b) than in public relations and more broadly, communication. Biologists, too, have explored coalition formation (Benenson, Markovitz, Thompson, & Wrangham, 2009). Cross-disciplinary studies may explain the reasons for and duration of broadcasting activists' coalition choices.

Coalitions commonly occur when a political party has insufficient power to succeed independently and forms alliances to achieve power blocs. Broadcasting activists may seek a government coalition or even the opposition to bring an issue to public attention, such as via early day motions (EDMs), as discussed later. They may ask them to place salient issues on their platforms. Children's broadcasting advocates have united politicians in the All Party Parliamentary Group (APPG) on Children's Media and the Arts: "approximately 80 parliamentarians, from both Houses and across the political spectrum . . . kept children's media and arts on the political agenda" (CMF, 2013).

Similarly, nongovernmental coalitions such as NVALA/MediawatchUK, Save Kids' TV (2006–2011), and Children's Media Foundation (CMF) have united individuals, groups, and other small constituencies. They may morph into new groups (i.e., Save Kids' TV became CMF) or bond ad hoc, issue by issue. Coalitions may mobilize via the Internet, meetings, or networking with other organizations. Save Kids' TV and successor CMF drew from professional associations such as Producers Alliance for Cinema and Television (PACT; 2013).

Historically, most coalitions existed for limited periods and specific issues, except for a few like NVALA and the Deaf Broadcasting Council (representing the UK's hearing impaired). The now-defunct Public Voice (2008) included VLV and CQT: respected, viable broadcasting groups allied to support PSB. It drew from some non-broadcasting groups as well. Consider the formation of the Citizens' Coalition for Public Service Broadcasting (CCPSB): "formed in the summer of 2009 . . . launched . . . on 2 November, 2009 . . . a broad mix of civil society groups, charities, arts and community organizations, together with other concerned individuals" (CCPSB, 2010, p. 1).

Many groups refused to form permanent coalitions. Despite some advantages, members' agendas may be weakened when absorbed into a larger cause (Albury, personal communication, January 14, 1997) and contention over provision of resources and division of responsibilities may arise. The decision to ally with others may only be made after careful cost-benefit analysis of each initiative. Kids' TV coalitions are discussed later in this chapter.

METHOD

This study builds on an initial study of six U.K. broadcasting–centered activist groups that sought greater accountability from broadcasters (Kovacs, 1998). The principal methods of the 1998 and follow-up studies were in-depth interviews with multiple stakeholders. In 1998, the 43 respondents included broadcasting executives at the BBC, Channel 4, and ITV, representatives of six activist groups, ministers of parliament (MPs), a Shadow Secretary, educators, policymakers, regulators, academics, public relations practitioners, journalists, and interested others (see Kovacs, 1998). As some of the original interviewees had moved on professionally, it was not always easy to get longitudinal data from them, but a number of interviewees provided data year after year. Flexible interview protocols were created for respective categories of respondents. The protocols loosely guided the interviews but overall, the questions were open ended. Subsequently, with changes in technologies, audience demographics, and other variables, questions were modified but the same loose direction and open-endedness applied.

In addition to interviews, the author collected primary data on campaigns, consultations, and tactics, coverage by the broadsheet press's journalists, organizational literature, consultation and regulatory documents, and archival and unobtrusive research in specialized libraries. After 2000, the author began to carefully monitor websites and electronic sources. Annual, supplementary U.K. research was expanded to attendance at government or Select Committee hearings, and additional unobtrusive methods.

The 1998 study had focused on six groups; the author subsequently sought to explore characteristics these U.K. activists shared with the broader NGO world (Kovacs, 2006), their regional and global influence, access to digital services and the impact of technologies, cultural integrity throughout the U.K., the future of PSB, and of course, children's television.

For the latter, the author interviewed Save Kids' TV's (SKTV) organizers, and later, those at the helm of CMF and the Children's Media Conference. The author's access to campaign coordination meeting notes, group e-mails, and communications regulator Ofcom's reviews of children's television (see Ofcom, 2013) helped clarify public relations strategies used to bring kids' TV issues to the fore.

RESULTS

Identifying key issues and key players who are affected by or who can affect them are critical strategies for successful public relations, as listed below.

Identification of Salient Issues. U.K. children's TV advocates have also identified adult content by children that has had an impact on the latter. Whitehouse's campaigns were concerned primarily with taste and decency issues—adult programming with potential negative moral effect on children and thus, by extension, other individuals, families, and British society (Whitehouse, 1967). Activists have sought to protect children from potentially damaging programs (MediawatchUK, 2014), advertisements (EURALVA, 2010; VLV, 2010a), and most recently, Internet content (CHIS, 2013).

Although VLV's primary concern has been the future of PSB, it has spearheaded annual conferences on children's television that drew illustrious speakers. SKTV and CMF have promoted distinctly British children's television that underscores national diversity, celebrates the uniqueness of indigenous culture, and provides children with a foundation for good citizenship.

The BBC has shouldered principal responsibility for developing children's content satisfying the above criteria. Nevertheless, Elstein (2012), among others, felt that the BBC, as a PSB, needed organizational change and competition, economic, and creative reasons to fulfill its mandate. To PSB supporters, however, the license fee and sustaining original kids' and other public service content was paramount.

Concerns about Declining Production and Lack of Home-Grown Programs. Ofcom's reports (2007, 2011) confirmed reduced public service obligations and declining indigenous production, with only 1% British-originated children's television programs in 2006 (Ofcom, 2007), many of which were reruns (Childs, personal communication, June 3, 2009). Declining funding for indigenous U.K. programs, including children's programs, continued. By 2011, the BBC overwhelmingly led the production of U.K. kids' drama (Ofcom, 2013, p. 34). The BBC's percentage of factual programming exceeded that of the commercial channels, but its Trust (2008) suggested that if the BBC incorporated more multicultural elements into its children's shows, it would be of greater value to ethnic minorities. The varied public relations strategies employed by U.K. groups on behalf of children's television are listed and illustrated later.

Public Relations Strategies Used to Shift Public Policy for Children's Television. Activists generated dialogue around the adult broadcasting environment, the climate it created, its impact on children, and the future of U.K. children's television. The latter conversations were primarily shared by elites. At a time when production revenues dipped and public service obligations declined, activists framed the issues plaguing kids' TV.

In an age of pre-electronic activism, Mary Whitehouse's NVALA depended on letter writing, although it shared other strategies (e.g., petitions) with later campaigns, such as SKTV (2008), which used accrued, diverse skills of individual members and industry groups. SKTV's numerous submissions to regulators, engagement of politicians and journalists through forums, and political lobbying catalyzed a major government review and consultation on children's television. This strongly suggested the link among activist public relations, the public sphere, deliberation, and civil society processes.

Choice of Media Outlet and Its Impact. Mary Whitehouse's media presence, particularly in the tabloids, subjected her to derision, perhaps for her appearance as much as for her moral absolutism. This quite possibly had a negative impact on the long-term viability of NVALA and successor MediawatchUK.

BBC executives (Graham, personal communication, February 5, 1997; Stevenson, personal communication, February 6, 1997) characterized NVALA as not truly representative, and thus not entitled to having its policy agenda take precedence over that of others. They also objected to Mary Whitehouse expecting changes that were not within the broadcasters' remit. In addition, they suggested her personality style and persistence made it difficult for those whom she sought out to deal with her. Finally NVALA's research was considered less credible than that of groups like VLV. These interviewee observations were important in as much as they helped the author understand that an effective activist group: (1) needs to be seen as representing a broad interest; (2) must respect the constraints of the broadcasters; (3) must engage in rapprochement (Kovacs, 1998, identified seven dimensions of successful relationships); and (4) must present credible, well-supported arguments (Mitchell, personal communication, January 22, 1998).

Validation over Time. Although this chapter provides an overview of children's television activists' success rather than a point-by-point analysis, the 1998 study's findings are worth noting. Identifying key publics and building strategic relationships over time is more successful for an activist group than short bursts of activity and celebrity (e.g., photos in the tabloids) that do not cultivate those key relationships built on mutual interests.

Long-term relationships are invaluable (Hon & Grunig, 1999; Ledingham & Bruning, 2000, Sallot & Johnson, 2007). When activists cultivate relationships with journalists, they may gain broadsheet column inches or coverage in the media pages of the *Guardian* and the *Financial Times* (e.g., Maggie Brown [2010], Raymond Snoddy [2007]). These journalists add legitimacy to a media issue and may get involved beyond their reporting duties. This ongoing interest by respected journalists in the VLV agenda, including children's issues, contributed to its long-term viability and level of interest by government, Parliament, and others—outcomes, in part, of a respectful relationship, as described earlier.

Raising Kids' TV Issues in Parliament: Engaging Parliament and the House of Commons Select Committee. The Select Committee's engagement in the debate attested to the significance of children's television, despite the absence of pressure from the "average" British citizen. The Department of Culture, Media, and Sport (DCMS) Select Committee Report (on testimony from NGO groups) stated, "we believe that U.K.-produced content plays an important role in maintaining children's cultural identity . . . it . . . is important that there remains a significant amount of UK-produced children's programming on commercial channels as well as the BBC" (DCMS, 2007).

Public sector activist strategies used to engage members of Parliament echoed those of 1998, when rhetorical framing, used in media advocacy (Wallack et al., 1993), lobbying, letter/petition writing, working, consultation, and written/oral public testimony were prevalent. Exponential expansion of Internet/Web-based capabilities increased mobilization of members, posting of files, exchanges of ideas/documents, networking among group members, and notably, outreach to potential members and affected publics. Interestingly, late into the first decade of the millennium, most activists still engaged heavily in face-to-face or voice-to-voice communication. Perhaps it is culturally specific to the U.K., but activists still largely pursued their agendas through interpersonal communication and are dependent on good relationships, prefaced by identifying key players.

Relationship Building and Identification of Key Parties and Venues to Strategically Target Them. When SKTV was active (2006–2011), the targeting of key individuals in these institutions would have been likely: (1) the DCMS Convergence Think Tank (a review of digital services and domestic programs); (2) the House of Lords; and (3) senior civil servants. SKTV's ancillary efforts would have included a consultation paper to a body conducting a review, a message to the House of Lords, and other measures (SKTV, 2012). With SKTV inactive, succeeded by CMF, relationships with a key body are crucial—the AAPG on Children's Media and the Arts (2014), an informal cross-party group without legislative status that also includes members from outside Parliament. CMF acts as secretariat for this group (CMF, 2014).The group submitted a report on children's online activities, and posted a newsletter on various media-related topics.

Political and Prominent Connections in Choice Venues. Activist NGOs were adroit at navigating the political system and involving politicians and celebrities in their campaigns. They frequented party conferences and invited key politicians and civil servants to public media-centered forums. The latter, in turn, voiced activists' questions in Parliament, motions, and other legislative maneuvers. This is what Mills (personal communication, January 24, 1998) referred to as a "virtuous circle."

Coalitions. It was explained earlier why coalitions appealed to some activists and not others. A number of coalitions cultivated relationships with journalists and others empowered to make changes. They also organized conferences and forums to which politicians, civil servants, journalists, and other opinion makers were invited. In short, coalitions used all tactics at the disposal of indi-viduals and groups. Hutt (2007) identified VLV's creation of "a coalition of concerned individuals, opinion formers and representative organizations, to act as a catalyst for ideas and actions." Among the opinion formers was Lord David Puttnam, renowned producer. The two coalitions below are the most prominent in the realm of children's TV in the last decade. One is inactive.

The SKTV coalition of producer- and broadcasting-based pressure groups and notables was coordinated by Childs (personal communication, June 3, 2009), a former kids' TV producer and consultant, and chaired by Anna Home (personal communication, June 14, 2007), former head of BBC Children's Television. It drew support from distinguished individuals includ-ing author Philip Pullman (Hill, 2007), VLV, the International Broadcasting Trust (IBT), the U.K. Coalition for Cultural Diversity of Expression, Society of Authors (SA), the Writers' Guild of Great Britain, Authors' Licensing and Collecting Society (ALCS), Equity (Actors), the British Academy of Film and Television Arts (BAFTA), Producers' Alliance for Cinema and Television (PACT), the Broadcasting Entertainment Cinematograph and Theatre Union (BECTU), the Directors' and Producers' Rights Society (DPRS), Action for Children's Arts (ACA), and the Musicians' Union (MU). It represented a wide range of interests and skills.

SKTV: Its Consultations, Events, and Successors. SKTV (2010) participated in the May 2010 consultation to the BBC Strategy Review. It campaigned for "a new online and broadcast service for children . . . high-quality, UK-produced content missing from broadcast schedules and websites . . . an online community for UK children, providing interaction and participation around content made by professionals and the kids themselves."

SKTV also catalyzed the Children's Television Conference in Sheffield and worked in tandem with CCPSB. It subsequently phased out of that event as of late 2011, and CMF became its successor (CMF, 2014), although Childs (personal communication, June 3, 2009) still oversees the conference.

SKTV Campaign Coordination, Outreach, and Activities by Supporters. Campaign coordination meeting notes documented the plurality of voices involved in the campaign, the careful attention paid to their suggestions, and the multiplicity of tactics suggested and used at any given time. These included lobbying the Parliamentary Performers and Writers All Party Group. At one such annual lobby/social event, performing artists had "buttonholed politi-cians." In the previous Parliament, there was an early day motion (EDM #1375) on children's television. VLV also sought support from MPs and civil servants.

VLV. Significantly, VLV, a broad-based, all-issue membership-based group, actively promoted children's issues for years. Founded by Jocelyn Hay in 1983 to save BBC Radio 4, it defends PSB. Hay created the VLV Forum for Children's Television, which holds conferences, and lobbies broadcasters, government, and Ofcom regarding children's programs. According to Hutt (2007), VLV should be credited for catalyzing the Ofcom review. Hay's (personal communication, June 14, 2008) overtures to key civil servants, conferences, and other tactics, she said, "put the issue on the public agenda" for SKTV to promote. This reinforces support for proactive public relations.

Rhetorical Framing of Issues. Hay (2007) framed the VLV agenda: "It is vitally important therefore that we not only alert all those with an interest in the welfare of children to the dangers that these cuts pose but also encourage them to engage in debate at this time." She said, "Our children are our future . . . We must persuade the politicians . . . to provide programs that nurture them) (Hay, quoted in VLV, 2007, p. 3).

Support From Influential Individuals. Tongue (2007), a former member of the European Parliament, wrote to the *Guardian* about *BBC Jam*'s (digital broadband curriculum) suspension. She argued that "there has been a failure to defend an individual public space and resource that would give access to those, particularly on low incomes, to . . . curriculum support." Other elites also donated time, resources, and/or talent.

VLV Lobbying. Hutt (2007) noted that "As a result of its lobbying, VLV can claim much credit for Ofcom's decision to launch its current review of the state of children's television in the U.K." Activist lobbying resulted in MPs raising issues for early day motions and other tactics.

EDMs. Early day motions (EDMs) are formally submitted for debate (but rarely debated) in the House of Commons and publicize the views of individual MPs, an event or campaign, and/or garner parliamentary support for an issue (U.K. Parliament, 2007). EDM #1375 reads as follows:

> This House recognises that children's television production provides significant public value; appreciates . . . high quality British television programmes . . . [and] believes that plurality of provision . . . is essential in ensuring quality."

Adjournment Debate. The debate in Westminster Hall was opened by MP Neil Gerrard on December 4, 2007, initiated by the Performers' Alliance Parliamentary Group, with support from PACT. Across political parties, consensus on the need to protect children's TV in the U.K. prevailed. (SKTV, 2007). This reinforced the value public relations places on credible spokespersons.

Petitions. On its website, SKTV publicized a petition posted by PACT and encouraged visitors to sign it; the petition was linked to a government e-petition website). The petition read: "We the undersigned petition the Prime Minister to ensure that UK children have access to a wider range of high quality, UK-made public service kids' television programmes that reflect the rich diversity of UK culture." It had garnered 3,873 signatures before its 2008 deadline. Its destination was Prime Minister Gordon Brown. One constituency was disinterested in the issue, and another did not respond rapidly enough, so the petition lacked the signatures to spur policy chance. In this situation, allied groups disregarded coalition leaders.

Allied Activities .Aside from mobilizing parent groups, activists focused more on press activity, celebrity support to generate press interest, and reaching young people themselves thorough outreach to schools and large organizations such as the Scouts. VLV engaged in these activities but sought to involve university students, given its own aging membership and leadership (Hay, personal communication, September 12, 2006).

Letter Writing. Although electronic writing campaigns have met with some success, earlier campaigns sent "hard copies" (i.e., letters) en masse via the postal service. Mary Whitehouse was adroit at mobilizing church and volunteer groups to write to the MPs, the minister in charge of broadcasting, the regulators, and of course, the broadcasters. Contemporary activists, including parents, are encouraged to write to MPs about their concerns. PACT had access to an automated system for locating MPs and sending pre-generated letters to an e-mail address (Childs, personal communication, June 3, 2009).

Conferences and Forums. An Ofcom seminar followed the regulator's report (2007) and VLV's conference on kids' TV. VLV organized an event on "The Role of the Media in Contemporary Childhood" (Hutt, 2007). Groups unaffiliated with the SKTV coalition hosted the Westminster Media Forum and a co-sponsored event by the Social Market Foundation and PACT. CMF's (2013) conference in Sheffield was a core event drawing hundreds.

Testimony Before Select Committee. Hay's (personal communication, June 14, 2008) testimony before the House of Lords Select Committee regarding media ownership referred to children's TV. Select Committees of both Houses of Parliament report oral and written testimonies and make policy recommendations.

European Connections and Comparative Policies. Tongue (2007) suggested at an SKTV meeting that the European Union's (EU) Television without Frontiers Directive (now the Audiovisual Services Media Directive), which dictates quotas for content of European origin, be invoked before the government. The official quota for original, indigenous programs is 51%, where practicable. Perhaps, she felt, such a reminder might move the government to enforce the statute.

Policy Proposals to Ofcom. At a 2007 meeting, Childs discussed SKTV's response to Ofcom's call for consultation after its (2007) report was published.

SKTV called for a funded online destination to commission new programs for 6–15 year olds. It "would also feature interactive and participatory enhancements." SKTV had fundraised toward engaging a digital communications consultancy company that would tap experts from among SKTV activists "to generate a completely new approach to children's broadcasting" (Childs, personal communication, June 3, 2009). Channel 4 was approached.

Web Use. Among other links (recall the direct link to the petition) and informational items on its website, SKTV also created a compilation video of the best children's programs to show what would be lost if children's TV were to deteriorate. Other activist groups used their sites to post newsletters, events, consultation documents, information for new or prospective members, and other information of interest, including essay contest information (VLV).

A wide range of strategies were used by activists. Those groups that appeared to have a wider appeal used the Web and other technologies to their advantage, but focused on relationship building with its membership base, credible journalists, MPs and civil servants, academics, and other well-placed individuals. Basic strategies listed under earlier headings remained fairly constant but specific tactics often varied according to the type of issue, the urgency, and the available resources. I will now discuss and interpret the results and "tease out" what public relations can and should offer broadcasting activists working in the public interest.

DISCUSSION

The public interest regarding children's television has prompted a steady flow of activism from groups on opposite ends of the moral and political spectrum, some of which are coalitions that represent a still broader spectrum. To the extent that these groups can transcend their differences and organize effectively to address an issue whose "whole is greater than the sum of its parts" (e.g., the future of children's television, writ large, as opposed to a single issue, such as the impact of reduced ad revenues on children's drama) demonstrates the commitment of these groups to the public sphere and public policy change. It is true that issues in children's television have been aggravated by loss of commercial advertising, declining revenues for commercial TV, competition from online gaming and Internet content, and other barriers to attainment of activist goals.

The crisis of the recession was preceded, quite a bit earlier, by a focused attack on violent images, foul language, sexual suggestiveness, and outright pornography (Whitehouse, 1967). Even looming concerns about online content have been overshadowed by a greater concern for the future of PSB (Kovacs, 2003) in an era of commoditization of childhood and exponentially available, cheap imported programming. British NGOs see their quest for funding sources for production and distribution of quality, indigenous children's television as critical and within reach. British activists perceive this as a policy issue of first-order magnitude for this generation of children and the civil society. Matters of this weight call for public relations research, planning, and implementation to create the environment for and generate interest in public deliberation. They also call for strategic relationship building with target publics and other constituencies.

In a participatory democracy, diverse publics must negotiate among each other, process new information, identify new entities of importance to their cause, and come to a consensus as to what will benefit society and therefore what needs to be protected. Only through building strategic relationships with those publics, providing a public forum and a public sphere in the public interest where people gather to discuss children's television issues, will these issues become front-of-mind experiences for people who truly have a stake in these matters and can help shape public policy. Only then can children's television take its rightful place among compelling issues that move society in a positive direction. With the freedom to shape the discourse comes the responsibility to communicate fully and transparently to all interested publics. Public relations practitioners, and other parties concerned with children's television and its impact, should aim to communicate fully and transparently to stakeholders, and wherever possible to encourage democratic, public deliberation and achieve some level of consensus among them. They should proactively seek and engage in positive relationships with all stakeholders in this matter, in the public interest and for the betterment of civil society.

At the same time, activists feel they must persevere to find a practical solution that will be a vehicle for the preservation of indigenous children's media. Clearly, in the current economy, the caliber of indigenous children's television that they desire cannot survive without financial and artistic support. To the activists, British children's values, perspectives, and futures are profoundly bound up with their media. Their comments and actions reflect their belief that a healthy U.K. democracy cannot survive without engaged, informed, and inherently British children—the adults of tomorrow.

Public relations' role in facilitating children's broadcasting activism in the U.K. has been to call attention to and rally resources toward the recognition and protection of quality, indigenous children's media. The British groups and coalitions mentioned here are the proactive links among relevant actors and empowered bodies who can change children's TV policies and allocate funding. Their public relations has been at least effective enough to position the compelling issues concerning children in the public's eye. Although clearly some of those who have catalyzed the discourse and set the terms of discussion are industry figures and creative talent, and some will stand to gain from funding for new children's productions, it would be cynical and rather unfair to attribute their relentlessness in advancing these issues to pure self-interest. These activists' efforts should be further researched in a few years to know how their concern for the citizens of tomorrow will play out and what, if any, consequences there will be for those whose livelihoods depend on children. But in the meantime, the data suggest that public relations, as auxiliary to democratic deliberation, can and does generates discourse in the public sphere about preserving quality, indigenous programs for the next generation of citizens.

It is only fair to close with limitations of the study and its historical methodology. Some actors (e.g., Mary Whitehouse and some of her generation) are no longer alive and therefore unable to present their perspectives in a fuller way. Similarly, the groups and individuals discussed in this chapter have been evaluated in terms of their engagement with certain defunct institutions (e.g., the Independent Television Commission and Broadcasting Standards Council) and inactive leadership, who no longer can provide firsthand knowledge. Their communications would seem cumbersome, ineffective, and incomplete by today's standards. Finally, although the sample is substantial, with multiple repeat interviewees, it still represents an elite group of respondents who may not share the sentiments or characteristics of more grassroots U.K. activist groups, nor the demographics of average British citizens. Nevertheless, the study does have value in showing the power over time and progress advocacy can make in generating discourse about important issues, and is a potential template for influencing policy in other cultures.

REFERENCES

BBC. (1992). *Annual report and accounts and guide to the BBC*. London: BBC.

BBC Trust. (2008). *The operation of the Window of Creative Competition (WOCC)*. First Biennial Review by the BBC Trust.

Benenson, J.F., Markovitz, H., Thompson, M. E., & Wrangham, R.W. (2009). Strength determines coalitional strategies in humans. *Proceedings of the Royal Academy, 276*(1667), 2589–2595.

Brown, M. (2010, June 14). Fears grow over funding for children's television. *Guardian*. Retrieved November 2, 2010, from http://www.guardian.co.uk/media/2010/jun/14/childrens-television-funding-fears

Castells, M. (2000). *The power of identity: The information age: Economy, society, culture* (vol. II). Oxford, UK: Blackwell.

Children's Charities' Coalition on Internet Safety [CHIS]. (2013). Comments on the EU Commission's Green Paper on a Converged Audiovisual World (Submission to European Commission). Retrieved October 30, 2013, from http://www.chis.org.uk/2013/08/19/comments-on-the-eu-commission-s-green-paper-on-a-converged-audiovisual-world

Citizens' Coalition for Public Service Broadcasting [CCPSB]. (2010). *A response to the BBC Trust consultation on the BBC strategy review putting quality first. The BBC and public space. Proposals to the BBC Trust*. London: CCPSB.

Children's Media Foundation [CMF]. (2013). *The children's media yearbook*. London: CMF.

Children's Media Foundation [CMF]. (2014). Previous CMF events. Retrieved April 29, 2014, from http://www.thechildrensmediaconference.com/events-archive/

Crawford Committee. (1926). *Report of the broadcasting committee (cmd 2599)*. London: HMSO.

Department of Culture, Media, and Sport [DCMS]. (2007). Select Committee on Culture, Media and Sport—First Report (point #14). Retrieved April 28, 2014, from http://www.publications.parliament.uk/pa/cm200708/cmselect/cmcumeds/36/3610.htm

Doh, J. P. & Teegan, H. (2003). *Globalization and NGOS: Transforming business, government, and society*. Westport, CT: Prager.

EURALVA. (2010). Activities. Retrieved November 3, 2010, from http://www.euralva.org/pages/activities.shtml

Gamson, W. A. (1961). A theory of coalition formation. *American Sociological Review, 26*(3), 366–373.

Garnham, N. (1992). The media and the public sphere. In C. Calhoun (Ed.), *Habermas and the Public Sphere* (pp. 359–376). Cambridge, MA: MIT Press.

Habermas, J. (1991). *The structural transformation of the public sphere: An inquiry into a category of bourgeois society*. Boston, MA: MIT Press.

Hay, J. (2007, Autumn). Letter regarding children's television crisis. *Voice of the Listener and Viewer Newsletter.*

Hiebert, R. (2005). *Commentary. Public Relations Review, 31*(1), 1–9.

Hill, A. (2007, May 26). Children's TV is social poison, says top novelist. *Guardian* (UK News).

Hon, L. C., & Grunig, J. E. (1999). *Guidelines for measuring relationships in public relations*. Gainesville, FL: Institute for Public Relations.

Horrie, C., & Clarke, S. (1994). *Fuzzy monsters: Fear and loathing at the BBC*. London: Mandarin.

Hutt, R. (2007, May 15). Children's TV under spotlight. *PA Regional Newswire for English Regions.*

Jakubowicz, K. (1991). Musical chairs? The three public spheres in Poland. In P. Dalgren & C. Sparks (Eds.), *Communication & citizenship: Journalism and the public sphere in the new media age* (pp. 155–175). London, UK: Routledge.

Kovacs, R. (1998, May). *Pressure group strategies and accountability in British public service broadcasting*. Unpublished doctoral dissertation, University of Maryland, College Park.

Kovacs, R. (2003). The broadcasting public sphere: Enduring issues, enduring relationships, enduring activists. *Journal of Communication Management, 7*(3), 209–238. London: Henry Stewart.

Kovacs, R. (2006, Winter). An interdisciplinary bar for the public interest: What CSR and NGO frameworks contribute to the public relations of British and European activists. *Public Relations Review, 32,* 429–431.

Kovacs, R. (2013, June). *Public relations for the next generation: An historical perspective on activism on behalf of children's broadcasting initiatives*. Paper presented to the Fourth Annual International History of Public Relations Conference, Bournemouth, UK.

Kovacs, R., & Tongue, C. (2008, March). *For the sake of our children: Corporate social responsibility, public relations, and the crisis of British children's television*. Proceedings of the Eleventh Annual International, Interdisciplinary Conference of the Institute for Public Relations, Miami, FL.

Ledingham, J. A., & Bruning, S. D. (Eds.). (2000). *Public relations as relationship management: A relational approach to the study and practice of public relations*. Hillsdale, NJ. Lawrence Erlbaum Associates.

MediawatchUK. (2014). *Mary Whitehouse: A household name*. Retrieved April 25, 2014, from http://www.mediawatchuk.com/our-history/

Museum of Broadcast Communications (2013). British television. Retrieved October 9, 2013, from http://www.museum.tv/archives/etv/B/htmlB/britishtelev/britishtelev.htm%E2%80%8E

Ofcom. (2007, October 3). *The future of children's television programming*. London: Office of Communications.

Ofcom. (2013). *Public service broadcasting report 2013: Annex Information Packet F-Children's Report*. London: Ofcom.

Palmer, S. (2006). *Toxic childhood*. London: Orion.

Pimlott, J.A.R. (1951). *Public relations and democracy*. Princeton, NJ: Princeton University Press.

Public Voice. (2008). Retrieved May 6, 2008, from http://www.public-voice.org.uk/

Pullman, P. (2006). Save Kids' TV [Blog archive]. Retrieved October 31, 2013, from http://www.savekidstv.org.uk/news/philip-pullman-offers-support/

Russell, K. (2007). *Corporate public relations and democracy: Arthur W. Page and the FCC, 1935–1941*. Paper presented to the Annual Conference of the Public Relations Division of AEJMC, Washington, D.C.

Sallot, L. M., & Johnson, E. A. (2007). Investigating relationships between journalists and public relations practitioners: Working together to set, frame, and build the public agenda, 1991–2004. *Public Relations Review, 32*(4), 151–159.

Save Kids' TV [SKTV]. (2007, December 20). Adjournment debate. Retrieved April 29, 2014, from http://www.savekidstv.org.uk/news/parliamentary-debate/

Save Kids' TV [SKTV]. (2008, January 31). *Minutes of Save Kids TV meeting.*

Save Kids' TV [SKTV]. (2010). Save Kids' TV—Campaigning for the best in children's media. Retrieved November 2, 2010, from http://www.savekidstv.org.uk/

Save Kids' TV [SKTV]. (2012). Action and events. Retrieved February 1, 2012, from http://www.savekidstv.org.uk/events/

Snoddy, R. (2007, April 2). Children's TV needs rescuing—but where are the people who can do it? *Independent.*

Tongue, C. (2007, March 27). Letter to the editor regarding suspension of *BBC Jam. Guardian.*

U.K. Parliament. (1990). *Broadcasting Act*. London: HMSO.

U.K. Parliament. (2007). EDM 1375—Children's television. Retrieved March 20, 2012, from http://www.parliament.uk/edm/2006–07/1375

Van Beest, I., Van Dijk, E., & Wilke, H. (2004a). The interplay of self-interest and equity in coalition formation. *European Journal of Social Psychology, 34*, 547–565.

Van Beest, I., Van Dijk, E., & Wilke, H. (2004b). Resources and alternatives in coalition formation: The effects on payoff, self-serving behaviour, and bargaining length. *European Journal of Social Psychology, 34*, 713–738.

VLV. (2007, August). The crisis in children's television. *Voice of the Listener and Viewer Bulletin, 90*, 4.

VLV. (2010a). Information regarding the British Action for Children's Television Archives. Retrieved November 2, 2010, from http://www.vlv.org.uk/pages/news-publications.php.

VLV. (2010b). Invitation to VLV talk by Joe Godwin, BBC Children's. Retrieved April 26, 2014, from https://www.jiscmail.ac.uk/cgi-bin/webadmin?A3=ind1009&L=MECCSA-POLICY&E=quoted-printable&P=18225&B=—B_3367815778_368687&T=text%2Fhtml;%20charset=ISO-8859-1

Wallack, L., Dorfman, L., Jernigan, D., & Themba, M. (1993). *Media advocacy and public health: Power for prevention*. Newbury Park, CA: Sage.

Whitehouse, M. (1967). *Cleaning up TV. From protest to participation*. London: Blandford.

Whitehouse, M. (1993). *Quite contrary. An autobiography*. London: Pan Books.

Wilson, H. H. (1954). *Pressure groups: The campaign for commercial television in England*. New Brunswick, NJ: Rutgers University Press.

16 Digging for Victory Gardens
A Comparative Analysis of the U.K. and U.S. World War II Gardening Campaigns

Cheryl Ann Lambert

World War II (WWII) placed an enormous strain on the food supply of allied countries including the United Kingdom and the United States. Seventy-five percent of the food supply in the United Kingdom was imported by ship, so German U-boat submarines blocking transport led to imminent danger of starvation (Gibbs, 2013). In the United States, more than 25 percent of food production including 50 percent of canned and dried fruits was needed to feed troops, allies, and civilians during the war (Gibbs, 2013). To alleviate the strain placed on food supplies, government agencies in the United Kingdom and the United States launched individual gardening propaganda campaigns (Witkowski, 2003; Ginn, 2012). In the United Kingdom, the Ministry of Information (Ginn, 2012) and the Ministry of Agriculture (British Library Board, 1941) initiated *Dig for Victory!* In the United States, the Office of War Information launched the *Victory Gardens* (Office of War Information, 1943c). Although the campaigns were similar, they differed because of access to food, gendered cultural roles, and citizen responsibilities.

The purpose of the present study is to gain insights about campaigns by analyzing them through a narrative paradigmatic lens. Countrywide campaigns contain some of the same elements that smaller campaigns do: audience assessment, message clarity, evaluative measures. This study has value for communications practitioners charged with developing campaigns where benefits are not immediate; for example, in public health programs. Strategic approaches used during WWII could be effective for practitioners in the current environment to facilitate behavior change. For academics, the study could advance a stream of rhetorical research investigating cultural stories from the war. The U.K. Mass Observation archive of citizen surveys and diaries during the war[1] (Collingham, 2011, p. xv) can be culled for research material. Practitioner and academic perspectives about the potential of propaganda could shift in light of the campaigns of the present study. At least 20 million military deaths were blamed on starvation, malnutrition, and associated diseases during WWII (Collingham, 2011). Food that was grown in response to gardening campaigns might have prevented some deaths.

LITERATURE REVIEW

A Brief History of Wartime Gardening Campaigns. The United Kingdom and the United States launched gardening campaigns during World War I with little success[2] (Smith, 2013), but the campaigns in WWII facilitated altogether different results.

The Dig for Victory campaign was a natural progression of the Cultivation of Lands (Allotment plots) Order of 1939, through which the United Kingdom encouraged citizens to produce food at home. The Order enabled councils to take over vacant grounds (Krzanaric, 2007; Smith, 2013) and keep livestock with permission. The United Kingdom also invested in failing farms (Gibbs, 2013), converting parks and playing fields into Allotments. Trespassing became a statutory offense (Smith, 2013). By 1939, 12.9 million acres of land were under cultivation in the United Kingdom (Smith, 2013, p. 66).

The Ministry of Agriculture and the Ministry of Information officially launched Dig for Victory in 1940, extending the *grow their own* call to Allotment and household gardens (British Library Board, 1941; Krznaric, 2007). The goal was to provide food for families and neighborhoods and to free up space for war materials on merchant ships (Wilkins & Wilkins, 2011). Thus, the Dig for Victory campaign was situated in a national security agenda (DeSilvey, 2003). Public areas such as domestic gardens, public parks, and even the lawn outside the Tower of London were eventually transformed into Allotments (Wilkins & Wilkins, 2011; Gibbs, 2013). The Scottish Gardens and Allotments Committee monitored participation and demanded explanations when citizens did not meet growth projections (DeSilvey, 2003).

When the U.S. Victory Garden campaign began in 1940, its stated purpose was offsetting food shortages among farmers and food processers (Office of War Information, 1943c). The Office of War Information focused mainly on individual gardening efforts. There was no government land set aside for growing food; instead, Victory Garden messaging encouraged citizens to grow gardens in backyards, community spaces, schools, and farms (Office of War Information, 1943d). By 1943, 20 million households were producing more than 40% of the vegetables Americans consumed (Office of War Information, 1943d; United States Department of Agriculture, 2011).

In the United Kingdom, more than six million private and community gardens were growing more than one million tons of vegetables by 1943 (Wilkins & Wilkins, 2011). These gardens produced one-fifth of the total vegetable supply in the United Kingdom that year (Office of War Information, 1943c). Thanks to Dig for Victory, 10% of all U.K. food production came from Allotments and private gardens by 1944 (Krznaric, 2007). By this time, the United Kingdom was importing a fraction of the food it had just 5 years prior (Smith, 2013, p. 66). In the United States, 18.5 million Victory Gardens were grown in 1944. Survey respondents told the U.S. Department of Agriculture they grew gardens to help the war, get better vegetables, and save money. The government attributed the largest commercial crop in its history to the Victory Gardens campaign ("The Facts," 1945).

In the United Kingdom, Dig for Victory had a major impact on wartime food production and helped offset food scarcity (Krznaric, 2007, p. 8). The country was able to cut its reliance on food imports in half. By the end of 1945, there were 1.4 million (Gibbs, 2013) to 1.5 million (Krznaric, 2007) Allotments in the United Kingdom.

Dig for Victory planners remained focused on increasing U.K. domestic food production by expanding campaign participation. But in the United States, Victory Garden messaging softened by 1945. United States citizens were no longer compelled to grow gardens; instead, they were encouraged through messages of saving money, eating healthier, or the joy of gardening ("The Facts," 1945). The accessibility of food and proximity of war shaped perspectives in each country: "While both countries endured rationing and the grief of losing hundreds of thousands of young men, the conflict remained remote for most people in the United States, causing far less deprivation and suffering than in Britain or occupied Europe" (Olson, 2010, p. 229).

Theoretical Framework. Initially posited by Fisher (1984) as an alternative to the traditional rational perspective, narrative paradigm holds that people are storytellers who use informed, differential reasoning to communicate and make decisions. Decision making is informed by history, biography, culture, and character; reasoning is informed by people as narrative beings whose ongoing narrative choices enable them to construct and reconstruct their realities. People create and share stories to give order to the human experience. These stories enable them to foster shared perspectives with others to form shared (community) narratives. Shared narratives become artifacts of each person's social reality.

Fisher (1984) advanced *narrative rationality* as an alternative to traditional rationality. Narrative rationality involves two related concepts: *narrative probability* and *narrative fidelity*. In narrative probability, people are inherently able to understand what constitutes a coherent message (story). A speaker must establish common ground with the receiver through coherent messages to foster narrative probability. Thus, when people determine the credibility of a message based on its consistency with their own belief systems, they are demonstrating narrative fidelity. According to the narrative paradigm, people are active participants in the world around them. They choose among fictive and factual stories they encounter, they participate in formulating the meaning of stories, and they judge narrative quality. These capabilities indicate the audience determines narrative fidelity.

Fisher (1984) contends that probability and fidelity are culturally acquired; therefore, narrative holds contextual meaning for individuals, communities, and cultures. All communities have key story-makers and storytellers, but all stories hold equal value: "There is no evidence to support the claim that 'experts' know better than anyone else" (p. 10). Although few scholars have applied narrative paradigm to wartime gardening campaigns (e.g., Lambert & Wang, 2013), insights from oral war histories suggests the narrative paradigmatic approach holds promise:

> Through paying attention to the micro-histories from within this [World War II] period, we have begun to explore the relationship between the rhetoric and reality through giving voice to the lived and embodied experiences of those people who are often hidden within the grander histories.
>
> (Harvey & Riley, 2009, p. 514)

As a qualitative communication researcher, the author selected secondary sources because of their relevance to the phenomenon of study (Lindlof & Taylor, 2011). These sources situated the dataset in the larger body of knowledge. The author arrived at an initial explanation of the campaigns by arranging the academic literature thematically.

Several scholars (e.g., Witkowski, 2003; Yesil, 2004) have identified the representations of household chores as military service in wartime gardening campaigns. The approach gave Americans a sense of participation, according to Witkowski (2003). Research about the roles of women in Victory Gardening during WWII reinforced the value of household chores: The "rhetoric did not merely remind working women of their traditional place; more importantly it implored non-working women to join the war effort—if not by donning an overall then by planting a Victory Garden" (Yesil, 2004, p. 110).

Research indicates that visuals in wartime gardening campaigns were utilized to evoke emotions. Witkowski (2003) stated that Victory Garden poster campaigns tapped into the American psyche through simple, recognizable characters. The U.S. government depicted the message of frugality for abundance during WWII. One Victory Garden poster included in Witkowski's (2003) analysis featured overflowing vegetables. Some advertisers used images of plenty to sustain war-weary Americans, according to Young (2005). Her analysis of WWII advertising revealed that themes of sacrifice and consumption coexisted.

Scholarship about Dig for Victory indicates the campaign initially faced an image problem. Citizens disliked the term Allotment, which called to mind government set-asides and unattractive plots of land "tended by an older stratum of society, particularly men over forty and old age pensioners" (DeSilvey, 2003, p. 2). Some believed Allotments were suited for lower-income people who could not otherwise afford fresh fruits and vegetables. Analysis of a wartime diary revealed that gardening was not initially enjoyable to a British woman (Gillespie, Cornish, Aveling, & Zittoun, 2008). In later entries, her opinion about Dig for Victory changed. According to the scholars, she eventually considered herself an active participant in the war effort. The following research question is posed for this study:

RQ: What shared community narrative emerged from WWII gardening campaigns?

METHOD

Historical research necessitates reliance on primary data, evidence developed during the historical period under study (Daymon & Holloway, 2002). Despite limited access to long-distance primary data, digitization of archives and university library collections have enhanced historical research capabilities (Witkowski & Jones, 2006). "Historians of public relations . . . often carry out their research in conjunction with a case study approach, collecting data about either an autonomous case or an example of a larger phenomenon" (Daymon & Holloway, 2002, pp. 189–190). The author employed comparative analysis (Azarian, 2011) to explore WWII gardening campaigns. In comparative analysis, two or more cases are explicitly contrasted in regard to a specific phenomenon to explore parallels and differences among cases. The cases in the present study were the Dig for Victory and Victory Garden campaigns; therefore, the author explored parallels and differences among the campaigns in regard to WWII-related food shortages. Comparative analysis also involves comparing specific events. Rather than "seek regular causal patterns with ordered sequences of the historical transition in question" (Azarian, 2011, p. 119), the author compared the contexts of each country that led to the development of the campaigns. By exploring the campaigns in context, the author gained insights about differential campaign development. Since typologies based on case differences and similarities have been effective in comparative analysis, the author developed a typology of the wartime gardening campaigns as shown in Table 16–1.

Conducting comparative analysis requires systematic investigation to arrive at understanding, explanation, and further conclusions. The investigation involved first locating primary sources in print and broadcast archival records as well as digitized reproductions of original materials. For the purposes of transparency (e.g., Witkowski & Jones, 2006), primary data sources are identified in Table 16–2.

Table 16–1   Communication Typology of Wartime Gardening Campaigns.

Source	Message	Channels	Receiver	Encode/Decode
United States: Office of War Information	Victory Gardens	Print: Posters Broadcast: Radio, movies Face-to-face: Victory Garden leaders	Female "Victory gardeners"	Progress reports
United Kingdom: Ministry of Information & Ministry of Agriculture	Dig for Victory!	Print: Posters Leaflets Broadcast: Radio, movies Face-to-face: Sermons, speeches	Male "Victory diggers"	Wartime Social Survey

Table 16–2 Primary Data Sources for "Digging for Victory Gardens" Project.

United Kingdom	United States
The wartime social survey (Box & Thomas, 1944)	"Save waste fats" poster (Bureau of Industrial Conservation, 1942)
Learning timeline infographic (1941)	Statement (Bureau of Operations, c. 1942)
Dig for Victory video (National Archives, 1942)	*Progress report of the Bureau of Intelligence* (Kane, 1943)
"Dig for plenty" poster (National Archives, 1944)	"Food is a weapon" poster (Office of War Information, 1943a)
Dig for Victory campaign photographs (Telegraph, 1941)	"Help bring them back to you" poster (Office of War Information, 1943b)
"British documentaries and the war effort" (Waley, 1942)	"How the homefront fights" poster (Office of War Information, 1943c)
"Dig for Victory: Foot-on-spade" poster (Ministry of Agriculture, c. 1940)	*Poster distribution bulletin* (Office of War Information, 1943d)
"Dig for Victory: Sailor boy" poster(Ministry of Agriculture, c. 1940)	"We'll have lots to eat this winter" poster (Office of War Information, 1943e)
"Use spades not ships" poster (Ministry of Agriculture, c. 1940)	"Where our men are fighting" poster (Office of War Information, 1943f)
"Dig on for Victory" poster (Ministry of Agriculture, c. 1943)	"Work on a farm . . . this summer" poster (Office of War Information, 1943g)
Dig for Victory anthem (Wilkins & Wilkins, 2011)	*The Facts About 1945 Victory Gardens* (Office of War Information, 1945)
"We want your kitchen waste" (Ministry of Information, c. 1940)	*Victory Gardens: WWII Gardening Tips* video (Internet Archive, 1944)
"Your own vegetables all the year round . . ." (Ministry of Information, c. 1940)	*Victory Garden Leader's Handbook* (U.S. Department of Agriculture, 1943)
". . .every available piece of land must be cultivated" (Ministry of Information, c. 1940)	"Food" poster (U.S. Food Administration, 1943a)
"Grow for winter as well as summer" (Ministry of Agriculture, c. 1940)	"Save" poster (U.S. Food Administration, c. 1943b)
"Those who have the will" poem (Wilkins & Wilkins, 2011)	*How to make posters that will help win the war* study (Young & Rubicam, Inc., c. 1943)

As the instrument in qualitative research (McCracken, 1988), the author employed thematic analysis to study the primary data sources. Analysis involved identifying themes through pattern recognition whereby emerging themes became categories for analysis (Fereday & Muir-Cochrane, 2006). In the first stage, the author examined data through several close readings for related words, phrases, or sentences (Lindlof & Taylor, 2011), writing initial ideas. After grouping the data by category, the author developed a preliminary understanding of the garden campaigns (Riessman, 2005). In the final analysis stage, the author interpreted meanings through narrative paradigm. Results of this analysis are identified next.

FINDINGS

The U.S. and U.K. governments urged citizens to make personal sacrifices during WWII. Government agencies delivered wartime gardening messages via the media and through photographs, speeches, records, books, and even sermons (Jowett & O'Donnell, 1992). In some cases, propaganda was utilized to censor messages; in others, to encourage behavior (L'Etang, 1998, p. 431). In Dig for Victory and Victory Gardens, the governments facilitated behavioral change. Seven thematic categories emerged from analysis of the campaigns: aesthetic components; public feedback; civilian soldier; structured involvement; gender representations; notable experts, and multilevel participation. Details about each category are described next.

Aesthetic Components. Both countries hired professional artists to develop war garden campaign visuals. Commercial artwork that typically took weeks in the United Kingdom was completed in one week for Dig for Victory. Artistic work was deemed important enough that the Ministry of Agriculture recalled some artists from military duty to design visuals. The Ministry spent £4 million on campaign publicity in 1942, £120,000 on posters, art, and exhibitions. "Extra designs were pre-prepared to cope with short lead-times and the changing events of war" (National Archives, 1942). In the United States, the Office of War Information hired hundreds of New York City–based artists to develop Victory Garden posters (Witkowski, 2003).

Anthropomorphic components were typical of campaign visuals. The Victory Garden poster "Where our men are fighting" (Office of War Information, 1943a) re-imagined food as soldiers; cartons of food parachuted into battle alongside soldiers. The Dig for Victory poster "Grow your own food" (Wilkins & Wilkins, 2011) depicts two images in one: A spade in the soil on one half, a ship on the other. The poster tagline "Spades not ships!" reinforced the message. Likewise, the Ministry of Agriculture replicated a Dig for Plenty poster message with an illustration of a colorful box of winter vegetables (National Archives, 1942).

Films promoting wartime gardening displayed differential visuals. In the United States, *Victory Gardens* (Internet Archive, 1944) was upbeat in tone and lasted 20 minutes. The U.K. Dig for Victory film, broadcast by the Ministry of Information to Allotment and Produce Associations, was somber and shot in black-and-white (Waley, 1942). Continuity was central in other campaign visuals. The foot-on-spade illustration appeared in pamphlets and in the corner of Dig for Victory posters as a slogan. Campaign visuals—particularly those that were repeated—became artifacts of viewer realities (e.g., Fisher, 1984). The more that citizens encountered campaign messages, the more they were able to exchange stories, shared perspectives, with one another.

Public Feedback. The U.K. Ministry of Information collected citizen responses to WWII in general and campaigns in particular (National Archives, 1942) via the Wartime Social Survey. The Ministry of Agriculture evaluated responses to the Dig for Victory campaign by surveying home gardeners and Allotment holders (Box & Thomas, 1944). Campaign changes might have occurred in response to evaluations. The Dig for Victory slogan, which ran through most of WWII, focused on the benefits of home-grown food. When the United Kingdom adopted the Dig for Plenty slogan in promotional materials, it might have been to assure citizens of an abundant future (National Archives, 1942). The United States pursued a different kind of feedback to the Victory Garden campaign. The head of the Office of War Information (Horten, 1996) commissioned research exploring war posters in Canada (e.g., Young & Rubicam, c 1943). He used results to develop designs for U.S. propaganda posters. Since people use informed, differential reasoning to communicate and make decisions (Fisher, 1984), obtaining public feedback for a campaign aligns with narrative paradigm.

Civilian Soldier. Citizens in the United Kingdom were invited to serve on the "garden front" by participating in Dig for Victory. The Victory Garden campaign included more prominent opportunities for the so-called civilian soldier. The *Victory Garden Leader's Handbook* conveyed reader responsibilities:

> When we were attacked by the enemy, the nation had on hand splendid stocks of most foods and fibres [*sic*], and our farmers were in a position to increase their production. We were able to throw this wealth of food ammunition into the battle of civilization.
>
>   (United States Department of Agriculture, 1943, p. 1)

The U.S. Department of Agriculture reiterated the message: "Food production is war production" (1943). "How the homefront fights" (Office of War Information, 1943c), a workbook for Victory Gardens, identified opportunities for civilian soldiers: They could serve in the "crop corps," "civilian defense," or a veritable army of suburban gardeners (p. 44). The announcer for the Victory Garden video (Prelinger Collection, 1944) addressed viewers as Victory Gardeners, thereby ascribing the soldier identity. A yard sign in the video reinforced the role: "Food and freedom . . . our family will grow a Victory Garden in 1942 . . . realizing the importance of reserve food supplies, we will produce and conserve food for home use" (Internet Archive, 1944). The patriotic voiceover at the conclusion of the video is accompanied by a waving American flag and soaring background music: "No work, no turnips. No work, no tank, no flying fortress, no victory. Bear that in mind all you Victory Gardeners and work . . . for victory!" (Internet Archive, 1944)

Based on narrative paradigm (Fisher, 1984), it is unclear whether citizens in either country applied narrative rationality to the citizen soldier theme. Campaign planners would have had to establish common ground with the public for probability; the public would then determine message quality.

Structured Involvement. Dig for Victory and Victory Gardens enabled structured citizen involvement in war gardening. People are actively involved in constructing their own realities (Fisher, 1984), so campaign structure could have given order to the experience. In the United Kingdom, Dig for Victory leaflets were developed to deliver the message that people had enough to eat, and that morale was kept high (British Library Board, 1941). A poster produced by the U.K. Ministry of Agriculture, "Grow for winter as well as summer" (c. 1940), doubled as an information guide. It designated vegetables by season and included contact information for the Ministry. The Victory Garden campaign included government publications and promotional videos (Internet Archive, 1944) with gardening information for amateur gardeners. The *Victory Garden Leader's Handbook* contained information about garden types, publicity, and details about planting season (United States Department of Agriculture, 1943). Community volunteers could use Victory Garden campaign workbooks as well. The Victory Garden promotional video (Internet Archive, 1944) features one community volunteer showing a family how to cultivate their garden.

Gendered Representations. An iconic image from the Dig for Victory campaign captured a close-up shot of a shovel partway in soil secured by a sturdy shoe worn by a boy wearing cuffed pants. The *foot-on-spade* was one of many images of gendered constructions. One Dig for Victory poster features a little boy in a sailor suit; "Dig on for Victory" depicts a pipe-smoking man loaded down with vegetables and a rake (Wilkins & Wilkins, 2011). Gender was even evident in a Dig for Victory anthem, in which listeners were assured their muscles would "grow big" while they were "avoiding any squirming worms" in the garden (Wilkins & Wilkins, 2011). Female gender roles were most prevalent in the Victory Garden campaign. Some posters depicted mothers and daughters (Office of War Information, 1943e) working together. Many men were away fighting, so these images reflected what viewers were experiencing. A war-era poster about the importance of conservation also reinforced traditional gender roles: A female shopper asks the male butcher for advice in the U.S. poster "Save waste fats" (Bureau of Industrial Conservation, 1942). These differential gendered constructions likely held narrative rationality for viewers in the United Kingdom and the United States (e.g., Fisher, 1984). Without common ground, narrative plausibility could not occur.

Notable Experts. Notable experts were essential components of both war gardening campaigns. At the start of the Dig for Victory campaign, an estimated 3.5 million U.K. radio listeners tuned in for advice from celebrity gardener Cecil Henry Middleton (Gibbs, 2013; Smith, 2013). Of equal importance in the U.K. was the Minister of Food, Lord Frederick Woolton. Thanks to his status—Lord Woolton was responsible for promoting better eating and the benefits of rationing—a vegetable-only recipe was named in his honor. Authors are split on whether the dish was popular (Smith 2013) or not (Wilkins & Wilkins, 2011). In the United States, novice gardeners were encouraged to contact experts such as the county agricultural agent, veteran gardeners, or local garden clubs for assistance (Office of War Information, 1943c). Experts held prominence in the Victory Garden promotional video: It opens with a quote from the U.S. Secretary of Agriculture and identifies the County Home Demonstration Agent as one whose gardening talents exceeded those of viewers (Internet Archive, 1944). According to Fisher (1984), all communities have key story-makers and storytellers, and all stories have equal value. Thus, the narrative paradigm offers an alternative to expert status that aligns with this theme.

Multilevel Participation. Multilevel participation in Dig for Victory and Victory Gardens emerged as the final thematic category. In the United Kingdom, the Royal Family replaced rosebuds with vegetables in a Dig for Victory garden (Gibbs, 2013). In the United States, First Lady Eleanor Roosevelt grew a Victory Garden on the South Lawn of the White House to support Americans fighting in WWII (Burros, 2009). The gesture by Mrs. Roosevelt was initially criticized by the U.S. Department of Agriculture (Obama, 2012), but her decision was likely informed by U.S. history and her own character (e.g., Fisher, 1984). Even soldiers began participating in gardening campaigns: U.K. soldiers grew gardens on station posts out of boredom; American soldiers followed with gardens at their posts (Smith, 2013). By sharing the gardening experience, U.K. and U.S. soldiers formed a community narrative (e.g., Fisher, 1984). United Kingdom campaign planners extended Dig for Victory through a parallel campaign for children. The campaign included cartoon characters Doctor (Smith, 2013) or Captain Carrot, Potato Pete, songs, and cookbooks (Gibbs, 2013). The following Dig for Victory lyrics could have appealed to adults or children:

> Those who have the will to win,
> Cook potatoes in their skin,

Knowing that the sight of peelings,
Deeply hurts Lord Woolton's feelings.

(Wilkins & Wilkins, 2011)

Anthems, poems, and nursery rhymes in garden campaigns lend merit to the narrative paradigm assertion that people are essentially storytellers (Fisher, 1984).

DISCUSSION

What shared community narrative emerged from WWII gardening campaigns? Through personal sacrifice, individuals demonstrated a new kind of patriotic service to their country.

With propaganda one might expect a simplistic message; after all, the goal of such campaigns is to facilitate particular behavior. By hiring professional artists to design garden campaign visuals, the United Kingdom and the United States revealed how important aesthetic components were in Dig for Victory and Victory Garden outreach. As with previous research (Witkowski, 2003), the present study indicates that visuals in both wartime gardening campaigns were utilized to evoke emotions. Thus, messages alone were not sufficient for campaign success. Visuals conveyed a message all their own. Replication of foot-on-spade visuals in the Dig for Victory campaign provided regular reminders to U.K. citizens. Aesthetic variety was also a hallmark of the Dig for Victory campaign. Messages were delivered via nursery rhymes, anthems, and films.

The United Kingdom and the United States analyzed public feedback to Dig for Victory and Victory Gardens. This approach counters the notion that propaganda is one sided. It can be argued that the inclusion of citizen perspectives transformed the campaigns from propaganda into public information. The governments demonstrated concern about the impact of campaign messages. According to Gillespie and colleagues (2008), citizen feedback revealed a substantial shift in perspective about Dig for Victory. Current campaign planners should note that expansive programs can effectively incorporate evaluation.

The civilian soldier category suggests that the U.K. and U.S. governments reconstructed patriotism. Participating in Dig for Victory and Victory Gardening was re-imagined as serving the country outside the military. Previous scholars have explored similar phenomena (e.g., Witkowski, 2003; Yesil, 2004). Unfortunately, perceptions about gardening might have had unintended consequences. Citizens who were unaccustomed to the rigors of gardening (e.g., Gillespie et al., 2008) might have felt duped by messaging that implied simplicity when cultivating a garden could be anything but. The civilian solder theme proved effective in bringing the public mindset into alignment with government focus. Public–private alignment might have aided the U.K. and U.S. governments in related issues such as equitable rations and energy conservation. Advertisers effectively constructed images of plenty to sustain war-weary Americans (Young, 2005).

The level of control the U.K. and U.S. governments held was evident by structured involvement in the gardening campaigns. This thematic category might be because of the lack of control that the U.K. and U.S. governments had over so many aspects of the war. The structure of Dig for Victory and Victory Gardens afforded them at least some semblance of control. The organizational rigidity could also have been a response to the limited success during the World War I gardening campaigns. Findings suggest citizens adhered to strict gardening guidelines. The U.K. government surely wanted to avoid Dig for Victory worsening food shortages.

The limited options for women in military service could explain the emergence of gendered representations in study findings. In the United States, women could participate through growing, cultivating, and serving food from Victory Gardens. Thus, they could simultaneously serve as nurturer and provider of the household. Yesil (2004) found that war gardening rhetoric reinforced traditional female roles in the home and presented gardening as a new normal. The gender differentiation between the United Kingdom and United States campaigns was unexpected. The Dig for Victory campaign, initially designated for men, gradually extended to children and even unemployed adults. The outreach beyond able-bodied men might have been necessitated by food shortages. In the United States, roles and responsibilities fell along distinct gender lines in campaign messaging: Gardening was for women and farming was for men. This delineation enabled farm and food processors to maintain traditional roles.

Dig for Victory program planners might have utilized notable experts to signify how critical food shortages were. Subject matter experts had credibility that ordinary citizens perhaps did not. The profiles of both campaigns might have been raised by including perspectives from experts, thus appealing to elite segments of the public. In the United Kingdom, a new audience profile could dispel the idea that Allotments were for low-income people (DeSilvey, 2003).

Participation of people from various walks of life appears to contradict the previous category. Improving the reach of the campaign would have disengaged citizens who already shunned the idea of Allotments in Dig for Victory (DeSilvey, 2003). Given the dire need for food in the United Kingdom, it would seem logical for the Dig for Victory to reach the widest audience possible. The question remains as to whether campaigns should be tailored to appeal to various classes of people, or whether experts should be the hallmark of campaigns to foster credibility among viewers. Ongoing evaluation about program success would be ideal for either approach, as long as campaigns are adjusted accordingly.

CONCLUSION

The access the author had to U.K. archival material limited findings of the present study. Academic scholars should partner with researchers in the United Kingdom in the future for firsthand access to analyze materials that have not yet been digitized. Scholars could also conduct analysis diaries from the Mass Observation study (e.g., Gillespie et al., 2008). Studying multiple diary entries would reveal insights about how other citizens experienced the Dig for Victory campaign. Future research into the phenomena should include extended time in the field, perhaps with the assistance of grant funding, to ascertain whether Dig for Victory and Victory Gardens were developed in tandem. The lack of an overt connection leaves a gap in the study findings.

Agencies in both countries addressed concerns arising from WWII; however, it is understandable why the U.K. campaign was conceptually different than the U.S. campaign. Dig for Victory could not have been effective in the United States, nor could the Victory Gardens campaign have worked in the United Kingdom. These similar campaigns only worked in context. The U.K. Dig for Victory campaign was a necessity, but the U.S. Victory Garden campaign was not essential. U.K. citizens were facing immediate physical danger because of the proximity of bombs and food shortages. The relationship of the two countries to food was pre-determined by the Lend-Lease agreement. Despite similarities, the Dig for Victory and Victory Garden campaigns were vastly different in social and cultural context.

NOTES

1. The Mass Observation was developed to record the views of ordinary British citizens. Nearly 3,000 people responded to questionnaires or sent in diary passages in installments during WWII. The material is held at the Mass Observation archive at the University of Sussex. All citizens are identified by pseudonyms (Collingham, 2013, p. xv).
2. The term "victory garden" originated with the conclusion of World War I. The government renamed what had been called "war gardens" to what was deemed better suited to the hoped-for result of WWII (Miller, 2003).

REFERENCES

Primary Data Sources

Box, K., & Thomas, G. (1944). The wartime social survey. *Journal of the Royal Statistical Society, 107*(3/4), 151–189.
British Library Board. (1941). *Learning timeline: Sources from history* [Infographics about the Dig for Victory campaign]. Retrieved December 1, 2012, from http://www.bl.uk/learning/timeline/item107597.html

Bureau of Industrial Conservation: War Production Board. (1942). *Save waste fats.* [Poster]. Propaganda posters collection. Howard Gotlieb Archival Research Center at Boston University, MA.

Bureau of Operations Office of Facts and Figures. (c. 1942). [Statement]. William Bennett Lewis Collection. Howard Gotlieb Archival Research Center at Boston University, MA.

Internet Archive (Prelinger Collection). (1944). *Victory Gardens: WWII gardening tips.* [Video file]. Retrieved November 15, 2012, from http://archive.org/details/victory_garden

Kane, R.K. (1943, January 12). *Progress report of the Bureau of Intelligence.* [Memorandum]. William Bennett Lewis Collection. Howard Gotlieb Archival Research Center at Boston University, MA.

National Archives (Ministry of Information and Ministry of Agriculture). (1942). *Dig for Victory* [Video file]. Retrieved November 15, 2012, from http://www.nationalarchives.gov.uk/theartofwar/films/dig_victory.htm

National Archives (Ministry of Agriculture). (1944). *Dig for plenty.* [Poster]. Retrieved December 1, 2012, from http://www.nationalarchives.gov.uk/theartofwar/inf3.htm

Office of War Information. (1943a). *Food is a weapon.* [Poster]. Propaganda Posters Collection. Howard Gotlieb Archival Research Center at Boston University, MA.

Office of War Information. (1943b). *Help bring them back to you.* [Poster]. Propaganda Posters Collection. Howard Gotlieb Archival Research Center at Boston University, MA.

Office of War Information. (1943c). *How the homefront fights.* [Victory Gardens]. William Bennett Lewis Collection. Howard Gotlieb Archival Research Center at Boston University, MA.

Office of War Information. (1943d). *Poster Distribution Bulletin.* [Bulletin]. William Bennett Lewis Collection. Howard Gotlieb Archival Research Center at Boston University, MA.

Office of War Information. (1943e). *We'll have lots to eat this winter.* [Poster]. Propaganda Posters Collection. Howard Gotlieb Archival Research Center at Boston University, MA.

Office of War Information. (1943f). *Where our men are fighting.* [Victory Gardens]. Propaganda Posters Collection. Howard Gotlieb Archival Research Center at Boston University, MA.

Office of War Information. (1943g). *Work on a farm . . . this summer.* [Poster]. Propaganda Posters Collection. Howard Gotlieb Archival Research Center at Boston University, MA.

Office of War Information. (1945). *The facts about 1945 Victory Gardens.*

Telegraph. (1941). *Dig for Victory: Vegetable growing during WWII in pics.* [Photographs from the Dig for Victory campaign]. Retrieved December 1, 2012, from http://www.telegraph.co.uk/gardening/howtogrow/9967597/Dig-for-victory-vegetable-growing-during-WWII-in-pics.html

U.S. Department of Agriculture. (1943). *Victory Garden leader's handbook.*

U.S. Food Administration. (c. 1943a). *Food.* [Poster]. Propaganda Posters Collection. Howard Gotlieb Archival Research Center at Boston University, MA.

U.S. Food Administration. (c. 1943b). *Save.* [Poster]. Propaganda Posters Collection. Howard Gotlieb Archival Research Center at Boston University, MA.

Waley, H.D. (1942). British documentaries and the war effort. *Public Opinion Quarterly, 6*(4), 604–609.

Young & Rubicam, Inc. (c. 1943). *How to make posters that will help win the war* [Study of Canadian War Posters]. William Bennett Lewis Collection. Howard Gotlieb Archival Research Center at Boston University, MA.

Secondary Data Sources

Azarian, R. (2011). Potentials and limitations of comparative method in social science. *International Journal of Humanities and Social Science, 1*(4), 113–125.

Burros, M. (2009, March 19). Obamas to plant vegetable garden at White House. *New York Times*. Retrieved December 9, 2012, from http://www.citizenstrade.org/ctc/wp-content/uploads/2011/05/20090319_obamastoplantvegetablegarden_nyt.pdf

Collingham, L. (2011). *The taste of war: World War II and the battle for food*. New York, NY: Penguin.

Daymon, C., & Holloway, I. (2002). *Qualitative research methods in public relations and marketing communications*. New York, NY: Routledge.

DeSilvey, C. (2003). Cultivated histories in a Scottish allotment garden. *Cultural Geographies, 10*, 442–468.

Fereday, J., & Muir-Cochrane, E. (2006) Demonstrating rigor using thematic analysis: A hybrid approach of inductive and deductive coding and theme development. *International Journal of Qualitative Methods, 5*(1). Retrieved January 29, 2012, from http://ejournals.library.ualberta.ca/index.php/IJQM/article/view/4411/3530

Fisher, W. R. (1984). Narration as a human communication paradigm: The case of public moral argument. *Communication Monographs, 51*, 1–21.

Gibbs, M. (2013, April 16). How "Dig for Victory" campaign helped win the War. *Telegraph*. Retrieved December 1, 2012, from http://www.telegraph.co.uk/earth/environment/9996180/How-Dig-for-Victory-campaign-helped-win-the-War.html

Gillespie, A., Cornish, F., Aveling, E.-L., & Zittoun, T. (2008). Conflicting community commitments: A dialogical analysis of a British woman's World War II diaries. *Journal of Community Psychology, 36*(1), 35–52. doi:10.1002/jcop.20215

Ginn, F. (2012). Dig for victory! New histories of wartime gardening in Britain. *Journal of Historical Geography, 38*, 294–305.

Harvey, D., & Riley, M. (2009). "Fighting from the fields": Developing the British "National Farm" in the Second World War. *Journal of Historical Geography, 35*, 495–516.

Horten, G. (1996). "Propaganda must be painless": Radio entertainment and government propaganda during World War II. *Prospects, 21*, 373–395. doi:10.1017/S0361233300006591

Jowett, G. S., & O'Donnell, V. (1992). *Propaganda and persuasion*. Newbury Park, CA: Sage.

Krznaric, R. (2007). *Food coupons and bald mountains: What the history of resource scarcity can teach us about tackling climate change* [Occasional paper]. New York, NY: Human Development Report Office.

Lambert, C. A., & Wang, Y. (2013, June). *Planting messages: A narrative paradigm analysis of the World War II Victory Garden campaign*. Paper presented at the annual International History of Public Relations Conference, Bournemouth University, Bournemouth, UK.

L'Etang, J. (1998). State propaganda and bureaucratic intelligence: The creation of public relations in 20th century Britain. *Public Relations Review, 24*(4), 413–441.

Lindlof, T. R., & Taylor, B. C. (2011). *Qualitative communication research methods*. Thousand Oaks, CA: Sage.

McCracken, G. (1988). Nine key issues: Issue 4: Investigator as instrument. In M. L. Miller, J. Van Maanen, & P. K. Manning (Series Eds.), *Qualitative research methods: Vol. 13. The long interview* (p. 20). Beverly Hills, CA: Sage.

Miller, C. (2003). In the sweat of our brow: Citizenship in American domestic practice during World War II—Victory Gardens. *Journal of American Culture, 26*(3), 395–409.

Obama, M. (2012). *American grown: The story of the White House kitchen garden and gardens across America*. New York, NY: Crown.

Olson, L. (2010). *Citizens of London: The Americans who stood with Britain in its darkest, finest hour*. New York, NY: Random House.

Riessman, C. K. (2005). Narrative analysis. In N. Kelly et al. (Eds.), *Narrative memory & everyday life* (pp. 1–7). Huddersfield, UK: University of Huddersfield. Retrieved December 1, 2012, from http://eprints.hud.ac.uk/4920/

Smith, D. (2013). *The spade as mighty as the sword: The story of the Second World War "Dig for Victory" campaign*. London: Aurum Press.

U.S. Department of Agriculture (2011). About us. *National Institute of Food and Agriculture*. Retrieved December 1, 2012, from http://www.csrees.usda.gov/qlinks/extension.html

Wilkins, D., & Wilkins, W. (2011, May). *Home sweet home front*. Retrieved December 1, 2012, from http://www.homesweethomefront.co.uk/web_pages/hshf_dig_for_victory_pg.htm

Witkowski, T.H. (2003). World War II poster campaigns: Preaching frugality to American consumers. *Journal of Advertising, 32*(1), 69–82.

Witkowski, T.H., & Jones, D.G.B. (2006). Qualitative historical research in marketing. In R. W. Belk (Ed.), *Handbook of qualitative research in marketing* (pp. 70–82). Cheltenham: Edward Elgar.

Yesil, B. (2004). "Who said this is a man's war?" Propaganda, advertising discourse and the representation of war worker women during the Second World War. *Media History, 10*(2), 103–117.

Young, D.G. (2005). Sacrifice, consumption, and the American way of life: Advertising and domestic propaganda during World War II. *Communication Review, 8*, 27–52.

New Media Challenges and Opportunities

17 Tweeting Charities
Perceptions, Resources, and Effective Twitter Practices for the Nonprofit Sector

Jeanine D. Guidry, Gregory D. Saxton, and Marcus Messner

Social media have become ubiquitous. Two-thirds of adult Internet users now use social networking sites, a number that has doubled since 2008 (Duggan & Brenner, 2013). As of the start of 2014, Facebook had 1.3 billion monthly active users who spend 640 million minutes using the service each month; Twitter had 645 million registered users with 58 million tweets sent daily; and YouTube reported that 4.25 billion daily video views and 65 hours of video are uploaded every minute (statisticbrain.com, 2014a; 2014b; 2014c). Relative newcomers Instagram and Pinterest reported 150 million and 70 million users, respectively (Bennett, 2014). Given these staggering numbers, nonprofit organizations have increasingly come to adopt social media to connect and engage with a "wired" populace.

At the same time, academic research on how nonprofit organizations should use social media is only just beginning to address the key issues confronting them. Scholars are starting to get a sense of why organizations are adopting social media (Nah & Saxton, 2013), along with the frequency with which they engage in dialogic engagement strategies (Waters, Burnett, Lamm, & Lucas, 2009). However, little is known about best practices (Messner et al., 2013) or about the barriers and challenges to the effective organizational use of social media. The study presented in this chapter presents an exploratory analysis that seeks to address these issues in two ways. First, by building on nascent research into best practices of social media use (Guidry, 2013) and the organizational determinants of social media practices (Nah & Saxton, 2013), the study examines the relationship between key organizational factors and measures of the successful use of Twitter. Second, a survey was carried out to study nonprofit managers' perceptions of the barriers and challenges to social media use.

LITERATURE REVIEW

Social Media and Public Relations. The emergence of social media has created new possibilities for interpersonal and organizational communication. A decade ago Kent and Taylor (2002) recommended online communications as an ideal avenue for fostering dialogue. Social media platforms have since created new avenues for organizations to connect with their publics through real-time dialogic and feedback mechanisms (Lovejoy, Waters, & Saxton, 2012).

Social media has also changed the face of public relations. Traditional public relations practice has been unidirectional from the PR professional or organization to the intended public. Perhaps one of the most relevant aspects of the social media revolution is that organizations and their stakeholders can now engage in direct online conversations. It is crucial for nonprofits to understand what works best in social media in order to optimize their efforts and reach the most positive outcomes.

Nonprofits and Social Media. Social media platforms allow nonprofits to directly engage with their audiences and build communities around their causes (Messner et al., 2013). Over the past few years, large nonprofits have almost universally adopted social media, arguably at a more rapid pace than the business world and academia. But when it comes to small and medium-sized nonprofits, studies have found that these nonprofits lag behind their larger counterparts in the rate of social media adoption (Guo & Saxton, 2014).

Social media offer many potential benefits for nonprofit organizations. Notably, social media have the potential to be dynamic relationship-building tools (Dumont, 2010). In addition, social media platforms allow stakeholders to self-organize and collaborate in support of an organization's mission (Keim & Noji, 2011). Social media platforms also offer nonprofits an additional approach to fundraising through strategies like crowdfunding, through which individuals across the globe can network and pool their resources to support efforts by others. Potential donors are solicited by someone in their social network, and the donors are therefore often more likely to trust the solicitor (Saxton & Wang, 2013).

Despite the benefits offered by social media, nonprofit organizations must approach this tool with realistic expectations. A study of mid-sized nonprofit organizations by Ogden and Starita (2009) expressed several often-heard cautions, for instance that most videos on YouTube have fewer than 100 views and that many of the fundraising campaigns on Facebook Causes failed to raise any money. It has also been argued that the more social media grows and spreads, the more "noise" is present: "When everyone is publishing and broadcasting, no one is reading or watching" (Ogden & Starita, 2009, p. 10).

While nonprofits in general acknowledge the importance of online interactivity and dialogue, they mostly use social media as a one-way communication channel. Admittedly, many nonprofits lack the time and resources to properly manage their social media platforms, but just creating a profile without maintaining it and without using it to interact with publics will yield at best limited results. Overall, research suggests that, so far, nonprofits have struggled to take advantage of the interactive nature and possibilities of social media (Waters et al., 2009).

How Nonprofits Use Twitter for Effective Public Relations. Founded in 2006, Twitter is a microblogging service that allows users to share information in 140 characters or less. The character limit imposed by the platform makes it possible to send messages, known as "tweets," to and from cell phones and other mobile devices as text messages; the messages also appear in the account holder's Twitter newsfeed on their desktop computer, laptop, or tablet. There are five primary technological tools available through tweets: direct messages, retweets, hyperlinks, hashtags, and user mentions. People now commonly use the service for news updates, shared experiences, and dialogue. In fact, Twitter's growth has been explosive, from 1.3 million registered users in March 2008 to 241 million active monthly users at the end of 2013 (Twitter, 2014).

Unsurprisingly, considering Twitter's relatively brief existence, existing academic research into its use is limited. Several studies have focused on how nonprofits use the various Twitter communication tools (Guo & Saxton, 2014). Of the few studies available, most have only focused on the characteristics of nonprofits' Twitter use, especially with respect to dialogic engagement (Waters & Jamal, 2011; Lovejoy & Saxton, 2012). These have found that, similar to Facebook, nonprofit organizations primarily use Twitter for one-way messages and fail to capitalize on the interactive nature of the platform. A study of news organizations refers to this broadcast model as "shoveling tweets," sending out as many tweets as possible without much consideration for whether and how followers may respond (Messner, Linke, & Eford, 2012).

Still, some recent research has shown nonprofit organizations' improved engagement on social media as compared to, say, websites. For instance, using an original coding scheme in which tweets are considered informational, promotional and mobilizational, or dialogic and community building, Lovejoy and Saxton (2012) found that 25.8% of all tweets sent by a sample of large nonprofit organizations were dialogic and community building in nature.

Another recent study that analyzed Twitter engagement of leading health sector nonprofits found that, although these organizations are improving in their use of Twitter, nonprofits are still in need of best-practice guidelines to better engage with their publics on Twitter (Messner et al., 2013). In response, Guidry (2013) highlighted a number of uses that seemed to indicate best practices in Twitter engagement strategies. This research study builds on these studies in identifying a core set of best practice measures. Our first research question is:

RQ1: Which organizational features are related to the successful use of Twitter?

Organizational Factors and the Successful Employment of Social Media. Lack of resources, specifically time and staff, is the most common barrier to the successful use of social media (Briones, Kuch, Liu, & Jin, 2011). Non-profits are often stretched thin with small staffs unable to fully support large social media efforts. The study by Briones and colleagues (2011) indicated that it is often a challenge to get board members, who tend to be from an older generation, to understand the need for social media. While the per-centage of older adults that use social media steadily increases, it still lags behind other age groups (Zickuhr & Madden, 2012).

While the available literature is limited, there is reason to believe that having a large number of followers on Twitter is positively correlated with increased Twitter activity. Saxton and Wang (2013) compared traditional and online fundraising and found that the more fans an organization has, the more funds are raised through the Facebook Causes application. The authors call this the "social network effect." The organizations' fans reach expanding circles of online friends in their own social networks, which ultimately increases both word-of-mouth and charitable contributions (Saxton & Wang, 2013).

Several studies also indicate that small and medium sized nonprofits lag behind their larger counterparts in terms of social media adoption (Dumont, 2010; Nah & Saxton, 2013). Engagement requires a certain level of organi-zational capacity that many of these nonprofits simply do not have. Young (2012) found a significant correlation between budget size and the amount of time devoted to social media, concluding that larger organizations spend more time on social media than smaller ones.

Organizational Perceptions of Social Media. There is little evidence in the existing literature concerning why organizational leaders choose to use any social media platform. Current literature has mainly focused on content and outcomes, but very little on why social media are being used. One key finding from exploratory research suggests nonprofit social media managers often have limited time available for Twitter management and engagement (Young, 2012). It is thus important to know what they perceive to be the greatest benefits and pitfalls of the use of Twitter in their daily practice.

In the aforementioned study by Briones and colleagues (2011), 40 Ameri-can Red Cross employees answered questions about how they used social media to build relationships. The interviewees consistently referred to open two-way dialogue being essential to building relationships. They empha-sized the role of two-way communication in finding out what the public is thinking and how the public thinks the organization can improve. Other respondents described Twitter as a helpful tool to keep track of news and technological developments. Social media in general was seen as helpful for communicating with volunteers, funders, and community members in humanitarian crisis situations. Local media outlets also monitored the Red Cross Twitter feed and contacted the organization to develop stories.

A survey by Young (2012) of 125 nonprofit human service organizations of all sizes in Richmond, Virginia, showed that nearly half of the respondents felt that social media has enhanced the relationship between their organization and its stakeholders or the general community. Furthermore, 60% of organizations agreed that social media offers new opportunities to interact with both people and other organizations. Less than 50% viewed social media as a helpful tool for fundraising (Young, 2012).

In effect, several studies have delved into organizational perceptions of social media use. Such research has primarily focused on the potential benefits of social media use. This study adds to and expands on existing research by focusing not only on the benefits but also the challenges and pitfalls of social media use. Our second research question is:

RQ2: How do nonprofit social media managers perceive the use, benefits, and challenges of Twitter for their organizations?

METHOD

Sample. A sample of large, primarily U.S.-based nonprofit organizations was used. These organizations, in spite of the ease of use and relative low cost of social media implementation, are more likely than smaller organizations to have a significant presence on Twitter (Lovejoy & Saxton, 2012). Specifically, this study examined organizations from the most recent *Nonprofit Times 100* list in 2011. Of the top 50 organizations on that list, 25 were randomly chosen. In addition, 25 nonprofits were randomly selected from the *Top Nonprofits on Twitter* list (Top Nonprofits, 2012), a list of the 50 nonprofits with the most Twitter followers. Since eight organizations in the sample were present on both lists, an additional eight organizations were randomly drawn, four from each list.

Data Gathering and Analysis Plan. The research design for this study consisted of two different strategies: the statistical analysis of tweets sent by the 50 organizations and an Internet survey sent to these organizations' social media managers.

Statistical Analyses. For the statistical analyses, during the eight-week period between June 14 and August 9, 2012, content from the Twitter accounts of these 50 organizations was sampled during a constructed two-week time period. Each day of the week was randomly selected twice within the eight-week period. This produced a sample of the following 14 non-consecutive days: June 14, 20, 23, 26, 29; July 1, 3, 5, 19, 16, 23, 27; and August 1, 4. On each of these days, all tweets and retweets by each of the 50 organizations were collected. This resulted in a sample of 3,415 total tweets.

These tweets were first coded for a series of best-practice variables and then aggregated to develop a series of organizational-level measures. Specifically, based on prior research (Guidry, 2013) that identified a series of best practices in nonprofit engagement on Twitter, the coders analyzed each of the organizations in terms of their performance in the following 11 best-practice areas:

focus on others by using external mentions and external hyperlinks in order to get stakeholders to retweet the original tweet

keep tweets simple and short in order to engage stakeholders in conversation

use more complex tweets in order to get stakeholders to retweet or favorite the original tweet

ask questions and use direct replies in order to engage stakeholders in conversation

use more public education than marketing tweets to get stakeholders to retweet or favorite the original tweet

use more call-to-action than event promotion or fundraising tweets in order to get stakeholders to retweet or favorite the original tweet

use photos instead of videos in tweets in order to get stakeholders to retweet the original tweet

tweet more on weekends in order to get stakeholders to retweet or favorite the original tweet

thank stakeholders for their input retweets and mentions in order to engage them in conversation

ask stakeholders to retweet tweets in order to engage them in direct conversation

use a dedicated hashtag in order to get stakeholders to retweet the original tweet.

Based on these Twitter practices, the following organizational-level variables were created: mean number of external mentions per tweet; mean number of external hyperlinks per tweet; mean complexity of tweets sent; total number of questions; percentage of all tweets that are questions; total number of direct replies; percentage of all tweets that are direct replies; total number of weekend tweets; percentage of all tweets sent on the weekend; mean number of dialogic messages/tweets; number of tweets sent; and the number of users the organization is following.

Because the study attempted to examine which organizational factors are related to the successful organizational use of Twitter, coders also analyzed a series of financial and other measures for each of the 50 organizations. These variables were taken from each nonprofit's Form 990, an informational tax form that most U.S. tax-exempt organizations must file annually. Measures include such variables as total number of employees and volunteers, total assets and revenues, program service revenues, and fundraising expenses.

These organizational variables were related to the best-practice variables in order to explore which organizational features seem to be related to the successful use of Twitter. Since seven of the organizations were based outside the United States, the Form 990 was not available for them and the sample for statistical analyses was therefore reduced to 43 organizations. A combination of Pearson's *r* correlation tests and *t*-tests were used to analyze the relationships between these organizational factors and the Twitter best-practice measures.

Internet Survey. A survey instrument was also developed for this study based on previous research in this area (Young, 2012). The purpose of this survey was to provide context on how the social media managers of the 50 organizations in this study perceive the use of Twitter in their communication with organizational stakeholders.

The survey was administered through the Internet survey tool SurveyMonkey and contained 20 questions. Seventeen were closed-ended questions, including three demographic questions, three questions about the nature of the respondents' organizations, and 11 questions about the respondents' Twitter use. The remaining questions were open ended and invited input on what the respondents perceived as being beneficial and challenging about the use of Twitter.

RESULTS

The Relationship Between Organizational Factors and Best Practices in Twitter Use. The analyses reveal several interesting relationships between organizational factors and effective Twitter usage. To start, while prior studies have shown a strong connection between an organization's total assets and the ability to successfully leverage IT resources into improved organizational performance (Hackler & Saxton, 2007), this does not seem to be as clearly the case with social media. Unlike previous technologies (e.g., computerization), the findings of this study show that the successful deployment of social media platforms is not as dependent on the financial resources an organization possesses, with few significant relationships between financial assets and the best-practice measures.

One of the strongest predictors of effective Twitter usage was the number of volunteers engaged with the organization. The number of volunteers, ranging from 15 for CamFed to 22 million for the American Heart Association, seems to be a significant predictor of a nonprofit's use of several core best practices. The number of volunteers is strongly and positively correlated with the total number of dialogic tweets, $r(41) = .893$, $p < .01$; with the average number of dialogic tweets, $r(41) = .509$, $p < .01$; with the number of tweets that included an external mention, $r(41) = .580$, $p < .01$; with the total number of tweets that contained a question, $r(41) = .598$, $p < .01$; and with the proportion of tweets that include a direct reply, $r(41) = .528$,

$p < .01$. These are all indicators of best practices related to an organization focusing on its stakeholders and publics. In addition, the number of volunteers was negatively correlated with the average number of marketing tweets an organization sent out, $r(41) = -.306$, $p < .05$. This is related to the best practice of sending out more public education tweets as opposed to marketing tweets.

We also found a number of interesting relationships with the proportion of an organization's tweets that was sent out on the weekend, which was positively and significantly correlated with the organization's total assets, $r(41) = .382$, $p < .05$; the number of employees, $r(41) = .349$, $p < .05$; and total program service revenue, $r(41) = .342$, $p < .05$.

General Survey Results. The survey produced 16 responses from the 50 organizations, for a 32% response rate. Given the relatively low number of responses, caution must be taken in generalizing the results. Nevertheless, the survey provides a window into the sentiments about using Twitter held by a sample of nonprofit social media managers. All 16 respondents were the designated Twitter handlers for their organization. The cultural, domestic needs, health, and international needs sectors were represented by three organizations each, two were religious in nature, one focused on the environment, and one on youth.

Twelve of the respondents (75%) were female and four (25%) were male. The majority of respondents ($n = 11$, 68.8%) were 30 to 39 years old, while 25% ($n = 4$) were between 18 and 29 years old, and one was between 40 and 49 years old. Of the respondents, 68.8% ($n = 11$) indicated that their nonprofit organization employed more than 100 people, 12.5% ($n = 2$) that their organization employed between 50 and 100 people, and 18.8% between 20 and 49 people ($n = 3$).

Organizational Perceptions. Of the respondents, 43.8% ($n = 7$) have used Twitter in their nonprofit organization for 3 to 5 years, and 12.5% ($n = 2$) have been tweeting on behalf of their organization for more than 5 years— an impressive length, considering Twitter itself has only been around since 2006. Roughly a third of respondents (31.25%, $n = 5$) have been tweeting on behalf of their organization for 1 to 2 years, with the remaining 12.5% ($n = 2$) doing so for less than a year. All respondents tweet at least several times daily on behalf of the organization, and all but one respondent use Twitter privately in addition to their professional use.

When asked what type of content their organization usually shared on Twitter, all of the respondents stated they shared photos from community and organization projects. All of the respondents also indicated they shared links to the organization itself. The majority of the nonprofits tweeted out links to specific information, as well as videos from community and organization projects (both 93.5%, $n = 15$). 62.5% ($n = 10$) sent out organization newsletters and similar information, while 56.3% ($n = 9$) tweeted out links to other organizations. Fifty percent ($n = 8$) replied they shared posts about quotes, Twitter chats, pictograms, free resources, Bible verses, survivor stories, and relevant news articles.

Reasons for Using Twitter. When asked to indicate all the reasons their organizations use Twitter, the 16 respondents provided a total of 85 responses. A vast majority (93.8%, $n = 15$) indicated their organization uses Twitter to engage with the community, as well as for fundraising (87.5%, $n = 14$). A slightly smaller portion of the nonprofits uses Twitter to promote services or events or to demonstrate transparency and accountability (both 81.3%, $n = 13$). The majority of organizations also report using Twitter to communicate and collaborate with others (75%, $n = 12$) and to engage new donors (68.8%, $n = 11$). Less common was the use of Twitter to recruit volunteers (43.8%, $n = 7$).

General Perceptions of Twitter. Looking at the social media managers' opinions about their use of Twitter, most respondents indicated they strongly or somewhat agreed that Twitter added to their communications workload. None of the respondents said Twitter lightened their workload, but all except one responded that Twitter created new opportunities for them to reach out to their organization's stakeholders, as shown in Table 17–1.

Perceptions of the Benefits and Challenges of Twitter. The survey also included two open-ended questions. The first one asked what the respondents found most beneficial about the use of Twitter for the communications purposes of their organization. The answers were diverse and gave an indication of the diverse needs of the nonprofits in this study.

Many of the reported benefits related to Twitter's ability for real-time communications, with respondents touting "the ability to get the word out immediately" and "reach . . . a broad audience quickly," stressing "the timeliness—we can communicate about things happening in real time." A second benefit concerned the potential to reach new stakeholders: "Twitter makes our large organization smaller—people can ask us their questions and get answers in non-PR/marketing lingo." Others similarly noted that, with Twitter, "we are able to directly engage with people," and that Twitter helps in "reach[ing] a unique segment of our audience who may not get our messages any other way," in "reaching out to people who do not know us," in "reaching people frequently, wherever they are," and in "making connections with other people talking about similar issues." A third category focused on some of Twitter's unique characteristics, including "the frequency the medium allows, as compared to blogging or Facebook status updates," "Twitter makes it easy to reach out to the customer directly," and "it's the easiest way to reach fans."

When asked what they found most challenging about the use of Twitter, social media managers focused heavily on time-related challenges, including

Table 17–1 Perceptions about Twitter for Nonprofit Organizations.

	Strongly agree	Somewhat agree	Neither agree nor disagree	Somewhat disagree	Strongly disagree	Don't know	Total
The use of Twitter has added to my communications workload	37.50% $n = 6$	25% $n = 4$	31.25% $n = 5$	6.25% $n = 1$	0% $n = 0$	0% $n = 0$	$n = 16$
The use of Twitter has made my workload lighter	0% $n = 0$	0% $n = 0$	50% $n = 8$	18.75% $n = 3$	31.25% $n = 5$	0% $n = 0$	$n = 16$
The use of Twitter has created new opportunities for me to reach out to our organization's stakeholders	62.50% $n = 10$	37.50% $n = 6$	0% $n = 0$	0% $n = 0$	0% $n = 0$	0% $n = 0$	$n = 16$
The use of Twitter has created new ways for me to communicate with our organizations stakeholders	56.25% $n = 9$	37.50% $n = 6$	6.25% $n = 1$	0% $n = 0$	0% $n = 0$	0% $n = 0$	$n = 16$
I find Twitter intuitive to use	43.75% $n = 7$	43.75% $n = 7$	0% $n = 0$	0% $n = 0$	0% $n = 0$	0% $n = 0$	$n = 16$
I find Twitter awkward to use	0% $n = 0$	6.25% $n = 1$	12.50% $n = 2$	31.25% $n = 5$	50% $n = 8$	0% $n = 0$	$n = 16$

the difficulties associated with "staying engaged everyday" and "hav[ing] to move quickly to be relevant." The issue of "noise" and attention (Ogden & Starita, 2009) was also prevalent, with respondents complaining about "getting heard through all the clutter" and the "competition for user attention with millions of other Twitter accounts." Needing more manpower was also frequently mentioned, with respondents citing the "need . . . [for] more people to answer all questions coming in," that "it's a lot to take on to do it right," and "to use Twitter to its full extent, we would need more people/ time." Finally, respondents noted the challenges imposed in "being precise, concise, informative, and helpful in 140 characters," with the "character limits mak[ing] it hard to communicate bigger-picture ideas."

DISCUSSION

This study focused on objective and subjective factors related to the successful organizational use of Twitter. Organizations with more volunteers were more consistent users of a list of Twitter best practices that included using external mentions, questions, and direct replies. Subjectively, the social media managers expressed both appreciation for Twitter as a platform as well as frustration with its functionality. The nonprofits in this study seemed not just aware but convinced of the increased significance of Twitter in their public relations efforts, in line with the more general findings by Wright and Hinson (2012).

While there does not seem to be a clear organizational profile for a nonprofit that uses the Twitter best practices mentioned above, there do seem to be some interesting characteristics related to individual best practices. Smaller nonprofits—with fewer employees and volunteers, and lower total assets—send more marketing tweets compared to public education tweets, which can be an indication of using Twitter more like a one-way broadcast channel. Nonprofits with more volunteers tweet more messages of a dialogic nature—more direct replies, more questions, and more external mentions. It seems that nonprofits with more volunteers are better versed in communicating with these volunteers, and therefore also with their Twitter followers.

According to the survey respondents, most social media managers are fairly experienced in their field. More than half have been tweeting for their nonprofit for 3 years or more—almost half the age of Twitter itself. All tweeted at least daily, and several reported tweeting more than 30 times a week. All but one use Twitter privately in addition to professionally.

A relatively large proportion of the respondents—almost 70%—use Twitter to engage new donors; close to 90% use Twitter for direct fundraising. While fundraising through Twitter may very well work for these organizations, exploring this concept was beyond the limits of this study and should be further explored in future research. For creating other types of engagement, however, fundraising tweets are not effective. Less than 1% of all conversation tweets focused on fundraising, and less than 4% of the most retweeted messages did. Considering the importance of conversations, it was encouraging to observe that virtually all respondents used Twitter to actively engage their communities, and 75% used it to communicate and collaborate with others. Combined with the results of another recent study (Lovejoy et al., 2012), there seems to be an increasing awareness of the importance of two-way communication on social media platforms, an encouraging shift from the earlier emphasis on asymmetrical communication between nonprofits and their stakeholders (Waters et al., 2009; Waters & Jamal, 2011).

The nonprofit social media managers surveyed considered the immediacy of Twitter both a blessing and a curse. When asked what they found most beneficial about Twitter, the majority mentioned the ability to reach both existing and new audiences quickly. Being required to communicate quickly, however, was the other side of a double-edged sword. Twitter is in many ways a new language to be learned, with respondents mentioning the challenges of "being precise, concise, informative, and helpful" in 140 characters or less. Finding training opportunities in how to "speak Twitter" may be an important task for social media managers.

CONCLUSION

A few limitations of this study should be considered. First, the sample was limited to the largest U.S. nonprofit organizations and nonprofits with the most Twitter followers. Future studies might focus on a sample of smaller and medium-sized organizations. Second, this study focused exclusively on the general nonprofit sector, providing an overview of the field. Future research into the use of Twitter among nonprofits should consider specific groups such as human service organizations, environmental nonprofits, nonprofits in the health sector. Other segments of the nonprofit sector may provide insight that cannot be gleaned from the data in this study.

Despite the limitations, this study provides unique insights into how managers perceive social media and on the organizational features that facilitate or hinder effective social media use. Given the considerable costs in time, money, and human resources needed to launch a sustained and successful social media presence, such insights are increasingly vital.

In the end, as described by our study's respondents, social media present an exciting opportunity to engage volunteers, donors, supporters, and others in the nonprofit's charitable work. Yet with the excitement and opportunity comes trepidation and frustration with the challenges associated with a new communication technology. Although we found financial assets in general to not be a critical barrier, Twitter has added to workloads, there are shortages with expertise and human resources, and training has been "on the job." Our findings thus suggest a shift in thinking is called for—to effectively leverage tools like Twitter, nonprofits need to afford their social media managers sufficient tools, training, and time.

REFERENCES

Bennett, S. (2014). Pinterest, Twitter, Facebook, Instagram, Google+, LinkedIn—Social media stats 2014. Retrieved April 12, 2014, from http://www.mediabistro.com/alltwitter/social-media-stats-2014_b54243

Briones, R. L., Kuch, B., Liu, B. F., & Jin, Y. (2011). Keeping up with the digital age: How the American Red Cross uses social media to build relationships. *Public Relations Review, 37*(1), 37–43. doi:10.1016/j.pubrev.2010.12.006

Duggan, M., & Brenner, J. (2013). *The demographics of social media users—2012.* Washington, DC: Pew Internet & American Life Project. Retrieved June 20, 2014, from http://www.pewinternet.org/2013/02/14/the-demographics-of-social-media-users-2012/

Dumont, G. E. (2010). *Nonprofit engagement of social networks.* 2010 ARNOVA conference.

Guidry, J. P. D. (2013). *A tale of many tweets: How stakeholders respond to nonprofit organizations' tweets.* Master of Professional Studies thesis, George Washington University, Washington, DC.

Guo, C., & Saxton, G. D. (2014). Tweeting social change: How social media are changing nonprofit advocacy. *Nonprofit and Voluntary Sector Quarterly, 43*(1), 57–79. doi:10.1177/0899764012471585

Hackler, D., & Saxton, G. D. (2007). The strategic use of information technology by nonprofit organizations: Increasing capacity and untapped potential. *Public Administration Review, 67*(3), 474–487.

Keim, M. E., & Noji, E. (2011). Emergent use of social media: A new age of opportunity for disaster resilience. *American Journal of Disaster Medicine, 6*(1), 47–54.

Kent, M., & Taylor, M. (2002). Toward a dialogic theory of public relations. *Public Relations Review, 28*(1), 21–37.

Lovejoy, K., & Saxton, G. D. (2012). Information, community, and action: How nonprofit organizations use social media. *Journal of Computer-Mediated Communication, 17*(3), 337–353. doi:10.1111/j.1083–6101.2012.01576.x

Lovejoy, K., Waters, R. D., & Saxton, G. D. (2012). Engaging stakeholders through Twitter: How nonprofit organizations are getting more out of 140 characters or less. *Public Relations Review, 38*(2), 313–318. doi:10.1016/j.pubrev.2012.01.005

Messner, M., Jin, Y., Medina-Messner, V., Meganck, S., Quarforth, S., & Norton, S. (2013). 140 characters for better health: An exploration of the Twitter engagement of leading nonprofit organizations. In H. N. Al-Deen & J. A. Hendricks (Eds.), *Social media and strategic communications.* Basingstoke, UK: Palgrave Macmillan.

Messner, M., Linke, M., & Eford, A. (2012). Shoveling tweets: An analysis of the microblogging engagement of traditional news organizations. *ISOJ Journal, 2*(1), 76–90.

Nah, S., & Saxton, G. D. (2013). Modeling the adoption and use of social media by nonprofit organizations. *New Media & Society, 15*(2), 294–313. doi:10.1177/1461444812452411

Ogden, T., & Starita, L. (2009). Social networking and mid-size nonprofits: What's the use? *Philanthropy Action.* Retrieved May 23, 2012, from http://www.philanthropyaction.com/articles/social_networking_and_mid-size_nonprofits_whats_the_use

Saxton, G. D., & Wang, L. (2013). The social network effect: The determinants of donations on social media sites. *Nonprofit and Voluntary Sector Quarterly.* Advance online publication. doi:10.1177/0899764013485159

statisticbrain.com. (2014a). Facebook statistics. Retrieved April 12, 2014, from http://www.statisticbrain.com/facebook-statistics/

statisticbrain.com. (2014b). Twitter statistics. Retrieved April 12, 2014, from http://www.statisticbrain.com/twitter-statistics/

statisticbrain.com. (2014c). YouTube statistics. Retrieved April 12, 2014, from http://www.statisticbrain.com/youtube-statistics/

Top Nonprofits. (2012). Top nonprofits on Twitter. Retrieved May 23, 2012, from http://topnonprofits.com/lists/top-nonprofits-on-twitter/

Twitter. (2014). Twitter reports fourth quarter and fiscal year 2013 results [Press release]. Retrieved April 23, 2014, from https://investor.twitterinc.com/releasedetail.cfm?ReleaseID=823321

Waters, R.D., Burnett, E., Lamm, A., & Lucas, J. (2009). Engaging stakeholders through social networking: How nonprofit organizations are using Facebook. *Public Relations Review, 35*(2), 102–106. doi:10.1016/j.pubrev.2009.01.006

Waters, R.D., & Jamal, J.Y. (2011). Tweet, tweet, tweet: A content analysis of nonprofit organizations' Twitter updates. *Public Relations Review, 37*(3), 321–324. doi:10.1016/j.pubrev.2011.03.002

Wright, D.K., & Hinson, M.D. (2012). *Examining how social and emerging media have been used in public relations between 2006 and 2012: A longitudinal analysis.* Paper presented at the BledCom Conference, Bled, Slovenia.

Young, J.A. (2012). *The current status of social media use among nonprofit human service organizations: An exploratory study.* Doctoral dissertation, Virginia Commonwealth University, Richmond. Retrieved from https://digarchive.library.vcu.edu/handle/10156/3775

Zickuhr, K., & Madden, M. (2012). Older adults and internet use. Retrieved October 29, 2013, from http://www.pewinternet.org/2012/06/06/older-adults-and-internet-use/

18 Nonprofits' Use of Facebook
An Examination of Organizational Message Strategies

Moonhee Cho and Tiffany Schweickart

Defined as "online resources that people use to share content: video, photos, images, text, ideas, insight, humor, opinion, gossip, news" (Drury, 2008, p. 274), social media has become a popular and indispensable element of people's daily life. Compared to traditional media, social media provides organizations with the potential benefit of engaging with other social media users. Such a two-way communication mechanism offered by social media creates a platform for ongoing dialogue and long-term bonds between an organization and its constituents. In other words, social media provides an organization with an opportunity to foster dialogic communication and build relationships with its key publics. Facebook, one of the most popular social media platforms, offers more engagement opportunities than ever before with the introduction of the Timeline.

Emphasizing the opportunity to explore new implications for organizational communication, many public relations scholars have extensively explored the role of social media as a tool for dialogic communication or managing relationships. However, even though Bortee and Seltzer (2009) argued that "organization comments in dialogic spaces" (p. 318), an additional strategy to the original dialogic communication principles, produced dialogic outcomes, there is a lack of research attempting to explore what types of messages or content is communicated through social media. Only Waters and Jamal (2011) and Lovejoy and Saxton (2012) have examined organizational message strategies on Twitter. Even though previous studies have found that information sharing is the most frequently used strategy, compared to dialogic communication or relationship management strategies, these findings are limited to Twitter, which, in nature, is used for real-time information updates. Given that Facebook is used more as a social engagement tool than Twitter (Garun, 2012) and considered a leading social media platform (Smith, 2013), it is imperative to investigate organizational message strategies on Facebook to understand the ways in which organizations communicate and build relationships with their constituents via social media. To this end, this study employs the four models of public relations proposed by Grunig and Hunt (1984) as a framework for exploring the types of message strategies nonprofit organizations use on Facebook. In doing so, this study will give a snapshot of current social media use by nonprofit organizations.

LITERATURE REVIEW

Social Media as an Effective Tool for Organizational Communication.
Social media is becoming increasingly popular in the modern world. Since its advent, social media has grown fast and influenced the daily lives of individuals in various ways, such as news consumption, communication, and interaction (Perdue, 2012; Pew Research Center, 2012). Almost 80% of active Internet users in the United States visit social media sites (Nielsen Report, 2011). Technological advancements, such as a smartphones and tablet PCs, allow individuals to access social media more easily with one click in downloaded applications.

Social media includes a variety of applications with distinct functions and structures, such as social network sites (SNSs) (e.g., Facebook, MySpace, and LinkedIn), blogs, Wikipedia, online message boards or forums, content communities (e.g., YouTube, Flickr), and microblogs (e.g., Twitter). Of the various types of social media, SNSs are the most popular and high profile social media types (Nielsen Report, 2011). For example, in October 2012, Facebook reached a total of one billion users (Huffington Post, 2012), meaning approximately one in every seven people in the world has a Facebook account.

Social media has also influenced the ways organizations communicate with their publics. Nearly 85% of American social media users expect that organizations should not only be present but also interact with their constituents in social media (Cone Business in Social Media Research, 2008). Nielsen Report (2011) found that 53% of individuals visit a brand's social media. Meeting constituents' expectations, many organizations actively use social media. According to eMarketer (2012), almost 90% of U.S. marketers use social media. This means that most companies, from small to large, use social media as marketing tools even though there is no clear evidence of how social media contributes to their bottom line (Paine, 2009). Twitter, blogs, LinkedIn, and Facebook are the top social media sites used by marketers (Stelzner, 2009).

Potential benefits offered by social media to organizations have been well documented. By connecting organizations or brands with constituents, social media helps them build brand awareness and loyalty (Gunelius, 2011). More importantly, social media offers an opportunity for the interaction, collaboration, and creating/sharing of various types of digital content among users (Universal McCann, 2008). In other words, social media is an indispensable tool for an organization to foster dialogic communication and build quality relationships with its key constituents (Kent & Taylor, 1998; Briones, Kuch, Liu, & Jin, 2011; Rubin, 2012). Grunig (2009) argued that social media has a crucial role in effective public relations practices, such as reaching global publics, implementing two-way symmetrical communication, and building relationships with publics.

Nonprofit Organizations' Use of Social Media. The nonprofit sector, like other sectors, has been proactive in adopting social media. According to Barns and Andonian (2011), nonprofit organizations leave corporations' standing in utilizing social media for a communication channel. With social media, nonprofit organizations can expand their reach to constituents, share organizational news, recruit supporters, and stay connected with key constituents. Although still in its infancy, some large nonprofit organizations have begun to utilize social media as a fundraising tool (Flandez, 2011). Some nonprofits also incorporate advanced social media or online techniques, such as online or social media games, for accomplishing organizational goals. Social gamers can raise funds for nonprofit organizations while being entertained (Ilsen, 2012). Indeed, being social is no longer optional for nonprofit organizations (Fine, 2011). Anticipating potential benefits—tangible and intangible—offered by social media, many nonprofits look for ways to utilize various types of social media or develop social media strategies to meet organizational missions.

Often under financially restricted circumstances, many nonprofit organizations adopt new technology or media to engage with their constituents in cost-effective ways. In this same thread, nonprofit professionals welcome various types of social media as a cost-effective channel for communicating/interacting with constituents. Moreover, social media offers nonprofit organizations an opportunity to engage with individuals without any time or geographical restrictions. Social media has become an essential tool for nonprofit organizations that have been faced with various challenges, such as increasing competition within and between sectors, declining governmental support, and declining public trust (Broom, 2009). While nonprofit organizations' adoption and use of social media is influenced by various internal and external factors surrounding the organizations, such as organizational strategies, capacity, governance, and external situations (Nah & Saxton, 2012) or the existence of a public relations department (Curtis et al., 2010), the increase in adoption and use of social media by nonprofit organizations is apparent. Through social media, nonprofits can disseminate organizational updates, solicit public support, and build/maintain relationships with their constituents in a cost-effective manner. Highlighting the values of social media to the nonprofit sector, many professionals urge nonprofit organizations to utilize social media tools and also provide some practical guidelines based on their own experiences and insights from successful or failed cases.

Communication Strategies for Social Media: Gaps between Theory and Practice. Both practitioners and academic scholars emphasize the value of social media, which helps organizations better engage with their key stakeholders. Among various theories, Kent and Taylor's (1998) dialogic communication and Hon and Grunig's (1999) relationship-building theory have been spotlighted in exploring the role of new media. First, Kent and Taylor's (1998) dialogic communication framework offers five principles (dialogic loop, usefulness of information, generation of return visits, intuitiveness/ ease of interface, conservation of visitors) to promote dialogic communication between an organization and its constituents. Although the dialogic framework was conceptualized for the purpose of guiding communication via websites, it is indeed applicable, and potentially more suitable to be employed for blogs and social networking sites (Seltzer & Mitrook, 2007). Recent studies utilizing the dialogic communication framework include studies of environmental activist groups on Facebook (Bortree & Seltzer, 2009), the use of social media by the American Red Cross (Briones et al., 2011), environmental weblogs (Seltzer & Mitrook, 2007), and political candidates' use of Facebook (Sweetser & Lariscy, 2008). Bortree and Seltzer (2009) added a dialogic strategy (organizational engagement) to organizational dialogic strategies, stating that organizations are able to post to their own sites to encourage dialogue. This addition highlights the importance of exploring the notion of engagement with social media.

Similarly, Hon and Grunig's (1999) relationship management theory has also been highly underscored in social media studies because of social media's built-in nature of interactivity. There are several scholars who embrace the notions of relationship management theory in new media settings, such as Fortune 500 company websites (Ki & Hon, 2006), websites of advocacy groups (Waters & Lord, 2009), and online relationship building during a crisis (Sweetser & Metzgar, 2007).

However, even though Bortree and Seltzer (2009) found that organizational engagement through posting/updating on social media "exhibited the most significant relationships with [dialogic] outcomes" (p. 318), dialogic communication strategies hardly focus on the specific message content communicated through social media (Waters & Jamal, 2011). Moreover, neither dialogic communication strategies nor relationship management strategies value one-way communication, while premising symmetrical communications as the goals of organizational communication (Waters & Williams, 2011). In fact, despite its potential or unique nature of interactivity, many studies found that organizations fail to utilize the interactive nature of social media, but rather use it as additional communication tools to disseminate information to constituents (Bortree & Seltzer, 2009; Waters & Jamal, 2011; Lovejoy & Saxton, 2012). These findings confirm "gaps between organizational relationship-building goals, implementation of online strategy, and actual dialogic engagement" (Bortree & Seltzer, 2009, p. 317).

Four Models of Public Relations: A Framework to Understand Message Strategies on Facebook. While Lovejoy and Saxton (2012) attempted to portray nonprofit organizations' Twitter message strategies based on an inductive approach and proposed three major functions of social media message (i.e., information, community, and action), they failed to distinguish press agentry and public information as different types of one-way communication. Thus, applying the four models of public relations that embrace both one-way and two-way communication, the current study explores how nonprofit organizations communicate with their constituents.

Grunig and Hunt (1984) proposed the four models of public relations that describe the evolution of public relations practice. With two dimensions of direction (one-way vs. two-way) and balance (asymmetry vs. symmetry), public relations practices can be categorized with four models: press agentry (one-way asymmetry), public information (one-way symmetry), two-way asymmetry, and two-way symmetry. As a primitive practice, press agentry disseminates emotional messages that are mainly used for manipulation, and reflects little formative research on constituents' opinions by organizations. For example, postings of emotional messages or pictures to draw public attention are based on the press-agentry model. Public information, still a one-way approach without any feedback channel, conveys trustful messages to constituents. Reporting an organization's own news/ updates or sharing relevant information about third-party organizations is an example of a public information–based message. While both two-way models provide feedback channels, the two-way asymmetry model uses market research to better persuade constituents and create influential messages, whereas the two-way symmetry model pursues legitimate conversations between an organization and its constituents in an attempt to create a mutual understanding. Asking Facebook users to participate in surveys or polls is based on two-way asymmetry model, whereas expressing gratitude for support or direct communication with a specific group of people is rooted in the two-way symmetry model.

Organizations' efforts and values of research to better understand publics increase as public relations practices moves from press agentry to the two-way symmetrical model (Grunig & Hunt, 1984). Of the four models of public relations, the two-way symmetrical communication approach is optimal to build quality relationships between an organization and its publics given that public relations practice with this approach requires an organization's efforts to conduct research and listen to publics' opinion as well as manage conflicts through dialogues (Hon & Grunig, 1999; Grunig, 2009).

Even though the four models have been recently criticized by some public relations scholars (Sha, 2007; Laskin, 2009), these models are still useful for depicting various public relations practices. Forecasting the future of public relations, Grunig (2009) argued that emerging media helps public relations practitioners utilize the generic principles of public relations, including the four models of public relations, rather than challenging the principles. More importantly, dialogic communication principles, which are heavily adopted by many social media researchers in the public relations discipline, are restricted to only two-way symmetrical communication (Kent & Taylor, 1998), and most studies found organizations' heavy use of one-way communication even in new media. Thus, it is more appropriate to adopt the four models of public relations to test message/content strategies in social media.

Recently, Waters and Jamal (2011) and Waters and Williams (2011) adopted the models to understand organizational messages on Twitter. More specifically, in their study of Twitter use by nonprofit organizations, Waters and Jamal (2011) found that nonprofit organizations are predominantly using Twitter to convey one-way messages, and in doing so, they are not utilizing "the interactive nature and dialogic capabilities of the social media service" but "sharing information instead of relationship building" (p. 323). Furthermore, a study of Twitter use by government agencies revealed similar results: the use of one-way communication for sharing information rather than the more desirable two-way symmetrical communication between organizations and constituents (Waters & Williams, 2011). The findings of both studies are based on the organizational messages on Twitter, which, by nature, have distinctive features of a real-time information network (Twitter, n.d.), compared to Facebook which is conversation-oriented based on social friendships. Even though both Twitter and Facebook are the most popular social media, distinctive features of each may warrant different message strategies. Given that there is no attempt to examine the message strategies on nonprofit organizations' Facebook pages, applying the four traditional models of public relations as the framework of message strategies, the following research question is posited:

RQ1: To what extent do nonprofit organizations incorporate the four models of public relations on Facebook?

Furthermore, given the various nature and purpose of nonprofit organizations, this study is interested in examining if the type of an organization has an impact on the type of model or message strategies used on Facebook. Thus, the second research question is as follows:

RQ2: Is there any difference between organizational types and the use of the four models of public relations?

In addition, given that social media, including Facebook, allows an organization to utilize digital communication resources, such as photos, hyperlinks, and videos, the study further explored the following questions:

RQ3: To what extent do nonprofit organizations utilize digital communication resources on their Facebook posting?

RQ4: Are there any differences between organizational message strategies and the use of digital communication resources?

METHOD

Sampling Procedure. To answer the research questions, a quantitative content analysis was used. Defined as "the systematic, objective, quantitative analysis of message characteristics" (Neuendorf, 2002, p. 1), content analysis has been widely used to investigate the content communicated through media. This study used the 2011 Nonprofit Times 100 as a sample framework, which contains the 100 largest nonprofit organizations in the United States by total revenue. Of the sample frame, 87 nonprofits have Facebook pages and 73 actively use Facebook, having regular updates and utilizing engagement functions. Thirty-six nonprofit headquarters Facebook pages were randomly selected for final data analysis. A total of 678 Facebook postings from 36 nonprofits, uploaded in a period of 20 days in October 2013 were examined. All the messages were collected within a week and saved as spreadsheet given the evolving nature of the Internet.

Coding Procedures. Nonprofit organizations were categorized into eight types (i.e., arts and culture, education, environment and animals, health, human service, international, public-societal benefits, and religion), defined by the National Center for Charitable Statistics (NCCS).

Waters and Jamal's (2011) coding schema was adopted and modified slightly to measure organizational message strategies on Facebook, given that the coding schema was created to measure public relations strategies on Twitter. The primary strategy was identified and coded when messages contained multiple message strategies. To measure the uses of digital communication resources on Facebook posting, the coders checked presence/absence of items of digital communication resources (i.e., comment, photo, nonprofit website, hyperlinks excluding the nonprofit's website, and video). Then, the total number of digital communication resources on each posting was calculated by summating the numbers of presence of digital communication resources. In addition, the study identified how many publics liked the nonprofit organizations' Facebook pages. Two well-trained coders conducted data collection, and the intercoder reliability between the coders was satisfactory and acceptable. Cohen's kappa coefficients ranged from .92 to .93.

RESULTS

The sampled nonprofit organizations represented a wide range of nonprofit organizations: Arts and culture ($N = 1$, 2.8%), education ($N = 2$, 5.6%), environment and animals ($N = 2$, 5.6%), health ($N = 8$, 22.2%), human service ($N = 10$, 27.8%), international and foreign affairs ($N = 7$, 19.4%), public/society benefit ($N = 4$, 11.1%), and religion ($N = 2$, 5.6%). The average of the number of "likes" of the sampled nonprofit organizations was 164,033.66 ($SD = 192,366.61$), with the wide range between 1,652 and 655,830. The nonprofit organizations posted approximately two new updates on their own Facebook each day.

To answer the first research question, frequency counts were checked. As Table 18–1 shows, public information was the most widely used of the four public relations models ($N = 331$ or 48.8%). More specifically, the majority

Table 18–1 Frequency of Nonprofit Organizations' Facebook Posts by the Four Models of Public Relations.

Message strategies (four models of public relations)	Operational definition	N	%
One-way models of public relations			
Press agentry	Use of emoticons to express emotion and words that express emotion/sharing emotional pictures or stories	55	8.1%
Public information	Providing updates and announcements from nonprofit organizations by using Facebook/providing information or reports from other organizations/ beneficiary update	331	48.8%
Two-way models of public relations			
Two-way asymmetry	Promoting organizational events/ asking for specific feedback, opinion, participation in a survey or online forum, donations, volunteers/product sale/asking to become involved with the organization by using social media/ lobbying and advocacy	206	30.4%
Two-way symmetry	Using publicly posted direct messages using Facebook name tags/fostering dialogue/giving recognition and saying "thank you"	86	12.7%

of the messages under the public information model ($N = 272$ or 82.18%) were updates or announcements of organizational news, including beneficiary updates. The rest of the messages shared information or reports from other organizations or anything of potential interest to Facebook friends. The second predominant model was two-way asymmetry ($N = 206$ or 30.4%), followed by two-way symmetry ($N = 86$ or 12.7%). Whereas the majority of two-way asymmetry model messages were asking constituents to learn how to help or to be involved with the organization, asking for participation in online forums, or soliciting donations/volunteers, the majority of two-way symmetry model messages were giving recognition and saying "thank you" to supporters, a key element of stewardship (Kelly, 2001). Nonprofits rarely used the press agentry model, which seeks to convey organizational emotions ($N = 55$ or 8.1%).

Research question two asked whether there were differences in the four models of public relations depending on the type of organizations.

A chi-square analysis showed that there were differences between organization types and the use of the four models of public relations, χ^2 (21, $N = 678$) $= 72.65$, $p < .01$. Looking closely at the results, except for education, environment and animals, and religion, the remainder of the organizations (i.e., arts and culture, health, human service, international and foreign affairs, and public/society benefit) followed the patterns of message strategies found in the first research question: public information was the most frequently used model, followed by two-way asymmetry, two-way symmetry, and press agentry. Even though those three types of organizations use public information and two-way asymmetry models the most, they used press agentry more often than two-way symmetry.

Research question three addressed to what extent nonprofit organizations utilized digital communication resources in their postings. By summating the total number of digital communication resources used in each posting, the study found that nonprofit organizations used multiple digital communication resources in each posting rather than a single resource (i.e., comment only, photo only, hyperlink only, or video only). More specifically, of the total of 678 postings, more than half of postings used one of the digital communication resources besides comments ($N = 432$ or 63.72%) whereas 85 postings (12.54%) used single-resource postings, as shown in Table 18–2. Only one posting used all four digital communication resources, including comment, nonprofit's own website, other hyperlink, and photo.

Table 18–2 Frequency of Nonprofit Organizations' Use of Digital Communication Resources on Facebook.

Total number of digital communication resources used	Digital communication resources	N	%
1	Comment only	50	7.37%
	Photo only	16	2.36%
	Nonprofit's own website only	14	2.06%
	Other hyperlink only	4	0.59%
	Video only	1	0.15%
Subtotal		85	12.54%
2	Comment + photo	107	15.78%
	Comment + nonprofit's own website	175	25.81%
	Comment + other hyperlink	123	18.14%
	Comment + video	27	3.98%

(Continued)

Table 18–2   (Continued)

Total number of digital communication resources used	Digital communication resources	N	%
Subtotal		432	63.72%
3	Comment + photo + nonprofit's own website	135	19.91%
	Comment + photo + other hyperlink	18	2.65%
	Comment + photo + video	1	0.15%
	Comment + nonprofit's own website + other hyperlink	1	0.15%
	Comment + nonprofit's own website + video	2	0.3%
	Comment + other hyperlink + video	3	0.44%
Subtotal		160	23.60%
	Comment + photo + nonprofit's own website + other hyperlink	1	0.15%
Subtotal		1	0.15%
TOTAL number of postings		678	100%

Research question four further addressed whether there is any difference between message strategies and the total number of digital communication resources used. The one-way analysis of variance (ANOVA) test result showed that there was a difference between the posting message strategies and the total number of digital communication resources used, $F(3, 675) = 3.58$, $p < .05$. More specifically, based on a Tukey's HSD post-hoc test of multiple comparisons, the study found that the press agentry model used less digital communication resources than public information ($p < .01$) or two-way asymmetry messages ($p < .05$). However, there was no difference between press-agentry and two-way symmetry–based postings.

DISCUSSION

The main purpose of this study was to explore how nonprofit organizations use Facebook by applying Grunig and Hunt's (1984) four models of public relations as a framework to assess message strategies. Based on the

Nonprofits' Use of Facebook 291

content analysis of top nonprofit organizations' Facebook posts, this study found that the public information model is the most frequently used message strategy adopted by nonprofit organizations, followed by two-way asymmetry, two-way symmetry, and press agentry. Even though there were some deviations observed in the use of the four models depending on the organizational types, the majority of nonprofit organizations use social media to disseminate information as their primary purpose. Despite the opportunity to further engage with constituents through the Timeline feature, nonprofit organizations still heavily rely on Facebook as a form of disseminating information about their organization to their constituents, rather than fully embracing the engagement features as tools for two-way communication.

This finding supports previous research (e.g., Bortree & Seltzer, 2009; Waters & Jamal, 2011; Lovejoy & Saxton, 2012) that nonprofit organizations predominantly use social media to share information based on the public information model. Utilizing multiple forms of information, such as video, images, and other types of social media, nonprofit organizations provide Facebook users with organizational or other relevant information. Many scholars expressed concerns about the limited utilization of two-way communication via social media by nonprofit organizations (Bortree & Seltzer, 2009; Waters & Jamal, 2011; Lovejoy & Saxton, 2012). A possible reason for the predominant use of public information is the limited resources that nonprofits have. As Briones and colleagues (2011) found, nonprofit organizations have endured challenges to actively utilize social media for relationship building due to a lack of resources or approval from boards of directors that may not value social media activities. Given these circumstances, it is hard to use social media for building relationships and generating ongoing conversation because it takes more effort than simply distributing messages or information. Proposing a hierarchy of organizational messages that may lead engagement between an organization and its constituents, Lovejoy and Saxton (2012) viewed information sharing as "a core activity to attract" social media users (p. 350), which is the initial level to be further developed to build community and ask to take action for the organizational mission. Applying Lovejoy and Saxton's notion, nonprofit organizations in this study used Facebook to lay the groundwork for building relationships with their key constituents.

However, unlike the findings of Waters and Jamal (2011), nonprofit organizations in this study utilized two-way models—both asymmetry and symmetry— more than press agentry. The study also found that, except for three types of organizations (i.e., education, environmental and animal, and religion), nonprofit organizations used the press agentry model the least. This indicates that nonprofit organizations do in fact use Facebook to facilitate two-way communication, compared to Twitter, which is designed for real-time information updates. Put another way, nonprofit organizations take advantage of Facebook's Timeline feature and engagement features that offer users a better understanding of those organizations. By documenting chronologically organized contents and ongoing conversations between organizations and their constituents, the Timeline feature enables nonprofits to build relationships on Facebook.

The study further explored how nonprofit organizations incorporated digital communication resources when communicating with their publics on Facebook. The study found that nonprofit organizations tried to utilize the virtue of social media that makes them easy to add digital communication resources in creating social media messages. In particular, public information and two-way asymmetrical postings utilized more digital communication resources than press agentry–based messages. By having supplementary information such as related links, photos, and video clips, nonprofit organizations can provide publics with detailed information that ultimately better inform or convince publics.

The current study not only portrays current public relations practices in the social media era but also offers some theoretical implications. Whereas most existing studies of public relations in new media circumstances adopted Kent and Taylor's (1998) dialogic communication or Hon and Grunig's (1999) relationship management approaches, these two theoretical frameworks are limited to two-way symmetrical communication, not exhaustive in describing other types of public relations practices. Dialogic communication is rooted from two-way symmetrical communication, as Kent and Taylor (1998) argued that the "relationship between two-way symmetrical communication and dialogic communication can be seen as one of process and product" (p. 323). Also, two-way symmetrical communication is the foundation of relationship cultivation strategies (Hon & Grunig, 1999). Even though these two theoretical approaches well describe potential benefits of new media for cultivating organization–public relations, many empirical studies found that organizations are limited in their use of these new media environments. Revealing the predominant use of one-way communication, more specifically, the public information strategy, this study confirms the gaps between organizational goals of relationship management and actual practice of online communication (Bortree & Seltzer, 2009).

While many organizations heavily rely on one-way communications to motivate passive publics to active, Grunig (2009) argued that this information-disseminating strategy is not effective for building organization–public relationships because most passive publics neither pay attention to organizational messages nor recall the messages. In discussing the future of public relations, Grunig (2009) further asserted cognitive responses (e.g., images, reputation) of an organization held by publics can be managed by managing communication that aims to build quality relationships with publics.

This study's findings also support that, rather than being dated (Sha, 2007; Laskin, 2009), the four models of public relations practices describe well today's public relations practices even in an age of new media, although some variations exist. As Grunig (2009) asserted, emerging media including social media does not challenge the excellence paradigm, but facilitates to build relationships between an organization and its publics if public relations practices utilize the capacity of new media.

CONCLUSION

In sum, revisiting the state of social media adoption and use by the nonprofit sector, the study explored how nonprofit organizations use Facebook. While nonprofit organizations still use social media as subsidiary to traditional media to disseminate information, nonprofit organizations are trying to widen the social media function to build a dialogic communication with publics. Also, nonprofit organizations attempt to incorporate digital communication resources into messages to offer concrete information to their publics.

Some limitations of this study should be acknowledged. The first concern is related to the samples studied. By focusing on top nonprofit organizations, the study is limited in generalizing the findings to small or medium-sized nonprofit organizations. Although the study included nonprofit organizations that support various social issues, the study excluded educational institutions, such as public universities. Given that, unlike traditional media or organizational media, social media users can create messages and share them with organizations, future research may investigate message strategies and digital communication resources used by publics on social media. In addition, while the study took a quantitative approach, future research based on a qualitative inquiry is recommended, such as qualitative analysis of comments made by constituents, or in-depth interviews with constituents to explore their motivations for engaging with organizations.

REFERENCES

Barns, N. G., & Andonian, J. (2011). The 2011 Fortune 500 and social media adoption: Have America's largest companies reached social media plateau? *Center for Marketing Research*. Retrieved October 18, 2012, from http://www.umassd.edu/cmr/studiesandresearch/2011fortune500/

Bortree, D. S., & Seltzer, T. (2009). Dialogic strategies and outcomes: An analysis of environmental advocacy groups' Facebook profiles. *Public Relations Review, 35*(3), 317–319.

Briones, R., Kuch, B., Liu, B. F., & Jin, Y. (2011). Keeping up with the digital age: How the American Red Cross uses social media to build relationships. *Public Relations Review, 37*(1), 37–43.

Broom, G. M. (2009). *Cutlip & Center's effective public relations* (10th ed.). Upper Saddle River, NJ: Prentice-Hall.

Cone Business in Social Media Research. (2008). Cone finds that Americans expect companies to have a presence in social media. *Business Wire*. Retrieved October 15, 2012, from http://www.businesswire.com/news/home/20080925005160/en/Cone-Finds-Americans-Expect-Companies-Presence-Social

Curtis, L., Edwards, C., Fraser, K. L., Gudelsky, S., Holmquist, J., Thornton, K., & Sweetser, K. D. (2010). Adoption of social media for public relations by nonprofit organizations. *Public Relations Review, 36*(1), 90–92.

Drury, G. (2008). Opinion piece: Social media: Should marketers engage and how can it be done effectively? *Journal of Direct, Data and Digital Marketing Practice, 9*(3), 274–277.

eMarketer. (2012, July 18). Social media usage plateaus among marketers. Retrieved October 30, 2012, from http://www.emarketer.com/Article.aspx?R=1009197&ecid=a6506033675d

Fine, A. (2011). Social media are no longer optional. *Chronicle of Philanthropy, 23*(17), 22.

Flandez, R. (2011). Big charities gear up to use social media to raise money. *Chronicle of Philanthropy, 23*(17), 16.

Garun, N. (2012, March 14). Study: Facebook engages fans and followers more than Twitter. *Digital Trends.* Retrieved October 10, 2012, from http://www.digitaltrends.com/social-media/study-facebook-engages-fans-and-followers-more-than-twitter/

Grunig, J. E. (2009). Paradigms of global public relations in an age of digitalization. *Prism, 6*(2). Retrieved February 20, 2012, from http://praxis.massey.ac.nz/prism_on-line_journ.html

Grunig, J. E., & Hunt, T. (1984). *Managing public relations.* New York, NY: Holt, Rinehart, and Winston.

Gunelius, S. (2011). *30 minute social media marketing.* New York, NY: McGraw Hill.

Hon, L. C., & Grunig, J. E. (1999). *Guidelines for measuring relationships in public relations.* Gainesville, FL: Institute for Public Relations.

Huffington Post. (2012, October 4). Facebook has 1 billion users, Mark Zuckerberg announces in a status update. Retrieved October 10, 2012, from http://www.huffingtonpost.com/2012/10/04/facebook-1-billion-users_n_1938675.html?utm_hp_ref=technology

Ilsen, S. (2012, July 24). A new form of volunteering: How social gamers are raising funds for nonprofits. *VolunteerMatch.* Retrieved March 2, 2013, from http://blogs.volunteermatch.org/engagingvolunteers/2012/07/24/a-new-form-of-volunteering-how-social-gamers-are-raising-funds-for-nonprofits/

Kelly, K. S. (2001). Stewardship: The fifth step in the public relations process. In R. L. Heath (Ed.), *Handbook of public relations* (pp. 279–289). Thousand Oaks, CA: Sage.

Kent, M. L., & Taylor, M. (1998). Building dialogic relationships through the World Wide Web. *Public Relations Review, 24*(3), 321–334.

Ki, E. J., & Hon, L. C. (2006). Relationship maintenance strategies on Fortune 500 company web sites. *Journal of Communication Management, 10*(1), 27–43.

Laskin, A. V. (2009). The evolution of models of public relations: An outsider's perspective. *Journal of Communication Management, 13*(1), 37–54.

Lovejoy, K., & Saxton, G. D. (2012). Information, community, and action: How nonprofit organizations use social media. *Journal of Computer-Mediated Communication, 17*(3), 337–353.

Nah, S., & Saxton, G. D. (2012). Modeling the adoption and use of social media by nonprofit organizations. *New Media and Society, 15*(2), 294–313.

Neuendorf, K. A. (2002). *The content analysis guidebook.* Thousand Oaks, CA: Sage.

Nielsen Report. (2011). State of the media: The social media report Q3 2011. Retrieved October 30, 2012, from http://blog.nielsen.com/nielsenwire/social/

Paine, K. D. (2009). *How to set benchmarks in social media: Exploratory research for social media, lessons learned*. Gainesville, FL: Institute for Public Relations.

Perdue, E. (2012, March 15). What's next? Social media has changed the way we communicate. *News-Herald*. Retrieved October 29, 2012, from http://www.thenewsherald.com/articles/2012/03/15/news/doc4f60d31a43ff0634185453.txt

Pew Research Center. (2012, September 27). In changing news landscape, even television is vulnerable trends in news consumption: 1991–2012. Retrieved October 20, 2012, from http://www.people-press.org/2012/09/27/in-changing-news-landscape-even-television-is-vulnerable/

Rubin, T. (2012, June 18). How to create real relationships with social marketing. *Mashable*. Retrieved October 20, 2012, from http://mashable.com/2012/06/18/social-marketing-relationships/

Seltzer, T., & Mitrook, M. A. (2007). The dialogic potential of weblogs in relationship building. *Public Relations Review, 33*, 227–229.

Sha, B. (2007). Dimensions of public relations: Moving beyond traditional public relations models. In S. Duhé (Ed.), *New media and public relations* (pp. 3–26). New York, NY: Peter Lang.

Smith, C. (2013, November 29). The planet's 24 largest social media sites, and where their next wave of growth will come from. *Business Insider*. Retrieved October 2, 2014, from http://www.businessinsider.com/a-global-social-media-census-2013-10

Stelzner, M. A. (2009). Social media marketing industry report: How marketers are using social media to grow their businesses. *WhitePaperSource.com*. Retrieved October 20, 2012, from http://www.whitepapersource.com/socialmediamarketing/report/

Sweetser, K. D., & Lariscy, R. W. (2008). Candidates make good friends: An analysis of candidates' uses of Facebook. *International Journal of Strategic Communication, 2*, 175–198.

Sweetser, K. D., & Metzgar, E. (2007). Communicating during crisis: Use of blogs as a relationship management tool. *Public Relations Review, 33*, 340–342.

Twitter. (n.d.). The fastest, simplest way to stay close to everything you care about. Retrieved October 20, 2012, from http://twitter.com/about

Universal McCann. (2008). Power to the people: Social media tracker wave 3. Retrieved March 1, 2013, from http://www.scribd.com/doc/25109686/International-Social-Media-Research-Wave-3

Waters, R. D., & Jamal, J. Y. (2011). Tweet, tweet, tweet: A content analysis of nonprofit organizations' Twitter updates. *Public Relations Review, 37*(2), 321–324.

Waters, R. D., & Lord, M. (2009). Examining how advocacy groups build relationships on the Internet. *International Journal of Nonprofit and Voluntary Sector Marketing, 14*, 231–241.

Waters, R. D., & Williams, J. M. (2011). Squawking, tweeting, cooing, and hooting: Analyzing the communication patterns of government agencies on Twitter. *Journal of Public Affairs, 11*(4), 353–363.

19 Compassion International and Pinterest

Developing Brand Personality and Demonstrating Stewardship through Visuals

Carolyn Mae Kim and John Keeler

In today's world there are more devices connected to the Internet than there are people, and 40% of people socialize more online than they do in a face-to-face setting (Bennett, 2013). As a result, publics engage with organizations in ways that have never before been possible. Ennes (2011) stated that organizations that used social media most effectively realized that it "is a conversation, not a monologue . . . they met their customers where they already were, using four or more social media channels—including multimedia sharing, review sites, discussion forums, and blogs" (Slide 7).

One social network platform that has garnered increased levels of attention is Pinterest. Launched in March 2010, it quickly became the one of most popular social networks in the United States. The image-based platform's explosive popularity and user interaction made it an attractive choice for brands seeking to establish and build relationships with their consumer base (Sutter, 2012).

As is the case of many social media platforms in their early stages, little academic research exists to provide any explanatory or predictive theories that can enhance organizational use of this social network platform. There is a need for case studies on such platforms as Pinterest that "produce the type of concrete, context-dependent knowledge that research on learning shows to be necessary to allow people to develop from rule-based beginners to virtuoso experts" (Flyvberg, 2011, p. 302). A case study of an organization's use of Pinterest to help achieve its branding and other marketing and public relations goals also contributes to the development of "epistemic theory, that is, theory that is explanatory and predictive" (Flyvberg, 2011, p. 302).

This chapter examines how Compassion International uses Pinterest to engage with the public to cultivate sponsors through a relational centered fundraising process. Compassion International, a Christian nonprofit based in Colorado Springs, is a holistic child sponsorship organization that partners with churches in 26 countries to bring children out of poverty. With sponsorships of over 1.4 million babies, children, and students, they are ranked by Forbes as the 16th largest charity in the United States ("The 100 Largest U.S. Charities," 2013).

As with all nonprofit organizations, Compassion International's relationship with sponsors is of critical importance. Because the organization is largely funded through child sponsorships, their entire business model depends on initiating and sustaining relationships with sponsors. Compassion's usage of Pinterest provides an excellent case for examining how organizations, particularly nonprofits, can utilize this social media platform to foster brand communities. Compassion's use of Pinterest had generated a reported monthly follower growth of 10 to 15 percent in late 2013 (personal correspondence with Chris Giovangnoni, 2013), but they also were an early adopter of the platform. While the Pinterest platform itself is still growing and adapting, causing organizations to adjust their approach to the social site, examining Compassion's success can provide theory and application insight for those developing brand communities.

LITERATURE REVIEW

Social Media. Social media of many types are part of the fabric of today's culture. It is estimated that at least 82% of the world is now reachable via social media ("It's a Social World," 2011). Organizations are preparing for the economic impact this will have, as it is estimated that by 2015 "brands will be generating 50% of their web sales through social media and digital platforms" (Pring, 2012).

In the last several years organizations have embraced the fact that these technologies have created new ways for individuals to interact and share information (Hansen, Shneiderman, & Smith, 2010). These methods of sharing and interacting have also altered the way that organizations engage with their publics (Hanna, Rohm, & Crittenden, 2011). They have had to utilize a new "bottom up" approach to influencing consumers, donors, and other publics because the people are "more trusting of their own opinions and the opinions of their peers" as a result of the social media landscape (Hanna et al., 2011, p. 267). Daily through social media, "billions of people create trillions of connections" (Hansen et al., 2010, p. 3). This focus on a "bottom up" perspective is reflected in the fact that publics have become actively involved with brand messages, products and causes—not mere consumers. Mike DiLorenzo, the Director of Social Media Marketing and Strategy for the National Hockey League explains, "Social networks aren't about Web sites. They're about experiences" (Wyshnyski, 2009).

Pinterest. Since its launch in 2010, Pinterest hit 10 million users faster than any other independent social site (Gilbert et al., 2013). It quickly became the third most popular social media site (Ngak, 2012), as over 25% of Fortune Global 100 companies created a Pinterest account (Honigman, 2012). With over 70 million users, not only is Pinterest prominent in the social media world, it is a huge site for driving traffic online (Semiocast, 2013). In October 2012, it was announced that Pinterest had surpassed Yahoo to become the fourth-largest driver of digital traffic (Chacos, 2012). By the end of 2013, Pinterest became the third most popular "sharing channel" (Marvin, 2014). With 70% of users citing the goal of gaining "inspiration on what to buy" as the main reason for using Pinterest, organizations and public relations professionals have turned attention to understanding the influence on audience opinions, values, beliefs, and behaviors that this new platform yields (Fogel, 2014). Users also expressed the preference to interact with brands or retailers via Pinterest as opposed to the larger platform of Facebook (Hongiman, 2012).

Pinterest is a site that centers on visuals. Users create boards, which serve as categorizations for images that they "pin" to the board. Each image can have an explanation and a URL that guides other users to more information. Interaction includes following, repinning someone else's content onto a personal board, liking a pin, or commenting on a pin. Interaction on Pinterest is of interest to organizations as user behavior has started to be studied with the maturing of the social network. Recently over 80% of pins were repins, meaning that the majority of interaction on the site is a response to other users' content (Honigam, 2012). Additionally, 80% of Pinterest users are women (Bullock, 2013). Over 20% of all users who engage via Facebook-connect login to Pinterest daily and spend an average of 16 minutes on the platform (Honigam, 2012). Organizations are seeing that the majority of time (83.9%) is spent pinning and 15.5% is spent looking at brands' boards. Very little time (0.6%) is spent commenting (Honigam, 2012). These findings show that users on Pinterest are highly engaged with brand content, often sharing information among peers through repinning that leads to purchase decisions and opinions that are significant to organizations. It is the interaction among individuals and their sharing and influence on each other that makes Pinterest and other social media especially attractive and valuable to marketers and public relations professionals. These users can form or be encouraged to form what is known as a "brand community."

Brand Communities. The term "brand community" refers to the formation of people in the digital world around a brand, organization, or cause. It is a term taken from relationship marketing theory (Morgan & Hunt, 1994). The main idea behind brand communities and management of those digital relationships is the fact organizations need to sustain strong relationships by utilizing the technology to meet customers' desires and needs in order to thrive (McKenna, 1991). It is within this effort that brand communities are derived. Muniz and O'Guinn (2001) describe a brand community as a "specialized non-geographically bound community, based on a structured set of social relationships among users of a brand" (p. 412). Brand communities are made up not only of the relationship between a customer and an organization, but also between individuals who are affiliated with the brand community (McAlexander, Schouten, & Koenig, 2002). In the digital world, brands are able to develop a more robust "brand personality" that allows users to become more attached, engaged, and attracted to the brand (Aaker, 1997). Additionally, activities that take place within a brand community can generate additional value and energize the relationships around a brand (Schau, Muniz, & Arnould, 2009). As a visual platform, Pinterest is especially suited for relationship building as much of the interaction is entirely user driven and created, allowing brand communities to thrive.

Stewardship of Relationships. For any organization desiring to develop a brand community fostering relationships is critical. This seems to be especially true for nonprofit organizations such as Compassion International that rely on charitable giving. Organizations need to be willing to commit time and resources with donors in order to have a long-term relationship (O'Neil, 2007). The process of relationship management with donors is something that Kelly (1998) calls "stewardship." This concept is based on Greenfield's (1991) definition of donor relations, which is to "establish the means for continued communication that will help to preserve their interest and attention to the organization" (p. 148). Kelly (1998) argued that the process by which that communication would be provided is stewardship. This idea is also shared by Horton (1981): "The idea of stewardship is often in our minds, of course—reporting back to donors on the benefits derived from their gifts" (p. 267). Additionally, Greenfield (1991) is among many scholars and practitioners who have said that there is too much focus on asking for money, and "more time and attention should be given to the relationships needed to sustain donor interest" (p. 17). Kelly (1998) argues for stewardship to be a holistic process that requires staff managers to be "agents of accountability, guardians of gifts, and the organization's conscience" (p. 434). This kind of additional interaction is what Hon and Grunig (1999) describe in their four stages of stewardship Reciprocity is the way an organization demonstrates gratitude toward the donor. Responsibility entails maintaining trust by acting with integrity and doing what the organization is committed to doing. Reporting is the element of dispensing information with the publics about the ways in which support was used. Finally, relationship nurturing is the process by which an organization continues to develop deeper and more robust ties with an individual donor in the hopes of establishing a long-term relationship (Waters, 2009). Pinterest allows stewardship in each of the categories through the engagement of pins. Boards can be dedicated to thanking publics (reciprocity), showing results of interaction with the publics and initiating ongoing values with the publics (responsibility and reporting), and by engaging with members of the brand community through repins (relationship nurturing). Compassion International's approach to Pinterest, which will be discussed more below, has been not only to foster new relationships via boards but also sustain existing ones using this exact approach.

Three overarching research questions guided this case study of Compassion International's use of Pinterest:

> RQ1: In what ways does Compassion's use of Pinterest suggest ways nonprofit organizations can use the social network platform to connect better with donors?

RQ2: Does Compassion's use of Pinterest offer best practices that non-profits can utilize on Pinterest to build brand communities?

RQ3: What other general applications to brand development and theory does Compassion's use of Pinterest provide?

METHOD

Compassion International Background. Compassion International, the focus of this case study on Pinterest, was started by Everett Swanson in 1952 in the war-torn country of Korea. Swanson had seen the needs of the many orphans and developed an organization to allow people in the United States to care for those children (Compassion International, 2014b). Today, Compassion is helping more than 1.4 million children in over 26 countries. They continue their development work by helping children and communities in places like Burkina Faso, India, Togo, El Salvador, Haiti, and many other locations (Compassion International, 2014b).

There are three child development models Compassion utilizes in developing nations to help children. First, there is the "Child Survival Program," which helps mothers during pregnancy and in the early development of the child's life to ensure they have a strong start. Once a child passes infancy, they can be enrolled in the "Child Sponsorship Program," where they can be sponsored. They receive food, education, medical help, and training through the local church until they finish high school. Finally, completing the goal of developing strong communities that are self-sustaining, there is a "Leadership Development Program" that helps these students go to college and return to their local community as a leaders (Compassion International, 2014a). These historical foundations and ways of engaging global poverty are extensions of Compassion International's mission statement: "In response to the Great Commission, Compassion International exists as an advocate for children, to release them from their spiritual, economic, social and physical poverty and enable them to become responsible and fulfilled Christian adults" (Compassion International, 2014c).

Data Collection and Analysis. This case study employed qualitative analysis of Compassion's Pinterest site, shown in Figure 19–1. The beginning stage included analysis of Compassion's structure, value, and focus on social media overall. This was done through an interview with the organization's social media marketing program manager. After providing the framework through which Compassion engaged with users around the world, Compassion's Pinterest platform was analyzed for content and activity. To conduct the analysis, each board was reviewed. It was found that there were six major categories of boards: initiating new donor relationships; maintaining current donor relationships, examples of Compassion's work; humanitarian

Figure 19–1 Screenshot of Compassion International's Pinterest Profile.

efforts; lifestyle boards; and group contributor boards. After identifying the overarching categories, each board was analyzed for specific metrics, including number of pins, number of repins, and comments within Pinterest.

RESULTS

Compassion's Pinterest Use and Growth Profile. Compassion's approach to Pinterest is consistent with their focus on relationship, particularly with donors and sponsors. An early adopter on Pinterest, Compassion's involvement started in September 2011. As of October 10, 2013, Compassion had 7,411 followers on Pinterest, was following 5,382 users, had 1,524 pins, 327 likes, and 35 boards.

Recently Compassion's Pinterest followers were growing by an average of 10 to 15 percent each month (personal correspondence with Chris Giovangnoni, 2013). A key component of Pinterest is the creation of boards and pinning of content. An interesting aspect of Compassion's Pinterest use is strong engagement with those connected to them through the social network. While organizations are typically seeing around 70% of user questions, complaints, and compliments ignored on social media (Baer, 2012; Bennette, 2013), Compassion has purposefully determined that managers of their Pinterest presence will proactively engage with users not only on their own site but on the Pinterest boards of users (personal correspondence with Chris Giovangnoni, 2013). This strong, intentional interactive component on the platform is perhaps one reason why they are experiencing such a large percentage of growth.

As previously mentioned, the boards that Compassion International created can be broken into six categories: Initiating Relationships; Maintaining Relationships; Lifestyle; Compassion Work; Humanitarian Efforts and Group Contributions. Additionally, there are a couple of group boards; Compassion did not create them but is now a contributor to their content as a result of an invitation from the originating organization. Analysis of the pins on each of these boards provides a picture of how Compassion's presence is contributing to the brand community and building trust and loyalty among the members of the brand community.

The boards and pins that Compassion uses on Pinterest directly engage users, and foster relationships within the brand community and with the organization. The pins that receive the most interaction involve a relational component—either to help the sponsor connect better with the sponsored child or to help the sponsor better display their active involvement with the sponsored child (such as the framing of letters received from a sponsor child for one's home). The most popular board, "Letter Writing," which is shown in Figure 19–2, has a high number of "repins." The top repin for the board is a "how to draw" animals printable graphic to send to a sponsored child. Other top boards include a tutorial on making a photostrip bookmark, ideas on making frames to display letters from a sponsored child, a long-distance hug idea, and a map to show a sponsored child where their sponsor lives.

Pinterest Strategy. Compassion's strategy on Pinterest, as with its other efforts to stimulate social presence online, is primarily about adding value to their audience. Along the same philosophical premise as Compassion's blog, their Pinterest use again is designed to help sponsors feel more closely connected to their children and also to the organization (personal correspondence with Chris Giovangnoni, 2013). Compassion's blog is the primary vehicle for all of the social activities. Social media links, including Pinterest, end up driving

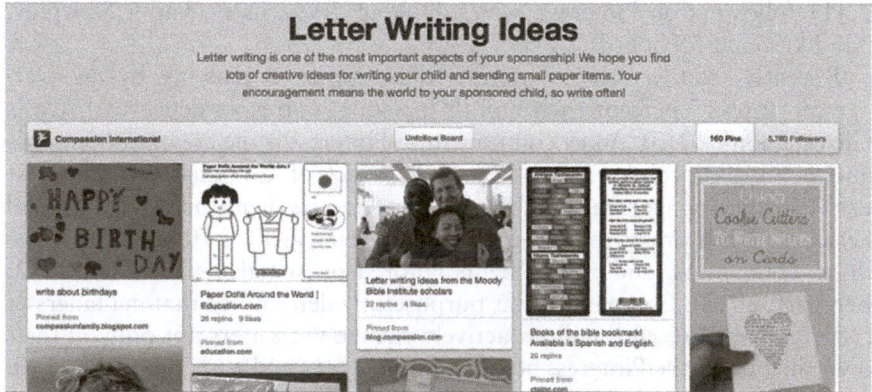

Figure 19–2   Screenshot of Compassion International's "Letter Writing Ideas" Pin Board.

users back to the content of the blog. Pinterest and other social media platforms also follow the categories and topics of the blog in a well-integrated branding or public relations strategy. Chris Giovangnoni, the social media program manager for all Compassion social media initiatives, explains what principles guide Compassion's content selections:

> At the center are our children. Stories focusing on individual children aren't just meant to be about that specific child. They're meant to represent the friends your child plays with. And in the blessed instance when the story is about your child, we share with you the extra photos and information we have but didn't publish. Since it's difficult to always hit the bullseye, we can help connect you with your child emotionally by providing insight into what life is like in a typical child development center in the child's country so, by extension, you have a better idea of what your child's daily life is probably like.
>
> (Giovangnoni, 2012)

The goal of Compassion's digital connections with the blog and social media is to "bridge the geographic distance" between sponsors and their children as well as develop an understanding of the ways Compassion works on a global scale. This approach to content creation allows Compassion to strategically develop and post information that fosters the brand community.

Two volunteers manage Compassion's Pinterest account. The volunteers are given broad guidelines of what to post or not post. But, like the rest of Compassion's philosophy, the approach to volunteer management is to empower these brand ambassadors to share the story of Compassion. This is the heart of Compassion's social media strategy and their Pinterest strategy specifically. It is the ability for individual users to share their stories and relationships. The fact that Compassion has two volunteers on Pinterest shows the high value management that Compassion places on this platform. No other social media platforms used by the organization utilized two volunteers. This is simply an indication of the "unique appeal that Pinterest has for users" (personal correspondence with Giovangnoni, 2013).

DISCUSSION

Compassion's Pinterest Use to Connect via Visuals. Compassion's Pinterest use confirms the growing importance of visuals in the social media world. It is no secret that photos outperform text. Pinterest has capitalized on this value by creating a platform completely around visuals. As a visuals-based social media platform, Pinterest has the benefit of bridging the global community in ways that other platforms have yet to do. Beninatto (2013) points out that part of this value lies in the fact that "the image unadorned by words speaks across borders, past languages" ("The Image Needs No Interpreter," para. 1).

Zahedi & Bansal (2011) suggest "images are more primal in human sensory communication than written words. In an era of increasing de-Westernization of the Web, it becomes even more important to configure Web site images with care and insight . . . pictures are easier to process than text" (p. 192). On top of bridging international barriers, the photo also meets the desire of many on social media to be less self-focused and more attentive to other topics. Brand communities are telling stories, sharing values, and advocating for brands that they believe in, all in the visual realm. "Today's consumers have progressed from sharing information to image-driven information. Brands must recognize and respond to this trend to maintain their place in consumer conversations" (Allen, Woodward & Lamp, 2012, p. 16).

Compassion capitalized on the value of images in order to achieve growth in and engagement with their brand community comprised of donors. For example, several of their images are of children within projects that Compassion helps. The visual impact of a child and the state of their living conditions are all exemplified within one pin—there is no need for a long explanation of the value of Compassion or the reason why people need to help these kids. Additionally, as a global organization, Pinterest allows the brand community members to break down geographical barriers and connect via visuals around a common cause, goal, passion, and need. As Compassion sponsors share images of their trips to projects, the kinds of gifts they might mail to sponsor children, the letters they have received, and other graphics that illustrate the value of Compassion, they form stronger connections and unity within the brand community. This is a principle that other nonprofits can easily integrate into their Pinterest strategy to better relate to their donors or other publics.

Compassion's Pinterest Use and Best Practices. One area that this case study of Compassion seems to point to is the ability of Pinterest to uniquely contribute to the creation of value within a brand community (Schau et al., 2009). Users within this platform consistently benefit organizations or brands through repinning and thereby advocating products, services, or causes. This also supports the theory that user practices within a brand community generate value for the members of that brand community. Compassion has tapped into the power of the "bottom up" approach for relationship influence discussed by Hanna and colleagues (2011, p. 267). Several boards instituted by Compassion are the stories of particular sponsors and their experiences. Because social media is often about experiences (Wyshnyski, 2009) and not about a controlled advertising presence, boards that cater toward the stories of users, rather than the organization, build a strong brand community. This is one way that Pinterest builds additional value for Compassion sponsors through brand community practices. Schau and colleagues (2009) suggest that the activities that take place in a brand community not only generate value but also emotional commitment to an organization or activity. By participating with others in Compassion's Pinterest community, users are exposed to practices such as writing a sponsor child, sending gifts, taking a trip to visit a sponsored child, and a multitude of other activities that lead to a closer connection with the child. The result, from an organizational standpoint, is stronger retention of sponsors based on a stronger sponsor relationship. Pinterest similarly can be used by other nonprofit organizations to stimulate value and emotional commitment within a brand community or connecting donors or other publics with the organization.

Encouraging Value and Emotional Commitment. People often build relationships with brands in the same way they would form relationships with each other people in a social context. The relationship is created through a series of interactions that build rapport, trust, and connection (Aggarwal, 2004). The sequence of interactions that is developed between the brand and the brand community on Pinterest involves pins, repins, likes, and shared boards. In the case of Compassion, the organization strategically fostered their brand personality and engagement with the organization as well as generating tangible actions among the brand community members. By 2020, Compassion's goal is to grow from 1.4 million sponsored children to 4 million. Based on connection with the brand personality and the activity of the community, Compassion has seen that new sponsorships have resulted based on repins by community members. This illustrates the value of organizations creating content that those in the brand community will repin. This is a specific tactic for nonprofits to use on Pinterest in order to build trust, as users often defer to recommendations of friends in the social world.

Brand Communities Gratitude and Stewardship by Nonprofits on Pinterest. Finally, the theory that the expression of gratitude within a brand community develops a long-term relationship and desire to continue giving has strong application with Pinterest, something that was clearly evident in the Compassion case. The ability to express and share about a cause or brand actually can produce more connection to the organization and result in continued giving and other expressions of gratitude—volunteering, for example, which is a huge focus for nonprofits (Palmatier, Jarvis, Bechkoff, & Kardes, 2009). The expression of gratitude is directly in line with Kelly's (1998) concept of reciprocity within stewardship. Additionally, especially for nonprofits, the relationship nurturing of donors is essential to the survival of the organization. The case of Compassion's use of Pinterest shows that allowing a brand community to express gratitude via pins or repins is one way that organizations can steward the relationship. Also, boards that illustrate the use of funds from sponsors via visuals of projects that children are in, activities of the organization, and usage of donations are all affirmations of the value the sponsor has to the organization and the integrity of the brand, which are opportunities that Kelly (1998) emphasizes within donor retention theory to show reporting and responsibility. Compassion's approach to Pinterest provides a roadmap for other nonprofits to utilize boards in strategic ways for relationship building with sponsors through Kelly's (1998) four tenets: reciprocity, responsibility, reporting, and nurturing.

Nonprofit Applications for Pinterest. Compassion's use of Pinterest provides additional insights about how social media in general, and Pinterest in particular, relate to what scholars have theorized about brand communities and their development. First, Pinterest, with its highly visual form and repinning function, seems to be an excellent way to foster a brand community through the creation of shared meaning, even when the community extends across diverse and widespread geographic and cultural boundaries. The activities that users participate in on the platform also can generate a sense of affiliation, connection, and value. Organizations should carefully consider what boards would best stimulate the development of shared values around a brand and how pins can also enhance those values. Establishing precise objectives for each of these boards and identifying values that seem to ideally relate to the organization's products, services, or cause, as well as the characteristics of existing or potential consumers, donors, or other publics would seem essential. Additionally, the Compassion case suggests that nonprofit organizations promoting their brands through Pinterest should consider the type of interaction and community dialogue that they hope to enhance through their Pinterest presence. For nonprofits, the ability for users to share gratitude is a pivotal application. Any brand development strategy involving Pinterest or other social media must, however, encourage brand communities to champion the brand. This enhances trust and long-term relationships with those individuals within the brand community.

CONCLUSION

This study provided a great deal of insight into Pinterest but was limited in scope. It focused on Compassion International, a single but sizeable nonprofit organization, at a particular point in time as it actively and innovatively employed Pinterest as a social media marketing tool. The study also concentrated on the types of Pinterest boards used by Compassion and their particular purposes and content but did not deal directly with users of these boards and their perceptions of them.

The scholarly research on Pinterest at this point is limited. Pinterest is growing in popularity, and its unique characteristics as a social network platform suggest the need for many types of studies, including those that focus on uses of the social network by nonprofit organizations. Because social media is continuing to thrive, and the process of audiences preferring visual images over text is only growing, it would be beneficial to conduct more research into this platform using various methodologies. Specifically, it would be interesting to study brand communities and the influence of pins across a spectrum of organizations. This would help to create broader and more generalizable practical and theoretical applications for the use of this platform and relationship building dynamics. Also, it would be interesting to develop a user-focused study, rather than an organizational study, in order to understand perspectives and beliefs that individuals hold regarding the value of brands, community, pins, repins, comments, likes, and activity on the Pinterest platform.

In a digital environment where brand communities are swayed primarily through interaction with other users versus the brand, it is more important than ever that both business and nonprofit organizations strategically engage audiences on social media. Pinterest is the latest platform that users are flocking toward and it only makes sense for organizations to establish a presence there. With photo sharing far outpacing text sharing on social media, Pinterest holds enormous potential for the development and advancing of relationships between organizations and brand communities. The dividing line between organizations who are successful and those that simply pile on one more social media platform profile after another will be the ability to intentionally cultivate content that encourages interaction and sharing. Sharable value is the new standard for content on social media. Organizations that understand this will flourish as the brand communities strengthen relationships and commitment toward the organization.

REFERENCES

Aaker, J.L. (1997). Dimensions of brand personality. *Journal of Marketing, 34*(3), 347–356.

Aggarwal, P. (2004). The effects of brand relationship norms on consumer attitudes and behavior. *Journal of Consumer Research,* 31(1), 87–101.

Allen, D., Woodward, J., & Lamp, M. (2012). Show me a story: How visual content is transforming social media. *Public Relations Tactics, 19*(5), 16.

Baer, J. (2012). 70% of companies ignore complaints on Twitter. *Convince and Convert.* Retrieved May 21, 2013, from http://www.convinceandconvert.com/social-media-strategy/70-of-companies-ignore-customer-complaints-on-twitter/

Bennett, S. (2013). 100 amazing social media statistics, facts and figures [Infographic]. *Media Bistro.* Retrieved May 21, 2013, from http://www.mediabistro.com/alltwitter/100-social-media-stats_b33696

Beninatto, R. (2013, March 12). Image vs. word: Why Pinterest wins at social marketing for global brands. *Moravia.* Retrieved May 25, 2013, from http://info.moravia.com/blog/bid/275600/Image-vs-Word-Why-Pinterest-Wins-at-Social-Marketing-for-Global-Brands

Bullock, L. (2013, May 24). 10 Pinterest tips and tools to help grow your business. *Mari Smith.* Retrieved May 25, 2013, from http://www.marismith.com/10-pinterest-tips-and-tools-to-grow-your-business/

Chacos, B. (2012). Pinterest drives more than window shopping. *PC World.* Retrieved May 23, 2013, from http://www.pcworld.com/article/2012749/pinterest-drives-more-than-window-shopping-survey-shows.html

Compassion International. (2014a). Child development model. Retrieved January 10, 2012, from http://www.compassion.com/child-development-model.htm

Compassion International. (2014b). FAQ—frequently asked questions. Retrieved January 10, 2012, from http://www.compassion.com/about/faq.htm

Compassion International. (2014c). Mission statement. Retrieved January 10, 2012, http://www.compassion.com/mission-statement.htm

Ennes, M. (2011). Social media: What most companies don't know. *Harvard Business Review.* Retrieved May 23, 2013, from http://hbr.org/web/slideshows/social-media-what-most-companies-dont-know/1-slide

Flyvberg, B. (2011). Case study. In N. Denzin & Y. Lincoln (Eds.), *The Sage handbook of qualitative research.* Los Angeles, CA: SAGE.

Fogel, E. (2014, February 13). Three ways to increase your nonprofit's social media engagement. *MarketingProfs.* Retrieved March 4, 2014, from http://www.marketingprofs.com/articles/2014/24397/three-ways-to-increase-your-nonprofits-social-media-engagement

Gilbert, E., Bakhshi, S., Chang, S., & Terveen, L. (2013). " 'I need to try this'?: A statistical overview of Pinterest. *Proceedings of the SIGCHI Conference on Human Factors in Computing Systems,* Paris, France. S.l: Association for Computing Machinery.

Giovangnoni, C. (2012). Where do you want to go? The Compassion blog "rethunk." *Compassion International.* Retrieved May 18, 2013, from http://blog.compassion.com/compassion-international-blog-where-do-you-want-to-go-the-compassion-blog-rethunk/

Greenfield, J.M. (1991). *Fund-raising: Evaluating and managing the fund development process.* New York, NY: Wiley.

Hanna, R., Rohm, A., & Crittenden, V.L. (2011). We're all connected: The power of the social media ecosystem. *Business Horizons, 54,* 265–273.

Hansen, D., Shneidermann, B., & Smith, M.A., (2010). *Analyzing social media networks with NodeXL: Insights from a connected world.* Boston, MA: M. Kaufmann.

Hon, L.C., & Grunig, J. (1999). *Guidelines for measuring relationships in public relations.* Gainesville, FL: Institute for Public Relations Research.

Honigman, B. (2012). 100 fascinating social media statistics and figures from 2012. *Huffington Post.* Retrieved May 22, 2013, from http://www.huffingtonpost.com/brian-honigman/100-fascinating-social-me_b_2185281.html

Horton, A.J. (1981). Acknowledgement of gifts and volunteer efforts. In F. D. Pray (Ed.), *Handbook for educational fund raising: A guide to successful principles and practices for colleges, universities, and schools* (pp. 265–268). San Francisco, CA: Jossey-Bass.

"It's a social world: Top ten need-to-knows about social networking and where it's headed." (2011). *ComScore.Com.* Retrieved May 20, 2013, from http://www.comscore.com/Insights/Presentations-and-Whitepapers/2011/it_is_a_social_world_top_10_need-to-knows_about_social_networking

Kelly, K. (1998). *Effective fund-raising management.* Mahwah, NJ: Lawrence Erlbaum Associates.

Marvin, G. (2014, January 16). Propelled by women, Pinterest beats out email in social sharing for first time [Report]. *Marketing Land.* Retrieved March 4, 2014, from http://marketingland.com/propelled-by-women-pinterest-beats-out-email-in-social-sharing-for-first-time-report-70834

McAlexander, J.H., Schouten, J.W., & Koenig, H.F. (2002). Building brand community. *Journal of Marketing, 66,* 38–54.

McKenna, R. (1991). Marketing is everything. *Harvard Business Review, 69,* 65–79.

Morgan, R.M., & Hunt, S.D. (1994). The commitment-trust theory of relationship marketing. *Journal of Marketing, 58,* 20–35.

Muniz, A. M., & O'Guinn, T. C. (2001). Brand community. *Journal of Consumer Research, 27*, 412–432.

Ngak, C. (2012, October 22). Pinterest CEO says key to success was marketing, not engineering. *CBS News*. Retrieved March 4, 2014, from http://www.cbsnews.com/news/pinterest-ceo-says-key-to-success-was-marketing-not-engineering/

O'Neil, J. (2007). The link between strong public relationships and donor support. *Public Relations Review, 33*(1), 99–102.

Palmatier, R. W., Jarvis, C. B., Bechkoff, J. R., & Kardes, F. R. (2009). The role of customer gratitude in relationship marketing. *Journal of Marketing, 73*, 1–18.

Pring, C. (2012, March 21). 100 social media, mobile and internet statistics for 2012. *TheSocialSkinny.Com*.RetrievedMay20,2013,fromhttp://thesocialskinny.com/100-social-media-mobile-and-internet-statistics-for-2012/

Schau, H. J., Muniz, A. M., & Arnould, E. (2009). How brand community practices create value. *Journal of Marketing, 73*, 30–51.

Semiocast. (2013, July 10). Pinterest has 70 million users. More than 70% are in the US. *Semiocast.com*. Retrieved February 4, 2014, from http://semiocast.com/en/publications/2013_07_10_Pinterest_has_70_million_users

Sutter, J. (2012, April 9). Report: Pinterest is third most-visited social site. *CNN Tech*. Retrieved May 23, 2013, from http://www.cnn.com/2012/04/06/tech/social-media/pinterest-third-social-network/

The 100 Largest U.S. Charities. (2013). *Forbes*. Retrieved February 4, 2014, from http://www.forbes.com/companies/compassion-international/

Waters, R. D. (2009). Measuring stewardship in public relations: A test exploring impact on the fundraising relationship. *Public Relations Review, 35*, 113–119.

Wyshynski, G. (2009, October 29). Inside NHL's social media innovations, growing pains. Retrieved May 21, 2013, from http://sports.yahoo.com/nhl/blog/puck_daddy/post/Inside-the-NHL-s-social-media-innovations-growi?urn=nhl,199092

Zahedi, F. M., & Bansal, G. (2011). Cultural signifiers of web site images. *Journal of Management Information Systems, 28*(1), 147–200.

20 Foundations
Creating Social Change through Technological Innovation

Geah Pressgrove and
Brooke Weberling McKeever

For nearly two decades, scholars have lauded the potential and lamented the failure of the Internet to achieve civic and social engagement (e.g., Kelemen & Smith, 2001; Mitra & Watts, 2003). Early research on the adoption of new media tools, specifically websites, indicated that organizations develop Web presences because they feel they need to in order to stay competitive (Miller, 2001). Further, research indicates that public relations practitioners, who were often asked to provide input for this new medium, joined the cyber-bandwagon without research-based target audience driven objectives (White & Raman, 2000). The rush to join the online cloud accelerated in the first decade of this century, when the Web entered a second generation of participatory online activity, commonly referred to as Web 2.0. This era was marked by the rise in popularity of user-generated content in the form of blogs, and the birth of free social networking sites defined by their ability to create social connections through user participation (Song, 2010).

In recent years, the exponential expansion of digital communication tools has captured the attention of public relations scholars and practitioners alike. Most studies about the public relations uses of new media for civic and social engagement focus on service-oriented nonprofits or corporate social responsibility campaigns of profit-seeking entities. Although an important part of the nonprofit sector, foundations have been largely overlooked in this research. Yet, these philanthropic organizations provide instrumental support to service-oriented nonprofits in terms of grant funding for programmatic efforts, training to develop leadership capacity, advocacy on their behalf in policy discussions, and education to enhance the viability of the sector. As a result, nonprofit organizations look to foundations not only as a source of funding but also as a resource for innovation. Through foundation funding and shared knowledge, nonprofits are able to empower stakeholders toward behavioral change, engage the public sphere in the democratic process through discussion of policy implications, invest in social change within their communities of influence, and affect media coverage of key issues (Holtz, 1999). For these reasons, this study examines foundations' use of Web 2.0 strategies as a public relations tool to advance civic and social engagement.

LITERATURE REVIEW

Quantitative inquiry has begun to explore and document the Web 2.0 strategies used by public relations in the nonprofit sector to stimulate social and behavioral change. However, this line of inquiry has focused almost exclusively on service-oriented Section 501(c)(3) entities (see e.g., Kent, Taylor, & White, 2003; Waters et al., 2009). Across the board, findings have indicated that nonprofits are not using the interactive power of the Web to its full potential and often fail to acknowledge and invest the necessary ongoing resources to take full advantage of this important communication vehicle. However, these types of quantitative inquiry are insufficient for documenting the motivations and expectations surrounding the use of new media strategies, and how these strategies are managed online. In light of foundations' leadership positions in cause-related research as well as their role as a primary funding source for a wide array of nonprofits, it is important to gather perspective on these issues from the professionals who work for these organizations.

The Role of Foundations. First, distinctions between foundations and service-oriented 501(c)(3) nonprofit organizations are worth noting. Although rarely providing direct service in the public domain, these grant makers rely on and invest heavily in the nonprofit sector to achieve success related to their missions. According to the Communications Consortium (2004), foundations are making unprecedented investments in communication strategies in order to educate and mobilize Americans in support of social and/or behavioral change. However, the benefactors of this substantial investment, nonprofit organizations, need more than grant funding from foundations to achieve success. As the next generation of citizens comes of age in a time of online and mobile technologies, the viability of these organizations will be determined in part by their transparency, interactivity, and collaborative communication made possible by Web 2.0 (Tapscott, 2009). Thus, foundations must also model best practices in online communication, contribute innovative planning solutions, and promote proven tactics to enhance programs and projects of their grantees.

The recent economic downturn has limited many foundations' ability to sustain previous levels of grant making, forcing nonprofits to stretch limited dollars further. In 2009, the charitable sector experienced its steepest decline in support in over 50 years. In the years since, giving has increased incrementally year over year; however, at the current growth rate, total charitable giving will not return to the 2007 high for another six years (Kalugyer, 2013). These decreases in funding have led many foundations to refocus their fiscal priorities on technology literacy initiatives, increased foundation-based public engagement through social media, and streamlining service offerings online. These tools allow the foundations to reach targeted, localized audiences with immediate and timely communications, while stimulating discussions and collaborations.

Theoretical Framework. The primary theoretical lens applied to this study is derived from the seminal multiyear study resulting in the theory of "Excellence in Public Relations" (Grunig & Hunt, 1984). This expansive body of scholarship has been referred to as a general theory of public relations (Kim & Lan, 2010). This theory tells us that excellent communications departments know how to engage in two-way communication with stakeholders, while using cutting-edge expertise in public relations research (Dozier, Grunig, & Grunig, 1995, p. 123). Further, according to some scholars (Grunig, Grunig, & Ehling, 1992), public relations strategies contribute to organizational effectiveness and have monetary value when they build quality long-term relationships with strategic constituencies. These authors posit that this happens when the senior public relations manager is a member of the dominant coalition and can help shape goals and determine strategic external publics for the organization.

In two-way symmetrical communication, which is the preferred model according to excellence theory (Grunig, 1992, p. 528), "organizations—and especially the dominant coalition—should adjust and adapt to publics upon whom survival and growth depends" (Dozier & Ehling, 1992, p. 182). This concept emphasizes the role of both communication officers and top executives at foundations supporting the efforts and initiatives of the nonprofits the foundations fund.

Further, while foundation communication officers are expected to have the tools and knowledge to create excellent communications, it is also imperative that senior management understand the role and function of communication (Dozier et al., 1995). Thus, this chapter relies on in-depth interviews conducted with senior staff as well as communication officers of foundations, regardless of whether they are considered part of the dominant coalition. More specifically, responses from these in-depth interviews should shed light on foundations' use of Web 2.0 strategies as a way of modeling public relations excellence by helping us answer the following research questions:

RQ1: How and why are foundation leaders using Web 2.0 strategies to communicate with various organizational stakeholders?

RQ2: How do foundation leaders view the allocation of resources for online communication, and how are they measuring success?

RQ3: Among foundation leaders, what are the perceived barriers or challenges related to implementing digital communication strategies?

METHOD

This chapter takes a qualitative approach to studying foundations concentrated in one southern state. The sampling frame for the study was the trade association for foundations working in the state. Foundation members of this association fall into four main categories: independent foundations with endowed funds focused on a particular geographic region or social issue; health legacy foundations funded through endowments typically created by hospital systems; community foundations serving a particular geographic area; and corporate giving programs operating as the social responsibility arm of for-profit entities. Annual grants for foundations in the study range from $100,000 to more than $5.5 million. Funding concentrations vary and include service to particular geographic areas, and those focused on particular social issue(s) including health, education, cultural affairs, and the environment. These foundation and grant types mirror national data and definitions provided by the Council on Foundations (2011), a national membership-based organization of more than 2,000 foundations. Corporate giving programs, because of their affiliation with and guidance from for-profit entities, were excluded from this study.

Sample. Open-ended interviews were conducted with foundation chief executive officers and communication directors who use online strategies as part of a communications plan for the organization. Additional investigation of the online strategies employed by the foundation provided context for developing categories used in the analysis. The researchers interviewed these experts either by phone or in person for 30 minutes to one hour.

Participants were carefully selected to assure representation from different foundation types, annual giving levels, geographic areas, and funding focus areas. Using these criteria assured maximum variation and allowed the researcher to identify normative usage of communication technologies among foundations. Four foundation CEOs and three communication officers representing a total of six foundations agreed to participate in the interviews.

Analysis. A qualitative textual analysis of transcribed in-depth interviews and foundation-related online communication was conducted. Open coding to extract concepts from the raw data occurred in three waves. First, upon completion of each phone interview, field notes were taken to notate themes from each interview. After completion of transcription, the researcher listened to the interviews while reviewing the transcription documents and a second set of field notes were compiled to outline themes emerging from a second review of the interviews. Axial coding, or crosscutting data, was then achieved by merging the two sets of field notes while concurrently reviewing the new media forums (websites and social media) employed by each foundation. This process led to the integration of information into categories or bins with multiple themes, concepts, dimensions, and properties contributing to the overarching key concepts, constructs, or blocks of content.

Next the researcher color coded the categories identified through open coding and reviewed the printed transcripts. Pertinent responses to interview questions were highlighted and theoretical memos were notated on the documents. This allowed for data reduction into the previously defined categories, and made further comparison between responses possible. At this point, the researcher returned to the online forums where foundations managed a public presence to compare key interview commentary to the actual online presence.

Throughout the analysis, special attention was paid to the foundations' mission, purpose for engaging in new media strategies, the scope of the new media tools employed, and maturity of online communication efforts. Validity was achieved through triangulation of data found in online sites, between foundation types, and within individual foundations between communication officers and CEOs.

FINDINGS

The foundation leaders and communication officers interviewed for this chapter universally agreed there is utility in online communication to achieve their mission. Recognizing that their role is more than just funding, these foundations are seeking to engage a wide array of internal and external constituencies including grantees, other foundations, media and policymakers, to name a few. Their efforts to better understand the potential for these channels are focused on elevating the visibility of the sector, bringing attention to important issues, sharing resources, educating existing and potential stakeholders, and promoting collaboration. Further, these foundations, once seen as "towers on a hill," hope to now use the participatory potential of online communications to break down barriers, transparently provide information, and innovate.

Leading by example, the foundation executives interviewed indicated that they have turned to participatory new media solutions including mass e-mail communication, interactive websites, informational blogs and podcasts that invite public commentary, participatory social media tools, training sessions delivered as webinars or by satellite feed, and online collaboration portals to facilitate discussions. Despite the broad range of type, focus area, and assets, insights from these foundations coalesced around several key themes related to their decisions to allocate resources to various strategies and desired outcomes associated with incorporating new media tools into communication campaigns. In the results below, we allow the executives to speak for themselves related to each of our research questions and provide additional support from the analysis of online content posted by the foundations that participated in the study.

The first research question asked how foundation leaders use Web 2.0 strategies to communicate with organizational stakeholders. Generally, foundation leaders seem to be using online communication to extend access to information, to advance their mission, and to interact with multiple stakeholders who may not be geographically proximal. Specific examples and participants' comments are described under these headings below.

Extend Access to Information. The foundation leaders interviewed indicated having had a website for some time, but most entered the participatory social media environment within the last two to three years. They now view their websites as an *information hub* or *repository*, with dialogue occurring on several social media platforms that are connected as spokes to the main website hub. Further, these executives saw the opportunity to develop *collaborative workspaces* that streamline the grants processes on the front end, and after funding, improve efficiency of nonprofits by creating spaces for nonprofits to work together. A final theme that emerged in discussions related to information access was related to the importance of *resource sharing* across key constituencies (e.g., staff, grantees, media).

Information Repository. A visit to these foundations' websites shows a variety of ways to connect to their social media platforms and join in dialogue with the foundations. This cross-promotion is an important strategy to achieving success online. As one foundation leader with 20 years of experience articulated, "we repackage information for distribution across a long list of online platforms and mass media outlets, but ultimately it all links back to our website for more information." Echoing the important role of the organization's website, a communication officer with three years of experience explained the strategic nature of information dissemination:

> The crux of our information is on our website. The crux of the people we want to engage are on Facebook. We're never going to get 8,000 people check out the site every day, but if I can tap into five places that most of those people already check every day, it's going to be the same effect.

Collaborative Workspace. Beyond housing information, the organization's website provides an important role in increasing efficiency of the grant-making process. Adopting the national trend of only accepting online grants applications, many foundations have been able to engage additional nonprofits seeking grants and better work with allocations committees by developing online tools. As one foundation leader with six years of experience put it, "we don't want everyone to jump through hoops to do their work. This online process means more people can participate in doing good in the community."

In line with this collaborative workspace model, one foundation indicated that for the rural geographic area they serve, connecting with popular online social networks was not the right answer. However, they have developed an online nonprofit collaboration portal designed and facilitated by the foundation. This foundation leader, with seven years of experience, indicated that this "increases their knowledge of the work of their peer community organizations, increases service awareness within the community, and decreases competition for available resources."

Resource Sharing. Another way that foundations are seeking to achieve their mission is to post content on information-sharing websites, and provide links to information sources through their own communication channels. As one communication officer with five years of experience put it, "If there's a website that shares best practices of foundations and nonprofits, we want to put our work on there . . . and we know we're not all knowing, so we share other [organizations'] resources and information to help educate our nonprofits."

Mission Advancement. Foundation leaders saw new media tools as a way to advance their mission in a number of ways. First, they seek to achieve goals of *capacity building*, by advancing the awareness and knowledge of issues that affect nonprofit leaders and grantees. Additionally, these foundations seek to *facilitate collaboration* both within the sector among nonprofits, as well as across the community, state, and nation. Further, these foundations seek to expand *crowdsourcing* opportunities, or gain input on projects, by soliciting insight from the public at large, and stakeholders specifically, online. A final way that these foundations hope to advance their mission-based objectives is by *positioning* their staff and leadership as experts and demonstrate their reach through effective use of technology-based communication.

Capacity Building. This theme refers to the conceptual approach to development that allows foundations to focus on understanding the obstacles that inhibit nonprofits from reaching their potential, while enhancing the nonprofits' abilities to achieve measurable and sustainable results. As one communication officer with two years of experience indicated, participatory media offers "many directions to improve engagement with important information, and hopefully our mission in general." A foundation leader with 15 years of experience articulated the dueling opportunity and threat in this way:

> Funders have to look at ways to help nonprofits become more sophisticated, knowledgeable and proactive moving forward, because if they're not, they're going to be left behind and it's not only going to be a missed opportunity. It's going to have a negative impact on their organization.

Facilitating Collaboration. While foundations recognize the potential of new media to segment audiences, personalize communication tactics, and localize outreach efforts among like-minded groups, they see these opportunities as a way to build bridges. One communication officer with five years of experience poignantly stated that foundations must "show what we're doing, let other people know . . . tell them how to participate." Realizing the interconnectedness of communities and states, another communication officer indicated that online communications are "about making those connections and developing those relationships beyond our sector and really educating other people . . . to bring about change in our community." Similarly, foundation executives saw their role in facilitating collaborations as innovators capable of creating opportunities and enhancing awareness. A foundation leader with 15 years of experience indicated that it was more than simply reminding the reader of the organization's mission, but helping them to see the people behind the mission:

> The opportunity with changing technology and the desire to share what we have learned, is to teach and inform about how that poor person pushing a cart got there. We can do it in a way that potentially influences more people from the everyday citizen, the policy-maker, the rural poor communities, or the capital city.

Crowdsourcing. Another key theme related to the utility of Web 2.0 strategies that emerged from foundation interviews was the concept of crowdsourcing. Foundation leaders recognize the value of multiple opinions and have begun using the two-way communication potential of new media to source opinions from a variety of audiences in new media forums. As one foundation leader with 20 years of experience put it, "it's shaping our story telling and helping us figure out what are the things that people react to." Another foundation leader with 15 years of experience indicated that the old "ivory tower" way of foundation thinking was no longer practical or effective:

> If you want to know something, ask everybody. We believe the best decisions are informed decisions, and we make better decisions not in a vacuum or an ivory tower, but with other people. New media gives a voice to those other people.

Positioning. Other foundation leaders saw new media strategies as a way to "increase legitimacy" of their work, "demonstrate the reach of the foundation," and position "foundation staff as a group of experts." Echoing sentiments associated with breaking down barriers and elevating visibility of the foundation, one communication officer with five years of experience said, "some people have the perception that we just sit in here and four times a year we make grants . . . we use this to also show what we're doing in the community."

Many foundations advance their mission in this way by using multiple authors for their online posts, which concurrently allows them to position the dominant coalition as experts. As one foundation leader with seven years of experience put it, these posts allow readers to "see the foundation staff as being a group of experts on these specific areas where they focus." Other foundations use online tools to help demonstrate their geographic reach. One foundation leader with 20 years of experience said, "I try very hard when I'm out of the office to post and reinforce how many places we work in this region."

Interaction With Stakeholders. Reviewing these foundations' online spaces that are open for public commentary provides evidence that these foundations seek to create channels of communication by presenting information that is timely and relevant, while also relying on photos and videos to share the story of their work in the communities they serve. When asked about the interplay between sharing information and engaging discussion, two key themes that reflect theory emerged. These themes related to *seeking engagement*, or two-way dialogic communication, versus serving as a *communication conduit*, a much more asymmetrical provision of information.

Seeking Engagement. Foundation leaders felt that the potential of participatory communication channels provided a way to "build trust and support" through transparent dissemination of information, "start the conversation" about what was going on in the community, allow "opportunities for feedback," and "attract new audiences while engaging existing donors and grantees." Across the board, study participants felt these outcomes increased efficiency and effectiveness of the foundation. They were, however, candid that often the goal and the outcomes do not meet. In fact, a review of these foundations participatory online presences revealed a lack of public commentary. While one foundation leader with 20 years of experience indicated a desire for a "conversation more than using a megaphone to stand up and announce something," he also noted that the organization was not yet at a state where they were getting a lot of reaction.

Communication Conduit. Further, foundation executives indicate that dialogue is not always the goal. Many foundation leaders saw new media's best role as a way to extend their nonprofit's programmatic abilities by providing resources and sharing research conducted by the foundation or other credible sources. An analysis of the volume of posts that disseminate expertise garnered from other organizations reaffirms this point, as a large volume of content on organization's participatory platforms originated elsewhere. These foundation leaders indicated that serving as a curator of content "allows nonprofits a one-stop shop for connecting with the right resources without having to search or recreate the wheel." One foundation leader with 15 years of experience said: "We have the resources . . . and knowledge of the issues that affect the sector. I see it as our job to get this information to the nonprofits working in the trenches in a timely way."

Exploring the potential of technology-based communication has resulted in positive gains for the sector according to study participants. By using these tools they have seen success in terms of expanded outreach and fostering thinking around issues by reaching stakeholders wherever they might be geographically. As one foundation leader with 15 years of experience indicated: "It's all about access. We don't want people to just have access to the information by being in person here. We want to provide them access through other methods." Some ways that these nonprofits are providing access to information include satellite trainings, podcasts, online workshops, and web-based resource centers. One communication officer with five years of experience lauded training access by discussing the advantages:

> We used to have these great nonprofit workshops that were free and open statewide. Then we realized what a sacrifice it was for people to drive all the way here to take part, so we now have the technology for satellite training sessions.

Fiscally Fundamental. The second research question asked how foundation leaders view the allocation of resources for online communication, and how they measure success in these endeavors. Generally, foundation leaders view online communication as an investment in the organization's mission and future, and thus far, they seem to be measuring success qualitatively, through trial and error approaches and through anecdotes and referrals.

Foundation leaders in this study recognize that while many new media technologies may be free in the initial sign-up phase, their maintenance and effective use requires a multipronged allocation of resources. Foundation executives described the expense as an *investment* that they feel they need to make because they have the resources and staff to do so. More specifically, foundation allocation of resources for experimenting with online communication strategies was described as a "costly value-added" service to the nonprofit sector. To measure the extent of the expense, one foundation went so far as to audit marketing staff time and found that approximately "20 percent of marketing staff time is spent on social media engagement." Staff time, however, is not the only form of investment in understanding the potential of online portals for participatory communication. One communication officer with five years of experience described the investment in terms of "perception versus reality" and indicated that foundations felt it was their "job to figure out what works." Echoing this sentiment, a foundation leader with 15 years of experience highlighted the depth of dollars allocated by ticking off a list of hardware, software, training, consultants, staff time, and development of distance learning programs needed to "develop the most up-to-date opportunities in the latest and greatest way." Another foundation leader with 20 years of experience outlined the fiscal investment in this way:

> We definitely are wasting effort on this because we are exploring it and we're probably investing more than nonprofits can do because we have the luxury of doing it. . . . We're investing fairly heavily in professional development at this point without much oversight and just trying to do it by focusing someone on what, in the long run, is our electronic strategy.

However, these leaders also indicated that modeling innovation can enhance overall efficiency and increase fiscal responsibility in the nonprofit sector. In their view, online strategies provide "advantages over some mass media and direct mail approaches" that lacked the ability to target messages, and frequently had long production schedules. One foundation leader with 15 years of experience described the use of technology as a reflection of the fiscal responsibility and viability of a nonprofit.

> It's interesting to me how many hundreds of print newsletters I get a year. By the time I receive it I think it is outdated information . . . (and) a terrible waste of money. It tells me a bit about the health, well-being and innovative savvy of a nonprofit based on what I get from them. Let's communicate in a way that's not in the dinosaur ages.

Measuring Success. Whereas most foundation activities and grant-funding allocations include rigorous success measurement protocols, the *trial and error approach* to communication technology initiatives has led to measurements of return on investment that are more qualitatively focused. In fact, many foundations see *anecdotal stories* as measures of success, while other foundations indicated that *referrals* were effective measures of success of online strategies.

Trial and Error. Foundation leaders commented both about their reservations and the opportunities for measuring success. One foundation leader with 20 years of experience indicated that it was hard to say "what successful might look like" and added, "we're jumping off a cliff a little bit not really knowing how to measure this." One communication officer indicated that the challenge of using standard quantitative metrics, such as "number of fans or followers or comments," was that there was no way to assess if " people are appreciating the information—are they finding it useful?" Relating it back to influencing social change, a foundation leader with 15 years of experience qualified this trial and error approach in this way:

> We haven't boiled it down to this messaging strategy is best for this segment, this is best for this one and so on. It's more about looking at goals broadly and seizing opportunities to inform and impact every day.

Anecdotal Stories. Foundation leaders also felt that the dynamic nature of their online presence meant that simple counts and tallies were insufficient measures. In their description of online success, they most often shared stories about personal contacts. One communication officer with five years of experience indicated that "a lot of times people comment in person to me about our activity in new media and what they've seen . . . verbally, but not within the mechanism." Yet another communication officer with two years of experience said: "What's really exciting for us now is when misinformation is put up, how quickly our friends jump to defend and correct." A foundation leader with 20 years of experience articulated that online communication reinforces in-person communication and vice versa:

> I'll go to an event and someone will come up from across the room and tell me she knows me because of my blog post; or we'll have an event and post it only on Facebook and 200 people will show up. Sometimes these people are lurkers. They sit in the background and never comment, then they show up and introduce themselves. Human connection has always been, and will always be, an important part of what we do.

Referrals. Success was also described in terms of referrals to connect with the foundation, a reality that foundation leaders saw as adding validity. A communication officer described the following as an example of how they capitalize on the credibility of referral marketing:

> You'd be more motivated to look at something because I sent it to you and you trust me. . . . So we ask our board members if they'll forward these things and kind of promote us and be our brand ambassadors.

Risks and Challenges. Of course, implementing new media strategies in a participatory environment is not without its challenges and risks for these foundations. Therefore, the final research question asked about the perceived barriers or challenges related to implementing digital communication strategies. Responses related to this question revealed three themes surrounding concerns of *information control*, increased *staff burden*, and *balancing personal contact* that has been the hallmark of their success.

Information Control. In the past, foundations have been protected from commentary and feedback of the public at large by channeling their work through nonprofits. However, new media has opened them up in a way that is outside of their comfort zone. A foundation leader with 20 years of experience described using social media to talk about the organization's work without filtering as "a bit like doing acrobatics without a net." A communication officer with five years of experience indicated that this uneasiness was not just about the lack of control over information, but also a function of "opening yourself up to more people that want money from you." Another foundation leader with 15 years of experience described the challenge as a supply and demand problem, indicating that decreased dollars for allocation coupled with increased communication results in more demand without the ability to supply funding, which sets "unrealistic expectations" in the sector.

Staff Burden. A review of the frequency and content of posts presented by foundations in their online forums revealed several interesting phenomena. Often postings are inconsistent, with posts appearing in stacks on a single day within a narrow window of time. These postings are regularly followed by gaps of several days before the next posting. Additionally, information is frequently recycled information from other sources, or images without descriptive support copy.

When asked about this, foundation leaders offered several explanations. One reason foundation leaders offered was that the volume of information disseminated and consumed in new media forums is "cumbersome to manage while doing our work." The participatory potential of these communication vehicles means that staff is tasked with regulating comments, surfing other profiles, and maintaining their online presence. Reflecting on the added responsibility of social media monitoring, one communication officer said: "We're to the point of capping how much we can actually do in a day . . . it's mind boggling the amount of information that is conveyed per second." One foundation leader with 15 years of experience indicated that "it's a double edge sword. It's an opportunity, but it's a curse too, because if you have it and don't use it, it becomes stale and could hurt you."

Balancing Personal Contact. Some foundation leaders describe new media as more sterile than in-person communication, and believe this is a challenge to relationship building. A foundation executive with six years of experience said, "the worst aspect [of Web 2.0] is you lose the personal contact. My people are going to gain more from personal contact with others than they are with just straight-up information." In a business where personal connection can be life changing, foundation leaders are concerned that online communication will "result in a whole new set of barriers." As one foundation leader with 15 years of experience put it: "When your work involves communities of people, it's hard to figure out how typed words and pretty pictures can support, rather than replace, human connection."

CONCLUSIONS

It is apparent that foundation executives and communication officers who participated in this study take seriously their role as leaders and fiscal stewards of the nonprofit community as it relates to the potential of Web 2.0. While perhaps not approached with the same rigorous system of checks and balances as other actions, their new media strategies seek to elevate this sector. These foundation leaders' comments illustrate a constant striving to provide resources and opportunities that meaningfully motivate social and behavioral change in their communities of influence.

Recognizing the power and promise of technology-based communication tools, they continue to invest in using participatory Web 2.0 strategies to motivate change, and elevate the aptitude of the sector. While these leaders are grappling with the best way to innovate and communicate within the context of technology-driven communication mediums, they are not daunted by the associated risks and challenges. As of yet, it is still an imperfect science;

however, they play a significant role in bringing to fruition the possibility and progress of online communication for the nonprofit sector.

Further, these foundation leaders are not simply jumping on the bandwagon of social media; they are integrating technology across their mission-based strategies. Whether it is through increasing access by providing satellite training sessions, enhancing collaboration by facilitating a portal for online communication, or investing in their own staff to test the potential of the mediums, they are doing more than merely launching an online presence. They are seeking ways to invigorate the sector by making the tools work for them.

Indeed, the foundations that participated in this study seem to be practicing "excellence in public relations" as the Grunig and Hunt (1984) theory suggests. However, while they are still learning the ropes of these ever-changing media, they are sometimes promoting two-way symmetrical communication yet other times engaging in one-way asymmetrical information sharing. They are using the tools differently, depending on the audience and capability for interactivity, and they are experimenting with many media in an attempt to do the trial-and-error work their nonprofit partners may not have the time, staff and/or resources to do. They are reaching people they may not have reached before, even though that sometimes opens them up to additional demands, and they (like many others) are still learning how to measure the success of their investments in these media as it relates to advancing their organizational missions.

Limitations. This study was very limited in scope, as it focused only on foundations in one state. Although these organizations were selected to reflect the various sizes and types of foundations found elsewhere, it is important to note that they were not randomly selected, and they are based in only one state. Future research should seek to replicate these findings with additional foundations, or pursue other methods including surveys, focus groups, or experiments, to continue to explore thoughts and reactions to these and similar topics not only on behalf of other foundations but also on behalf of foundations' many stakeholders. As mentioned, foundations are often neglected in nonprofit-related research, making them a valuable focus for future research.

REFERENCES

Communication Consortium Media Center. (2004). Guidelines for Evaluating Nonprofit Communications Efforts. Washington, DC. Retrieved November 15, 2013, from http://www.mediaevaluationproject.org/Paper5.pdf

Council on Foundations. (2011). Retrieved November 15, 2013, from http://www.cof.org/

Dozier, D. M., & Ehling, W. P. (1992). Evaluation of public relations programs. In J. E. Grunig (Ed.), *Excellence in public relations and communication management* (pp. 159–184). Mahwah, NJ: Lawrence Erlbaum Associates.

Dozier, D. M., Grunig, L. A., & Grunig, J. E. (1995). *Manager's guide to excellence in public relations and communication management.* Mahwah, NJ: Lawrence Erlbaum Associates.

Grunig, J. E., & Hunt, T. (1984). *Managing public relations.* New York, NY: CBS College.

Grunig, L. A. (1992). Activism and public relations. In J. E. Grunig (Ed.), *Excellence in public relations and communication management* (pp. 503–530). Mahwah, NJ: Lawrence Erlbaum Associates.

Grunig, L. A., Grunig, J. E., & Ehling, W. P. (1992). What is an effective organization. In J. E. Grunig (Ed.), *Excellence in public relations and communication management* (pp. 65–90). Mahwah, NJ: Lawrence Erlbaum Associates.

Holtz, S. (1999). *Public relations on the Net: Winning strategies to inform and influence the media, the investment community, the government, the public, and more!* New York, NY: Amacom.

Kalugyer, A. D. (2013). Giving USA: Charitable donations grew in grew in 2012, but slowly, like the economy. Retrieved November 13, 2013, from http://www.philanthropy.iupui.edu/news/article/giving-usa-2013

Kelemen, M., & Smith, W. (2001). Community and its "virtual" promises: a critique of cyberlibertarian rhetoric. *Information, Communication & Society, 4*(3), 370–387.

Kent, M., Taylor, M., & White, W. (2003). The relationship between Web site design and organizational responsiveness to stakeholders. *Public Relations Review, 29,* 63–77.

Kim, J., & Lan, N. (2010). Seeing the forest through the trees: The behavioral, strategic management paradigm in public relations and its future. In R. Heath (Ed.), *The SAGE handbook of public relations* (pp. 35–57). Thousand Oaks, CA: SAGE.

Miller, D. (2001). Measuring effectiveness of your Intranet. *Strategist, 8,* 35–39.

Mitra, A., & Watts, E. K. (2003). Theorizing cyberspace: the idea of voice applied to the internet discourse. *New Media & Society, 4*(4), 479–498.

Song, F. W. (2010). Theorizing Web 2.0: A cultural perspective. *Information, Communication & Society, 13*(2), 249–275.

Tapscott, D. (2009) *Grown up digital: How the net generation is changing your world.* New York, NY: McGraw Hill.

Waters, R. D., Burnett, E., Lamm, A., & Lucas, J. (2009). Engaging stakeholders through social networking: How nonprofit organizations are using Facebook. *Public Relations Review, 35*(2), 102–106.

White, C., & Raman, N. (2000). The world wide web as a public relations medium: The use research, planning, and evaluation in website development. *Public Relations Review, 25,* 405–419.

Afterword

Richard D. Waters

In the foreword to this volume, Cutlip, Center, and Broom's (2000) definition of public relations was provided and used as a basis for helping the nonprofit sector overcome its fiscal, accountability, technology, and human resource challenges. The preceding 20 chapters covered a range of nonprofit topics, ranging from fundraising and volunteer management to community outreach and advocacy. Yet, their undertones all refer back to the classic definition: "the management function that establishes and maintains mutually beneficial relationships between an organization and the publics on whom its success or failure depends" (Cutlip et al., 2000, p. 6).

The three key components of that definition—management function, mutually beneficial relationships with publics, and success or failure—are illustrated throughout the chapters in this book. The research highlights important insights for nonprofit sector leaders and scholars about the role of public relations strategy and activity in nonprofit organizations. For public relations theory to grow, it is necessary to analyze these perspectives through multiple communication lenses and not exclusively base our theoretical development on corporate communication.

MANAGEMENT

Public relations is a management function aiding counsel to an organization's leaders so that decisions can be made without solely thinking about the internal outcomes and consequences of those decisions. Information brought by public relations practitioners to the boardroom concerning external stakeholders is critical for the practice of excellent public relations as outlined by Dozier, L.A. Grunig, and J.E. Grunig (1995). As a result, public relations practitioners must be proactive boundary spanners constantly surveying the horizon for potential issues that the organization may face resulting from internal and external stakeholders' behavior.

As Hilary Fussell Sisco, Randi Plake, and Erik Collins discussed, organizations that fail to be proactive and plan for public relations activities risk losing organizational stability and decreasing longevity. Although their research focused on crisis management plans within religious institutions, the overarching message that pervades their study is that public relations practitioners cannot simply be reactive to what is going on in their organizations. To overcome the accountability challenge, nonprofits must be forward thinking and devise even the simplest plans to remain proactive and alert. With that mentality, public relations practitioners are able to help nonprofits carry out their programs and services without encroaching on other departments' domains, as Christopher Wilson and Sarabdeep Kochhar point out.

Public relations practitioners must be boundary spanners to stay abreast of activities surrounding an organization's operating environment. The various organizational roles discussed by Natalie Tindall, Richard Waters, and Kathleen Kelly highlight the importance of having multiple touchpoints to an organization's stakeholders. The expert prescriber is isolated within an organization and carries out the programming alone without the assistance of others, while the problem-solving process facilitator brings others within and outside of the organization together to design and carry out the programming. As relationship management becomes a dominant paradigm in public relations thought, practitioners must think of ways to build ethical relationships so that future engagement is likely. Shannon Bowen and Diana Sisson found that alumni were more likely to respond to initiatives when they felt their personal relationship with the university was strong. Boundary spanners, like the fundraiser enacting the problem-solving process facilitator role, create those stronger relationships by keeping them involved and informed.

Keeping the public informed about organizational events and breaking situations was the subject of two chapters in the book. Emily Kinsky, Nicholas Gerlich, Kristina Drumheller, and Marc Sollosy found that the public supported Planned Parenthood in the wake of cancelled funding from Susan G. Komen for the Cure, primarily because of their rapid sharing of news as to what was unfolding with the partnership. Similarly, Suzanne Horsley saw an organization's willingness to share information as being one of the biggest factors in the implementation of the crisis-adaptive public information model. As part of the accountability challenge facing the nonprofit sector, news that impacts both internal and external stakeholders must be shared whether through the executive director or other communications staff.

Tim Penning's study on the public relations capacity of nonprofit organizations' boards of directors highlights an important issue facing the human resource challenge of nonprofits. Nonprofit organizations, especially the many small organizations with budgets less than $100,000, may not have someone qualified to serve as the public relations representative. In this situation, nonprofits must recruit someone versed in public relations to serve on the board and provide the much-needed communication counseling. Nonprofit boards should include a diverse spectrum of organizational constituents culturally as well as professionally. This includes someone who can offer insights on technology adoption, as Geah Pressgrove and Brooke

McKeever note that the usage of new technologies can help an organization achieve its mission. A volunteer could also serve as the catalyst for using new technologies. Organizations simply cannot hide behind technology fears if they want to remain proactive and practice excellent public relations. The minimization of technological fear by having a trusted voice to turn to for assistance is an important first step in overcoming the technological challenge nonprofits face.

MUTUALLY BENEFICIAL RELATIONSHIPS

Although public relations practitioners provide management with information needed to create a hospitable environment for organizational action, they also play a key role in creating and maintaining relationships with stakeholders that provide positive outcomes for both parties. One could argue that relationships are more important for nonprofit organizations than public agencies or for-profit corporations. Relationship building is the foundation that nonprofits can use to overcome the fiscal, accountability, and human resource challenges they face. Surveying the entire nonprofit landscape, donations from fundraising efforts represent 20% of the overall income for the sector; this amount is substantially larger for organizations that do not charge fees for programs or services. More than 60 million individuals gave nearly 8 billion hours of volunteer service work to the sector in 2012. Without individuals' donations and volunteer work, nonprofits would not be able to provide the quality and quantity of programs and services to their constituents that they currently do.

However, these are not the only relationships that matter for nonprofits. Grant writing is a necessity for nonprofits as they seek ways to diversify their revenue streams; however, the distribution of funds, as Giselle Auger points out, is not the only function that foundations have. Foundations facilitate many connections in the nonprofit community as they introduce nonprofit leaders working on similar missions to each other and encourage cooperation to address social issues. Brigitta Brunner and Giovanna Summerfield discuss the value of connections and cooperative efforts in the community. Their research on the town-and-gown connectivity highlights relationship building as a contributing factor to getting buy in and participation from both sides of the relationship.

Drawing on results from in-depth interviews, Jennifer Vardeman-Winter reveals a variety of strategies that community outreach and client caseworkers can use to strengthen the relationship between an organization and underserved community members. These relationships are often difficult to create because of multiple factors, including institutional skepticism, ethnic and cultural barriers, and the pride and self-esteem of those offered assistance. Denise Bortree also discusses institutional factors that hinder relationships between a nonprofit and its volunteers. She notes that male and female volunteers experience the nonprofit organization–volunteer relationship differently and that the use of organizational and personal inclusion strategies must be done in a manner that makes both genders feel involved with the organization at the social, work group, and departmental levels.

Carolyn Kim and John Keeler highlight that while formal volunteers provide assistance in carrying out a nonprofit's programs and services, relationships built over social media can also be used to achieve a nonprofit organization's mission. In their chapter, they discussed Compassion International's use of Pinterest as a channel for stewardship activities. However, the most popular board focuses on the letter writing that can be done between organizational supporters and the children they support overseas. In this instance, social media has built relationships that help an organization provide emotional support and demonstrations of care and concern not by volunteers but by the public at large.

THE SUCCESS OR FAILURE OF PUBLIC RELATIONS

The relationship management paradigm first advocated by Ferguson (1984) provides strategies for the creation and cultivation of relationships with organizational stakeholders. But the true test of relationship building comes down to whether the relationship is allowed to grow through both parties' active participation, or whether the organization manages the relationship so that stakeholders' involvement is stifled. A nonprofit's orientation toward relationship building will influence whether their public relations efforts succeed or fail.

Jeanine Guidry, Greg Saxton, and Marcus Messner's chapter on the perceptions of Twitter reiterate the importance of organizational orientation toward relationships. Nonprofit leaders that viewed social media and Twitter more favorably were more likely to see increased engagement and interactivity with these followers online. Through online conversations and by spreading institutional messages, social media engagement increased the level of online and offline initiatives, including public awareness and advocacy to increased revenue through donations and event participation.

Despite these successes, the overall level of engagement on social media platforms remains low. Moonhee Cho and Tiffany Schweickart examined status updates on Facebook using Grunig and Hunt's (1984) four models of public relations. More than half of those messages were one-way in nature, although they were more fact based than self-serving. Nonprofits did seek participation by their social media followers through the two-way asymmetrical model, but only 1 in 10 messages was a true attempt at having a conversation over Facebook.

Social media engagement levels differed significantly based on the type of messaging that the nonprofit used. Liz Gardner, Trent Seltzer, Andrea

Phillips, and Rachel Page used an experimental design to test how different message sources were viewed by the public. Their finding that organizational stories were viewed as being more credible than news stories may help explain why one-way, public information–style messaging on Facebook was dominant. The results of this experiment reiterate the importance of messaging and cultivation strategies. Public relations theory can result in successful organizational efforts if the practitioners take the time to plan their behaviors proactively and move away from organization-centric behaviors and messaging. Ensuring that messages are stakeholder centric increases the likelihood that the messages are heard and acted on.

The outcome of message framing—as discussed by Ben Benson and Bryan Reber regarding the wind energy debate and in Erich Sommerfeldt and Sifan Xu's discourse analysis of ACT UP's congressional testimony—rests upon the believability of the messages and whether the message source is seen as trustworthy and honest. Through these two content analysis projects, research shows that the level of public support hinged on what type of message strategies were used in the activism efforts. Loud, confrontational messaging yielded significantly different levels of public support than messages grounded in calm and reason. That does not mean that there is not a place for challenging and difficult-to-face messages by nonprofits.

As Rachel Kovacs found in her historical discussion of the Children's Broadcasting Initiatives' activism efforts, public relations strategies, messaging, and tactics must be planned according to the overall timeline of a social movement. Grassroots and social movements often use loud, brash messaging initially to attract media and political attention; as the media validate and highlight an issue, organizational messaging tends to become more mainstream and less confrontational so that it is more understood and accepted by the public. Cheryl Lambert highlights that the media can be bypassed and still achieve public acceptance. The propaganda used during the "Dig for Victory" and "Victory Gardens" campaigns during World War II included aesthetic visuals on posters as well as anthems and nursery rhymes to draw in audiences. The use of these communication strategies helped rally support around British and American efforts to support the war effort without having to turn to traditional journalism outlets.

Although we live in an environment that thrives on the 24-hour news cycle, nonprofit organizations may find it easier to legitimize their missions and messaging without mainstream news media. Social media have helped flatten the media landscape: organizations can take their messaging directly to the public rather than having to go through news gatekeepers. This direct-to-consumer messaging may also help explain the prevalence of public information messages on Facebook and the perceptions that nonprofit leaders have toward Twitter. Regardless of their approach to spreading their messages and building public awareness about their missions, nonprofit organizations need sound public relations efforts to create organizational success.

Although its historical beginnings may have been founded in publicity and emotionally charged messaging, public relations has evolved into a function that helps manage issues and cultivate relationships with internal and external stakeholders to ensure organizational successes and longevity. As illustrated in this volume, nonprofit organizations are utilizing public relations strategy, messaging, and tactics in every department within the organization and at every level of the organizational structure. Whether the focus is public awareness and education, client and volunteer outreach, or fundraising, public relations efforts keep the nonprofit sector running strong. These efforts are carried out by volunteers working to deliver programs and services, employees managing organizational processes, and executive directors and boards of directors providing oversight and strategic planning for the nonprofits.

Given the strong connections between nonprofit organizations and public relations, it is only appropriate that the next wave of public relations scholarship prominently features nonprofit studies. Scholars in the public relations discipline have built a solid body of knowledge and a range of theories over the past 40 years. By examining these perspectives through the unique fiscal, effectiveness, technological, and human resource challenges that face nonprofit organizations, our theories can be challenged, tested, and pushed to their limits. The 20 studies presented in this volume provide strong evidence that public relations theory and nonprofit organizations are intertwined. The next 40 years of our scholarly inquiry into public relations will no doubt be influenced by the work presented here and this call for further examination of how nonprofit organizations' management, decision-making, and communication efforts are guided by public relations theory.

REFERENCES

Cutlip, S. M., Center, A. H., & Broom, G. M. (2000). *Effective public relations.* Upper Saddle River, NJ: Prentice Hall.

Dozier, D. M., Grunig, L. A., & Grunig, J. E. (1995). *Manager's guide to excellence in public relations and communication management.* Mahwah, NJ: Lawrence Erlbaum.

Ferguson, M. A. (1984). *Building theory in public relations: Interorganizational relationships.* Paper presented to the Association for Education in Journalism and Mass Communication, Gainesville, FL.

Grunig, J. E., & Hunt, T. (1984). *Managing public relations.* New York, NY: Holt, Rinehart, and Winston.

Contributors

Giselle A. Auger, APR (Ph.D., U. of Florida) is an assistant professor of Public Relations in the Journalism and Multimedia Arts Department of McAnulty College of Liberal Arts at Duquesne University in Pittsburgh. Her research focuses on transparency, nonprofit communication, strategic use of social media, and academic dishonesty. She enjoys the intersections of practice and academia and making theory and research applicable to her students.

Ben Benson finished his master's in Journalism and Mass Communication with an emphasis in PR at the University of Georgia in 2011. His research examined how environmental activist groups can enhance their environmental messaging for key stakeholders. Previously, he received a bachelor's in journalism and economics at the University of Oregon. Today, Ben works as an account executive at Waggener Edstrom Worldwide on the Microsoft account.

Denise Sevick Bortree (Ph.D., U. of Florida) is an associate professor in the department of advertising/public relations and a senior research fellow for the Arthur W. Page Center. Bortree researches and writes on nonprofit organizational communication and sustainability. She has authored more than 25 peer-reviewed journal articles that have been published in journals such as *Journalism and Mass Communication Quarterly*, *Journal of Public Relations Research*, *Nonprofit Management and Leadership*, *Public Relations Review*, the *International Journal of Nonprofit and Voluntary Sector Marketing*, and the *International Journal of Volunteer Administration*.

Shannon A. Bowen (Ph.D., U. of Maryland) is a Full Professor in the School of Journalism and Mass Communications at the University of South Carolina. She sits on the Board of Trustees of the Arthur W. Page Society and the Board of Directors of the International Public Relations Research Conference. Bowen researches public relations ethics and won the Jackson Jackson and Wagner Behavioral Science Research Prize, the Heath

Outstanding Dissertation Award, and is a Page Legacy Scholar, who was inducted into the *PRNews* Measurement Hall of Fame in 2014.

Brigitta R. Brunner (Ph.D., U. of Florida) is a professor in the School of Communication & Journalism at Auburn University. She has served as a College of Liberal Arts Engaged Scholar, Associate Director for the Public Relations program, Imagining America Research Fellow, Auburn University Provost's Fellow, Southeastern Conference Academic Leadership Development Program Fellow, Plank Center for Leadership Educator Fellow, and Journalism and Mass Communication Leadership in Diversity Program Fellow. Brunner teaches public relations courses at both the graduate and undergraduate levels.

Moonhee Cho (Ph.D., U. of Florida) is an assistant professor in the School of Advertising and Public Relations at the University of Tennessee's College of Communication & Information. Her research focuses on public relations management of both for-profit and nonprofit organizations, social media, public empowerment, and strategic corporate philanthropy. A former fundraiser and nonprofit public relations manager in South Korea, she was named the Emerging Scholar by the Association for Research on Nonprofit Organization and Voluntary Action in 2010.

Erik L. Collins (Ph.D., Syracuse U.; J.D., Ohio State U.) is an associate professor at the School of Journalism and Mass Communications at the University of South Carolina. He previously served as a senior public relations manager for major corporations including Miller Brewing Company and Philip Morris Incorporated.

Kristina Drumheller (Ph.D., U. of Missouri) is an associate professor of communication studies at West Texas A&M University. Her primary areas of teaching are in organizational communication, consulting, and training and development. Her research interests include crisis communication, media effects, and leadership. She is a principal in the collaborative research group Media Buffs with research focusing on organizational crisis communication, mobile app trends, and consumer ethnocentric tendencies.

Liz Gardner (Ph.D., U. of Missouri) is an assistant professor of public relations at Texas Tech University, where she teaches campaign planning, research methods, and nonprofit public relations. Her research examines health communication, media psychology, and nonprofit public relations. Prior to joining the faculty at Tech, she worked in a variety of public relations roles in Raleigh and Atlanta.

R. Nicholas Gerlich (Ph.D., Indiana U.) is the Hickman Professor of Marketing at West Texas A&M University. His research interests are in social media, e-commerce, nostalgia, and fandom. He teaches Evolutionary Marketing and Market Research. Dr. Gerlich has researched and published numerous articles exploring faculty and student involvement with and evaluation of online teaching as well as exploring consumer shopping orientation and their locus of control, as well as risk aversion and its effect on personal use of e-commerce.

Jeanine D. Guidry is a Ph.D. student in the Social and Behavioral Health program at Virginia Commonwealth University, as well as an affiliate graduate researcher at the Center for Media+Health. Her research interests include the use of social media in health and nonprofit communications. Her work has been published in the *Journal of Social Marketing* and in *Corporate Communications: An International Journal*. She has also presented at the Association for Education in Journalism and Mass Communication, International Public Relations Research, and Digital Disruptions in Multimedia Journalism conferences.

J. Suzanne Horsley (Ph.D., U. of North Carolina–Chapel Hill) is an associate professor in the Department of Advertising and Public Relations at the University of Alabama. Her research focuses on crisis and disaster communication in the public and nonprofit sectors. In September 2012 she was named a White House Champion of Change for her disaster public affairs work with the American Red Cross and for her incorporation of service learning in her classes.

John Keeler (Ph.D., U. of Texas) is a professor in the Strategic Communication and Journalism Department in the graduate School of Communication and the Arts at Regent University. His research and teaching specializes in organizational communication, media, church and culture, history of communication, new communication technologies, public relations and advertising.

Kathleen S. Kelly, APR, Fellow PRSA (Ph.D., U. of Maryland) is an internationally recognized authority on public relations and fundraising. She is the author of two award-winning books and more than 70 articles, book chapters, monographs, and refereed papers. Her research interests focus on organization–public relationships, particularly donor relations. Dr. Kelly has 17 years of professional experience as a fundraiser and public relations practitioner.

Carolyn Mae Kim, APR (Ph.D., Regent U.) teaches Public Relations at Biola University in the department of Journalism & Integrated Media. Her specialties include social media, public relations, brand credibility and digital strategy. She is an accredited public relations professional who regularly speaks and writes on social media strategy, search engine optimization, and public relations education.

Emily S. Kinsky (Ph.D., Texas Tech U.) is an assistant professor in the Department of Communication at West Texas A&M University, where she teaches courses related to advertising, public relations, design, and new media. Her research interests include crisis communication, social media, and portrayals of public relations. She helps advise WTAMU's Ad/PR Society and National Broadcasting Society.

Sarabdeep K. Kochhar (Ph.D., U. of Florida) is the Director of Research at the Institute for Public Relations (IPR). She also holds the position as the Associate Director of Measurement and Analytics at APCO Worldwide. At APCO, she serves as a strategic counsel for clients on measurement and evaluation. At IPR, she is the chief research strategist, advising and leading the Institute on priorities and research programs. She has several years of professional work experience in both public and private sectors. She has authored book chapters and refereed conference papers, received the top paper award from PRSA Educators Academy, the Chester Burger Award for Excellence in Public Relations from PRSA, and the Ketchum Public Relations Research Award by IPR.

Rachel Kovacs (Ph.D., U. of Maryland) is an adjunct associate professor at the City University of New York, where she has taught media and public speaking courses and developed online curricula. Her areas of research specialization are international public relations, NGO activism, and corporate social responsibility. She has advised a national award-winning PRSSA campaign, and received top paper awards from PRSA's Educators Academy and the Institute for Public Relations.

Cheryl Ann Lambert (Ph.D., U. of Tennessee) is an assistant professor in the College of Communication at Boston University. She pursued her doctorate after working for seven years in corporate communications at Sears, Roebuck and Co. Her academic scholarship exploring representations of public relations and health has been informed by her practitioner and academic experience.

Brooke Weberling McKeever (Ph.D., U. of North Carolina–Chapel Hill) is an Assistant Professor in the School of Journalism and Mass Communications at the University of South Carolina. McKeever's primary teaching and research interests are nonprofit public relations and health communication. She has worked in PR, marketing, and fundraising for an agency in Chicago and for organizations including St. Jude Children's Research Hospital.

Marcus Messner (Ph.D., U. of Miami) is an assistant professor of mass communications in the Richard T. Robertson School of Media and Culture at Virginia Commonwealth University and the executive director of the Center for Media+Health. His research agenda explores the adoption and use of social media platforms in journalism and public relations and has been published in such journals as *Mass Communication & Society*, *Journalism Studies*, *Newspaper Research Journal*, and *Public Relations Journal*.

Rachel E. Page received her master's in mass communications from Texas Tech University in 2013. Her thesis focused on the use of Twitter in crisis communication, and her research interests include news media, popular culture theory, and social media and online user communication. She currently works at the Lubbock Avalanche-Journal as a copy editor, laying out pages for print and updating the website and social media pages.

Timothy Penning, APR (Ph.D., Michigan State U.) is a full professor in the School of Communications at Grand Valley State University where he teaches public relations courses. He continues to practice public relations as a consultant with his own business, Penning Ink. He was named "Distinguished Practitioner" by the West Michigan Chapter of the Public Relations Society of America in 2001 and 2005. He is active with the Public Relations Society of America, having served as president of the West Michigan chapter in 2004 and on its board for seven years.

Andrea L. Phillips, APR, is a Ph.D. candidate at Texas Tech University. She has spent 20 years developing and directing public relations and marketing communications efforts in nonprofit, corporate, and agency settings. She teaches public relations at Middle Tennessee State University as an assistant professor. She holds bachelor's and master's degrees from Texas Christian University, an MA from Dallas Theological Seminary, and is owner of FTF Marketing Communications.

Randi Plake received her master's in public relations from Quinnipiac University. She is the co-owner of Grand Street Creative, a consulting agency that offers creative services including public relations, social media, graphic design, and marketing, with an emphasis on church crisis management. She has previous experience in higher education and nonprofit public relations.

Geah Pressgrove (Ph.D., U. of South Carolina) is an Assistant Professor at the Reed College of Media at West Virginia University. Her primary research and teaching interests include public relations, nonprofit advocacy, strategic communications, and social media. Pressgrove worked at an integrated marketing communications agency for over a decade executing strategies for myriad clients.

Bryan H. Reber (Ph.D., U. of Missouri) is the C. Richard Yarbrough Professor in Crisis Communication Leadership at the Grady College of

Journalism and Mass Communication, University of Georgia. He teaches introduction to public relations, public relations writing, public relations management, and public opinion. He is coauthor of three top-selling public relations textbooks. His research focuses on public relations, activism, crisis communication, and health communication.

Gregory D. Saxton (Ph.D., Claremont Graduate U.) is an associate professor in the Department of Communication at the University at Buffalo, SUNY. His research on nonprofits' use of new and social media has been published in such journals as *New Media & Society, Journal of Communication, Public Administration Review, Nonprofit and Voluntary Sector Quarterly, Journal of Computer-Mediated Communication*, and *Public Relations Review*.

Tiffany Schweickart is a Ph.D. student in the College of Journalism and Communications at the University of Florida. She graduated from the University of South Florida in 2013 with a Master of Arts in mass communications. Her research interests include political public relations, strategic communication, organizational message strategies, and crisis communication.

Trent Seltzer (Ph.D., U. of Florida) is an associate professor of public relations in the Texas Tech University College of Media & Communication. His research focuses on social media, agenda building, framing, and relationship management in political contexts and has appeared in *Public Relations Review, Journal of Public Relations Research, Journalism & Mass Communication Quarterly, International Journal of Strategic Communication*, and PRSA's *Public Relations Journal*.

Hilary Fussell Sisco (Ph.D., U. of South Carolina), is an associate professor of public relations at Quinnipiac University. She has published 15 refereed journal articles in various premier academic journals in public relations and mass communication and has presented 30 refereed research papers at international and national conferences. She previously worked in nonprofit and higher education public relations. Her research agenda focuses on nonprofit organizations and crisis communication.

Diana C. Sisson is a Ph.D. candidate in the School of Journalism and Mass Communications at the University of South Carolina. Her research interests include public relations, reputation management, and ethics. Sisson's work has been presented at the International Public Relations Research Conference. Previously, Sisson worked in digital public relations in the healthcare industry, specifically social media strategy and web content management.

Marc Sollosy (D.B.A., Kennesaw State U.) teaches strategic management, international management, and ethics at Marshall University in

Huntington, West Virginia. After a successful career spanning more than 30 years in industry, he returned to academia and earned his Doctorate of Business Administration. His research interests include strategic management, marketing, international management, ethics, and pedagogy. He has written a number of publications, including two book chapters in strategy.

Erich J. Sommerfeldt (Ph.D., U. of Oklahoma) is an assistant professor in the Department of Communication at the University of Maryland, College Park. His research centers on activist group communication, civil society, social capital, and social network analysis. He was the co-recipient of the 2011 PRIDE Award for Best Article of the Year from the Public Relations Division of the National Communication Association.

Giovanna Summerfield (Ph.D., U. of Florida) is the Associate Dean for Educational Affairs in the College of Liberal Arts at Auburn University, where she also serves as Professor of Italian and French languages and literatures. She is a College of Liberal Arts Engaged Scholar at Auburn and an Imagining America Research Fellow. She has published extensively on the long eighteenth-century French and Italian literature, religious and philosophical movements, Mediterranean studies, and women's studies. Her latest book is *The Politics of Poetics: Poetry and Social Activism in Early-Modern through Contemporary Italy.*

Natalie T.J. Tindall (Ph.D., U. of Maryland) is an associate professor in the Department of Communication at Georgia State University. She currently serves as the chair of the public relations division in the Association for Education in Journalism and Mass Communication. Dr. Tindall has undertaken research in areas including identity, diversity, and power in the public relations function; identity and health messages; fundraising and philanthropy; organizational culture and stereotypes within historically Black fraternities and sororities; and the intersection of public relations and marketing to minority health.

Jennifer Vardeman-Winter (Ph.D., U. of Maryland) is an assistant professor in the Jack J. Valenti School of Communication at the University of Houston, where she teaches courses in public relations theory and management as well as critical and cultural public relations. She is widely regarded for her health communication and multicultural feminist research and has published in numerous journals, including *Public Relations Review*, *Health Communication*, and the *Journal of Public Relations Research*.

Richard D. Waters (Ph.D., U. of Florida) is an associate professor in the School of Management at the University of San Francisco, where he teaches courses on strategic communication in the graduate business administration and nonprofit administration programs. Author of more than 75 peer-reviewed publications, Waters currently serves as the associate editor of *Case Studies in Strategic Communication*. Additionally, he serves on seven editorial review boards for public relations and nonprofit management journals.

Christopher Wilson (Ph.D., U. of Florida) is an assistant professor at Brigham Young University in Provo, Utah, where he teaches public relations coursework. Prior to earning his doctorate, he worked in a variety of public relations capacities for West Valley City, Utah, and as the public relations manager for the Brigham Young University Museum of Art. He has won top paper awards for his research from the International Institute for Public Relations Research Conference and the Association of Educators in Journalism and Mass Communication.

Sifan Xu is a Ph.D. student in the Department of Communication at the University of Maryland, College Park. He earned his B.A. in Communication from the University of International Relations in China. He is interested in the public relations practices of activist groups and nongovernmental organizations, strategic issues management, and civil society.

Index